T0261438

Engines of Order

The book series RECURSIONS: THEORIES OF MEDIA, MATERIALITY, AND CULTURAL TECHNIQUES provides a platform for cuttingedge research in the field of media culture studies with a particular focus on the cultural impact of media technology and the materialities of communication. The series aims to be an internationally significant and exciting opening into emerging ideas in media theory ranging from media materialism and hardware-oriented studies to ecology, the post-human, the study of cultural techniques, and recent contributions to media archaeology. The series revolves around key themes:
– The material underpinning of media theory
– New advances in media archaeology and media philosophy
– Studies in cultural techniques

These themes resonate with some of the most interesting debates in international media studies, where non-representational thought, the technicity of knowledge formations and new materialities expressed through biological and technological developments are changing the vocabularies of cultural theory. The series is also interested in the mediatic conditions of such theoretical ideas and developing them as media theory.

Engines of Order

A Mechanology of Algorithmic Techniques

Bernhard Rieder

Amsterdam University Press

This publication is funded by the Dutch Research Council (NWO).

Chapter 1 contains passages from Rieder, B. (2016). Big Data and the Paradox of Diversity. *Digital Culture & Society* 2(2), 1-16 and Rieder, B. (2017). Beyond Surveillance: How Do Markets and Algorithms 'Think'? *Le Foucaldien* 3(1), n.p.

Chapter 6 is a heavily reworked and extended version of Rieder, B. (2017). Scrutinizing an Algorithmic Technique: The Bayes Classifier as Interested Reading of Reality. *Information, Communication & Society* 30(1), 100-117.

Chapter 7 is a reworked and extended version of Rieder, B. (2012). What Is in PageRank? A Historical and Conceptual Investigation of a Recursive Status Index. *Computational Culture* 2, n.p.

Cover illustration: The full text of this book, represented as a *feature vector*. © Bernhard Rieder

Cover design: Suzan Beijer
Lay-out: Crius Group, Hulshout

ISBN	978 94 6298 619 0
e-ISBN	978 90 4853 741 9
DOI	10.5117/9789462986190
NUR	670

Printed and bound by CPI Group (UK) Ltd, Croydon, CR0 4YY

Table of Contents

Acknowledgements

This book has been long in the making and has benefited from many different inputs. I would first like to thank the Recursions series editors – Anna Tuschling, Geoffrey Winthrop-Young, and, in particular, Jussi Parikka – for their many valuable remarks and suggestions. Maryse Elliott from Amsterdam University Press has been an invaluable help in guiding me through the whole editorial process. Eduardo Navas's constructive comments on the manuscript were much appreciated. I am also grateful to Carolin Gerlitz, Sonia de Jager, Janna Joceli Omena, Niels Kerssens, Emillie de Keulenaar, Thomas Poell, Gernot Rieder, Guillaume Sire, Michael Stevenson, and Fernando van der Vlist for reading drafts at various stages of completion and providing critical feedback.

I want to thank Thomas Brandstetter, Dominique Cardon, Mark Coté, Nick Couldry, José van Dijck, Nigel Dodd, Matthew Fuller, Paolo Gerbaudo, Paul Girard, Andrew Goffey, Olga Goriunova, Sanne Kraijenbosch, Camille Paloque-Berges, Jean-Christophe Plantin, Thomas Poell, Barbara Prainsack, Theo Röhle, Anton Tantner, Leon Wansleben, and Hartmut Winkler for conference and workshop invitations that allowed me to develop the ideas that run through this book. My thanks also go to my colleagues at the Mediastudies Department and the Digital Methods Initiative at the University of Amsterdam as well as my former colleagues at the Département Hypermedia and Laboratoire Paragraphe at Paris VIII University for the many stimulating conversations that shaped the following chapters.

Particular thanks are due to Richard Rogers and the Dutch Research Council (NWO) for making it possible to release this book through open access.

I dedicate this book to the memory of Frank Hartmann, whose passion for thinking technologies as media echoes through these pages.

Introduction

Abstract

The introduction chapter positions algorithmic information ordering as a central practice and technology in contemporary digital infrastructures, a set of techniques that serve as 'levers on reality' (Goody). While algorithms used in concrete systems may often be hard to scrutinize, they draw on widely available software modules and well-documented principles that make them amendable to humanistic analysis. The chapter introduces Gilbert Simondon's mechanology and provides an overview of the structure and argument of the book.

Keywords: algorithmic information ordering, information search and retrieval, mechanology, software-making

Over the last decades, and in particular since the widespread adoption of the Internet, encounters with algorithmic procedures for 'information retrieval' – the activity of getting some piece of information out of a collection or repository of some kind – have become everyday experiences for most people in large parts of the world. We search for all kinds of things on the open web, but also for products, prices, and customer reviews in the specialized databases of online retailers, for friends, family, and strangers in social networking services or dating sites, and for the next thing to read, watch, play, listen to, or experience in quickly growing repositories for media contents. There are at least three remarkable aspects to this spread of information seeking. First, computer-supported searching has sprawled beyond the libraries, archives, and specialized documentation systems it was largely confined to before the arrival of the web. Searching, that is, the act of putting a query into a form field, has become such a fundamental and ubiquitous gesture that a missing search box on a website becomes an almost disturbing experience. Second, what retrieval operates on – information – has come to stand for almost anything, from scraps of knowledge to things, people, ideas, or experiences. Digitization, datafication, and the capture of

Rieder, B., *Engines of Order: A Mechanology of Algorithmic Techniques*. Amsterdam: Amsterdam University Press, 2020

DOI 10.5117/9789462986190_INTRO

always more activities in software are, in the words of Netscape founder and venture capitalist Marc Andreessen (2011), 'eating the world'. Search has become a dominant means to access and order the masses of digital and datafied bits and pieces that clutter the environments we inhabit. Third, the deliberate and motivated act of formulating a query to find something is only one of the many forms in which information retrieval nowadays manifests itself. Automated personalization, localization, recommendation, filtering, classification, evaluation, aggregation, synthetization, or ad hoc generation of information are similarly pervasive practices that do not require explicit user input to select, sequence, arrange, or modulate some set of digital items. And retrieval techniques are no longer limited to producing result lists: they generate scores, suggest items, discard or promote messages, set prices, arrange objects and people in relation to each other, assemble texts, forbid or grant access, fabricate interfaces and visualizations, and even steer objects in the physical world. In short, various activities or gestures this book addresses under the broad notion of 'information ordering' have become both pervasive and subtle in terms of how they operate in the thickening layers of digital mediation.

The proliferation of these algorithmic practices has been accompanied by considerable efforts in the humanities and social sciences to investigate techniques and applications in terms of power and social significance. Early analyses of search engines already highlighted their political dimension, claiming that 'there is no such thing as algorithms without their own weight' (Winkler, 1999, p. 36). This meant that one could examine 'the wide-ranging factors that dictate systematic prominence for some sites, dictating systematic invisibility for others' (Introna and Nissenbaum, 2000, p. 171) from a point of view concerned with social impact and public interest. Beyond search, authors have called attention to 'moments of algorithmic judgement' (Graham, 2005, p. 576) that abound when 'code-based technologized environments continuously and invisibly classify, standardize, and demarcate rights, privileges, inclusions, exclusions, and mobilities' (Graham, 2005, p. 563). Terms like 'automated management' (Kitchin and Dodge, 2011), 'algorithmic ideology' (Mager, 2012), 'algorithmic governmentality' (Berns and Rouvroy, 2013), and, more recently, 'algorithmic accountability' (Diakopoulos, 2015) all subscribe to 'the central premise that algorithms have the capacity to shape social and cultural formations and impact directly on individual lives' (Beer, 2009, p. 994). This broad recognition of the 'relevance of algorithms' is not, however, a symptom of a sudden curiosity for the fundamentals of computational theory. It stems from a more specific interest in the particular instances where algorithms serve as 'a means to know what there is to know and how to know it, to participate in social and political discourse, and to familiarize ourselves with the publics in which we participate' (Gillespie, 2014, p. 167). Most of the techniques that sit at the center of these questions and concerns directly relate to the field of information ordering.

Search engines remain the most instructive illustration for the issues at hand since the tensions between their remarkable practical utility, their technical prowess, and their political relevance are so clearly visible. We intuitively understand that ranking web pages – and thus the services, contents, and viewpoints they stand for – is delicate business. But, as Grimmelmann (2009) argues, search engines face the 'dilemma' that they *must* rank in order to be useful. This imperative collides with the uncomfortable observation that there is arguably no technical procedure that can lay serious claim to producing assessments concerning ambiguous and contested cultural matters in ways that could be broadly accepted as 'objective'. In fact, whenever data are processed algorithmically, the transformation from input to output implies a perspective or evaluation that, through the coordination between data and what they stand for, is projected back into spheres of human life. Techniques for information retrieval become engines of order that actively intervene in the spaces they seek to represent (cf. Hacking, 1983).

The need to better understand the specificities of these processes becomes even clearer if we broaden the scope beyond everyday online experiences to activities where algorithms evaluate and inform decisions that can have dramatic effects, for example, in hiring, credit assessment, or criminal justice (cf. O'Neil, 2016; Christin, 2017; Eubanks, 2018). These emblematic and troubling applications point to a myriad of instances in business and government where procedures from the broad field of information ordering are used to inspire, choose, or impose a specific course of action.

The technical procedures involved are loaded, often implicitly, with specific ideas and attitudes concerning the domains they intervene in. Search engines evaluate the 'relevance' of information, news aggregators generate front pages according to various measures of 'newsworthiness', dating sites calculate 'compatibility coefficients' between members and order them accordingly, social networking sites filter friends' status updates based on quantified ideas of 'interest' or 'closeness', and microblogging services give prominence to 'trending' topics. In each of these cases, there is a framing of the application domain that implies various kinds of conceptual and normative commitments. This can involve a general allegiance to the broad epistemological 'style' (Hacking, 1985) of computation as a means of knowing; but it can also take more specific forms, for example, when psychological research on partnership satisfaction flows into the design of a matching algorithm or when the optimization objectives for a machine learning system are being selected on the basis of business considerations.

At the same time, technical procedures are more than just a means to efficiently enact values and ideas that are themselves nontechnical. Jack Goody (1977) argued that list-making, from the start an essential part of writing, 'gives the mind a special kind of lever on "reality"' (p. 109) by supporting mnemonics and, more importantly, by facilitating different operations of ordering and reordering pieces of text and, by extension, the things these pieces refer to. As Goody knew all too well, the advent of list-making meant not just a quantitative extension in cognitive capacity. More fundamentally, it stimulated the production and recording of knowledge, spurred modes of classificatory and hierarchical thinking, and supported more complex forms of social organization. As Peters (2015) argues, '[i]n list writing, serial order loosens its hold' (p. 290), with wide-ranging consequences. The information ordering techniques that have become so pervasive today share the transversal character and broad applicability of list-making and may prove to have equally fundamental repercussions for how we construct and relate to the world around us.

Like list-making, algorithmic ordering comes with a genuine operational substance that rarely boils down to a simple transposition of a manual method into computational form. A web search engine, for example, orders documents through iterative processing of vast amounts of distributed signals and the specific way it produces an aggregate appreciation of these signals defines an epistemic substance and character that has little to do with the knowledge practices that have defined libraries, encyclopedias, or archives over the last millennia. As Edsger Dijkstra, one of the central figures in the history of software, remarked about computers over 40 years ago:

> [T]he amount of information they can store and the amount of processing that they can perform, in a reasonably short time, are both large beyond imagination. And as a result, what the computer can do for us has outgrown its basic triviality by several orders of magnitude. (Dijkstra, 1974, p. 608)

Computers' capacity to run billions of data points through billions of iterations of small calculative steps means that they 'think' (Burrell, 2016) in ways that are not only opaque, but potentially *strange* and hard to fit into established categories. Techniques like machine learning, network algorithms, or relational database management systems are not just powerful means to produce and apply knowledge, to enact value preferences, or to control practice; they participate in the very definition of what knowledge, value, and practice mean and *can* mean, both through the conceptual resources they propose to think with and the actual interpretations and orderings they generate when applied in practice. We should consider the possibility that they challenge cultural modes and social institutions in more fundamental ways than the necessary discussions of algorithmic opacity or bias can lead us to believe.

The methods and procedures involved in actual practices are often hidden from our sight by technical and legal means, latched not even in black boxes but somewhere in the 'black foam' (Rieder, 2005) of systems whose contours are hard to delineate. But, paradoxically, they have also become highly accessible, in the sense that concrete implementations draw heavily on open reservoirs of technicity and knowledge that find their expression in scholarly publications, software libraries, and communities of practice gathering on websites like Stack Overflow. These reservoirs are neither hidden nor closed off and we are free to examine a steadily growing archive of techniques that enable computers to accomplish tasks that seem increasingly 'cultural' or 'intelligent' in nature. This book is an expedition into this archive and more specifically into the areas that deal with information ordering.

The actual makeup of Google's search ranking may indeed be 'unknowable' for a number of practical, commercial, and legal reasons, but, as shown in Chapter 7, the content, history, and substance of its most famous algorithm, PageRank, stands wide open. We may never get access to the concrete specifications of the machine learning methods behind the personalized filtering Facebook applies to its users' News Feed, but we can ask, as in Chapter 6, where machine learning comes from, what concepts and ideas it builds on, and how it operates in general terms. The second part of this book is thus dedicated to a series of investigations into specific 'algorithmic techniques', that is, into the defined-yet-malleable units of technicity and knowledge developers draw on when designing the function and behavior of computers acting in and on the world. Offering many different ways to order and organize information, they serve as levers on the 'reality' of a world eaten by software.

While this book draws heavily on work situated in the 'cultural techniques' tradition, an approach coming out of German media scholarship, there is at least one important difference. Unlike Young's (2017) inspirational take on the list, which follows a particular cultural form through various societal settings, I examine a set of techniques as they traverse what is maybe not a single cultural domain but nonetheless a somewhat demarcated practice:

software-making. The broader theoretical perspective guiding these probes will be discussed at length in part one, but the particular focus on technical creation calls for some background and clarification.

Toward Mechanology

This book is largely motivated by the remarkable spread of algorithmic information ordering but also translates a feeling of hesitation or uneasiness toward the way software is often presented and discussed in media studies and associated fields, or, more specifically, toward the emphasis on *code* as software's quintessential technical quality or substance. To be clear, understanding how written instructions produce machine behavior is fundamental to understanding software, but it is also a comparatively small step into the massive world of technicity software constitutes. Code is neither trivial nor transparent, but for any experienced developer it is a familiar means to access a domain of *function* that is vastly more complex than the term is able to address. Building a program or system is to craft a composite technical object, 'a being that functions' in the words of French philosopher Gilbert Simondon, who plays a central role in what follows. This may entail, today more than ever, the assemblage of many preexisting chunks of software. Code serves as the means to draw on an archive, to 'build-with', and to create in ways that are deeply relational and embedded. As I will argue over the following chapters, the world of software-making is structured around 'techniques', expressions of knowledge and technicity that enable developers to make computers *do* things that are more involved or complex than their 'basic triviality' suggests. This book does not presume any practical technical knowledge or experience, but it addresses algorithmic information ordering from the perspective of technical creation.

My own background plays an important role in this setup. While I have little formal training in any technical discipline, I have been developing software on a regular basis for a long time. I started to program when I was a still in high school, worked as a web developer during my university studies, and taught programming to students ranging from beginners to computer scientists at master's level for about a decade. I continue not only to code but to make software, nowadays mostly in the domain of digital methods for Internet research (Rogers, 2013). The part of the software landscape under scrutiny in this book, algorithmic information ordering, is not only socially relevant but also closely connected to the technical practice I have been pursuing over the last 20 years. As a web developer, I worked extensively with relational database management systems (Chapter 4) and I encountered advanced information retrieval techniques (Chapter 5) during my PhD in information and communication science at Paris 8 University when I was investigating the possibilities for 'society-oriented design' (Rieder, 2006). This work led to a system, procspace (Rieder, 2008), which used a variety of algorithmic methods to generate navigational pathways between documents to support a logic of connection, enrichment, and overview that breaks with the serial forms of order dominating search. The encounter with information retrieval, an established technical field that comes with a large body of well-documented methods, came as a shock: as an autodidact programmer I felt very comfortable when it came to writing code, but I was not fully aware how much I was missing. The techniques I discovered gave me a new sense of possibility and opened the door to forms of technical expression that have stimulated my imagination ever since. Although often more heavily mathematized than what I was used to, these techniques were relatively simple to implement and, like clay, could be modeled in countless ways. The entanglement between information ordering and the politically, culturally, and economically significant matters it is increasingly involved in became my principal research interest. This eventually led to work in digital methods, where I focused on studying online platforms that rely on algorithmic techniques in fundamental ways and, paradoxically, to a situation where I would apply similar techniques as analytical instruments to make sense of large sets of empirical data. The chapters about machine learning (Chapter 6) and network algorithms (Chapter 7) draw on this work.

The reason I mention these details is not to claim technical authority but to introduce and situate a perspective that has been fundamentally shaped by these experiences. This perspective is still uncommon in media studies and in the broader discussions of software or, to use the buzzwords of the day, of 'algorithms' or 'artificial intelligence'. Following Johanna Drucker's (2013) suggestion to give '[m]ore attention to acts of producing and less emphasis on product' (n.p.), my conceptual vantage point is software-making, a series of practices that increasingly revolve around the use of packaged function as a means to extend programmers' capabilities. It takes hardly more than an hour to install and set up PyTorch or TensorFlow, powerful open-source libraries for machine learning, and to have a first classifier trained. While some people will want to peek under the hood of these artifacts to make adaptations or simply out of intellectual curiosity, developers often draw on technicity and knowledge that they understand only in broad terms or not at all. What programming languages, software libraries, and similar artifacts do is to enable software-makers to step further faster, not merely regarding resource efficiency but in terms of what can be considered possible in the first place. Such packages widen the spaces of expressivity, broaden the scope of ambitions, but also structure, align, and standardize. Spelled out, stabilized, and 'frozen', algorithmic techniques spread through technical imaginaries and artifacts, and further into application logics and business models. They are *means of production*, not simply outpourings of computational principles or scientific ideas.

Algorithmic techniques are ways of making computers do things, of creating function, and their history is characterized to a greater extent by accumulation and sedimentation than by paradigm shifts or radical breaks. Certainly, methods and approaches are regularly superseded or fall out of fashion, but it is clear that the archives that inform and constitute software-making have grown vastly over time. While this book entertains a somewhat complicated relationship with the field of media archeology, another prominent approach coming out of German media theory, it indeed follows a selection of techniques into their historical trajectories to excavate some of the fundamental ideas that resonate through our technical present. But throughout these historical probes, I strive to keep an eye on the possibilities for variation, combination, and divergence that invariably emerge when a technique becomes part of a concrete technical object. The developer, in contrast to the computer scientist, philosopher of science, or science historian, neither looks at the reservoir of techniques from below, as an emanation of foundational mathematical principles, nor from above, as outpourings of scientific progress. The developer is right in-between, surrounded by technicity coming in all shapes and forms, and thus '*among* the machines that operate with him' (Simondon, 2017, p. 18).

To interrogate technology both in terms of its fundamental nature and from the perspective of technical practice is the task Simondon laid out for 'mechanology', a discipline or mode of thinking that would serve as a 'psychology' or 'sociology' of machines (Simondon, 2017, p. 160), capturing their 'interior life' and 'sociability' in terms that do not reduce them to an exterior finality or effect. As a general science of technology, mechanology would approach technical function as human gesture, examine technical creation as mediation between human beings and nature, and interrogate the *values* implied in mechanical operation itself. This book, suffice to say, is an attempt to develop a mechanological perspective on software and to apply it to the engines of order that increasingly adjudicate (digital) life.

Organization and Overview

The book is divided into two parts. The first part is dedicated to the theoretical and methodological foundations that inform and support the examination of four clusters of algorithmic techniques for information ordering in the second part.

The first chapter discusses central terms like 'information' and 'order', and it proposes the concept of 'engine' to point toward the infrastructural embeddings that have allowed techniques initially conceived for document retrieval to become pervasive mediators in online environments. While this book constitutes a humanistic exploration of technical substances rather than their practical application, the chapter pays tribute to the fact that the techniques under scrutiny have become prevalent in a specific situation, in *this* world and not another.

The second chapter then formulates a conceptual perspective on software, starting from an attempt to situate the project in relation to existing takes on the subject. But it is mainly dedicated to the presentation and appropriation of Simondon's philosophy of technology, which reserves a central place to technical creation and evolution. Here, we find an understanding of technicity as a domain of life that constitutes its own substance and regularity, whilst remaining a fundamental form of human gesture. Simondon's inductive view, which frames technology as multitude of technical objects rather than idealized techne, grounds the conceptual and analytical apparatus I then bring to the analysis of algorithmic techniques.

Chapter 3 builds on central ideas from Simondon's work, such as the distinction between invention and concretization and the delineation of technical elements, individuals, and ensembles, to conceptualize algorithmic techniques as the central carriers of technicity and technical knowledge in the domain of software. In dialogue with the cultural techniques tradition, it addresses them as methods or heuristics for creating operation and behavior in computing and discusses how they are invented and stabilized. Algorithmic techniques, in this perspective, are at the same time material blocks of technicity, units of knowledge, vocabularies for expression in the medium of function, and constitutive elements of developers' technical imaginaries.

The second part of the book then launches a series of probes into the history of algorithmic information ordering. These probes do not follow a single lineage or logic and cover different periods of time, but they come together in staking out an 'excavation ground' (Parikka, 2012, p. 7) that marks the 1960s and 1970s as the period where the fundamentals of contemporary information ordering were laid out. While Simondon's understanding of technology as human gesture and my emphasis on adaptation and variation lead away from certain core tenets of media archeology, I seek 'to investigate not only histories of technological processes but also the current "archaeology" of what happens inside the machine' (Parikka, 2012, p. 86). The goal is to excavate select roots of an increasingly technological present. The four clusters of algorithmic techniques examined share the characteristic that they are highly relevant to contemporary information ordering while remaining fundamentally understudied, both in their historical and conceptual dimension. Looking at the inception and evolution of algorithmic techniques allows us to examine them in a state of relative 'liquidity', where they have not yet been fully stabilized or 'frozen' into the canon, remaining precarious propositions that have to be explained and justified in terms that are absent from contemporary publications in the computing disciplines.

Chapter 4 serves as a topic-focused introduction that situates contemporary information ordering in a historical lineage that is largely absent from dominant narrations. Although the story starts off from standard takes on knowledge organization and classification in libraries and encyclopedias, it zeros in on the field of information retrieval, which develops in fundamental opposition to even the most visionary of library techniques, not merely in terms of technology and method, but regarding the idea of order itself. Coordinate indexing, the first and defining technique in this lineage, is explicitly designed to eliminate the influence of librarians and other 'knowledge mediators' by shifting expressive power from the classification system to the query and, by extension, to the information seeker. Order is no longer understood as a stable map to the universe of knowledge but increasingly as the outcome of a dynamic and purpose-driven process of ordering. Although equally foundational for the statistical tradition in information retrieval, the chapter closes by discussing coordinate indexing as a precursor of the relational model for database management, which underpins large swaths of contemporary information handling, from enterprise software to web platforms.

Chapter 5 investigates the early attempts in information retrieval to tackle the full text of document collections. Underpinning a large number of contemporary applications, from search to sentiment analysis, the concepts and techniques pioneered by Hans Peter Luhn, Gerard Salton, Karen Spärck Jones, and others involve not only particular framings of language, meaning, and knowledge, they also introduce some of the fundamental mathematical formalisms and methods running through information ordering, preparing the extension to digital objects other than text documents. The chapter specifically seeks to capture the considerable technical expressivity that comes out of the sprawling landscape of research and experimentation that characterizes the early decades of information retrieval. It also documents the emergence of a conceptual construct and 'intermediate' data structure that is fundamental to most algorithmic information ordering at work today: the feature vector.

Chapter 6 examines one of many areas where feature vectors play a central role. Machine learning is currently one of the most active domains in computer science and the wide availability of datasets and increasingly robust techniques have led to a proliferation of practical applications. The chapter uses the Bayes classifier as an entry point into the field, showing how a simple statistical technique introduced in the early 1960s is surprisingly instructive for understanding how machine learning operates more broadly. The goal is to shed light on the core principles at work and to explain how they are tweaked, adapted, and developed further into different directions. This chapter also develops the idea that contemporary information ordering represents an epistemological practice that can be described and analyzed as 'interested reading of reality', a particular kind of inductive empiricism.

Chapter 7 ventures into the field of network algorithms to discuss yet another way to think about information ordering. While Google's PageRank algorithm has received considerable attention from critical commentators, the vast intellectual landscape it draws on and contributes to is less well known. Graph algorithms are used in many different settings, not least in the social sciences, yet the technical and epistemological commitments made by graph theoretical formulations of 'real life' phenomena are hardly a subject of discussion beyond specialist circles. The chapter shows how algorithmic ordering techniques exploit and integrate knowledge from areas other than information retrieval and demonstrates how the 'politics' of an algorithm can depend on small variations that lead to radically different outcomes. The context of web search means that the various techniques covered in the second part of the book can be brought together into a shared application space, allowing for a more concrete return to earlier discussions of variation and combination in software.

The conclusion, finally, synthesizes algorithmic information ordering into a denser typology of ordering gestures, paying particular attention to the modes of disassembly and reassembly that inform the underlying techniques. The attempt to distill an operational epistemology from the cacophony of techniques begs the question whether we are witnessing the emergence of a new *épistémè* (Foucault, 2005), a far-reaching set of regularities that characterize how we understand and operationalize the very notion of order at a given time and place. Independently from how we answer this question, it is clearly impossible to avoid the more immediately pressing need to understand how the capacity to arrange individuals, populations, and everything in-between in highly dynamic and goal-oriented ways relates to contemporary forms of capitalism. To face this challenge, I come back to Simondon's mechanology and its broader cousin, technical culture, as a means to promote a 'widening' of technical imagination and appropriation. While certainly not enough to solve the many concrete issues surrounding advanced algorithmic techniques, an understanding of technicity as human gesture – albeit of a specific kind – can sharpen our view for the many instances where technology has become complicit in domination, for the reconfigurations of power relations that occur when new levers begin to operate in and on society, and for the increasing interdependence between technical critique and social critique.

Bibliography

Andreessen, M. (2011). Why Software Is Eating the World. *Wall Street Journal*, 20 August. Retrieved from http://online.wsj.com.

Beer, D. (2009). Power through the Algorithm? Participatory Web Cultures and the Technological Unconscious. *New Media & Society 11*(6), 985-1002.

Berns, T., and Rouvroy, A. (2013). Gouvernementalité algorithmique et perspectives d'émancipation. Le Disparate comme condition d'émancipation par la relation? *Réseaux 177*, 163-196.

Burrell, J. (2016). How the Machine 'Thinks': Understanding Opacity in Machine Learning Algorithms. *Big Data & Society 3*(1), 1-12.

Christin, A. (2017). Algorithms in Practice: Comparing Web Journalism and Criminal Justice. *Big Data & Society 4*(2), 1-14.

Diakopoulos, N. (2015). Algorithmic Accountability. *Digital Journalism 3*(3), 398-415.

Dijkstra, E. W. (1974). Programming as a Discipline of Mathematical Nature. *American Mathematical Monthly 81*(6), 608-612.

Drucker, J. (2013). Performative Materiality and Theoretical Approaches to Interface. *Digital Humanities Quarterly 7*(1), n.p.

Eubanks, V. (2018). *Automating Inequality: How High-Tech Tools Profile, Police, and Punish the Poor*. New York: St. Martin's Press.

Foucault, M. (2005). *The Order of Things: An Archaeology of the Human Sciences*. London: Routledge.

Gillespie, T. (2014). The Relevance of Algorithms. In T. Gillespie, P. J. Boczkowski, and K. A. Foot (eds.), *Media Technologies: Essays on Communication, Materiality, and Society* (pp. 167-195). Cambridge, MA: MIT Press.

Goody, J. (1977). *The Domestication of the Savage Mind.* Cambridge: Cambridge University Press.

Graham, S. D. N. (2005). Software-Sorted Geographies. *Progress in Human Geography* 29(5), 562-580.

Grimmelmann, J. (2009). The Google Dilemma. *New York Law School Law Review* 53, 939-950.

Hacking, I. (1983). *Representing and Intervening.* Cambridge: Cambridge University Press.

Hacking, I. (1985). Styles of Scientific Reasoning. In J. Rajchman and C. West (eds.), *Post-Analytic Philosophy* (pp. 145-163). New York: Columbia University Press.

Introna, L. D., and Nissenbaum, H. (2000). Shaping the Web: Why the Politics of Search Engines Matters. *The Information Society* 16(3), 169-185.

Kitchin, R., and Dodge, M. (2011). *Code/Space: Software and Everyday Life.* Cambridge, MA: MIT Press.

Mager, A. (2012). Algorithmic Ideology. *Information, Communication & Society* 15(5), 769-787.

O'Neil, C. (2016). *Weapons of Math Destruction: How Big Data Increases Inequality and Threatens Democracy.* New York: Crown.

Parikka, J. (2012). *What Is Media Archaeology?* Cambridge: Polity Press.

Peters, J. D. (2015). *The Marvelous Clouds: Toward a Philosophy of Elemental Media.* Chicago: University of Chicago Press.

Rieder, B. (2005). Networked Control: Search Engines and the Symmetry of Confidence. *International Review of Information Ethics 3*, 26-32.

Rieder, B. (2006). *Métatechnologies et délégation: pour un design orienté-société dans l'ère du Web 2.0.* PhD dissertation, Université Paris 8. Retrieved from https://tel.archives-ouvertes.fr/tel-00179980/.

Rieder, B. (2008). An Experimental Collaboration Tool for the Humanities: The Procspace System. In P. Hassanaly, T. Herrmann, G. Kunau, and M. Zacklad (eds.), *Supplement to the Proceedings of the 7th International Conference on the Design of Cooperative Systems, Carry-le-Rouet, France, May 9-12* (pp. 123-130). IOS Press: Amsterdam.

Rogers, R. (2013). *Digital Methods.* Cambridge, MA: MIT Press.

Simondon, G. (2017). *On the Mode of Existence of Technical Objects* (C. Malaspina and J. Rogove, trans.). Minneapolis: Univocal Publishing.

Winkler, H. (1999). Search Engines: Metamedia on the Internet? In J. Bosma (ed.), *Readme! Filtered by Nettime: ASCII Culture and the Revenge of Knowledge* (pp. 29-37). New York: Autonomedia.

Young, L. C. (2017). *List Cultures: Knowledge and Poetics from Mesopotamia to BuzzFeed.* Amsterdam: Amsterdam University Press.

Part I

1.   Engines of Order

Abstract
The chapter discusses central terms like 'information' and 'order', and it proposes the concept of 'engine' to point toward the infrastructural embeddings that have allowed techniques initially conceived for document retrieval to become pervasive mediators in online environments. While this book constitutes a humanistic exploration of technical substances rather than their practical application, the chapter pays tribute to the fact that the techniques under scrutiny have become prevalent in a specific situation, in *this* world and not another. To this end, the chapter discusses three critical trends: computerization, information overload, and social diversification.

Keywords: information ordering, computerization, information overload, social diversification, digital infrastructures

Although the various practices described as 'information ordering' have become ubiquitous parts of online experiences, the two notions making up the term are far from self-evident. Instead of providing strict definitions, however, I take 'information' and 'order' as starting points for an investigation into a domain of techniques that intervene in deeply cultural territory in ways that come with their specific framings and epistemological perspectives. Instead of asking what information and order *are*, I am interested in the operational answers enacted by algorithmic techniques. This means remaining at a certain distance from common uses of the vocabulary and concepts that characterize the fields associated with information ordering, itself already a somewhat uncommon term. Information scientists and readers familiar with volumes such as Svenonius's authoritative *The Intellectual Foundation of Information Ordering* (2000) or Glushko's recent *The Discipline of Organizing* (2013) will notice that my interpretative lens can differ substantially, despite the shared subject matter. This begins to manifest in seemingly small gestures, for example,

Rieder, B., *Engines of Order: A Mechanology of Algorithmic Techniques*. Amsterdam: Amsterdam University Press, 2020
DOI 10.5117/9789462986190_CH01

when glossing over paradigmatic distinctions between classification and categorization or between data, information, and knowledge. Instead of committing to particular definitions of these and other terms, I am interested in understanding how they inform and coagulate around specific 'problematizations' (Foucault, 1990, p. 10f.) of the domains they refer to and how they are strategically deployed in the construction and justification of techniques that produce epistemologically distinctive outputs. So far, I have used the term 'information ordering' very broadly, connecting it to tasks such as searching, filtering, classifying, or recommending items in online systems. The following section discusses information and order in sequence to address – rather than resolve – their vagueness.

Information Ordering

The techniques and practices discussed in this book hinge to a great extent on the term 'information' and the key role it plays in and around computing. My concern, however, is not the ontological question of what information is, but rather its practical role in different discourses and 'its apparent ability to unify questions about mind, language, culture, and technology' (Peters, 1988, p. 21). In the already somewhat restrained domain I will be investigating, the term has become a central instrument in the endeavor to bridge the gap between human practice and the workings of computing machinery. Here, the fact that information has no shared definition,[1] both in and across different epistemological sites, that it remains 'a polymorphic phenomenon and a polysemantic concept' (Floridi, 2015, n.p.), should not be seen as a failure or deficit but, on the contrary, as a strategic benefit when it comes to smoothening conceptual differences and bringing entire domains into the fold of computing.

As AI-researcher-turned-social-theorist Philip Agre has shown in great detail in his critique of artificial intelligence, polysemy – or, rather, the strategic arrangement of precision and vagueness – plays a productive role in technical work because it helps in binding human affairs to the technical

1   'Information is not just one thing. It means different things to those who expound its characteristics, properties, elements, techniques, functions, dimensions, and connections. Evidently, there should be something that all the things called information have in common, but it surely is not easy to find out whether it is much more than the name' (Machlup and Mansfield, 1983, p. 4f.).

world and the other way around. The following paragraph summarizes his pivotal argument:

> It is frequently said that technical practice employs an especially precise and well-defined form of language, but this is misleading. In fact, terms like 'knowledge,' 'planning,' and 'reasoning' are simultaneously precise and vague. Considered as computational structures and processes, these terms are as precise as mathematics itself. Considered as descriptions of human life, however, they are profoundly *im*precise. AI continually tries to assimilate the whole of human life to a small vocabulary. (Agre, 1997a, p. 48)

Agre's analysis details how artificial intelligence reduces the complex and ambiguous phenomenon of human 'action' to the much more contained notion of 'execution of plans', thereby opening up concrete pathways toward implementation in a working system, a fundamental requirement of the discipline (Agre, 1997a, p. 12). This involves conceptual work: plans are defined as mental structures that consist of subplans, going down a compositional hierarchy to a set of basic operations. The decomposition into small steps prepares a proclamation of equivalence between plans and computer programs (Agre, 1997a, p. 5f.). What is essential, here, is that this reductive, operational understanding of planning is used in such a way that it keeps the initial starting point, the rich world of human action, as a referent. If plans are programs and action the execution of plans, one can now – by definition – simulate human action. The gesture is supported by the idea that 'the proof is in the programming' (Agre, 1997b, p. 140), which leads to a form of tautological reasoning: a technical idea is true if one can build it, and if one cannot build it, it is not a technical idea and therefore has no merit in the field.

We can find comparable semantic operations in many areas of computer science, and the term 'information' often plays a pivotal role in connecting the worlds of humans and machines in similar ways. A well-known example can be found in Warren Weaver's introduction to Claude Shannon's *A Mathematical Theory of Communication*, published as a joint book in 1948 (Shannon and Weaver, 1964). Here, Weaver distinguishes 'three levels of communication problems', beginning with the *technical problem* (A), which is concerned with the fidelity of symbol transmission and thus the level where Shannon's mathematical definition and measure of information are situated. But Weaver then also postulates a *semantic problem* (B) that refers to the transmission of meaning and an *effectiveness problem* (C) that asks how conduct is affected by meaning. While he is somewhat prudent in this regard, he clearly wishes to extend Shannon's model from level A to levels B and C, which should only require 'minor additions, and no real revision' (p. 26). The statistical framing of information on level A finds its equivalence in 'statistical *semantic* characteristics' on level B, and the 'engineering noise' that troubles Shannon's technical transmissions becomes 'semantic noise' (p. 26). The communication of meaning is framed in similar terms as an encoding/decoding type operation. The engineering communication theory 'has so penetratingly cleared the air that one is now, perhaps for the first time, ready for a real theory of meaning' (p. 27). If meaning 'behaves' like information, it is to be investigated and conceptualized in similar terms, which, very concretely, suggests and requires 'a study of the statistical structure of language' (p. 27). What we end up with resembles the transformation Agre describes: a definition of meaning that does not fully reduce it to Shannon's notion of information but postulates a somewhat vague equivalence that enables and authorizes the transposition of the conceptual and analytical apparatus from one to the other. And, as an additional benefit, since that apparatus is mathematical in nature, there is now a clear path toward building a running system, for example, for the practical task of machine translation. The field of information retrieval broadly follows this program from the 1950s onward.

However, an important nuance has to be introduced at this point. The movement of 'absorption' or 'incorporation' of various aspects of human life into the space of computation is often discussed as *formalization* and critiqued as a reduction of an overflowing richness into the cold language of mathematical logic. Golumbia (2009), for instance, takes Chomsky's attempts to model the fundamental rules of language as a finite set of algorithms as his main example to show how 'computationalism' installs formal logic as both an analytical tool and a model for the workings of the mind itself. While Chomsky's work does not seek to build working systems for machine translation but to understand the fundamental principles of cognition (Katz, 2012), such explicit instances of 'high rationalism' have indeed radiated throughout the field of computing. But in many domains, for instance in information retrieval, the conceptual apparatus driving formalization can be surprisingly unambitious, subscribing to the pragmatic mindset of statistics rather than the rationalistic purity of logic. In the paper that first laid out what is now known as a Bayes classifier (Chapter 6), M. E. Maron (1961) programmatically states 'that statistics on kind, frequency, location, order, etc., of selected words are adequate to make reasonably good predictions about the subject matter of documents containing those words'

(p. 405), and this is basically all he has to say about the nature of language in that text. Although a logician himself, he considers the modeling of human language in mathematical logic to be an impasse and instead promotes Weaver's probabilistic perspective.[2]

Information retrieval shares AI's practical goal 'to make computers do humanlike things' (Swanson, 1988, p. 97), but it takes a different route to achieving it. The key referent on the 'human side' in tasks like document search is clearly something having to do with meaning and knowledge, but there is an almost comical desire to *not* develop any serious theory of these concepts and to stick to commonsense uses instead. Lancaster's (1968) classic definition of information retrieval creates even more distance by arguing that an 'information retrieval system does not inform (i.e. change the knowledge of) the user on the subject of his inquiry [but merely] on the existence (or non-existence) and whereabouts of documents relating to his request' (p. 1). Rather than commit to a theory of knowledge, information retrieval sits comfortably in a space where the relationship between knowledge and information is implied, but remains vague.[3] In the end, information's designated role is to be 'the essential ingredient in decision making' (Becker and Hayes, 1963, p. v) and this results-oriented epistemic 'attitude'[4] runs through the field to this day. For example, the famous Text REtrieval Conference (TREC) series, which has been organizing competitions in retrieval performance since 1992, is based on comparing participants' systems to known 'right answers', that is, to classifications or rankings that were manually compiled by experts. The primary goal is to attain or exceed human performance in situ rather than furthering deeper understanding of cognitive processes. Chomsky indeed argues that 'Bayesian this and that' may have arrived at some degree of practical proficiency, but 'you learn nothing about the language' (Katz, 2012, n.p.). His deep disdain for the statistical approach to machine translation is an indicator that the field of computing is characterized by real epistemological variation and disagreement. As Cramer argues, '[c]omputation and its imaginary are rich with contradictions, and loaded with metaphysical and ontological speculation' (Cramer, 2005, p. 125).

---

2   'Thus the goal of processing ordinary language by translating it (first) into a logical language brings with it more problems than prospects, and raises more questions than it answers' (Maron, 1963, p. 139).

3   'To impose a fixed boundary line between the study of information and the study of knowledge is an unreasonable restriction on the progress of both' (Machlup and Mansfield, 1983, p. 11).

4   I take this term from Desrosières (2001).

When it comes to the concept of 'order', we could again pursue formal definitions, pitting it against notions like entropy, but keeping a loose understanding means remaining open to the practical propositions made in the field. The OED broadly suggests that order is 'the arrangement or disposition of people or things in relation to each other according to a particular sequence, pattern, or method'. Order, in this definition, does not have the connotations of Cartesian regularity, uniformity, or immutability. And, indeed, the types of 'ordering' the techniques discussed in this book perform can be fuzzy, fragmented, and dynamic. They generally subscribe to probabilistic frameworks but also draw on other mathematical fields to deal with complexity and variation. Indeed, computing has been instrumental in shifting the problem of 'arrangement and disposition' from static conceptions of *order* to dynamic processes of *ordering*.

One way to think about such changing conceptions leads through Michel Foucault's *The Order of Things* (2005) and Deleuze's reading of that text merits particular attention. Here, the central term to delineate historical formations, each carrying its own specific understanding of order, is that of *épistémè*. Deleuze (1988) reads the classic *épistémè*, situated roughly in the seventeenth and eighteenth centuries, through the notion of 'unfolding' and couples it with what he refers to as the 'forces that raise things to infinity' (p. 128). Epitomized by Linnaeus's *Systema Naturae* (published in twelve editions between 1735 and 1767), divided in the kingdoms of animals, plants, and minerals, this *épistémè* is organized around categorization into a timeless system. Following the logic of representation, there is an incessant production of two-dimensional tables that establish the bounds of the order of things; concrete entities do not define this space, they are merely positioned on it through the attribution of identity and difference with other entities, in infinite variation.

Around 1800, the modern *épistémè* first appears as a perturbation of the classic order. There are irreducible and contingent forces – life, work, language – that break through the preset representational grids ordering the entities these forces are entangled with. In Darwin's work, for example, there is no predefined *regnum animale* ('animal kingdom') that covers all animals and their infinite variations. On the contrary, the tree of life starts with a single organism and the way it evolves is contingent and dependent on interactions between individuals and their specific environments. There is no eternal plan or order: life sprawls and disperses in different directions through successions of abundant yet finite variations. According to Deleuze (1988, p. 126f.), the modern *épistémè* is marked by an empiricism organized around the continuous 'folding' of the forces of life, work, and language. History is not simply variation on a constant theme, but a process of becoming. The order of things is the result of that process and no longer the unfolding of an eternal blueprint.

Rather than stopping at this point, Deleuze attempts to address a question Foucault famously evokes at the end of *The Order of Things*, asking what comes beyond the modern *épistémè*. It makes sense to quote the central passage of Deleuze's argument in full:

> Biology had to take a leap into molecular biology, or dispersed life regroup in the genetic code. Dispersed work had to regroup in machines of the third kind that are cybernetic and informatic. What would be the forces in play, with which the forces within man would then enter into a relation? It would no longer involve raising to infinity or finitude but a fini-unlimited, thereby evoking every situation of force in which a finite number of components yields a practically unlimited diversity of combinations. (Deleuze, 1988, p. 131, translation amended)

This notion of the 'fini-unlimited'[5] provides a compelling way to address the question of order – 'the arrangement or disposition of people or things in relation to each other' (OED) – and how it connects to the algorithmic techniques under scrutiny here. Foucault's *épistémès* are not only connected to particular visual forms of arranging, such as the table or the tree, but they contain specific ideas about the nature of order itself. In the classic period, order is thought to be pregiven, a 'God-form' (Deleuze, 1988, p. 125) that runs through the things themselves, constantly unfolding according to eternal, unchanging principles. The scholar observes, designates, and takes inventory; and although words and things are considered to be distinct, a well-built analytical language or taxonomy keeps them from falling apart by producing a correct account of a world 'offered to representation without interruption' (Foucault, 2005, p. 224). In the modern period, however, order is an 'outcome', something that is produced by the processes of life, work, and language.

How does the notion of the fini-unlimited incubate a third understanding of order? The crucial element, here, is the idea that a limited number of elements can yield an (almost) unlimited number of combinations or arrangements. As shown throughout the second part of this book, permutative

---

5   While the common translation of 'fini-illimité' as 'unlimited finity' may be more elegant than 'fini-unlimited', this amounts to a rather drastic change in emphasis. For a discussion of the topic from a different angle, see Galloway (2012).

proclivity is indeed a central characteristic of algorithmic information ordering: for any sufficiently complex dataset, the idea that 'the data speak for themselves' is implausible; developers and analysts select from a wide variety of mathematical and visual methods to *make* the data speak, to filter, arrange, and summarize them from different angles, following questions that orient how they look at them. Rather than ideas of a natural order, there are guiding interests that drive how data are made meaningful.

This argument is indeed central to two popular books by David Weinberger, *Everything Is Miscellaneous* (2008) and *Too Big to Know* (2012), which are almost manifestos for a fini-unlimited *épistémè*. Even if Weinberger's epistemic attitude and historical trajectory differ substantially from my own, we share the fundamental diagnosis that information ordering increasingly revolves around gestures of disassembly and reassembly that follow specific interests and desires: 'How we choose to slice it up depends of why we're slicing it up' (Weinberger, 2008, p. 82).

Indeed, it has become widely accepted that computers, whether we think of them as computing machinery or as digital media, encourage 'disaggregation and disassembly, but also reaggregation and reassembly' (Chadwick, 2013, p. 41). The central idea informing the relational model for database management, for example, is to cut data into the smallest parts possible to allow for dynamic recombination at retrieval time with the help of a powerful query language that makes it possible to make selections, calculations, or 'views' on the data. Outputs are selected and ordered based on the 'question' asked. The machine learning techniques discussed in Chapter 6, to give another example, provide the means to create information sieves inductively. By 'showing' a spam filter which emails are considered undesirable, the classifier 'learns' to treat each word or feature as an indicator for 'spamminess'. But no two users' classifier profiles will be exactly the same, not only because they receive different emails but also because they will have different definitions of what constitutes an *unwanted* message. This book traces such instances of a fini-unlimited in a manner that remains attentive to commonality yet refrains from singularizing a space of variation into a totalizing assessment.

My purpose, however, is not to postulate a new *épistémè*, a new understanding of order that would have emerged sometime after WWII, and then to show how this new formation has 'found its expression' in a range of algorithmic techniques. In line with the cultural techniques tradition, and in particular with Bernhard Siegert's (2013) radical formulation, I consider that order, as a concept, does not exist independently from ordering techniques and that any broad shift would have to be considered, first and foremost, as a consolidation in the network of ontic operations established by the techniques themselves. From a methodological perspective, this means that the concrete gestures of ordering and the technical, functional, and epistemological substance they carry are the necessary starting points.

Engines Ordering *This* World

While one can look at algorithmic information ordering techniques as a series of technical ideas, their role as 'epistemological operators' (Young, 2017, p. 45) acting on the world in significant ways cannot be understood without consideration for their embedding in ever-expanding infrastructures that play fundamental roles in mediating and constituting lived reality (Burrows, 2009, p. 451). As Peters argues, '[m]edia are not only devices of information; they are also agencies of order' (Peters, 2015, p. 1) in the sense that they support and organize social, political, and economic systems in specific ways. The functional substance of ordering techniques cannot be separated from their application to the bits and pieces of the 'real' world. They have become part of 'the connective tissues and the circulatory systems of modernity' (Edwards, 2003, p. 185) and their integration into larger 'operative chains' (Siegert, 2013, p. 11) binds their broad technical potential into more specific roles. My emphasis on technicity is therefore not in opposition to the perspective Peters (2015) calls 'infrastructuralism' (p. 33) but approaches the large systems that define and support modern life from the perspective of their smaller components.

The term 'engine' indeed serves to link the work done in particular locations or instances to its broader infrastructural embeddings. Donald MacKenzie's *An Engine, Not a Camera: How Financial Models Shape Markets* (2006) studies financial markets in these terms, connecting fine-grained attention for the substance or *content* of calculation with an appreciation of its role and performativity in larger systems. Financial theory, understood as a series of conceptual and mathematical models, is analyzed as 'an active force transforming its environment, not a camera passively recording it' (MacKenzie, 2006, p. 12). How investment markets are framed conceptually and methodologically has concrete consequences for individual (e.g., investment decisions) and collective (e.g., regulation, market design) choices and behavior. The performative dimension of a financial model, method, or theory is strengthened further when it becomes reified in software that defines operative modes directly (MacKenzie, 2010). Both the 'cognitive' and the 'mechanical' understanding of performativity can be fruitfully applied to information ordering, but the latter calls increased attention to forms of operation and automation that are particularly relevant.

Following Adrian Mackenzie's (2017a) take on machine learning, one could emphasize information ordering as a field of academic inquiry and an epistemic practice that is organized around mostly well-delineated steps, where a deliberately selected technique is applied to a contained dataset at a specific moment in time to generate a classificatory output. While this is certainly a common setup, the infrastructural perspective emphasizes a scenario where large-scale platforms capture, support, and channel human practice continuously and information ordering becomes a pervasive arbiter of real-life possibilities. Indeed, the degree to which calculative processes have penetrated into the fabric of contemporary societies is striking, although historiographical work (Beniger, 1986; Yates, 1989; Gardey, 2008) has clearly shown that data collection and analysis techniques have a long history, becoming steadily more central to organization, coordination, and control in business and government over the course of several centuries. Even modern-sounding approaches such as graph algorithms or machine learning have been around since at least the 1960s but were only widely taken up over the last two decades. The question why this has not happened earlier and why this is happening now on such a large scale can serve as an entry point into a deeper appreciation of the context algorithmic information ordering operates in. In the remainder of this chapter, I will thus establish a broader picture, beginning with an assessment of what has been called 'computerization' and followed by a discussion of 'information overload', the problem most often put forward by early information retrieval specialists. Taking a more sociological angle, I will then single out social diversification as a contextual factor that cannot be ignored.

Computerization

One of the reasons for the somewhat delayed adoption of algorithmic information ordering could be that computers were simply not powerful enough before the turn of the century, making the exponential growth in speed and capacity the principal driver. In his acceptance speech[6] delivered on receiving the Turing Award in 1972, Dijkstra (1972) noted that 'as the power of available machines grew by a factor of more than a thousand, society's ambition to apply these machines grew in proportion' (p. 862)

---

6   In computer science, award speeches are one of the few publication formats where broad 'discoursing' is not only allowed but encouraged.

and his argument cannot be easily dismissed: processing brawn is indeed a prerequisite for making certain applications of information ordering a feasible option. Another technical explanation could call attention to the growing availability of algorithmic techniques beyond university labs and specialized documentation centers. But instead of singling out individual 'causes', it makes sense to think about these elements as parts of a larger, self-reinforcing process of 'computerization'.

While the term has fallen out of fashion after its heyday in the 1970s and 1980s, speaking of computerization reminds us that digital media are not just sleek graphical interfaces for making and accessing various kinds of 'content' or 'data' or, but also machines that vary in shape and ability, offering a variable computational basis for the implementation of all kinds of forms, functions, and autonomous operation. The capacity to connect ever-expanding capabilities for storage, transmission, and processing to rich and sophisticated input and output interfaces connected to the world in myriad ways has allowed the computer to infiltrate and to constitute a large number of practices. This can be understood as a process of progressive mediatization, a 'deepening of *technology-based interdependence*' (Couldry and Hepp, 2016, p. 53) that is not limited to consumer devices and includes countless activities in business or government. While the term 'infrastructure' is not reserved for technical systems, it is clear that fewer and fewer practices are not channeled through computing in one way or another.

The web still constitutes the prime example for a pervasive, general-purpose infrastructure that affords access to media content and social interaction as well as myriad services that rely on its technical malleability to organize activities through end-user interfaces and backend coordination. The rapidly expanding entanglement of practices related to communication, coordination, consumption, and socialization with computing is realized through the design and adoption of 'activity systems that are thoroughly integrated with distributed computational processes' (Agre, 1994, p. 105). Facebook, for example, can be understood as a highly complex amalgamation of various layers and instances of hardware and software that, together, form a global infrastructure for 'socializing online' (Bucher, 2013). Agre (1994) argues that an activity is 'captured' in the technical and conceptual vocabularies computing provides when it is enabled and structured by software-defined and computer-supported 'grammars of action'. Since the way this happens is clearly not a mere transposition of previous forms of 'socializing' into a new environment, computerization must be seen as an 'intervention in and reorganization of [human] activities' (Agre, 1994, p. 107). Facebook is not a neutral or transparent means to make, maintain, and enact social relationships, but, 'by organizing heterogeneous relations in a specific way, constitutes a productive force' (Bucher, 2013, p. 481) that operates and mediates through an arrangement of deliberately designed forms and functions. Information ordering techniques become engines of *social* order when they operate and intervene in such environments, where '[t]hey may change social relations, but [...] also stabilize, naturalize, depoliticize, and translate these into other media' (Akrich, 1992, p. 222).

To consider the evolution of computing hardware from the mainframe to personal computers and further to mobile, networked, and integrated devices would be one way to analyze the deep incursions into the frameworks of human life computers have made. Notions like computerization and grammatization, however, seek to address the many different ways broad technical possibilities have been connected to a large variety of practices. If we follow Turing (1948) and Manovich (2013c) in framing computers both as universal machines capable of simulating all other machines and as 'metamedia' uniting various media forms in a single screen, software stands out as the principal means to create the fine-grained structures capable of capturing the components of highly complex activities such as online gaming or project management.

More recently, scholars have used the term 'datafication' to call attention to the process of 'taking information about all things under the sun – including ones we never used to think of as information at all, such as a person's location, the vibrations of an engine, or the stress on a bridge – and transforming it into a data format to make it quantified' (Mayer-Schönberger and Cukier, 2013, p. 15). This is clearly an important aspect to consider. The result of datafication has been the rapidly increasing production and availability of very large datasets that often comprise transactions (logged events or behavior) or other forms of nontraditional data such as traces of movement in navigational or physical spaces, social interactions, indications of cultural tastes, or sensor readings. This, in turn, stimulates demand for analytical capabilities. The accumulation of complicated yet highly expressive unstructured data in the form of textual communication, for example, has fueled interest in techniques like topic modeling or sentiment analysis that seek to make them intelligible and 'actionable', that is, applicable to decision-making.

However, speaking of computerization rather than datafication emphasizes that data accumulation enables forms of 'immediate' management that operate through interface modulation. The direct *application* of algorithmic ordering is made possible by the emergence of digital infrastructures and environments that allow for both data collection and output generation, in the sense that the structure and content of what appears on a screen or some other interface can be compiled in real time on the basis of data that may have been collected over extended periods of time. Differential pricing on the web provides an elucidating example: a user's location, software environment, browsing history, and many other elements can be situated against a horizon of millions of other users and their shopping behavior; this knowledge can then be used to estimate an 'optimal' sales price. The result of this calculation, made in the fraction of a second, can be directly integrated in the interface served to that user, showing an individualized[7] price for an item. Content recommendation, targeted advertising, or automated credit assessment are variations of the same logic.

This instant applicability of data analysis is a crucial step beyond traditional uses of calculation or 'mechanical reasoning' because it integrates and automates the sequence of collecting data, making decisions, and applying results. Human discretion is relegated to the design and control stages and expressed in technical form. Instead of merely detecting or describing some pattern, the results of algorithmic information ordering are pushed back into the software-grammatized spaces the input data were initially taken from, creating new and particularly powerful forms of 'an environmental type of intervention' (Foucault, 2008, p. 260). Algorithms become engines of order that intervene in the processes they analyze, creating feedback loops that direct behavior to realize specific goals. Whether we consider that the various trajectories of computerization, datafication, or 'platformization' (Helmond, 2015) converge into an 'accidental megastructure', an encroaching 'planetary-scale computing system' (Bratton, 2015, p. xviii) or not, it is clear that algorithmic information ordering can now rely on infrastructural conditions that constitute a favorable habitat.

Information Overload

Even today, however, algorithmic information ordering is most often not presented as a means to automate decision-making in integrated digital environments, but more modestly as a solution to the problem generally referred to as 'information overload'. The idea holds that computer-based, networked infrastructures consistently confront users with too much

---

7   A recent report by the White House summarizes: 'Broadly speaking, big data seems likely to produce a shift from third-degree price discrimination based on broad demographic categories towards personalized pricing and individually targeted marketing campaigns' (Executive Office of the President of the United States, 2015, p. 19).

information – too many documents, too many contents, products, or people, too much 'stuff' than could possibly be handled by any individual. These are the circumstances where algorithmic information ordering becomes the preferred solution. As Andrejevic argues, '[d]ata mining [...] comes to serve as a kind of "post-comprehension" strategy of information use that addresses the challenges posed by information overload' (Andrejevic, 2013, p. 41). Of course, neither the assessment that too much information is hampering understanding, nor the call for technical solutions are recent phenomena.

In 1945, when Vannevar Bush described his Memex, an imaginary personal information machine (Buckland, 1992), he famously argued that 'a growing mountain of research' was 'bogging down' scientists (Bush, 1945, p. 112). The idea that the production of printed material had outpaced human capacities indeed became the foundational assessment and problem space for information retrieval. Popular historian James Gleick's book *Information* does not mention the field by name but gives a concise description of what had become a universally accepted diagnosis around the middle of the twentieth century:

> *Deluge* became a common metaphor for people describing information surfeit. There is a sensation of drowning: information as a rising, churning flood. Or it calls to mind bombardment, data impinging in a series of blows, from all sides, too fast. (Gleick, 2011, p. 402)

The cognitive capacities of individuals, the assessment holds, are simply insufficient to deal with the masses of items the 'information society'[8] is confronting them with. While early lamentations concerned the proliferation of printed material, computer systems quickly became the main object of speculation. When Herbert Simon (1971) declares in the early 1970s that '[f]iltering by intelligent programs *is* the main part of the answer' (p. 72) to the information overload problem, he can already look back at two decades of research and experimentation in that direction.

With the advent of networked computing and the web in particular, the question of information abundance and overload is posed with renewed vigor and often in terms that register the widening of applications beyond document search and information retrieval. Chris Anderson's notion of 'infinite shelf space' (Anderson, 2006, p. 16), to name one take on the issue, initially refers to Amazon's seemingly bottomless catalogue, but is quickly extended to other domains covered by the web. In the domain of social

8   The popularization of the term is generally attributed to Machlup (1962).

interaction, for example, the end of the 'tyranny of locality' (Anderson, 2006, p. 16) has allowed burgeoning online communities and dating sites to overcome the limitations of physical distance, resulting in much larger pools of possible interlocutors. Here, as elsewhere, we find larger 'marketplaces' for all kinds of 'goods', not only larger archives of (text) documents. These developments indeed inform the remarkable expansion of the domain covered by information ordering. Although Beer (2016) rightfully argues that phenomena like 'big data' need to be seen 'as part of the long series of developments in the measurement of people and populations' (p. 9), many of the techniques involved have actually been adapted from technical lineages initially concerned with ordering text documents and not people. The crucial moment is the realization that any kind of entity or item can be handled in similar ways when fit into certain data representations. Once grammatized into an information system, 'a human being is merely a document like any other' (Ertzscheid, 2009, p. 33).

Contemporary Internet platforms certainly extend this logic significantly. Referring to online platforms as marketplaces emphasizes that there are units of exchange being made available in a way that each participant could, in theory, access every single one of them. The web makes documents available. Amazon makes consumer goods available. Spotify and Netflix, respectively, make music and audiovisual contents available. Uber makes units of transportation available, AirBnB of housing. Facebook, OkCupid, Meetup, and Monster all make people available, even if they do so quite differently. Since these services often dominate their specific niche and are generally much less limited in geographical and logistical terms than their offline equivalents, they can host large numbers of units and participants. The threshold for participating in online marketplaces is generally low: writing a message on Twitter, which could potentially reach millions of people, is almost effortless.

Building on Coase's (1937) theorization of transaction cost, authors like Ciborra (1985) and Agre (1994) have convincingly argued that information technology makes it easier to organize (economic) activities through markets rather than firms, since it affects all three of the main difficulties transactions have to overcome:

> The costs of organizing, i.e. costs of coordination and control, are decreased by information technology which can streamline all or part of the information processing required in carrying out an exchange: information to search for partners, to develop a contract, to control the behavior of the parties during contract execution and so on. (Ciborra, 1985, p. 63)

This reduction of transaction cost, which has also been recognized by popular authors like Clay Shirky (2008), has facilitated the emergence of the very large marketplaces for information, goods, and people we take increasingly for granted. And the prominent place the transaction cost approach gives to search clearly highlights the mediating role Simon's 'intelligent programs' are set to play in areas that have little to do with text documents. Large online platforms indeed rely heavily on data collection and algorithmic information ordering to filter, recommend, or personalize, that is, to connect users with the units on offer. By modulating the distance between *specific* participants and *specific* items, techniques perform 'navigational functions' (Peters, 2015, p. 7) or forms of 'programmed coordination' (Bratton, 2015, p. 41) in otherwise flat networks or markets. Spam filtering is an interesting example in this context: while unwanted mail is certainly not a new phenomenon, the extraordinarily low cost of sending huge quantities of electronic mail has multiplied the practice by orders of magnitude. The 'renaissance' of the Bayes classifier (Chapter 6) as a means to fight spam can be seen as an attempt to solve the problem without locking down the open, marketlike structure of the email system. Filtering is one way to manage connectivity and mass interaction.

Unsurprisingly, information retrieval has developed in close relationship with statistics, the principal field concerned with applying 'mechanical reasoning' to matters where *too many* individual units hamper under-standing. Statistical mechanics, for example, materialized when it became clear that a description of the empirical behavior of gases based on the measurement of individual molecules would be utterly impossible. Even if the behavior of every molecule in a gas were to be considered as fully deterministic – which quantum mechanics denies – it would be practically impossible to determine the position, direction, and velocity of all individual molecules and to calculate the myriad micro-interactions between them. Mechanical statistics proposed means to manage this disconnection and to conceive the *emergent* behavior of the whole in terms of statistical ensembles rather than individuals. Similarly, as Foucault (2009, p. 104) points out, the study of epidemics and economic dynamics in the nineteenth century undermined the dominance of the family as model for understanding and governing society. Instead, the 'population' – the term now used in statistics for sets of items of any kind – emerged as a proper conceptual entity seen as giving rise to phenomena and dynamics that could not be reduced to its constituent parts. Both molecules and people could no longer be described in deterministic terms when encountered as 'living multiples' (Mackenzie and McNally, 2013) too great in number to describe individual behavior and interaction. In both cases, statistics would resolve the supposed contradiction between uncertainty and control by providing the concepts and techniques to reason with and about such multiples. Statistics both challenges secure descriptions of the world by 'eroding determinism' and furnishes a new language and methodology to 'tame' the resulting uncertainty (Hacking, 1990). Notions such as regularity and variation, distribution and tendency, or dependence and correlation are means to move beyond cognitive overload by addressing 'the many' as statistical ensembles rather than individuals.

Information ordering turns statistical descriptions into engines that intervene in the processes they observe. Peters indeed reminds us that the history of statistics – etymologically the 'science of the state' – is not one of 'pure' mathematics but indeed always tied to practical applications and the realization of pragmatic goals:

> [R]ulers don't want to rule over an imaginary state: they need to make policy, control populations, tax incomes, raise armies. They need facts. And so, statistics arose as the study of something too large to be perceptible – states and their climates, their rates of birth, marriage, death, crime, their economies, and so on – and secondly, as a set of techniques for making those processes visible and interpretable. (Peters, 1988, p. 14)

Algorithmic information ordering relies heavily on statistical techniques to tame information abundance and largely subscribes to a pragmatic epistemology and ethos that seeks to make large quantities of information not only visible and interpretable, but also navigable, actionable, and (economically) exploitable. This line of reasoning leads us further down the rabbit hole into properly sociological territory.

Social Diversification

The enormous production of all kinds of information and the reduction of transaction cost that fuels the 'transition to market-based relationships' (Agre, 1994, p. 120) sit in the midst of social transformations that further exacerbate the perception that ours is a time of complexity, chaos, and disorientation, which makes information ordering – as a mechanism for both description and management – particularly attractive. The schematic assessment that follows remains superficial but adds a layer of explanation that points to deeper transformations than the 'information overload' and 'transaction cost' narratives can capture.

In Ulrich Beck's formulation, modernity, and the period since WWII in particular, is characterized by 'processes for the "diversification" and individualization of lifestyles and ways of life' (Beck, 1992, p. 91). The emergence of consumer capitalism has shifted the focus from production to consumption and brings forth an ever more fine-grained variety of commodities and experiences in virtually all areas of human life, from food to cultural goods and vacations. Societies adopting liberal democracy have seen many traditional social segmentations and taboos erode, continuously extending individuals' capacities to live lives that differ substantially from those lived by both previous generations and next-door neighbors. According to Giddens (1994), ours are decentered, nontraditional societies 'where social bonds have effectively to be made, rather than inherited from the past' (p. 107) and 'choice has become obligatory' (p. 76). One may rightfully wonder whether there is any 'real' difference between the many breakfast cereals available in supermarkets, but my objective is not to adjudicate whether these variations in patterns of consumption, in socioeconomic status, in geographical anchoring, in political and social values, in sexual preferences, in cultural identities and tastes, and so forth are meaningful or not. The argument I want to put forward is threefold: first, we live, at least on the surface, in societies characterized by high degrees of diversity in terms of lived lives; second, these lives increasingly unfold trough infrastructures that log and survey them in various ways, generating large amounts of data that reflect (some of) that diversity; third, these lived lives are patterned and not random. The last point requires particular attention.

The social sciences have spent the last 200 years trying to understand how individuals and society relate, how variation and commonality entwine to produce complex and dynamic arrangements that stabilize, form institutions, and so forth. The most common term used to address stability in society is that of *structure*, whether it is understood descriptively to denote nonrandomness or analytically to refer to actual social forces. The notion of social structure is at least partially tied to group membership, either externally attributed or used by actors to demarcate themselves. Categories along the lines of estate, class, caste, profession, and so forth are the result of historically produced (socioeconomic) classification and stratification that resulted in more or less consistent groups that shared characteristics and social standing, which, in turn, differentiated them from other groups. These segmentations have – at least in part – lost their 'binding force' (Giddens, 1994, p. 63) and structuring capacity, as well as their utility as descriptive concepts.[9] Established arrangements have been disrupted and new ones

9   In his introduction to the sociology of stratification, Saunders writes: 'Compared with the nineteenth century, when Marx developed his theory, the class system has become highly complex and differentiated' (1990, p. 85).

are more complex, dynamic, and opaque, beginning with the organization of labor, 'which has exploded into a multiplicity of activities and statuses, expressing subjectivities and expectations which cannot be reduced to the traditional concept of class' (Lazzarato, 2006, p. 187).

One may wonder in how far attempts to think social structure from the bottom up as multiplicities are reactions to these transformations. Simmel's (1908) 'social geometry' can already be seen as a way of conceptualizing *Vergesellschaftung* ('societification') from the individual, who, due to increasing social differentiation, enters into complex relationships with various others and is less and less confined to a primary group. The recent interest in Tarde's monadological understanding of society (Latour et al., 2012), as well as the continued popularity of other 'inductive' currents – including social exchange theory and social network analysis – can be seen as mere methodological trends or, more fundamentally, as attempts to grapple, conceptually and methodologically, with decentered societies that are grouping in more flexible, transient, and diverse ways. Rodgers indeed calls the recent decades an 'age of fracture', where the 'emergence of the market as the dominant social metaphor of the age' (Rodgers, 2011, p. 44) reinforces a trend toward forms of social organization that revolve around mass interactions between atomized individuals. As I will show in Chapter 7, graph analytical algorithms like PageRank draw heavily on such atomistic conceptualizations of society, but information ordering on the whole thrives on gestures of disassembly and dynamic reassembly.

In a situation characterized by social differentiation on the one side and ambivalent forms of global and local integration on the other, data collection and analysis promise to make the social legible and actionable, to reinstall mastery over societies that continuously create differentiations that no longer conform to traditional groupings and categorizations. This is, at least in part, where the demand for computational data analysis and algorithmic information ordering comes from. As complexity and opacity grow, the epistemic and commercial value of techniques that promise to produce viable descriptions and effective decisions grows as well. This promise, however, still hinges on the 'structuredness' of society in the sense that elements are arranged in increasingly complicated ways without devolving into randomness. Forms of coherence, commonality, and stability continue to exist even if they can no longer be reduced to conceptual pivots such as class. The emergence of what Couldry and Hepp (2016) call 'media-based' or 'mediatized collectivities' (p. 175) – which may well be assembled and ordered algorithmically – represents one vector of coagulation even as 'the spectrum of *possible* collectivities has increased fundamentally' (p. 175).

The 'fragmentation of audiences' (Andrejevic, 2013, p. 12) resulting from the proliferation of channels and outlets becomes an opportunity for those capable of reassembling fragments into addressable groupings.

Most importantly, if it has become difficult to speak of a 'working class' today, it is not because (economic) exploitation has disappeared, but because forms of exploitation have become too intricate and varied to summarize them easily into clear-cut sociological concepts. The transformations Wagner (2016) describes as a 'dismantling of organized modernity' (p. 109), where globalization and individualization have dissolved the binding forces of space and time (p. 120f.), yield a situation where 'formal domination' in terms of legal rights has given way to new kinds of domination that are often based on past formal privilege (p. 146f.), but also increasingly individual-ized. As Giddens (1994) remarks, individuals' capacity to make choices in virtually every sphere of life does not guarantee egalitarian pluralism since decision-making 'is also a medium of power and of stratification' (p. 76). And Bourdieu's (1984) assessment that different forms of capital – economic, social, and cultural – are connected means that, for example, years of education, level of income, and cultural tastes correlate. Forms of analysis that make it possible to describe and act upon such multivariate relationships spanning different domains of life 'tame' social complexity. A much-discussed study in attribute prediction based on Facebook Likes makes a clear case in point:

> Facebook Likes can be used to automatically and accurately predict a range of highly sensitive personal attributes including: sexual orientation, ethnicity, religious and political views, personality traits, intelligence, happiness, use of addictive substances, parental separation, age, and gender. (Kosinski et al., 2013, p. 5802)

One may rightfully interject that the researchers used contestable con-cepts, for example, concerning gender. But this critique risks missing what makes these techniques so attractive in operational settings: when the task is to make distinctions in a seemingly amorphous mass of customers or other entities, the epistemic objective is not disinterested, conceptually rich knowledge and not even getting classificatory predictions right every time; it is to make (quick) decisions that are more accurate than a coin toss,[10] speculative inferences that produce advantageous outcomes

---

10   There are, of course, many areas where higher precision is required, but this (slight) exag-geration should serve to highlight differences between epistemic requirements.

more often than not. And statistical techniques combined with rich data generally perform much better than that. The above-mentioned study was able to predict gender with an accuracy of 0.93 and sexual orientation with 0.88. In many commercial domains, a level of 0.51 would already be satisfactory. The targeting of advertisement, for example, does not have to be perfect to make it economically viable, merely better than purely random placement. There are many powerful techniques for producing such better-than-coin-toss performance at very little cost and these techniques have the additional benefit of providing an empiricist narrative that includes moments of testability and verifiability when effects, for example on click-through rates, can be directly observed. The integrated digital infrastructures or marketplaces discussed above reward economic actors capable of making even *slightly* better predictions than their competition.

For all intents and purposes, the technical environments we inhabit have become our 'real', and the data these environments generate so effortlessly reflect part of human reality. There would be many caveats to add at this point, but I still propose that we consider the possibility that the masses of collected data are not hallucinatory fever dreams, but somewhat spotty and skewed windows on complex societies that are increasingly grammatized and captured by the very technical structures that produce these data in the first place. Since Facebook is a dominant means for social interaction and organization, the data generated by the platform *reveal* our societies, at least particular aspects from particular vantage points. But Facebook's capacity to modify user behavior through interface design and algorithmic processing reminds us that integrated infrastructures are more akin to social *experiments*, controlled environments that can be modified at will, than to settings where sociality is merely observed. In digital spaces, the difference between representation and intervention collapses into a continuous feedback loop. This is why Zuboff (2019) describes 'surveillance capitalism', which seeks to derive monetary surplus from the datafication of human experience, as 'a market form that is unimaginable outside the digital milieu' (p. 15).

Information ordering techniques acting as engines of order that actively modulate relationships between users and circulating units of various kind operate on existing patterns and fault lines in diversified yet unequal societies. They arrange atomized individuals into ad hoc groups, to the point where 'the processes of social segmentation become flexible' (Lazzarato, 2006, p. 182) and follow the operational goals of the moment rather than a desire for stable, disinterested description. Large and small variations between (datafied) individuals can be read from vantage points tied to specific performance targets, such as longer time on site, higher click-through rates, lower loan default ratios, more productive employees, and so forth, but also integrated into broader activities, such as market research, product development, or strategic planning. Zuboff's (2019) extraction of 'behavioral surplus' is clearly not the only way algorithmic techniques can inform processes of value production, but the combination of infrastructural capture, data collection, and information processing indeed provides distinctive means to know and to act on complex societies on the basis of an empiricism that is epistemically biased in a way that the opposition between 'objective' and 'subjective' does not apprehend. Algorithmic techniques, just like other forms of mechanical reasoning, provide seemingly impartial ways to pursue deeply partial objectives.

Bibliography

Agre, P. E. (1994). Surveillance and Capture: Two Models of Privacy. *The Information Society 10*(2), 101-127.

Agre, P. E. (1997a). *Computation and Human Experience*. Cambridge: Cambridge University Press.

Agre, P. E. (1997b). Toward a Critical Technical Practice: Lessons Learned in Trying to Reform AI. In G. C. Bowker, S. L. Star, W. Turner, and L. Gasser (eds.), *Social Science, Technical Systems, and Cooperative Work: Beyond the Great Divide* (pp. 131-158). New York: Psychology Press.

Akrich, M. (1992). The De-Scription of Technical Objects. In W. E. Bijker and J. Law (eds.), *Shaping Technology/Building Society: Studies in Sociotechnical Change* (pp. 205-224). Cambridge, MA: MIT Press.

Anderson, C. (2006). *The Long Tail: Why the Future of Business Is Selling Less of More*. New York: Hyperion.

Andrejevic, M. (2013). *Infoglut: How Too Much Information Is Changing the Way We Think and Know*. New York: Routledge.

Beck, U. (1992). *Risk Society: Towards a New Modernity* (M. Ritter, trans.). London: Sage.

Becker, J., and Hayes, R. M. (1963). *Information Storage and Retrieval: Tools, Elements, Theories*. New York: John Wiley.

Beer, D. (2016). How Should We Do the History of Big Data? *Big Data & Society 3*(1), 1-10.

Beniger, J. (1986). *The Control Revolution: Technological and Economic Origins of the Information Society*. Cambridge, MA: Harvard University Press.

Bourdieu, P. (1984). *Distinction: A Social Critique of the Judgement of Taste* (R. Nice, trans.). Cambridge, MA: Harvard University Press.

Bratton, B. H. (2015). *The Stack: On Software and Sovereignty*. Cambridge, MA: MIT Press.

Bucher, T. (2013). The Friendship Assemblage: Investigating Programmed Sociality on Facebook. *Television & New Media 14*(6), 479-493.

Buckland, M. (1992). Emanuel Goldberg, Electronic Document Retrieval, and Vannevar Bush's Memex. *Journal of the American Society for Information Science 43*(4), 284-294.

Burrows, R. (2009). Afterword: Urban Informatics and Social Ontology. In M. Foth (ed.), *Handbook of Research on Urban Informatics: The Practice and Promise of the Real-Time City* (pp. 450-454). Hershey: Information Science Reference.

Bush, V. (1945). As We May Think. *Life Magazine*, 9 October, 112-124.

Chadwick, A. (2013). *The Hybrid Media System*. Oxford: Oxford University Press.

Ciborra, C. U. (1985). Reframing the Role of Computers in Organizations: The Transaction Costs Approach. In L. Gallegos, R. Welke, and J. C. Wetherbe (eds.), *Proceedings of the Sixth International Conference on Information Systems* (pp. 57-69). Chicago: Society of Information Management.

Coase, R. H. (1937). The Nature of the Firm. *Economica 4*(16), 386-405.

Couldry, N., and Hepp, A. (2016). *The Mediated Construction of Reality*. Cambridge: Polity Press.

Cramer, F. (2005). *Words Made Flesh: Code, Culture, Imagination*. Rotterdam: Piet Zwart Institute.

Deleuze, G. (1988). *Foucault* (S. Hand, trans.). Minneapolis: University of Minnesota Press.

Desrosières, A. (2001). How Real Are Statistics? Four Possible Attitudes. *Social Research 68*(2), 339-355.

Dijkstra, E. W. (1972). The Humble Programmer. *Communications of the ACM 15*(10), 859-866.

Edwards, P. N. (2003). Infrastructure and Modernity: Force, Time, and Social Organization in the History of Sociotechnical Systems. In T. J. Misa, P. Brey, and A. Feenberg (eds.), *Modernity and Technology* (pp. 185-225). Cambridge, MA: MIT Press.

Ertzscheid, O. (2009). L'Homme, un document comme les autres. *Hermès 53*(1), 33-40.

Executive Office of the President of the United States (2015). Big Data and Differential Pricing, February. Retrieved from https://obamawhitehouse.archives.gov/sites/default/files/whitehouse_files/docs/Big_Data_Report_Nonembargo_v2.pdf.

Floridi, L. (2015). Semantic Conceptions of Information. In E. N. Zalta (ed.), *The Stanford Encyclopedia of Philosophy* (Winter 2012 edition). Retrieved from https://plato.stanford.edu/entries/information-semantic/.

Foucault, M. (1990). *The Use of Pleasure: Volume 2 of the History of Sexuality* (R. Hurley, trans.). New York: Vintage Books.

Foucault, M. (2005). *The Order of Things: An Archaeology of the Human Sciences.* London: Routledge.

Foucault, M. (2008). *The Birth of Biopolitics: Lectures at the Collège de France, 1978-79* (G. Burchell, trans.). Basingstoke: Palgrave Macmillan.

Foucault, M. (2009). *Security, Territory, Population: Lectures at the Collège de France, 1977-78* (G. Burchell, trans.). Basingstoke: Palgrave Macmillan.

Galloway, A. (2012). Computers and the Superfold. *Deleuze Studies* 6(4), 513-528.

Gardey, D. (2008). *Écrire, calculer, classer. Comment une evolution de papier a transformé les sociétés contemporaines (1800-1940).* Paris: La Decouverte.

Giddens, A. (1994). Living in a Post-Traditional Society. In U. Beck, A. Giddens, and S. Lash (eds.), *Reflexive Modernization Politics, Tradition and Aesthetics in the Modern Social Order* (pp. 56-109). Stanford: Stanford University Press.

Gleick, J. (2011). *The Information: A History, a Theory, a Flood.* New York: Pantheon Books.

Glushko, R. J. (ed.). (2013). *The Discipline of Organizing.* Cambridge, MA: MIT Press.

Golumbia, D. (2009). *The Cultural Logic of Computation.* Cambridge, MA: Harvard University Press.

Hacking, I. (1990). *The Taming of Chance.* Cambridge: Cambridge University Press.

Helmond, A. (2015). The Platformization of the Web: Making Web Data Platform Ready. *Social Media + Society* 1(2), 1-11.

Katz, Y. (2012). Noam Chomsky on Where Artificial Intelligence Went Wrong. *The Atlantic*, 1 November. Retrieved from https://www.theatlantic.com.

Kosinski, M., Stillwell, D., and Graepel, T. (2013). Private Traits and Attributes Are Predictable from Digital Records of Human Behavior. *PNAS* 110(15), 5802-5805.

Lancaster, F. W. (1968). *Information Retrieval Systems: Characteristics, Testing and Evaluation.* New York: Wiley.

Latour, B., Jensen, P., Venturini, T., Grauwin, S., and Boullier, D. (2012). 'The Whole Is Always Smaller Than Its Parts': A Digital Test of Gabriel Tarde's Monads. *British Journal of Sociology* 63(4), 590-615.

Lazzarato, M. (2006). The Concepts of Life and the Living in the Societies of Control. In M. Fuglsang and B. M. Sørensen (eds.), *Deleuze and the Social* (pp. 171-190). Edinburgh: Edinburgh University Press.

Machlup, F. (1962). *The Production and Distribution of Knowledge in the United States.* Princeton: Princeton University Press.

Machlup, F., and Mansfield, U. (1983). Cultural Diversity in Studies of Information. In F. Machlup and U. Mansfield (eds.), *The Study of Information: Interdisciplinary Messages* (pp. 3-59). New York: John Wiley & Sons.

Mackenzie, A. (2017a). *Machine Learners: Archaeology of a Data Practice.* Cambridge, MA: MIT Press.

Mackenzie, A., and McNally, R. (2013). Living Multiples: How Large-Scale Scientific Data-Mining Pursues Identity and Differences. *Theory, Culture & Society 30*(4), 72-91.

MacKenzie, D. (2006). *An Engine, Not a Camera: How Financial Models Shape Markets*. Cambridge, MA: MIT Press.

MacKenzie, D. (2010). Unlocking the Language of Structured Securities. *Financial Times*, 18 August. Retrieved from https://www.ft.com.

Manovich, L. (2013c). *Software Takes Command*. New York: Bloomsbury.

Maron, M. E. (1961). Automatic Indexing: An Experimental Inquiry. *Journal of the ACM 8*(3), 404-417.

Maron, M. E. (1963). A Logician's View of Language-Data Processing. In P. L. Garvin (ed.), *Natural Language and the Computer* (pp. 128-151). New York: McGraw-Hill.

Mayer-Schönberger, V., and Cukier, K. (2013). *Big Data: A Revolution That Will Transform How We Live, Work, and Think*. London: John Murray.

Peters, J. D. (1988). Information: Notes toward a Critical History. *Journal of Communication Inquiry 12*(2), 9-23.

Peters, J. D. (2015). *The Marvelous Clouds: Toward a Philosophy of Elemental Media*. Chicago: University of Chicago Press.

Rodgers, D. T. (2011). *Age of Fracture*. Cambridge, MA: Harvard University Press.

Saunders, P. (1990). *Social Class and Stratification*. Routledge: London.

Shannon, C. E., and Weaver, W. (1964). *The Mathematical Theory of Communication*. Urbana: University of Illinois Press.

Shirky, C. (2008). *Here Comes Everybody: The Power of Organizing Without Organizations*. London: Penguin Books.

Siegert, B. (2013). Cultural Techniques; or The End of the Intellectual Postwar Era in German Media Theory. *Theory, Culture & Society 30*(6), 48-65.

Simmel, G. (1908). *Soziologie: Untersuchungen über die Formen der Vergesellschaftung*. Berlin: Duncker & Humblot.

Simon, H. A. (1971). Designing Organizations for an Information-Rich World. In M. Greenberger (ed.), *Computers, Communication, and the Public Interest* (pp. 37-72). Baltimore: Johns Hopkins University Press.

Swanson, D. R. (1988). Historical Note: Information Retrieval and the Future of an Illusion. *Journal of the American Society for Information Science 39*(2), 92-98.

Svenonius, E. (2000). *The Intellectual Foundation of Information Ordering*. Cambridge, MA: MIT Press.

Turing, A. M. (1948). *Intelligent Machinery*. National Physical Laboratory Report. Retrieved from http://www.alanturing.net/intelligent_machinery/.

Wagner, P. (2016). *Progress: A Reconstruction*. Cambridge: Polity.

Weinberger, D. (2008). *Everything Is Miscellaneous*. New York: Henry Holt.

Weinberger, D. (2012). *Too Big to Know*. New York: Basic Books.

Yates, J. (1989). *Control through Communication*. Baltimore: Johns Hopkins University Press.

Young, L. C. (2017). *List Cultures: Knowledge and Poetics from Mesopotamia to BuzzFeed*. Amsterdam: Amsterdam University Press.

Zuboff, S. (2019). *The Age of Surveillance Capitalism: The Fight for a Human Future at the New Frontier of Power*. New York: PublicAffairs.

2.   Rethinking Software

Abstract
This chapter formulates a conceptual perspective on software, starting from an attempt to situate the book in relation to existing takes
on the subject. It then moves to a presentation and appropriation of
Simondon's philosophy of technology, which reserves a central place
to technical creation and evolution. Here, we find an understanding
of technicity as a domain of life that constitutes its own substance and
regularity, whilst remaining a fundamental form of human gesture.
Simondon's inductive view, which frames technology as multitude of
technical objects rather than idealized techne, grounds the conceptual
and analytical apparatus then brought to the analysis of algorithmic
techniques.

Keywords: software studies, theory of software, philosophy of technology,
Gilbert Simondon

Taken together, computerization, information overload, and social diversification help us explain how algorithmic information ordering techniques
have come to play such prominent roles and call attention to at least some
of the social, political, and economic matters they have become entangled
with. But they do not provide a clear picture of the actual technical substance
that lurks behind words like 'processing', 'modulating', or 'ordering'. The
rest of this book is thus dedicated to the technicities that give functional
meaning to these terms, even if the shadow of their eventual application
cannot be ignored. This requires an understanding of *software*, as it defines
basic materialities and conditions of production. In this chapter, I begin
to carve out my own perspective in conversation with a number of intellectual signposts, in particular the philosophy of Gilbert Simondon, which
provides valuable clues for an understanding of software as historically
accumulated archive of technical possibilities and of software-making as
technical creation.

Rieder, B., *Engines of Order: A Mechanology of Algorithmic Techniques*. Amsterdam: Amsterdam
University Press, 2020
DOI 10.5117/9789462986190_CH02

Getting a Grip on Software

Philosophy, in particular in its Anglo-Saxon analytical tradition, has long been interested in the foundations, status, and fundamental possibilities and limitations of computing (cf. Colburn, 2000; Floridi, 1999). Subjects such as the distinction between hard- and software, the ontological character of computer programs, and the specific problems computation raises for logicians have been lively areas of study since at least the 1960s and 1970s. An important strand, in this context, is the discussion of the relationship between computing and the mind, famously epitomized by Dreyfus (1972) or Searle (1980), which asks whether computers could ever be capable of 'real' understanding and not just of performing clever tricks that succeed in fooling an observer. These thinkers work toward what I would call a *foundational* understanding of computing, which seeks to settle its ontological status in order to develop a clear, axiomatic basis that supports the deductive style of reasoning analytical philosophy favors.

Despite its very different grounding in what is often referred to as 'continental' philosophy, the field of *software studies*, a subfield or spin-off from media studies, often employs similar strategies. Following the broad roads opened by McLuhan (1964) and Kittler (1997a), authors like Berry (2011), Chun (2011), Hayles (2004), or Mackenzie (2006) have sought to assess the fundamental properties of computing in ways that frequently circulate around the notion of 'code' as the center of gravity. If one could clarify the specific character of this strange creature – written like text yet operating like a machine – one would be able to build all other aspects on these intellectual foundations. While the field has produced a series of attempts (e.g., Fuller, 2003; Gehl and Bell, 2012; Manovich, 2013c) to broaden the focus from computational foundations and experimentation at the margin to the mainstream of widely used software packages, volumes such as the *Software Studies Lexicon* (Fuller, 2008) illustrate a perspective that engages the nitty-gritty of technicity mostly through the basic building blocks of software and eschews the more compound or higher-level techniques and artifacts that populate software-making. In-depth discussion is often limited to the level of (short) code examples[1] and experiments, while the broader

---

1   It is telling that Berry's *Philosophy of Software* provides a complete implementation of Quicksort (2011, p. 48) in C, in order to discuss 'code aesthetics', but says nothing about what that code actually does or what kind of intellectual substance it carries. But without capturing the technicity of the method, there is simply no means to understand why this particular example is considered 'beautiful'. Incidentally, the code snippet, taken from Oram and Wilson (2007), would be an excellent example for discussing how Simondon's notion of concretization applies to software.

technical rationales driving the design and architecture of software artifacts and behavior remain in the background.

Using a somewhat clumsy analogy, one could say that most existing theorizations have approached software primarily through its manifestation as 'language', code, rather than as 'literature', that is, as the myriad of components and programs written in concrete settings for concrete purposes. Understanding how code operates is certainly crucial for getting a grip on software, but the actual landscape of existing objects does not follow teleologically from the mere existence of computing machinery and programmability. Similar to language, software allows for the expression of a wide range of ideas and aspirations, even if basic principles and historically sedimented trajectories of knowledge and technicity structure spaces of possibility. The basic principles of computation have indeed received considerable attention, but the vast pools of accumulated ideas, techniques, systems, or reservoirs of ready-made function have rarely been made matters of concern. Despite the many inspirations I take from strands of foundational reasoning, my goal is indeed to inquire into a small but highly significant portion of what *has been expressed* as software and what *continues to be expressed* when developers draw on available techniques to build programs.

If the notion of algorithm, which I will address in the next chapter, points toward a foundational definition of computation, the notion of algorithmic technique opens onto a vast, contingent, and heterogeneous landscape of words and things that clutter minds and solid-state drives. Because, ultimately, if our business is not with the very possibility of mechanical computation, but with software as a plethora of objects in-the-world, the question to ask becomes 'What is *in* an algorithm?', leading to an investigation into the methods and mechanisms that constitute and inform operation. The elegant concept of computation then quickly begins to bloat up with many different things: real computers, not just abstract Turing machines; real software, lodged in tight networks of other software, all written for a purpose; data that stand for *something*, outputs that have consequences. If software is indeed eating the world, then the world – culture, economics, politics, sociability, education, desire, and so forth – fills up software in return. Much like Latour's famous speed bump, we could argue that software 'is not made of matter, ultimately; it is full of engineers and chancellors and lawmakers, commingling their wills and their story lines with those of gravel, concrete, paint, and standard calculations' (Latour, 1994, p. 41). At the same time, what *is* the gravel of computation? computers? bits? code? How is software made and what is if made out of? Software-making can be, and certainly has been (Bowker et al., 1997), studied through a social scientific lens investigating work processes, social norms, situated learning, tacit knowledge, organizational structures, economic constraints, and so forth. But if there is no serious attention paid to the technical content of software, an approach limited to social or cultural embeddings risks treating technical objects as mere epiphenomena of social or cultural forces. If we consider that artifacts like Google's search ranking mechanisms have political relevance, the question *what* they do and *how* they do it necessarily involves a technical specificity that should not be ignored. An ethnographic workplace study of what used to be Amit Singhal's team[2] would probably yield highly interesting insights in its own right but would be hard pressed to understand how the mechanisms at work relate to the trajectories of technicity that enable and inform their actual operation. While important parts of software-making are indeed entangled with questions of process, convention, learning, and so forth, there is a properly technical substance that sits at the center of technical practice.

The scholarly traditions mentioned above have mostly attempted to describe this substance as a series of singular principles, but the last decades have certainly seen attempts to capture and theorize subdomains and their specificities. The dominant cultural interpretations of the technical and intellectual content of software clearly come in the form of popular science books written by journalists or computer scientists, such as Mac-Cormick's *Nine Algorithms That Changed the Future* or Domingos's *The Master Algorithm*. While these texts do an excellent job at relaying technical principles to a lay audience, their cultural analysis is mostly celebratory and based on what amounts to commonsense reasoning about society and culture. Agre's (1997a) *Computation and Human Experience*, which describes itself as 'a critical reconstruction of the fundamental ideas and methods of artificial intelligence research' (n.p.), remains a rare example for an attempt to produce a technically competent and theoretically informed appreciation of this particularly evocative part of computing. Works by scholars like Burrell (2016), Dourish (2017), and Mackenzie (2015, 2017a), however, have shown more recently that it is still possible to approach some of the most complex techniques in computing from a humanistic perspective with regard to their technicity and not just their social effects and entanglements. Their efforts to unpack, interpret, and critique the rationales informing actual technicities are invaluable and pioneering, raising the question why,

---

2   Amit Singhal is mentioned here by name because he was one of the last PhD students of a central figure in this book, Gerard Salton. Singhal left Google in 2016, allegedly over sexual misconduct, and the head of machine learning, John Giannandrea, took over the search division.

despite the immense public interest, such works remain exceedingly rare. Mackenzie's recent *Machine Learners* (2017a) constitutes a particularly involved attempt to work through the technical and intellectual content of a technical subdomain that sits at the very center of current debates. Although my theoretical perspective and approach deviate in important ways, our projects share not only some of their subject matter, but also a desire to discuss and situate software as a series of particular practices. While the anxieties formulated in popular volumes such as Pariser's *Filter Bubble* (2011), Pasquale's *The Black Box Society* (2015), O'Neil's *Weapons of Math Destruction* (2016), or Eubanks's *Automating Inequality* (2018) inevitably echo through humanistic work on software, the technicities involved and their specific operational and epistemological character merit attention in their own right.

In my own attempt to investigate the substance of information ordering, I broadly follow the perspective laid out by Lev Manovich, most clearly in *Software Takes Command* (2013c), which develops a historically informed analysis of what he calls 'cultural software' and, in particular, of specific techniques and application packages in the domain of media creation, such as Adobe's After Effects and Photoshop. Although Manovich is certainly interested in the fundamentals of computation, his focus is squarely on what comes *after* computation, when software pioneers begin to turn the computer into a 'metamedium' and implement a staggering array of forms and functions into the inviting windows of graphical user interfaces. While my domain of study is a different one, I very much build on the idea that computing is marked by a continuous, cumulative, and contingent process of evolution that is in large part the result of software-making:

> None of the new media authoring and editing techniques we associate with computers are simply a result of media 'being digital'. [...] 'Digital media' is a result of the gradual development and accumulation of a large number of software techniques, algorithms, data structures, and interface conventions and metaphors. (Manovich, 2013b, p. 34)

The computer may be 'undergoing continuous transformation' (Manovich, 2001, p. 64), but this transformation rests on historical processes of 'accumulation' that should not be seen as a singular stream, but as 'sedimented and layered', as 'a fold of time and materiality' (Parikka, 2012, p. 3) that produces complicated temporal patterns. This process concerns not only end-user functionality but runs through software-making itself. The constructive and cumulative 'archives' of technicity and knowledge shape the paths of possibility for the making of technical objects and even if they imply no teleology, they constitute the foundation for any future advancements.

The next section therefore turns to the philosophy of Gilbert Simondon to frame software as technology – not to neutralize its specificities, but to consider it as part of a fundamental mode of constructing and relating to the world, and to distill a number of conceptual and methodological resources for the analysis of concrete technical objects and their evolution. Certain distinctions, in particular between objective and objectal, between abstract and concrete, and between element, individual, and ensemble, make it possible to address algorithmic techniques for information ordering with regard to both their inner composition and their complex relational embeddings. These distinctions inform a perspective that understands the practice of software-making not primarily as 'writing code', but as the creation of technical objects, that is, of 'beings that function' (Simondon, 2017, p. 151). The recognition that technical creation is both *constructive* and *contingent* is central to this argument.

Software as Technology

Simondon's *Du mode d'existence des objets techniques*,[3] published in 1958 and translated as *On the Mode of Existence of Technical Objects* (Simondon, 2017), remains to this day one of the most striking attempts to make technology a matter of philosophical concern. What makes this text a timely read 60 years after its publication is the delineation of a technical mode and substance that are distinct – although not disconnected – from other domains of being. Technology is neither understood as a manifestation of

---

3   All of the conceptual work in this book has been based on the French original (Simondon, 1958). While I reference the English version (Simondon, 2017) for convenience, certain translations have been amended. Most importantly, I translate the French 'la technique', used as a categorical term, with 'technology' to make a clearer distinction with 'une technique' or 'les techniques', for which I use the term 'technique'. Simondon thinks technology from the vantage point of advanced *machinery* and not from *tools* such as hammers. The English term 'technology' connotes this emphasis on 'modern' technical objects better than the specialist term 'technics' used in the recent English translation. In general, Simondon puts little emphasis on strong ontological definitions or demarcations. The term 'techne' does not appear once in *Du mode d'existence des objets techniques* and central conceptual distinctions, for example, between technical element, individual, and ensemble, stem from an analysis of concrete machinery. Much care is taken to not absorb these concepts into an understanding of technology that totalizes the variety of technical objects into a singular logic.

a broad principle of thought such as instrumental rationality, nor as an outcome of social processes yielding functional responses to some needs or desires. But technology is also not framed as an external, autonomous force that stands separate from or even against human beings. On the contrary, is seen as one of the two fundamental 'phases'[4] – the other being religion – that characterize the mode of existence of the ensemble constituted by humans and the world after the breakdown of the original, integral mode that Simondon (2017) calls 'magical' (p. 169). Aesthetic thinking, ethics, and scientific knowledge rise from the tension between the two phases and serve to mediate between them (p. 174).

The details of Simondon's (2017) broader metaphysics are less important here than the conceptual developments that follow from them. At the outset, we find the diagnosis of a culture marked by an imbalance (p. 16) caused by the 'ignorance or resentment' (p. 15) of the central manifestation of modern technology, the machine. The popular debates on the power of 'algorithms' or artificial intelligence neatly illustrate what Simondon means: without robust technical understanding, our culture is condemned to oscillate between two contradictory attitudes: one that holds that technology is merely matter assembled to provide some utility and one that ascribes (hostile) intentionality to it (p. 17). Both attitudes reveal a technical illiteracy that locks our societies in 'alienation', keeping them from accessing the specific way of relating to the world technical creation constitutes. Even broader than its Marxist understanding, the term denotes the profound misapprehension of an entire domain of existence. While there are fundamental differences between Simondon and Heidegger, there is an element of *Seinsvergessenheit* ('oblivion of being')[5]: we treat technical objects as meaningful only in relation to a use and utility, ignoring the human reality they express and constitute. Unlike esthetic objects, they are not given right of residence in the world of signification (Simondon, 2017, p. 16).

Simondon's work is thus an attempt to fundamentally rethink (contemporary) technology as a proper domain of both being and meaning. In close contact with the technical and industrial world since his childhood, he seeks to 'recover' the significance of the material world, both mediated

4   Simondon understands the concept of 'phase' not temporally but in reference to the phase difference between two curves, that is, between $f(x) = \sin(x)$ and $f(x) = \sin(x) + \pi/2$. This means that they need to be understood in unison, even if they each has their specificity (cf. Simondon, 2017, p. 173).

5   Heidegger's (1962) critique targets the ontological reductionism manifest in attempts to narrow being to a single aspect, for example, Plato's designation of ideas as the domain of true existence.

and constituted by technology, for human existence. Emphasizing this conceptual and normative readjustment, Chateau argues that for Simondon '[t]echnicity is an essential mode in man's relation to the world: *it is an essential mode of existence for man*'.

The concept of 'technicity', the term used to conceive and address a specifically technical substance, undergirds this project, putting at its center the notion of 'function'. According to Simondon, '[w]hat resides in the machines is human reality, human gesture fixed and crystallized in working structures' (Simondon, 2017, p. 18), that is, structures that perform technical operations. This quote, however, should not be read as a concession to social constructivism, where human ideas and desires that are not themselves technical in nature are imprinted onto technical objects. On the contrary, Simondon (2014) attempts to delineate a domain of 'functional meaning' (p. 28) that rests on itself, where machines signify not only through *what* do, but, crucially, through *how* they operate. There is not something properly human on the one side that is transposed or translated into technical form on the other. Technicity itself, understood as organized functioning, is an intrinsically human mode of existence and evolution (cf. Simondon, 2014, p. 321). Simondon thus joins thinkers like Leroi-Gourhan (1993), who see technology, like language, as a fundamental trait of our species. Indeed, when Simondon (2017) argues that 'human beings communicate by what they invent' (p. 252), he does not mean that there is some kind of message encoded in the technical object, but anticipates McLuhan's (1964) famous one-liner: the object, its technical schema and functional makeup, *is* the message.

To be clear, Simondon postulates neither a cybernetic equivalence between human and machine through the notion of operation nor a confluence of technical and biological evolution (cf. Guchet, 2008). Rather, distinct orders of reality enter into contact through 'transduction': individuation, of both subjects and objects, happens when preindividual realities develop relations of mutual structuration (cf. Simondon, 1989, p. 24f.). Primacy is given to the relation over its parts, but heterogeneity is not erased. Identity, so to speak, can be seen as the metastable function of a dynamic system, as long as we understand that this does not mean that all relations are equivalent or that relations emerge spontaneously or 'promiscuously' (cf. Stiegler, 1989). A technical individual is, first and foremost, characterized by strong and stable *technical* or *causal* relations between the constitutive elements that establish and maintain its functioning. These relations constitute the *objective* mode of existence of a technical object, in opposition to its *objectal* mode, which marks a detachment from its producer and 'the beginning of a free adventure' (Simondon, 2014, p. 27) embedded in economic, social, and psychosocial relations.[6]

While Simondon concedes that social factors also affect the technical object during its evolution, he insists that the objective mode is already full of meaning and value, without considering use or finality (Simondon, 2014, p. 321). His position, here, has a normative component: early manifestations of consumer capitalism's tendency to package technical objects in endless variations of the same technicities clearly do not find Simondon's approval (cf. 2014, p. 27f.). A technical object may have a 'halo of sociality' as a 'psychosocial symbol' (Simondon, 2014, p. 29), but it already – and even primarily – signifies in its objective mode and thus constitutes a domain of expression in the form of operational structures.

Using the vocabulary of Actor-Network Theory, we could say that an object's technicity realizes 'its script, its "affordance", its potential to take hold of passersby and force them to play roles in its story' (Latour, 1999, p. 177). Simondon's philosophy, however, cautions us to not move too quickly to the heterogeneous but flat assemblages Actor-Network Theory conceives. In fact, Latour's more recent *An Inquiry into Modes of Existence* (2013) follows Simondon in arguing that such modes delineate their own substances in ways that are more profound than a mere incommensurability between language games, because they admit other beings than words into the fold of what makes a mode *specific* (Latour, 2013, p. 20). Being itself is marked by difference and, as Peters (2015) claims, '[o]ntology is not flat; it is wrinkly, cloudy, and bunched' (p. 30).

When it comes to technology, this means that one should be attentive to the specificity of an object's functioning, and, on a broader level, to the question of how technology defines its own forms of evolution and transmission. The latter, in particular, is essential for understanding software and software-making as embedded in processes of accumulation and sedimentation.

Technical Evolution

For Simondon (2017), technology is characterized by a complex process of evolution. This process includes a moment of inception, an 'absolute

---

6   While the conceptual separation between 'objective' and 'objectal' runs through all of Simondon's work on technology, he uses the latter term only in his lecture on the psychosociology of technicity (Simondon, 2014). My more explicit opposition between the two terms follows Chateau's (2014) interpretation.

beginning' (p. 44) of what he calls a 'schema'. He acknowledges that there is always a prehistory – my own rather meandering account of PageRank in Chapter 7 is a case in point – yet argues that the invention of the thermionic diode, for example, amounts to the creation of a new 'technical essence' that concerns, in this case, a particular way of producing asymmetric conductance. Fleming's idea to heat one of the two electrodes in a vacuum tube to assure that current can only travel in one direction then constitutes the beginning of a technical lineage that dominates electronics from the early 1900s to the arrival of semiconductor devices in the 1960s. Indeed, what constitutes the thermionic diode's essence is not merely the technical task it performs ('what it does'), since asymmetric conductance could already be produced by other means, but the specific technical principle it relies on ('how it does it'). The technical principle takes primacy since 'no fixed structure corresponds to a definite usage' (Simondon, 2017, p. 25). And, indeed, vacuum tubes acquire a whole range of initially unintended uses over time. This means that categorizations of technical objects based on use or finality cannot capture their objective dimension and that technical trajectories are not tied to single tasks but often run through many different applications and cultural segmentations. We will see this principle at work many times in the context of information ordering.

Putting the emphasis on technical schemas highlights the deep embeddedness and relationality of modern technology. Engines working with steam, combustion, or electricity, for example, may all perform the exact same work in certain conditions, but they are made out of different materials, have different sizes, weights, and operational properties, require different forms of maintenance and care, and depend on different energy infrastructures for their particular fuels. All of this means that each engine type is more compatible with certain modes of social and economic organization than with others. And these relational aspects are not static but change in conjunction with the specific evolutionary trajectories they trace over time. While it may be enough to describe an algorithm's behavior to establish its 'script' and to analyze its role in the *hic et nunc* of a particular setting, a deeper appreciation of computing as a technical domain has to consider schemas as 'units of becoming' (Simondon, 2017, p. 26, translation amended) that evolve and change their potentiality. Yet the way a technical trajectory unfolds is circumscribed by its technicity, even if there is no singular destination or telos (cf. Bontems, 2009). To speak with Wolfgang Ernst (2015), 'technical things form a self-referential subsystem that [...] disconnects itself from the broad "historical" time' (p. 186) and evolve according to their 'inner time' (*Eigenzeit*), their own temporality.

The notion of technical essence and the process of evolution are complicated by the observation that technical 'individuals', the level of integration Simondon (2017) associates with machines (p. 77), are made of technical 'elements' such as screws, springs, or diodes, which are the most immediate carriers of technicity (p. 73ff.). Individuals, which constitute operational units and are therefore closest to the human scale (p. 77), combine and arrange elements into functioning and integrated wholes, realizing technical schemata that evolve over time. As Chabot argues, for Simondon, '[t]echnological invention consists of assembling a coherent system from disparate elements' (Chabot, 2013, p. 14). Technical objects are made – and increasingly so – out of other technical objects.

The distinction between element and individual also allows for a lucid conceptualization of transmission or transversality between different trajectories, since elements are more 'universal' and can be put to use in very different individuals (Simondon, 2014, p. 327). Elements developed in one context often spread to others, further underscoring the task-independence of technicity, which will be particularly important when accounting for algorithmic techniques. At the same time, Simondon (2017, p. 21) argues that the locus of technicity has steadily 'moved up', to the point where contemporary societies are organized around technical 'ensembles' that combine many individuals into coordinated systems reliant on an exchange of information rather than energy. These ensembles – laboratories, factories, industrial networks – ensure the production of both elements and individuals. The trifecta of element, individual, and ensemble allows for a nuanced analysis of technology not as techne but as sprawling ecosystems of objects and trajectories that require inductive conceptualization rather than idealistic totalization. For Simondon, technology does not exist as a singular, but as a multitude of concrete technical objects (cf. Carrozzini, 2008, p. 9).

Another reason why Simondon's approach is attractive to students of contemporary technology is the attention paid to technical evolution *after* the invention of a technical schema or essence. Although common in studies of technology as economic and industrial endeavor, the matter is rarely tackled in philosophical accounts. Terms like 'lineage' or 'trajectory' indeed address how a schema evolves after its basic principles have been introduced and the particular pathway it follows relates to its technical specificity (cf. Simondon, 2017, p. 26). Evolution implies moving from an *abstract* state, that Simondon (2017) also calls 'analytical' (p. 29) or 'intellectual' (p. 49), toward a *concrete* state, where the interplay between elements has become 'a system that is entirely coherent within itself and entirely unified' (p. 29). 'Concretization', then, does not denote a movement from idea to physical artifact but the way technical objects shift their internal composition as they iterate from one version or instance of a schema to the next. The combustion engine can serve as an instructive example: early motors were characterized by strong functional separation between parts, each element having a single task in a functional chain (p. 27). Over many cycles of refinement, motors became more integrated, synergetic, and thus concrete. Elements started to take on multiple roles, such as the cylinder block performing heat regulation to reduce material strain and to keep the electrodes of the spark plug at optimal working temperature. Instead of being largely separate steps in a chain, the elements in a concrete technical object support and sustain each other. If a technical object is a 'theater of a certain number of reciprocal causal relations' (p. 32) that assure its operational functioning, concretization is the movement toward synergy, toward an optimal state of interaction between elements.

A schema's trajectory ends when this process has reached a point of saturation and no further optimizations can be made (p. 45f.). At that point, any improvement to task performance requires a new invention, a new essence or schema that, in turn, will begin its own march toward concretization. The switch from steam to combustion engines clearly marks such a moment.[7] Trajectories are defined by this process of evolution, not by tasks performed or by companies' changing product portfolios. Contemporary machines can tie together many trajectories: in the case of computing, it is clear that the shift from vacuum tubes to semiconductors inaugurates a new technical schema for central processing units, but other crucial elements, such as storage or input and output devices define their own evolutionary pathways.

Crucial for my discussion of software is Simondon's association of the abstract state of technical objects with *artisanal* modes of production and the concrete state with *industrial* modes. The former is 'analytical', closer to the world of ideas, and more open to deviation and new possibilities (p. 29). The latter is marked by functional closure and standardization. However, it is not standardization that drives concretization; it is concretization, as convergence toward an integrated state, that stabilizes the technical object internally and thereby makes it ready for industrial production. As a consequence of this stabilization, the concrete technical object determines its uses and 'acquires the power to shape a civilization' (p. 29), while the abstract, artisanal object is shaped by external needs and desires.

---

7   Simondon's analysis is actually more fine-grained and puts the diesel engine, which uses compression instead of spark plugs to ignite the fuel, in its own lineage.

However, technical evolution is not exclusively driven by internal con-cretization; it also involves adaptation to the geographical[8] and technical milieux, for example, through better reaction to climatic conditions or a more efficient use of production capacities. The technical object sits between the natural and the technical world and, through it, each world acts on the other (Simondon, 2017, p. 56). The idea that the natural world circumscribes the fundamental possibilities of technical functioning is certainly not uncommon. Wolfgang Ernst (2015), for example, argues that technologies can only be 'discursively constructed within the confines of matter and mathematical logic' (p. 196), which means that the 'technological time proper to media stands closer to the acculturated laws of nature than to historiography and the humanities' (p. 188). In Simondon's relational ontology, however, the difference between these two worlds is pushed into the background to make room for technical evolution as a fundamentally 'constructive' process (Simondon, 2017, p. 58).

Technical *invention* is different from internal concretization and adaptation to the environment. Invention means that technical objects realize or actualize their own 'associated milieu',[9] composed of natural and technical elements and relations that enable and sustain their operation. The creation of this third, this 'techno-geographic' milieu, points to the fundamental contingency that undergirds the evolution of technical objects: there is no teleology, no law of necessity that drives evolution, only feats of human intelligence that, in a sense, generate new materialities out of existing materialities. This is what Simondon means when he says that technical evolution is constructive: much like biological life has formed highly complex ecosystems that are populated by organisms capable of maintaining and reproducing themselves yet deeply enmeshed in various relations and interdependencies, technology has a 'fecundity' (Simondon, 2017, p. 45) to sprawl and to extend the possibilities of life itself. Terms like 'autopoiesis' or even Herbert Simon's (1996) analysis of complex systems as 'nearly decomposable' hierarchies, where every level develops properties that cannot be reduced to the level below, capture certain aspects of Simondon's

8   The term 'geographical' underscores how, for Simondon, abstract principles such as 'nature' have little interest since materiality is always a set of concrete circumstances in time and space.
9   The mixed, relational, and self-referential character of the associated milieu becomes explicit in the following quote: 'This simultaneously technical and natural milieu can be called an associated milieu. It is that through which the technical object conditions itself in its functioning. This milieu is not fabricated [*fabriqué*], or at least not fabricated in its totality; it is a certain regime of natural elements surrounding the technical being, linked to a certain regime of elements that constitute the technical being' (Simondon, 2017, p. 59).

thinking here, even if they do not sufficiently account for heterogeneity and transduction. New schemas sit on top of old schemas in an endless process of constructive expansion.

While Simondon is hardly clear on this point, there may very well be a 'ground floor' of irreducible physical structures, but since human beings exist as technical beings, we inhabit a world that is always already characterized by this relational state of overflow. Simondon's (2017) rather cryptic assertion that '[t]he mediation between man and the world becomes itself a world, the structure of the world' (p. 193) evokes the deeply constructive nature of technology and it is essential to emphasize that in this relational ontology, the normative force of structure, that is, the capacity of *what is already given* to make some things possible and others not, to make some things easy and others difficult, is not seen as a confinement, but as the very condition for an endless generation of new materialities, new schemas, new (technical) essences.

Because technology itself adds to the reservoirs of technicity, it is never just an application of science, even if its possibilities are subject to the laws of nature and concretization can be seen as a way to exploit these laws for the greatest efficiency (cf. Simondon, 2017, p. 39). But it is also never just a playground of cultural imagination. An idea describing a particular use or application is not a technical idea. Gene Roddenberry thought of a 'transporter' that can 'beam' things from one place to another, but he did not *invent* it and, therefore, his idea is not a technical idea and the transporter not a technical object. A technical object is a being that functions and a technical idea is one that assembles an associated milieu into a potential for operational functioning. And because the reservoir of what is given does not easily bend to our will, technical invention is *hard*.

Simondon's perspective has been called 'unbalanced' (Mills, 2011, n.p.) for giving priority to the objective over the objectal, that is, to technicity over economic, social, and psychosocial dimensions. However, seen in the context of Simondon's broader oeuvre, which dedicates much attention to psychosocial 'transindividuation', his work on technology can be seen as a normatively charged attempt to put culture and technicity on equal footing, framing both as 'techniques for human handling' (Simondon, 2014, p. 318) that imply their own 'modes of analysis' (p. 329). Actual technical objects, once they detach from their creators, connect technicity to specific tasks in specific settings and their contribution in this specific context is thus a shared product that can be analyzed along both lines. But technology and culture are 'unbalanced' (Simondon, 2017, p. 16) because we generally do not consider technicity as a genuine domain of meaning and a viable

avenue for the analysis of human existence. If philosophy has historically considered technology as either autonomous or defined by its use, in
Simondon's perspective it is neither. It is an 'expression of life' (Simondon,
2014, p. 321) that requires a *mechanology*, a mode of analysis that recognizes
its specificities.

The Technicity of Computing

My investigation into information ordering is largely inspired by the question
of how algorithmic techniques can be understood and investigated as what
Petersen (2015) calls 'functional expressions', human communication in
the form of function that exercises 'an action on man' (Simondon, 2014,
p. 318). This raises the question of how Simondon's perspective, formulated
in the 1950s, can be productively applied to the domain of computing. We
may require some adaptation and additional nuance, but his thinking can
certainly inspire a course toward an analysis of technicity that moves from
totalizing accounts to the universe of technical objects, sprawling and in
constant evolution. My objective, here, is not to 'rectify' Simondon's account,
but to continue what he set out to do, that is, to take technical objects
seriously as carriers of meaning and to ask what they can tell us about the
character of contemporary technology.

The distinction between element, individual, and ensemble can certainly
be read as part of a metaphysics of technology, but it can also be used as
a conceptual device orienting the analysis of specific technical domains.
While technicity resides on all three levels, there are important differences.
Elements can be seen as carriers of 'pure' or 'free' technicity (Simondon, 2017,
p. 74), because they are not yet combined into systems that, so to speak, put
certain *demands* on them. Individuals, on the other hand, are such stable
systems of organized elements (p. 74) and they require 'self-regulation'
(p. 73), that is, structural coherence capable of assuring their function
and stability over time. As part of an individual or machine, the element
is no longer an unconstrained potential, but part of a schema that defines
an associated milieu and, in turn, is defined by its relationship with the
regularities of existing natural and technical materialities. A good way to
think about this nuance is to consider that an element has no real scenario
of optimal function or failure, since it is not yet part of a context that defines
what that would mean. Whether a screw fulfills its role depends on the
structural weight or pressure it has to withstand when becoming part of a
specific object. We cannot say that a screw is too weak without knowing
what it is supposed to hold.

When considering computers as technical individuals, one can begin by pondering hardware as composed of various kinds of elements, from voltage regulators to semiconductor parts to cables and casing. But should we treat more stable and modular units such as processors, hard drives, and screens, which are themselves made of smaller parts, also as individuals? In Simondon's perspective, they play the role of elements, since they cannot function on their own and are therefore not tied to a specific operational context or milieu that determines the specific conditions they have to perform in. But how does software fit into this equation?

Given Simondon's impressive technical awareness, it is not surprising that computers already figure prominently in his work. They are discussed as part of a larger species of 'open' machines that possess a margin of indetermination and the capacity to receive information that is then used to set actual outcomes (Simondon, 2017, p. 154). Only living beings can give themselves information, but even a mechanical piano that plays a piece according to the holes in a paper roll has the capacity to actualize a potential in different ways (cf. p. 156). While the piano already comes with built-in 'schemas of decisions' (p. 154) that define the relationship between information and action, such schemas have to be programmed into the computer to tie incoming information to particular actions (p. 154). Software is thus fundamentally part of the machine, since it defines how it functions. The hardware remains element without the software, pure technical potential that needs other elements to become a functioning whole. That also means that programming is not simply a form of *adapting* a machine, it is an integral part of *making* a machine and, consequently, a genuine domain of technical creation and invention. The reverse holds true as well: without the hardware, software is but a technical element.

This perspective resonates with Turing's fundamental take on computation (1937), where any universal (Turing) machine can simulate any arbitrary (Turing) machine, the latter specifying the actual computational procedure to be executed. But for Simondon, only a physical computer can be a technical object that *functions*. As technical individual it is defined both by the software procedures it executes and by its physical capabilities, such as processing speed, storage size, networking equipment, and input/output modalities. All of these elements form the associated milieu that make the individual a 'networked object' (Guchet, 2001, p. 229) that draws preexisting potential together into function. We end up with a perspective that moves away from strict ontological distinctions between hardware and software or between digital and analog and instead gives primacy to the question of how various heterogeneous elements come together to form a machine.

This does not mean that we cannot treat software as a particular domain or type of element. What it does mean, however, is that we need to be cognizant that actual functioning is a relational outcome of elements assembled into working systems that are placed into particular objectal contexts. The constructive and relational character of technology quickly becomes evident when we look at actual objects and their trajectories.

As previously stated, a technical essence or schema has an absolute beginning. If we consider algorithms to be potential carriers of such technical schemas, we can take something like Tony Hoare's Quicksort and trace it back to roughly 1959, when Hoare was working on machine translation on visit at Moscow State University (Hoare, 2011). But Quicksort arrives at a point in time where computers not only exist, but exist at a certain stage of development, where the early programming language Autocode has been released, where other sorting algorithms have already been in use for years, and so forth. The availability of a programming language means that many of the basic elements needed to put Quicksort in place – a list-type data structure, looping functions, basic logical operators, string comparison features, etc. – were readily available and no longer had to be coded by each programmer herself in machine language. Against a somewhat naive reading of Kittler's (1997a) 'There Is No Software', where high-level programming languages represent a form of 'obscuring' or barring of access to the hardware (p. 150), Simondon would hold that the elements of technicity these languages provide constitute a 'more': more technicity, more possibilities, new techniques to integrate and ideas to draw on, trajectories of concretization in the form of highly optimized compilers, and so forth. Construction, not confinement. There is no base layer of technicity where the 'real' operations happen, only specific instances of natural and technical potentials that are being drawn together into a technical object. And this includes hardware: while we can reason about performance characteristics of sorting algorithms in abstract terms, Hoare (2011) himself argued that Quicksort responded to the particular challenges of sequential tape storage and the small working memory available at the time.

Quicksort may have been a genuinely new schema for sorting, but its invention occurred in an environment already full of technicity that forms a reservoir or archive for technical imagination to draw on:

> We can consider the technical imagination as being defined by a particular sensitivity to the technicity of elements; it is this sensitivity to technicity, that enables the discovery of possible assemblages; the inventor does not proceed *ex nihilo*, starting from matter that he gives form to, but from elements that are already technical. (Simondon, 2017, p. 74)

The compositional nature of technical invention is particularly obvious when considering computing's highly layered and modular character, which I will address in more detail in the next chapter.

Crucially, elements are not dissolved when forming individuals and they constitute their own trajectories. The combustion engine forms a lineage because there are certain functional principles that run through all combustion engines and these principles are different from the those that animate the steam engine, for example. In the domain of software, the C-family of programming languages or the many Unixlike operating systems are evocative and tangible candidates for such 'units of becoming' that carry a set of functional principles through the course of an evolution. Application packages, programming libraries, or toolkits may well be pondered in similar terms as they carry schemas from one version number to the next.

When dealing with complex software artifacts like operating systems, the distinction between element, individual, and ensemble becomes unstable, but remains analytically useful. The point of view of the element points toward technicity as fundamental technical potential or force in the sense that elements have the 'capacities for producing or undergoing an effect in a determinate manner' (Simondon, 2017, p. 75). The notion of the individual addresses how these 'pure' technical forces are integrated, how an associated milieu is formed and stabilized, how continuous operation is realized. A car defines such a mutually stabilized system of almost innumerable elements and a smartphone is no different in that regard. Hardware and software are assembled in a way that each element is adjusted to the others. The application software 'fits' the processor speed, memory capacities, screen dimensions, sensor arrays, and so forth. The battery size reflects the requirements of the hardware and the charging mechanism is designed to keep it from exploding by taking into account the chassis's capacity to evacuate heat. The operating system manages the hardware resources within their limits and assures that the applications stay out of each other's memory space. As part of an individual, each element binds and is bound at the same time.

Technical ensembles, on the other hand, constitute systems that are not characterized by the creation of an associated milieu, but rather by a form of coupling that merely connects outputs to inputs, while remaining separate in terms of actual functioning. There is no search for synergetic integration; on the contrary, each individual operates in its own milieu and interactions may produce unfavorable effects (Simondon, 2017, p. 66). In an artisan's workshop, a laboratory, or a factory, phenomena like heat transfer or electromagnetic induction from one object may detrimentally affect another and shielding or physical separation may be necessary, even if there is 'cooperation' in terms of overall operation. The relationship between individuals in an ensemble is therefore characterized by exchange of information rather than direct technical coupling (Simondon, 2017, p. 17). Simondon compares technical elements to organs, functional units that could not subsist on their own, and individuals to living bodies (Simondon, 2017, p. 62). In this analogy, ensembles appear as 'societies', characterized by more precarious or tumultuous dynamics of relation, stabilization, and perturbation. Computer networks connecting functionally separate machines are obvious candidates for technical ensembles, but the utility of the concept is broader. Simondon argues that technical and economic value are almost completely separate on the level of the element, while individuals and ensembles connect to broader realities such as social arrangements and practices. Ensembles, in particular, point to the fact that contemporary technology functions as a series of 'industries', highlighting the deep entanglement between technologies and economies, to the point where a whole 'geology' (Parikka, 2015) of technology becomes visible: almost everything on this planet, above ground and below, has become part of networks of production and consumption. These networks are organized through flows of information that assure communication and control.[10]

In Simondon's work, concretization is the march from a more abstract or modular state, where elements are arranged so that every part only fulfills a single function without synergy with the others, to a state of integration where mutual adjustments yield optimal functioning. The process implies an arrangement of technicities in a way that the technical properties of an element, which may well pose problem to the functioning of the whole, are turned into a benefit. Structural integrity, weight and size, heat evacuation, favorable operational conditions, reduction in cost and resource use during both construction and operation, and even aspects such as the degree of difficulty to produce or recycle an object: these are some of the lines the process of concretization travels along. While Simondon's conceptualization of technology from the state of the art of his time is one of its greatest strengths, it also means that there is a marked focus on energy use and, in particular, on the problem of thermal buildup as the principal plague

10   Simondon engages in a substantial dialogue with cybernetics, which he generally views favorably as a means to conceptualize and manage the dynamics of ensembles, but also considers as 'insufficient', because it neither conceives technology in its entirety, nor gives adequate attention to the specific nature of technical schemas. But it is clear that he sees a systems perspective grounded in a theory of information as essential to the understanding of technical ensembles (cf. Simondon, 2017, p. 160).

of industrial technology. Excess heat means energy loss, impediment to function, and, *in fine*, structural disintegration, all causing extra costs. Although Simondon never states this directly, the concrete technical object is, first and foremost, *efficient* when it comes to dealing with these problems.

Computers certainly face some of the same problems 'normal' machines do, since energy efficiency and heat evacuation are two of the most pressing issues hardware engineers struggle with. Moore's law, which holds that transistor density in integrated circuits doubles roughly every two years, can be seen as a metric for concretization that indicates efficiency gains in terms of performance, energy consumption, size, and material cost per unit. While we usually venerate invention as the creation of the genuinely new, there are good reasons Simondon dedicates so much space to concretization: the emergence of modern technology as a truly pervasive force would be unthinkable without it. From a formal point of view, the first general-purpose microprocessors of the 1970s are (almost)[11] identical to the chips powering today's smartphones. But steady progress in manufacturing has sped up processors by many orders of magnitude, to the point where the supercomputers in our pockets have become capable of extraordinary feats. Similar arguments can be made for storage technology, network bandwidth, or display capabilities. Concretization thus remains essential for understanding contemporary computing, even before we include the fact that the mass manufacture of computing devices raises urgent questions about energy use and waste production (cf. Parikka, 2011). But when moving to the domain of software, the notion needs to be interrogated more carefully.

Certainly, efficiency is far from irrelevant when it comes to software. But the material conditions of software introduce differences that cannot be ignored. As Reeves (1992) notes, software is *cheap to build*, because what he calls the 'design' of a program, its source code, is automatically transformed ('built') into machine code by a compiler – no raw materials and elbow grease are required to turn the blueprint into an artifact. But since every detail needs to be specified and programs can get extraordinarily complex, software is *expensive to design*. While Reeves's argument that a program's source code constitutes its design is certainly debatable, it echoes Turing's (1948) affirmation that in computing, '[t]he engineering problem of producing various machines for various jobs is replaced by the office

---

11   While all Turing-complete processors can calculate all computable functions, instruction sets have grown over time, often to address special-purpose logic blocks that accelerate certain calculations, for example, for video decoding, where fixed-function hardware enables higher video resolutions and compression rates at lower energy costs.

work of "programming" the universal machine to do these jobs' (p. 4). This means that the notion of concretization requires a different understanding of efficiency. This passage on the 'imperfection' of the abstract technical object highlights where Simondon's perspective requires adaptation:

> Because of its analytic character, [the abstract technical object] uses more material and requires more construction work; it is logically simpler, yet technically more complicated, because it is made up of a convergence of several complete systems. It is more fragile than the concrete technical object, because the relative isolation of each system […] threatens, in case of its malfunction, the preservation of the other systems (Simondon, 2017, p. 30, translation amended).

If we take a program that relies heavily on preexisting modules or libraries as an example for an abstract technical object, it is true that it may require more storage space, working memory, and processing power than purpose-built code. But the construction time aspect is completely reversed: since the compiler builds the actual technical object and reproduction comes down to mere copying, a more abstract or modular construction will be much faster and cheaper to create than a more concrete, optimized, and integrated object. Fewer lines of code are specifically written for a given program, even if the total number of lines grows.

The sharing of modular elements between projects also means that many different programs can benefit from the time invested in debugging, security, and performance tuning. Concretization in this broad sense of optimization therefore often focuses on the element, on transversal and reusable modules, packages, libraries, and frameworks, on operating systems that underpin all function, and on development tools such as programming languages and compilers that can greatly facilitate even complicated tasks such as parallelization. As I will argue in the next chapter, actual programs rely heavily on all of these things. One could go as far as to argue that much software is constructed like an ensemble in the sense that the collaborating units merely exchange information while remaining separate in most other aspects. Services like Facebook or Google Search, which rely on vast and distributed arrays of technicity, would be obvious examples, but even much more contained programs are designed around functional separation. These considerations further add to the fundamental ambiguity between element, individual, and ensemble when it comes to computing.

If software is easy to build but difficult to design, the issues coming up in design prime over those relating to material fabrication: how can code be organized in a way that it is easy to maintain, easy to debug or enhance, easy to reuse in other projects, or easy to transfer to other developers? How can complexity be contained or managed? In software, an abstract technical object that addresses these issues through a strategy of 'divide and conquer' (Dijkstra, 1974, p. 609) may well be more stable and 'perfect' than a concrete one. Crucially, the mass production of software is much less dependent on concretization since a less concrete program can be copied and distributed just as easily as a tightly integrated one. Even highly abstract or 'artisanal' programs may thus end up having extremely high adoption rates and contribute to a global standardization of functional patterns. This helps explain how the software landscape, seen as the sum of available software artifacts, can group around a limited number of 'superstar' applications yet host a staggering amount of variation and novelty at the same time.

Technical *evolution* is indeed tied to the invention of new schemata and to their concretization, but the landscape of actually existing technical objects is the result of a much wider relational process. Drawing on the same elements or technicities, different technical individuals are designed to fit different social, economic, functional, or aesthetic circumstances. Here, we find another important relationship with the particularities of technical creation. Indeed, the dimensions of abstract (or analytic) and concrete (or synthetic) connect to two modes of making, artisanal and industrial. The former implies a certain 'immaturity' in the sense that the technical object is first and foremost an object of use, necessary for daily life (Simondon, 2017, p. 103) and drowned in the particularities of a here and now that dominates the sensible universe of the craftsman (Simondon, 2017, p. 105). The latter marks a stage of 'maturity' that entails scientific rationality (p. 103) and a higher degree of detachment from the natural milieu (p. 105), resulting in the production of an industrial associated milieu where nature is largely dominated. The engineer inhabits a world of technicity that is not primarily shaped by human needs or uses, but one where 'needs mold themselves onto the industrial technical object, which in turn acquires the power to shape a civilization' (p. 29).

This characterization of the industrial mode of production in more than one way elicits Heidegger's (1998) portrayal of modern technology as *Gestell*, as a form of unveiling where science and mathematics 'challenge' nature with the sole purpose of extracting energy. While Heidegger promotes a return to the artisanal mode, Simondon suggests that we should pursue an outlook that incorporates both the artisanal and industrial modes and thereby achieves a relationship that is neither dominated nor dominating, but one of 'equality' (Simondon, 2017, p. 105f.). The level where this can be achieved most easily is that of the technical ensemble, which integrates trajectories of concretization yet remains open to the natural and social milieux. Here, Simondon proposes cybernetics as a starting point for thinking and regulating the modalities for information exchange (p. 119). But ultimately, it is the role of philosophy to introduce a mode of thinking into 'general' culture that is capable of incorporating technicity as a fundamental mode of relating to the world, thereby installing human beings as coordinators and inventors of machines: '[Man] is *among* the machines that operate with him' (p. 18). Simondon attributes to philosophy the role of fostering balance, homeostasis, and regulation through mediation between the theoretical and practical, the abstract and concrete, the idea and the concept, the ethical and the scientific, the technical and the religious (p. 221). To achieve this synthesis, technicity needs to be recognized as a means of human expression, which first requires a cultural sensitivity for technical objects as human creations. My emphasis on software-making is an attempt to respond to this challenge.

Software, in fact, is an area of technology where an intermingling between modes of creation is already a common phenomenon. The emphasis on abstraction and modularity on the one side and the ongoing movements of concretization on the level of tools and libraries on the other imply a constant copresence of artisanal and industrial modes. In fact, the abstract, artisanal character of software-making is *strengthened* by the ongoing concretization and optimization on the lower levels. The availability of robust operating systems that provide large amounts of baseline functionality, the spread of simpler and more expressive programming languages, and the proliferation of powerful code libraries for almost any purpose make complex capabilities such as 3D graphics or machine learning available to almost any programmer. The underlying trajectories of concretization support a high degree of liveliness and experimentation by providing masses of elements for the assembly of individuals and ensembles. Concretization and industrialization on one level enable abstraction and artisanal production on another. One area where this becomes particularly visible is the domain of custom software written for the here and now of a particular situation. These applications are often assembled out of standardized building blocks and adapted as practices evolve. Actors working in this domain have certainly developed various strategies – from project management to automated testing – to make their production methods more industrial but, to paraphrase Reeves, software work is largely design work and therefore tends to remain abstract, intellectual, and *open* to context. Software, in this sense, is more immediately susceptible to objectal requirements than industrial products developed on assembly lines.

Software as Technology

While Simondon's thinking may seem overly complicated, it proposes a rare take on the old debates between social and technical determinism that does not propose a 'middle ground' but seeks to move beyond the dichotomy altogether. Other than the distinctions between element, individual, and ensemble and between artisanal and industrial modes of technical creation, which are particularly useful for the analysis of concrete objects and settings, there are three main considerations that inform and orient my analysis of information ordering.

First, while Simondon sees technicity as a means of expression, it is not simply a surface where social forces, cultural imagination, or economic dynamics manifest to shape technical objects and their trajectories. They certainly do play crucial roles in orienting the objectal use and adaptation of technology, but technicity itself is an irreducible domain of life that constitutes the objective 'skeleton' all technical creation draws on. Technical objects have their specificity and, in Chateau's formulation, 'their technical mode of existence is not to be confused with their social or psychosocial mode of existence' (Chateau, 2014, p. 5). In line with Ernst's (2015) argument that 'radio reception is not only a cultural agreement, but a scaffolding of electromagnetism' (p. 194), the cumulatively constructed techno-geographic milieux Simondon describes are not merely projection spaces for imaginary applications or uses. It is out of the evolving space of technical potentiality that uses can emerge. The technical object becomes objectal on the basis of its technical objectivity: its psychosocial role as an object of everyday life is bounded by its technical or function capabilities. Certainly, there are questions regarding social adoption, the economics of production, and thick layers of symbolic understanding. The car has prodigious amounts of social meaning. But it only runs at the push of a pedal due to its technicity and without that capacity to propel, there would be no social role to play. To be clear, to consider the objectal mode of technical objects is not a 'mistake'. The mistake is to take the objective development of the car as a given, to take the very existence of the car as a development that needs no further explanation or interpretation beyond mentioning some technical milestones. To appreciate the radical proposal Simondon makes, we have to understand that technology is neither socially determined, nor autonomously following some internal telos. Its evolution is contingent, constructive, and relational. But it constitutes a mode of existence that is specifically technical, and it is as technicity that it constitutes an integral part of human life. The car is 'crystallized human gesture' (Simondon, 2017, p. 18) and more deeply 'ours' than a social constructivist position would admit. The problem, for Simondon, is that the dominant culture negates and ignores the possibilities afforded by technology to express life. Technology becomes *Gestell*, to speak with Heidegger, not because of its intrinsic character, but because it has been banished from the realm of 'noble' expressions to the domain of mere utility. A culture seeking to find an equilibrium would have to assign to technical objects a status similar to works of art or scientific theories, while recognizing that function is their principal mode of signification.

Second, Simondon's philosophy pushes our attention toward operation rather than materiality. His thinking is certainly of materialist persuasion, but the description of technicity as the domain of function, understood as arrangement and unfolding of reciprocal causality, emphasizes notions like process, behavior, interaction, or system over more static terminology. Here, Simondon's work shows strong affinities with cybernetics (Simondon, 2017, p. 16off.). However, if cybernetics is dedicated to describing behavior in informational terms and seeks to subsume everything into a singular layer of analysis, Simondon's ontology sees relations of various kinds between entities that keep their specificities. *How* a particular behavior is produced makes a difference. A working system may be described as an informational process only at the price of missing the level of technicity, where materiality and function intersect. A computer is the sum of its hard- and software, the combination of various technicities that determine its capabilities and tie it to the history of technical invention. Where cybernetics abstracts away from the particularities of underlying mechanisms, Simondon moves them to the center of attention – not to engage in an exercise of ontological categorization, but to trace how different heterogeneous elements assemble into a coherent whole. Taking this perspective into the domain of computing means inquiring into the components and relationships that enable a system to do what it does, to generate its particular behavior. This is where we will encounter algorithmic techniques as instances of technicity that render particular functions possible. Following Simondon, we have to give up the search for a 'base layer' of computation and renounce modes of description that subsume everything into singular principles. Instead we marvel at all the technicity that has been brought into being, at the mass of things already 'sayable' in the medium of function, at the 'statements' have been added to the archives of technicity. More than anything, Simondon's understanding of technology installs operation as a lush domain of cumulative creation.

Third, and drawing on the two previous points, this means that there are genuinely technical forms of imagination. Creators may be driven by all kinds of motives, but the construction of a technical object or the invention of a new schema require technical thinking and skill. The resulting artifact constitutes a transindividual relation that 'communicates' through the function it introduces into the world and this mode of expression requires an aptness that has to be acquired. The material reality of technicity is thus mirrored by a 'mental and practical universe' that humans come to know and draw on to create technical objects (Simondon, 2017, p. 252). Only afterwards does the technical expression become part of the lived realities of individuals and societies as it detaches from its creator to begin a 'free adventure' (Simondon, 2014, p. 27) as an object of use. As I will argue in detail in the next chapter, software-makers inhabit a knowledge domain that revolves around technicity, but also includes practical and normative notions concerning application, process, evaluation, and so forth. This domain cannot be subsumed into others.

These points together constitute a view of technology that emphasizes its internal substance and richness, without negating the myriad connections it forms and upholds. Such a perspective trades foundational arguments for inquiries into constructive accumulation. The reduction of computing to mechanical computation misses the technical substances and associated knowledge spheres that allow contemporary computers to do extraordinary things, including algorithmic information ordering. To inquire into these substances and to connect them back to other cultural domains is the task Simondon set for mechanology:

> In order to restore to culture the truly general character it has lost, one must be capable of reintroducing an awareness of the nature of machines, of their mutual relations and of their relations with man, and of the values implied in these relations. This awareness requires the existence of a technologist or *mechanologist*, alongside the psychologist and the sociologist. (Simondon, 2017, p. 19)

This book indeed develops a mechanological probe that demarcates and investigates a slice of technicity bounded by computation at the bottom and by the world of social purposes at the top. While hardly independent from these two boundaries, it constitutes a coherent domain that must neither be absorbed, à la Kittler, into the basic principle of computation, nor too readily into the organizational, political, and economic logics that dominate contemporary applications of computing. Ultimately, I hope to show that the domain of software retains a degree of openness that constitutes an opportunity for the emergence of a 'technical culture' (Simondon, 2017, p. 257). As Mercedes Bunz (2014), a keen reader of Simondon, argues, '[d]igitalization is happening, and instead of abdicating our responsibility, we must take our part more actively' (p. 54). A deeper understanding of software and software-making is one of the conditions for living up to this challenge.

Bibliography

Agre, P. E. (1997a). *Computation and Human Experience*. Cambridge: Cambridge University Press.

Berry, D. M. (2011). *The Philosophy of Software*. Basingstoke: Palgrave Macmillan.

Bontems, V. (2009). Gilbert Simondon's Genetic 'Mecanology' and the Understanding of Laws of Technical Evolution. *Techné: Research in Philosophy and Technology 13*(1), 1-12.

Bowker, G. C., Star, S. L., Turner, W., and Gasser, L. (eds.). (1997). *Social Science, Technical Systems, and Cooperative Work: Beyond the Great Divide*. New York: Psychology Press.

Bunz, M. (2014). *The Silent Revolution*. Basingstoke: Palgrave Macmillan.

Burrell, J. (2016). How the Machine 'Thinks': Understanding Opacity in Machine Learning Algorithms. *Big Data & Society 3*(1), 1-12.

Carrozzini, G. (2008). Technique et humanisme. Günther Anders et Gilbert Simondon. *Appareil*, 2, 1-12.

Chabot, P. (2013). *The Philosophy of Simondon: Between Technology and Individuation* (A. Krefetz, trans.). London: Bloomsbury.

Chateau, J.-Y. (2014). Présentation. In Simondon, G., *Sur la technique (1953-1983)* (pp. 1-21). Paris: Presses Universitaires de France.

Chun, W. H. K. (2011). *Programmed Visions*. Cambridge, MA: MIT Press.

Colburn, T. R. (2000). *Philosophy and Computer Science*. Armonk: M. E. Sharpe.

Dijkstra, E. W. (1974). Programming as a Discipline of Mathematical Nature. *American Mathematical Monthly 81*(6), 608-612.

Domingos, P. (2015). *The Master Algorithm: How the Quest for the Ultimate Learning Machine Will Remake Our World*. New York: Basic Books.

Dourish, P. (2017). *The Stuff of Bits: An Essay on the Materialities of Information*. Cambridge, MA: MIT Press.

Dreyfus, H. (1972). *What Computers Can't Do*. New York: Harper & Row.

Ernst, W. (2015). Technophysikalische and Symbolische Medienoperationen als Herausforderung der Historischen Zeit. In S. Haas and C. Wischermann (eds.), *Die Wirklichkeit der Geschichte* (pp. 185-204). Stuttgart: Franz Steiner Verlag.

Eubanks, V. (2018). *Automating Inequality: How High-Tech Tools Profile, Police, and Punish the Poor*. New York: St. Martin's Press.

Floridi, L. (1999). *Philosophy and Computing: An Introduction*. London: Routledge.

Fuller, M. (2003). It Looks Like You're Writing a Letter. In M. Fuller (ed.), *Behind the Blip: Essays on the Culture of Software* (pp. 137-165). New York: Autonomedia.

Fuller, M. (ed.). (2008). *Software Studies: A Lexicon*. Cambridge, MA: MIT Press.

Gehl, R. W., and Bell, S. A. (2012). Heterogeneous Software Engineering: Garmisch 1968, Microsoft Vista, and a Methodology for Software Studies. *Computational Culture 2*, n.p.

Guchet, X. (2001). Théorie du Lien Social, Technologie et Philosophie: Simondon Lecteur de Merleau-Ponty *Les Études philosophiques 57*(2), 219-237.

Guchet, X. (2008). Évolution technique et objectivité technique chez Leroi-Gourhan et Simondon. *Appareil 2*, 1-14.

Hayles, N. K. (2004). Print Is Flat, Code Is Deep: The Importance of Media-Specific Analysis. *Poetics Today 25*(1), 67-90.

Heidegger, M. (1962). *Being and Time* (J. Macquarrie, & and E. Robinson, Trans., trans.). London: SCM Press.

Heidegger, M. (1998). Traditional Language and Technological Language. *Journal of Philosophical Research 23*, 129-145.

Hoare, C. A. R. (2011). Interview by L. Thomas [tape recording], 8 September. Oral History of British Science, British Library. Retrieved from https://sounds.bl.uk/Oral-history/Science/021M-C1379X0052XX-0005V0.

Kittler, F. A. (1997a). There Is No Software. In J. Johnston (ed.), *Literature, Media, Information Systems: Essays* (pp. 147-155). Amsterdam: Overseas Publishers Association.

Latour, B. (1994). On Technical Mediation. *Common Knowledge 3*(2), 29-64.

Latour, B. (1999). *Pandora's Hope: Essays on the Reality of Science Studies*. Cambridge, MA: Harvard University Press.

Latour, B. (2013). *An Inquiry into Modes of Existence*. Cambridge, MA: Harvard University Press.

Leroi-Gourhan, A. (1993). *Gesture and Speech* (A. Bostock Berger, trans.). Cambridge, MA: MIT Press.

MacCormick, J. (2011). *Nine Algorithms That Changed the Future: The Ingenious Ideas That Drive Today's Computers*. Princeton: Princeton University Press.

Mackenzie, A. (2006). *Cutting Code: Software and Sociality*. New York: Peter Lang.

Mackenzie, A. (2015). The Production of Prediction: What Does Machine Learning Want? *European Journal of Cultural Studies 18*(4-5), 429-445.

Mackenzie, A. (2017a). *Machine Learners: Archaeology of a Data Practice*. Cambridge, MA: MIT Press.

Manovich, L. (2001). *The Language of New Media*. Cambridge, MA: MIT Press.

Manovich, L. (2013b). Media after Software. *Journal of Visual Culture 12*(1), 30-37.

Manovich, L. (2013c). *Software Takes Command*. New York: Bloomsbury.

McLuhan, M. (1964). *Understanding Media*. New York: McGraw-Hill.

Mills, S. (2011). Concrete Software: Simondon's Mechanology and the Techno-Social. *Fibreculture Journal 18*, n.p.

O'Neil, C. (2016). *Weapons of Math Destruction: How Big Data Increases Inequality and Threatens Democracy*. New York: Crown.

Oram, A., and Wilson, G. (eds.). (2007). *Beautiful Code: Leading Programmers Explain How They Think*. Sebastopol: O'Reilly.

Parikka, J. (2012). *What Is Media Archaeology?* Cambridge: Polity Press.

Parikka, J. (2015). *A Geology of Media*. Minneapolis: University of Minnesota Press.

Parikka, J. (ed.). (2011). *Medianatures: The Materiality of Information Technology and Electronic Waste*. Ann Arbor: Open Humanities Press.

Pariser, E. (2011). *The Filter Bubble: What the Internet Is Hiding from You*. New York: Penguin Press.

Pasquale, F. (2015). *The Black Box Society*. Cambridge, MA: Harvard University Press.

Peters, J. D. (2015). *The Marvelous Clouds: Toward a Philosophy of Elemental Media*. Chicago: University of Chicago Press.

Petersen, J. (2015). Is Code Speech? Law and the Expressivity of Machine Language. *New Media & Society 17*(3), 415-431.

Reeves, J. W. (1992). What Is Software Design? *C++ Journal 2*(2), 14-12.

Searle, J. (1980) Minds, Brains and Programs. *Behavioral and Brain Sciences 3*(3), 417-457.

Simon, H. A. (1996). *The Sciences of the Artificial* (3rd ed.). Cambridge, MA: MIT Press.

Simondon, G. (1958). *Du mode d'existence des objects techniques*. Paris: Aubier.

Simondon, G. (1989). *L'Individuation psychique et collective*. Paris: Aubier.

Simondon, G. (2014). *Sur la technique (1953-1983)*. Paris: Presses Universitaires de France.

Simondon, G. (2017). *On the Mode of Existence of Technical Objects* (C. Malaspina and J. Rogove, trans.). Minneapolis: Univocal Publishing.

Stiegler, B. (1989). Préface. In Simondon, G., *L'Individuation psychique et collective* (pp. i-xvi). Paris: Aubier.

Turing, A. M. (1937). On Computable Numbers, with an Application to the Entscheidungsproblem. *Proceedings of the London Mathematical Society 2*(1), 230-265.

Turing, A. M. (1948). *Intelligent Machinery*. National Physical Laboratory Report. Retrieved from http://www.alanturing.net/intelligent_machinery/.

3. Software-Making and Algorithmic Techniques

Abstract

The third chapter builds on central ideas from Simondon's work, such as the distinction between invention and concretization and the delineation of technical elements, individuals, and ensembles, to conceptualize algorithmic techniques as the central carriers of technicity and technical knowledge in the domain of software. In dialogue with the cultural techniques tradition, it addresses them as methods or heuristics for creating operation and behavior in computing and discusses how they are invented and stabilized. Algorithmic techniques, in this perspective, are at the same time material blocks of technicity, units of knowledge, vocabularies for expression in the medium of function, and constitutive elements of developers' technical imaginaries.

Keywords: software-making, algorithmic techniques, cultural techniques, software and abstraction

There remains a stark contrast between the increasingly accepted diagnosis that '[s]oftware structures and makes possible much of the contemporary world' (Fuller, 2008, p. 1) and the attention given to the actual technical and intellectual content mobilized by developers. If software has indeed become a technology of power, a means to 'conduct conducts' (Foucault, 2008, p. 186), it is surprising that critical analyses of concrete technical procedures remain rare. We have recognized that computers and software have considerable impact on human life, and we invest great effort in making sense of the ways they have affected various societal domains, from the economy to politics, art, and intimacy. But beyond attributions of sometimes very broad properties to 'the digital' or, more recently, to 'algorithms', scholars in the humanities and social sciences still rarely venture more deeply into the intellectual and material domains of technicity that hardware and

Rieder, B., *Engines of Order: A Mechanology of Algorithmic Techniques*. Amsterdam: Amsterdam University Press, 2020
DOI 10.5117/9789462986190_CH03

software developers invent and draw on to design the forms, functions, and behaviors that constitute technical objects and infrastructures. There is a clear preference for theorizing social, political, and cultural effects of software, often understood as a singular category, to the examination of the sprawling landscape of imagination and operation that informs technical enunciations in the first place.

Certainly, most people encounter software mainly in its running state, as fully formed interface, tool, or environment, and this level of experience is often enough to gain a sufficient sense of what the software *does* to assess its role in social and cultural practice. In the short run, we do not need to know anything about the architecture of Facebook's data centers to study how users integrate the service into their daily lives. However, in specific cases, such as the News Feed filtering mechanism, the way a particular task or function is performed may be indispensable for assessing its contributions and consequences. An apprehension of technical forms and, consequently, of technical possibilities can shed light on these cases. More importantly still, it can inform broader apprehensions of a world that increasingly constitutes and maintains itself technologically.

In this chapter, I venture deeper into the technical substance of computing and investigate how existing technicities form an infrastructure or a priori for software-makers. Beneath the infinite variation of technical forms, technical trajectories evolve at their own speed, resulting in broad arrays of elements that, taken together, constitute computing in its current state. The concept of 'algorithmic technique' plays a pivotal role in capturing some of the central units of technicity and knowledge that define this space of possibility.

From Cultural Techniques to Algorithmic Techniques

So far, I have used the term 'technique' without much specificity. The OED defines it as 'a way of carrying out a particular task' and this certainly captures aspects that are central to my project, in particular the idea that a technique is not necessarily defined by its outcome but rather by the manner of getting there. This involves specific gestures and, potentially, specific tools and materials that are combined and arranged in specific ways, often taking the form of a sequence of steps. A technique must thus be assembled or acquired before it can be brought into service. Techniques therefore have an origin, even if the time, place, and scenario of their inception may be spread out and difficult to reconstruct. If we follow Simondon's assessment that machines contain 'human gesture fixed and crystallized in working structures' (Simondon, 2017, p. 18), we can consider that techniques can be 'implemented' in technical form to carry out particular tasks in particular ways. As a technical individual, the machine takes over as the 'executor' of the technique, replacing human beings as 'tool bearers' (p. 78), leaving them the role of coordinator or 'organizer' (p. 80). However, the automatic loom neither 'learns' how to weave, nor does it carry out the task in the same way as a human being would, even if certain similarities remain. The loom weaves because someone arranged a series of technical elements into the specific 'reciprocal causal relations' (p. 32) that enable its operation. We can thus speak of *mechanical* techniques that are genuinely technical in the sense that they are carried out by a machine. They can implement nonanthropomorphic forms of operation but remain human creations as they are 'invented, thought and willed, taken up [*assumé*] by a human subject' (p. 252). The *algorithmic* techniques I will outline in more depth in this chapter are indeed of that kind: ways of carrying out tasks that are specified, designed, and materialized in software, but invented and arranged by human creators.

Cultural Techniques

The concept of technique, however, merits deeper conceptual appraisal before handing it over to concrete analytical application. The definition given so far supports a pragmatic use of the term but provides little when it comes to situating techniques in a wider conceptual space. The question I want to ask, therefore, is how 'mechanical techniques' can be understood 'as escalations of classical cultural techniques' (Ernst, 2013, p. 135), a central concept in German media theory over the last three decades that has more recently received significant attention in English-language scholarship. As Parikka (2013) rightfully argues, the concept of cultural technique (*Kulturtechnik*) can evoke a certain familiarity, begging the question whether '(German) cultural techniques [are] just like (Anglo-American) cultural practices' (p. 149) and asking how they relate to French traditions epitomized by authors like Mauss, Leroi-Gourhan, Bourdieu, or Latour. There are, however, several specificities that make cultural techniques an essential means to deepen the ad hoc definition given above. Rather than provide a systematic introduction, I want to highlight five aspects that are particularly relevant for this inquiry.

First, the authors dedicated to developing the concept emphasize the etymological relationship between *Kultur* and the Latin *colere*, which means

to tend a field or garden (Winthrop-Young, 2014, p. 380). This initial reference to agricultural practices already indicates a far-reaching conceptual
ambition that includes the material and environmental conditions cultural
techniques relate to. As Krämer and Bredekamp (2013) emphatically exclaim,
'[culture] is first and foremost the work with things – their cultivation – that
surround us on a daily basis' (p. 21). These 'things' evoke various materialities
and draw attention to the richness and contingency of the milieux we
inhabit. While significant attention has been given to cultural techniques
that relate to cognitive operations and media use,[1] the technical, broadly
understood as material forms of operation, is always close. But rather than
postulate equality between human and nonhuman agents, the cultural
technique concept emphasizes connections, couplings, and shifts that
span heterogenous domains, such as the material and the symbolic, linked
together as 'operative chains' (Siegert, 2013, p. 11). This allows for a nuanced
appraisal of things like calculation and computation, where the calculative
capacities afforded by the Hindu-Arabic numeral system are not seen as
mere anticipations of the computer but understood in terms of their own
procedurality. There is a mechanical dimension that runs through and
connects human cognition and skill to a symbolic system to enable 'manual'
computation in complex and dynamic ways (Krämer, 1988). If the cultural
technique tradition can, at times, appear as 'cultural practices enriched
with mathematics and a head-on engagement with technical and scientific
cultural reality' (Parikka, 2013, p. 6f.), this should not be understood as a mere
widening of the field of attention but as a more fundamental attribution of
substance to things like mathematical or technical procedures.

Second, although we find, particularly in more recent formulations
(Siegert, 2013, p. 8), a clear repudiation of the programmatic and somewhat
polemic assertion that 'media determine our situation' (Kittler, 1999, p.
xxxix), the cultural techniques concept retains the idea of an a priori in the
sense of both Foucault and McLuhan. Cultural techniques such as reading,
writing, or arithmetic shape the very foundations of culture by transforming
'what "everybody" can do' (Krämer and Bredekamp, 2013, p. 26). Echoing
Goody's (1977) assertion that writing 'gives the mind a special kind of lever
on "reality"' (p. 109), there is a clear understanding that cultural techniques

---

1   'Watching television, for instance, not only requires specific technological know-how but
also an equally medium-specific set of mental and conceptual skills, such as understanding
audiovisual referentiality structures, assessing the fictionality status of different programs,
interacting with media-specific narrative formats, or the ability to differentiate between
intended and unintended messages' (Winthrop-Young, 2014, p. 381).

constitute the fundamental capacities and modes of operation of cultures organized around specific media. According to Vismann (2013), '[c]ultural techniques define the agency of media and things' because they 'describe what media do, what they produce, and what kinds of actions they prompt' (p. 83). However, in contrast to McLuhan, cultural history is not written as a series of dominant media that would constitute and determine an archetype like 'typographic man' (McLuhan, 1962); in contrast to Foucault, there is no clear succession of *épistémè* that define regularities running through the different discursive formations of an era. Rather, we find a 'historically given micro-network of technologies and techniques' (Siegert, 2013, p. 11) that is pluralistic, dynamic, and marked by both continuities and discontinuities. Periodization is not impossible but needs to be aware of its contingent and analytical character.

Third, in Heidegger's terms, the ontic is given privilege over the ontological. More precisely, ontological concepts are seen as the products of the concrete operations of cultural techniques:

> Humans *as such* do not exist independently of cultural techniques of hominization, time *as such* does not exist independently of cultural techniques of time measurement, and space *as such* does not exist independently of cultural techniques of spatial control. (Siegert, 2013, p. 10)

This focus on the production of conceptual entities means that 'the study of cultural techniques takes aim at the materialities of ontologization' (Winthrop-Young, 2014, p. 387) in ways that eschew 'philosophical idealizations' (Siegert, 2013, p. 10), or, rather, tie the production of concepts to the ontic operations performed by cultural techniques. This idea is already present in Thomas Macho's early assertion that '[c]ultural techniques – such as writing, reading, painting, calculating, making music – are always older than the concepts that are generated from them' (Macho, 2003, p. 179). For Siegert (2007), who favors a particularly foundational interpretation, cultural techniques are 'media that process the observation, displacement, and differentiation of distinctions' (p. 31). A door, for example, is not the result of a distinction between inside and outside, but a technique 'involved in operationalizing distinctions in the real' (Siegert, 2013, p. 14) and thus instrumental to *producing* and *processing* the concepts of inside and outside. Such distinctions do not have to be binary and, if we inquire further, we find that doors, indeed, connect to a wider array of techniques for separating and shielding, such as walls, roofs, windows, and so forth. On the level of intellectual pragmatics, and in line with earlier tenets of German media theory, this translates into an emphasis on 'empirical historical objects' (Siegert, 2013, p. 10) as analytical starting points. In the context of my own investigation, this means that notions like 'information', 'order', and 'knowledge' are not to be treated as things that exist *as such*, but as shifting conceptual constructs that emerge in conjunction with the operation of techniques. Algorithmic information ordering, in this perspective, appears as a set of particular forms of 'distinction-making' that have the power to define broader cultural perceptions. I hesitate, however, to consider cultural techniques purely as 'preconceptual operations that generate the very concepts that subsequently are used to conceptualize these operations' (Winthrop-Young, 2014, p. 385). Operation, I would argue, may actually include concepts as operational agents and conceptualization itself can be seen as a specific cultural technique. In the second part of this book, we will encounter instances of conceptualization and formalization that affect techniques' capacities to connect and to travel from one domain to another.

Fourth, my emphasis on operational chains or networks is meant to counteract a tendency still present in earlier literature on cultural techniques to idealize techniques into singular conceptual substantives, like 'reading', 'writing', or 'calculating'. Early work goes as far as describing the 'use of computers' as *a* cultural technique (Krämer and Bredekamp, 2013, p. 25). Siegert already points more explicitly to variation when he argues that '[a]n abacus allows for different calculations than ten fingers; a computer, in turn, allows for different calculations than an abacus' (Siegert, 2013, p. 11). Additional differentiation is necessary, however, and I want to push further by arguing that the computer is not a singular technical object but, to use Manovich's take on the work of Alan Kay and Adele Goldberg, a 'metamedium' that is 'simultaneously a set of different media and a system for generating new media tools and new types of media' (Manovich, 2013c, p. 102). Computers – deliberately in plural – open onto a vast variety of objects, practices, and (cultural) techniques. Kittler's polemical bon mot that 'there is no software' (1997a) indicates a lingering tendency in German media theory toward a foundationalism that reduces computing to computation and thereby risks failing to adequately recognize the immense reservoirs of technicity and knowledge that have been formulated over the last 70 years. However, the focus on cultural techniques in its most recent formulation allows not only for a 'resolutely anti- or counter-Platonic stance' (Winthrop-Young, 2013, p. 8) when it comes to the relationship between the ontic and the ontological, but also for a 'de-idealization' of the ontic itself: instead of singular verbs like 'writing' or 'processing', there is room for substantial variation, and thus for a 'variantology' (Zielinski, 2006, p. 7) that considers technology and its conceptual correlates from Simondon's relational perspective and understands 'the computer' as 'a complex of calculator, software, peripherals, and network connections' (Coy, 2001, p. 18) defined by myriad trajectories of technical evolution.

Fifth, and crucial for my own purpose, authors like Krämer and Bredekamp argue that the rise of cultural techniques drawing on calculation, computation, and – more generally – mechanical operation leads to a separation between the capacity to put a technique into practice and the comprehension of its inner workings and conceptual underpinnings:

> There is a growing divide between 'knowing how' and 'knowing that'; skill and knowledge are going their separate ways. The daily use of operative signs removes the burden and complexities of interpretation. Calculus is always already a kind of 'mechanism of forgetting'. In order to calculate correctly, we don't need to be able to provide an answer to the question, 'What is a zero?' (Krämer and Bredekamp, 2013, p. 26)

This points toward an appreciation of computation as a form of 'externalization' that pushes cognition out of the 'invisible interiority' of the minds of individuals and makes it a 'distributive, and hence collective, phenomenon' (Krämer and Bredekamp, 2013, p. 26f.). The specific ways of carrying out tasks I have described as 'mechanical' techniques at the beginning of the chapter constitute both components for the operational chains formed by cultural techniques and vectors of externalization that widen the gulf between competent performance and a deeper understanding of the technicities or 'mechanics' involved. This dissociation characterizes the use of computers to a previously unseen degree. Graphical user interfaces and most user-facing functions are largely dissociated from underlying operational arrangements. The often lauded 'digital natives' are certainly competent users, but there is little reason to believe that this task-oriented competence translates into mechanological awareness. The cultural techniques concept, however, avoids dissolving the technical in a sociology of use and appropriation and, heeding the lessons of Kittler and others, keeps an eye on the reality of operation and on 'the rules of selection, storage, and transmission that characterize a given system of mediation' (Geoghegan, 2013, p. 4). The interface effects produced by algorithmic information ordering involve their own forms of dissociation and critical understanding therefore requires that we investigate the mechanisms at work below the surface.

Taking these five points together, cultural techniques provide an intellectual frame that allows for an integrated perspective on technical objects, practices, skills, signs, and emergent conceptualizations, following Simondon in rejecting an externalist understanding of technology, where machines and tools become part of human life purely trough their uses. Instead, there are networks of operation that do not imply a strict ontological hierarchy or division of labor. What counts are specific operational arrangements and their stabilization/destabilization over time; in that sense, even concepts can perform the role of elements that materialize, connect, and inform as part of larger chains.

Coming back to the initial question of this section, we can see that there are many different and historically contingent ways mechanical techniques and technical objects may enter into the equation, some of them in direct and continuous connection with human bodies, others through automation, autonomy, and delegation (Rieder, 2006). But even if the part technology plays in the unfolding of life does not follow a singular logic, technicity and technical evolution still figure as means to coagulate diverse forces into more stable configurations. The analytical task is to 'ask how, and under what conditions, cultural techniques strategically and temporarily consolidate these forces into coherent technologies' (Geoghegan, 2013, p. 14).

However, there is no specific attempt in the cultural techniques tradition to carve out a domain of technicity that has its own evolutionary character and mode of development. Lacking a distinction between an objective and an objectal dimension, it frames both techniques and technical objects not in terms of evolutionary trajectories but as series of singularities that seem to manifest almost spontaneously. Despite its apparent interest in the 'hard stuff' – symbolic systems, mathematical functions, processor architecture – the German tradition has yet to fully recuperate from the tendency to narrate history as a sequence of foundational technological 'plateaux' in the sense that fundamental incisions, like the invention of 'the digital computer' or 'computation', mark the arrival of a new logic that largely explains and determines what follows. The incessant evocations of Turing, Shannon, and von Neumann we find not only in Kittler's work compares unfavorably to the relative silence on anything that has happened in computer science and related disciplines in the last 70 years. Even the cultural techniques tradition, notwithstanding its willingness to engage seemingly banal objects like doors, remains uneasy when it comes to moving more closely into the meanderings of digital media that are not just Turing machines but almost intolerably full of 'stuff' awaiting further scrutiny. Although this lack of interest in contemporary technology has been noted,[2] the field remains

_____

2   'For all their apocalyptic poetry about Alan Turing's universal machine and Claude Shannon's schematic account of communication, Kittler and his most fervent disciples never had much to

wide open when it comes to applying the cultural techniques concepts to the technological material that fields like software studies (Fuller, 2008) or web search studies (Zimmer, 2010) regularly deal with. Practically, this requires the recognition that computation is a starting point that fueled an explosion of techniques and technologies following their own evolutionary trajectories; it also requires a much more fine-grained understanding of technical creation. The rest of this chapter is thus dedicated to discussing software-making in a way that brings Simondon's sensitivity to technicity into dialogue with cultural techniques.

Software-Making

One way to approach cultural techniques in the context of computing is to come back to the earlier understanding of the concept as skill or competence. We have seen that authors like Krämer and Bredekamp describe the *use* of computers as a cultural technique. But what if we inquire into the *making* of digital artifacts? This is by no means a straightforward project. Various disciplines, from electrical engineering to interface design, are involved in producing the myriad objects and trajectories that populate computing. These specialties differ substantially in terms of methods, concepts, materialities, and everyday practices. Even if we focus on the academic field of computer science, we find both highly different subject areas and competing definitions concerning the epistemological status of the discipline. Arduous debates continue to this day, even if 'since the 1970s, computing has typically been characterized as a combination of empirical, mathematical, and engineering traditions' (Tedre, 2011, p. 363). Entering into dialog with the cultural techniques tradition, German computer scientist Wolfgang Coy boils this distinction further down to 'construction and theory' (Coy, 2001, p. 16) and describes *Informatik* ('computer science') accordingly as both *Technik* ('technology') and *Wissenschaft* ('science'). He associates the former explicitly with *Handwerk* ('craft') and *Kunstfertigkeit* ('skillfulness') and assigns to the latter the task of gauging the fundamental possibilities and limitations of construction. While this characterization would be at least partially contested by computer scientists that frame their field as 'a discipline of mathematical nature' (Dijkstra, 1974) or as a natural science dedicated to 'the study of natural and artificial information processes' (Denning, 2007, p. 15), it has the considerable advantage of capturing the

say about media after the mid-1980s, when personal computers became a common presence in the domestic home' (Geoghegan, 2013, p. 3).

everyday realities encountered by the many graduates computer science courses churn out every year. That reality consists, as Coy argues elsewhere, in the programming of computers as a constructive gesture that results in making a machine perform a specific task:

> At the beginning there is the implementation of rule-based thinking and acting into a machine, that is, the idea of the program and, in its theoretical comprehension, the idea of the algorithm. Processes of thinking and associated action can be analyzed, described in exact terms, and handed over to a machine or a system of machines. (Coy, 2007, p. 33)

Coy (2007, p. 33) consequently defines computer science as a cultural technique that both creates and acts in increasingly technical environments, where computers process all kinds of data (and not just numbers), have constantly growing technical capacities (in terms of speed and storage capacity), are connected in networks (that span the globe), and serve a wide variety of purposes, in particular as 'media machines' and 'media of communication'. 'Computer people'[3] contribute to these environments mainly by making the machines and by formulating the 'thinking and acting' that goes into them in the form of software. In his acceptance speech for the Newell Award, Frederick P. Brooks, Jr., who oversaw the troubled development of IBM's OS/360 and wrote about the experience in his seminal book *The Mythical Man-Month* (1975), similarly called the computer scientist a 'toolsmith' and declared that '[w]e are concerned with making things, be they computers, algorithms, or software systems' (Brooks, 1996, p. 62). If we pass on the hardware aspect, somewhat improperly, to the field of electrical engineering, we can summarize that the central cultural technique computer science pragmatically concerns itself with is the making of computer programs, that is, of software.

If we further unpack this notion, we find programming proper, that is, the writing of the computer code that makes up a program. But there are clearly many other practices, skills, and, indeed, techniques that come into play, such as requirements analysis, software architecture, interface design, testing and debugging, deployment, maintenance, just to name a few. Some authors argue that running through all of these domains is something like

---

3   While there are good reasons to differentiate between computer scientists, software engineers, software designers, programmers, coders, hackers, and so forth, this book focuses on what connects all of these professions, namely technical creation. Agre (1994, p. 120) simply talks about 'computer people' and I favor the equally underspecified term 'software-makers'.

'computational thinking' which consists in 'reformulating a seemingly difficult problem into one we know how to solve, perhaps by reduction, embedding, transformation, or simulation' (Wing, 2006, p. 33). Connecting this idea with Coy's notion of 'description in exact terms', we could argue that there is both an internal and external dimension to making programs that maps onto Simondon's distinction between objective and objectal. Internal aspects are those concerned with technicities, with programming itself, with code, but also with questions of correctness, reliability, or easy maintenance. External aspects would be those that connect the program to the social world around it, which means not just inputs and outputs, but the specific forms of analysis that define and examine a 'problem' through the lens of the conceptual space computing brings with it. Agre (1994) uses the term 'capture' to explain how a process of description that relies on analytical techniques such as the entity-relationship model (Chen, 1976) or use-case diagrams[4] becomes a form of prescription when software is deployed, as it inevitably reorganizes how the task is carried out. The work of consultants, analysts, modelers, optimizers, or rationalizers specialized in capturing practices into technical form should therefore not be underestimated. But, ultimately, there is a technical substance, an internal or objective technicity, that demarcates a space of possibilities and limitations that the methods and practices dedicated to external or objectal aspects are ultimately bound to. Only what can be programmed can find its way into the scenarios, models, and formalizations used to design software as applications to be used in concrete settings. And for the vast majority of software developers, the existing reservoirs of technicity define the potentiality, the *vocabulary of possible function* that can be used to capture the world.

The question whether there are some things that 'computers can't do' (Dreyfus, 1972), that is, whether some behaviors cannot be programmed,[5] is certainly interesting, but there are also good reasons to ask instead what computers *can* do, that is, what can be programmed, here and now. The textbook answer that 'any computation that is realizable can be realized by a universal machine, provided that it is specified' (Newell and Simon, 1976, p. 117) again points toward the fundamental limits of computation but does little to help us understand why, for example, the weekly suggestions in Spotify are actually very good, at least in my own experience.

4   Use case diagrams are part of the Universal Modeling Language (UML), a very common tool for designing computer systems.
5   To be clear: certain algorithms may 'learn' a particular behavior or decision model from data or interaction, but that learning behavior still had to be programmed.

Apparently 'making good recommendations' is something that, as it stands, can indeed be programmed. The analytical philosopher and logician M. E. Maron (1963), whose Bayes classifier I will examine in Chapter 6, addresses this difference through a distinction between logic on the one side and methodology or heuristic on the other: logic may provide the language for proving a theorem, but it does not tell us how to discover new ones. In the same way, the computer furnishes an environment for the execution of software, but in order for the machine to actually *do* something, we have to come up with the 'methods, approaches, clues, tricks, heuristics' (Maron, 1963, p. 141) that allow us to formulate that behavior. And this capacity to 'make do' is historically contingent. Would a recommender algorithm like GroupLens (Resnick et al., 1994) have run on the very first computer? If we disregard the obvious limitations concerning storage and execution speed, the answer would have to be 'yes'. Yet it did not run on that first computer since nobody bothered to program it. *Could* somebody have programmed it? This question makes just about the same amount of sense as the question whether the Romans could have built a massage chair. To that we would reply that a whole series of technical and cultural elements would have to fall into place before anyone could begin to think about making a such a chair, elements that were apparently not present in Roman culture. With Foucault, we could say that the statement 'massage chair' was not 'sayable' in the Roman discursive formation. In our own discursive moment, however, both slavery and manual arithmetic have fallen largely out of the realm of the imaginable and acceptable. The invention of mechanical computation is the beginning of a constructive, contingent story, not its end point and the recommender system appears at moment when many other things have already fallen into place.

In their acceptance speech of the Turing Award, Allen Newell and Herbert Simon (1976) make the seemingly tautological argument that '[c]omputer science is the study of the phenomena surrounding computers' (p. 113), but they quickly add that these phenomena are, in fact, 'deep and obscure' (p. 114). What the work of Turing, Post, Church, and others amounts to, they argue, is the very mechanization of thought, which 'seemed still to inhabit mainly the heaven of Platonic ideals, or the equally obscure spaces of the human mind, until computers taught us how symbols could be processed by machines' (p. 125). Computer science, from this perspective, is the experimental and empirical study of symbol systems, which are seen as capable to the point of demonstrating 'intelligent action' (p. 118). While we may disagree with Newell and Simon's equation of humans and computers as symbolic systems and their view of intelligence as symbol processing, they connect with the 'tool-making' perspective in the sense that the phenomena examined are designed and 'artificial'. Both the practice and epistemology of computing revolve around 'knowledge about artificial objects and phenomena' (Simon, 1996, p. 3), which means that in computer science, by and large, what we know is what we can build, and vice versa – 'nothing is understood until it has been made into a working computer system' (Agre, 1997a, p. 12). There may well be a difference in outlook when it comes to defining the discipline, but the notion of building remains central: 'the scientist *builds in order to study;* the engineer *studies in order to build*' (Brooks, 1996, p. 62). This difference in finality may be a good way to distinguish (academic) theory from (commercial) practice, but both are entangled in the history and growth of constructive artificiality that continuously extends what can be built and what there is to know.

When I ask whether some behavior can be programmed, I am thus not referring to the fundamental mathematical question of what can and cannot be computed, but to our state of knowledge and capacity concerning the construction of function in the computer medium. This state is constantly expanding through technical invention – that is, the production of new technical schemas – and it diffuses throughout the larger world of software-making: today, any somewhat skillful computer programmer can go online and learn how to make a recommender system, or copy existing source code, or simply use one of the many existing modules.[6] In short, there are algorithmic techniques available that give certain practical expressions to the somewhat vague idea of 'making good recommendations'. If the goal of advanced information retrieval is 'to make computers do humanlike things' (Swanson, 1988, p. 97), the invention of algorithmic techniques is its principal vector of progress.

Algorithmic Techniques

When it comes to making software, programming takes a central place and we can certainly think of it as a cultural technique in the sense of a fundamental skill. Being able to read and write code, to work with constructs such as variables and basic data structures like lists, to arrange control flow via loops and conditional statements, to make use of different means for inputting and outputting data, and to master related aspects, for example, what it means to execute a program and how to do that, are things not too

---

6   There is, for example, an open-source project that grew directly out of GroupLens (Resnick et al., 1994), LensKit (http://lenskit.org).

dissimilar from language proficiency or the mastery of basic arithmetic. However, while programming is (mostly) still a fundamental requirement, the much broader practice of making software draws on a wide array of concepts and techniques that cover the already mentioned areas like requirements analysis, process and data modeling, software architecture, interaction design, project management, testing, maintenance, DevOps,[7] and many others. These are by no means minor subjects: the famous 'software crisis' of the late 1960s was prompted by the observation that '[i]n many sensitive areas, software is late, expensive, unreliable and does not work to specification' (Buxton, 1978, p. 23). The emergence of software 'engineering' as the 'systematic, disciplined, quantifiable approach to the development, operation, and maintenance of software' (IEEE, 1990) was the direct outcome of that crisis. The engineering approach places heavy emphasis on analysis, planning, modeling, testing, and documenting, to the point where '[s]oftware engineers probably spend less than 10% of their time writing code' (Laplante, 2007, p. 4). Over the years, there have been countless debates around the 'organizational' dimension of software development. In 1978 Buxton distinguished 'three main lines of thought as to how software should be designed and built, [...] the cottage industry, heavy engineering, and applied logic approaches' (Buxton, 1978, p. 24); Raymond (1999) famously opposed a 'cathedral' to a 'bazaar' development model; and the many iterative or 'agile' methodologies that have garnered so much interest over the last decade can not only look back on a rich history, but explicitly link the design process of technical artifacts to questions of power and democracy (cf. Bjerknes et al., 1987). For example, as Gürses and Van Hoboken (2018) have convincingly shown, modes of software development directly intersect with the way user privacy is imagined and implemented. These are clearly important issues. The one-sided emphasis on code and programming in media studies and adjacent fields is, in fact, quite limiting when it comes to painting a comprehensive picture of how software is made.

At the same time, the dense networks of technique and methodology that software development and engineering have woven over the last decades

---

7   Dyck et al. (2015, p. 3) define DevOps, a concatenation of development and IT operations as 'an organizational approach that stresses empathy and cross-functional collaboration within and between teams – especially development and IT operations – in software development organizations'. I mention DevOps specifically because it testifies to the complex integration between organizational and technical strategies; it is not just a set of organizational practices, but often associated with technical innovations such as *containerization*, where an entire solution stack is packaged together and virtualized in a way that it can be easily and quickly transferred from one machine to another. Docker is probable the most well-known product in this context.

necessarily tie back to software's *objective* dimension, that is, to the rich environment of technicity I have begun to address in the last chapter. This environment is populated by technical elements that software developers can appropriate in different ways to write programs that carry out certain tasks, provide particular functions, or demonstrate specific behaviors. While we cannot easily distinguish the various management and design practices from a properly technical substance in concrete circumstances, there is a backdrop of technical evolution that defines what computers can do at a given point in time. In the domain of software, I suggest that evolutionary trajectories form around what I have referred to as 'algorithmic techniques'. So, what are they more precisely?

Answering that question requires a closer look at the notion of 'algorithm', which I have mostly avoided so far, since the short definitions that abound in nontechnical literature provide a false sense of conceptual security by suggesting that a 'ground level' apprehension of computation provides an adequate understanding of the technicities at hand. I hope to have sufficiently shaken this belief at this point, making it safe to proceed. Interestingly, Donald Knuth's megaclassic *The Art of Programming*, which I will use as a guide into the question, initially also refrains from giving a definition and starts by *showing* an algorithm, namely this one:

> **Algorithm E** (*Euclid's algorithm*). Given two positive integers m and n, find their *greatest common divisor*, that is, the largest positive integer that evenly divides both m and n.
> **E1.** [Find remainder.] Divide m by n and let r be the remainder. (We will have $0 \leq r < n$.)
> **E2.** [Is it zero?] If $r = 0$, the algorithm terminates; n is the answer.
> **E3.** [Reduce.] Set $m \leftarrow n$, $n \leftarrow r$, and go back to step E1. (Knuth, 1997, p. 2)

Only afterwards do we learn that an algorithm is 'a finite set of rules that gives a sequence of operations for solving a specific type of problem' (Knuth, 1997, p. 4) and thereby has a similar meaning 'to that of *recipe, process, method, technique, procedure, routine, rigmarole*' (Knuth, 1997, p. 4). Knuth specifies five additional features, namely that an algorithm 1) has to terminate after a certain number of steps, 2) should be well defined, 3) can have some input, 4) must have one or several outputs, and 5) should consist of operations 'sufficiently basic that they can in principle be done exactly and in a finite length of time by someone using pencil and paper' (Knuth, 1997, p. 6). The last aspect actually makes a finer point concerning the theory of computability, but it also indicates that we are talking about abstract operations that can be carried out in different ways. Colburn's definition makes this difference more explicit:

> Ordinarily conceived, an algorithm is not a program but an abstraction of a problem solution in the form of a terminating sequence of steps, which when implemented in a programming language issues a list of computer instructions which carry out the solution steps. (Colburn, 2000, p. 168)

This distinction between an 'algorithm', a sequence of actions that can be described in a formal or not-so-formal language, and a 'program', an implementation of that sequence in a language that a computer can 'understand' and execute, is important (cf. Dourish 2016). At this point, however, I consider the ontological aspect of the distinction to be less relevant than its relation to the question of how algorithms manifest and 'travel'. The different ways algorithms are commonly presented are significant in that respect. An algorithm could be laid out in natural language, in mathematical notation, or as a flow chart – and, on a first level, a programming language is just another way of representing an algorithm. Here is my own description/implementation of Euclid's algorithm, written in JavaScript:

```
var m = prompt("enter number m")
var n = prompt("enter number n")
var r  = 1
while(r  !== 0) {
    r  = m % n
    if(r === 0) {
        alert(n)
    } else {
        m = n
        n = r
    }
}
```

This code can be copied and pasted in the JavaScript console of your favorite web browser and will run there. Note that the script asks for an input in the beginning – for a concrete implementation to function, there has to be some data the algorithm can work on.

Knuth's description and this small program are two representations of what most computer scientists would recognize to be the same algorithm. However, the JavaScript version has the specific characteristic that it can run on a computer, even if any programmer could produce an implementation based on Knuth's text, just like I did. The distinction between different forms of description and, in particular, between those that can be executed and those that cannot is certainly crucial to any ontological inquiry. But a perspective emphasizing the practice of software-making is less interested in pondering what an algorithm *is* than coming to a broader understanding what *goes into* concrete programs, written in concrete circumstances, which may end up performing the concrete operations that determine whether a post appears in a user's Facebook News Feed or not. The ambiguity between algorithm-as-abstraction and algorithm-as-program – and similar discussions[8] – is therefore not something I seek to resolve but would rather use as an analytical dimension for addressing different forms of technicity and technical knowledge. Indeed, while my focus is on mechanical techniques, I would like to recall that the priority the cultural techniques concept gives to operation not only resonates well with Simondon's understanding that machines are 'human reality, human gesture fixed and crystallized in working structures' (Simondon, 2017, p. 18), but, more generally, promotes the analysis of cross-cutting ontic performance over ontological idealization. In that sense, I prefer talking about forms of materialization rather than identifying specific techniques strictly with specific materialities. This has the advantage that techniques can be traced through shifting material manifestations and configurations, materiality becoming one analytical category among several.

In practical terms, algorithms are sequences of operations that programmers formulate or specify in programming languages in order to make a computer do something. This level of appreciation is too often the point where the critical engagement with algorithms as technical subject matter stops. Too many authors still think that understanding what an algorithm is, in principle, allows for a sufficient understanding of what algorithms do – or could do – in practice. But we have barely arrived at page 6 of Knuth's 2000+ page magnum opus! What is he writing about on the remaining pages? As Knuth explicitly states, his business is not with a 'theory of algorithms', that is, with the fundamental theory of computation we associate with authors like Turing or Church. Instead, he proposes an 'analysis of algorithms' that articulates 'the theory of the properties of particular computer algorithms' (Knuth, 1997, p. vi). What follows over five monumental

---

8   Another question that one could raise is whether a program is a single algorithm or a collection of algorithms. While I tend toward the latter, I am simply not convinced that the question is relevant for my analytical purposes.

volumes are therefore presentations and discussions of existing algorithms: *Fundamental Algorithms* (volume 1), *Seminumerical Algorithms* (volume 2), *Sorting and Searching* (volume 3), *Combinatorial Algorithms* (volume 4), and *Syntactical Algorithms* (volume 5, work in progress).[9] While the first volume does contain a chapter on what we would roughly call 'learning how to program', these passages do certainly not constitute anything close to the many beginner's tutorials one can find online. But more advanced subjects such as software architecture or process management are treated sparingly as well. Clearly, for Knuth, the art of programming consists in knowing how to solve problems with algorithms, which means *knowing algorithms*. Lots of them. This is what he seems to say: 'Programmer, you can invent your own solutions to problems, but you do not have to: for many problems there are existing solutions and here they are, this is how they work, these are their advantages, disadvantages and the most important things to consider when implementing them. Want to find the greatest common divisor of two integers? Here is Euclid's algorithm. Want to sort a list? Here are 20 ways of doing that, each a little different from the others.'

Are algorithms techniques in the sense that they carry out a particular task in a particular way? Yes, they most certainly are. Algorithms can be described as techniques that have one set of material properties when written in natural language in a book and another set when written in a programming language for execution on a computer. From here, a path forks over to software studies or, more particularly, to critical code studies, a field situated in the humanities that proposes 'that we can read and explicate code the way we might explicate a work of literature' (Marino, 2006, n.p.). While this is certainly an interesting proposition, I seriously doubt that most humanities scholars can realistically arrive at a level of technical acculturation that allows for a meaningful and context-aware reading of any but the most trivial pieces of code. This may well suffice in certain cases, but the field of information ordering, for example, relies on algorithms that require among other things a robust understanding of probability theory to decipher what is happening in a sequence of instructions. Knowing how to read code is rarely sufficient to understand the actual content of a program, at least not in domains where complex concepts and heuristics are articulated in the form of a program.

9   Another classic in computer science literature, Robert Sedgewick's *Algorithms* (1983), provides its own segmentation, which can be summarized through its chapter headings: mathematical algorithms, sorting, searching, string processing, geometric algorithms, graph algorithms, and advanced topics.

I will therefore use the term 'algorithmic technique' more specifically to target a space that is somewhat abstracted from the level of concrete algorithms, whether they are implemented in code or not. Going back to Knuth's work once more, I want to draw attention to the almost 400-page-long section on sorting, which, here, means 'marshaling things into ascending or descending order' (Knuth, 1998, p. 1) following a numerical system or the sequence of the alphabet. In the first part of the section dedicated to *internal* searching, which concerns lists of data small enough to fit into main memory, Knuth begins by distinguishing seven different 'types'. Since the given overview is particularly instructive for my purposes, I would like to quote it in full:

> A. *An insertion sort.* The items are considered one at a time, and each new item is inserted into the appropriate position relative to the previously-sorted items. (This is the way many bridge players sort their hands, picking up one card at a time.)
> B. *An exchange sort.* If two items are found to be out of order, they are interchanged. This process is repeated until no more exchanges are necessary.
> C. *A selection sort.* First the smallest (or perhaps the largest) item is located, and it is somehow separated from the rest; then the next smallest (or next largest) is selected, and so on.
> D. *An enumeration sort.* Each item is compared with each of the others; an item's final position is determined by the number of keys that it exceeds.
> E. *A special-purpose sort*, which works nicely for sorting five elements as stated in the problem, but does not readily generalize to larger numbers of items.
> F. *A lazy attitude*, with which you ignored the suggestion above and decided not to solve the problem at all. Sorry, by now you have read too far and you have lost your chance.
> G. *A new, super sorting technique* that is a definite improvement over known methods. (Please communicate this to the author at once.) (Knuth, 1998, p. 73)

This quote is interesting for a number of reasons. First, type E is a jab at programmers who think that they do not need to consult the record of existing techniques and can just come up with a sorting method on the fly. Knuth thus restates programming as a practice and discipline that may allow for 'wiggling through' occasionally, but actually has a serious body of knowledge that any respectable programmer should know (of). Second, the last type acknowledges that there is no end to invention/discovery, even if the domain of sorting has been studied excessively already and new breakthroughs are unlikely. Third, and most importantly, this is not simply a list of algorithms, but an effort to distinguish general approaches to the problem of sorting, such as inserting or exchanging. Each of the first four types, in fact, leads to several specific algorithms, Hoare's already mentioned Quicksort being one of four algorithms proceeding through exchange. These larger principles or strategies for solving a specific type of problem are what I think of as 'algorithmic techniques'.

Starting from the observation that the making of nontrivial[10] software draws on rich reservoirs of existing knowledge, I hope to use the concept to formulate an approach to the analysis of software that sits between broad theorizing and the empirical investigation of concrete applications of information ordering algorithms. This middle ground revolves around a large, constantly growing, yet finite set of possibly well-known approaches to the 'software problems' that underpin running systems. In the domain of information ordering, this may concern, for example, how to sort a list, how to classify a text message, or how to make a 'good' recommendation. Algorithmic techniques can be seen as technical elements that are combined into technical individuals, that is, into working systems. As standardized yet plastic approaches or methods, they form the technical center of software development practice and an important part of computer science education. In fact, learning how to program, in the sense of mastering a programming language, makes for only a small part of computer science training at university level. A much larger portion is dedicated to the many different and often math-heavy techniques that can be expressed in code and to the question of how to apply them to the famous 'real-world problems' students are set to encounter in concrete work settings. Wing's (2006) notion of 'computational thinking' is thus not only a broadly analytical outlook but includes the capacity to abstract from a concrete situation to a level where familiar techniques can be applied. To develop this specific 'sensitivity' may require years of training and practice. As Mackenzie (2017a) observes, much of the skill acquisition for practitioners of machine learning concerns 'not so much implementation of particular techniques [...] but rather navigating

---

10   This term may seem strange to a humanities audience, but, according to ComputerLanguage. com, '[n]ontrivial is a favorite word among programmers and computer people for describing any task that is not quick and easy to accomplish' (Nontrivial, n.d.). While the meaning is certainly vague, it is important to understand that not all programming is inherently difficult, and that many standard problems require little in terms of deep planning.

the maze of methods and variations that might be relevant to a particular situation' (p. 75f.). This brings software specialists in line with other 'methods experts' such as statisticians, operational researchers, or consultants who know and master a set of techniques that they can readily apply in diverse settings.

Indeed, actual algorithms are written in code to become (part of) programs that run in actual locations and with actual purposes. They will always imply an interpretation and contextualization of an algorithmic technique's objective content according to objectal settings. Concrete programs are, in this sense, the heavily mediated outcomes of situated encounters between algorithmic techniques and local circumstances. But if we want to get a hold of the technical substance of software, we need to single out and address the question of how it has become possible to express and design functional behavior such as 'ranking', 'learning', or 'recommending'. Many algorithmic techniques are sufficiently specific and remarkable to try and isolate their functional principles, even if we understand that they are eventually embedded in both larger technical systems and local application contexts.

For Simondon, technical thinking organizes around the knowledge of elements and builds up from there:

> In technical thinking, it is the element that is more stable, better known and in a certain sense more perfect than the ensemble; it is truly an object, whereas the ensemble always stays inherent to the world to a certain extend. Religious thinking finds the opposite balance: here, it is the ensemble that is more stable, stronger, and more valid than the element. (Simondon, 2017, p. 187)

In that sense, I take algorithmic techniques to be the technical elements that enable computers to perform *compound* or *complex* operation, made possible by computation but not reducible to it. This transcends common analytical grids, such as Simon's (1996) distinction[11] between state and process or Kittler's (1997b) assessment that media transmit, store, and process information, and focuses on the question of how transversal and transductive technical arrangements are capable of producing certain behaviors. Lev Manovich, one of the few scholars in the humanities invested in approaching the landscape of techniques as a proper object of study,

---

11   This distinction finds a parallel in Wirth's (1976) famous assessment 'Algorithms + Data Structures = Programs'.

makes a distinction between a 'cultural layer' and a 'computer layer', which helps clarify the issue:

> The examples of categories on the cultural layer are encyclopedia and a short story; story and plot; composition and point of view; mimesis and catharsis, comedy and tragedy. The examples of categories on the computer layer are process and packet (as in data packets transmitted through the network); sorting and matching; function and variable; a computer language and a data structure. (Manovich, 2001, p. 46)

This distinction is useful, in particular if the cultural layer is understood to include categories that diverge from the traditional repertoire of media forms and involve elements that evoke Peters's 'logistical media' (2015, p. 37). In the case of the subject matter addressed in the second part of this book, this concerns tasks such as retrieving information, grouping items, attributing relevance, assessing risk or aptitude, and recommending contents, products, or people. Although I am hesitant to oppose culture and computation, it is worthwhile to think about algorithmic techniques as the technical schemas at work in the computer layer that make it possible to actually perform such tasks on the cultural or interface layer.

Importantly, even for moderately complex operations, there is rarely an analogous relationship between the underlying technical schemas and the behavior on the interface. This fuels the dissociation between 'knowing how' and 'knowing that' Krämer and Bredekamp (2013, p. 26) refer to when they argue that 'ability and knowledge split up' under circumstances of increased mechanization. We can certainly see that a program like Google Lens is able to recognize objects in an image, but this does not help us in the slightest to understand how the currently most effective[12] algorithmic technique for doing so, convolutional neural networks, actually work. This prompts the question of how to think of technical knowledge in the context of software-making.

Techniques and Technical Knowledge

Before launching into that question, I have to address an important ambiguity, namely the difference between an understanding of cultural techniques as 'the skills and aptitudes involved in the use of modern media'

---

12   Such claims to leadership are generally made through competitions, such as the ImageNet Large Scale Visual Recognition Challenge.

(Winthrop-Young, 2014, p. 381) and the theoretically more sophisticated definition as 'preconceptual operations that generate the very concepts that subsequently are used to conceptualize these operations' (Winthrop-Young, 2014, p. 385). This distinction raises the uncomfortable question of the subject, which cannot be avoided when talking about knowledge, skill, or experience. I will deal with this issue by embedding the former perspective into the latter, in the sense that I understand what is commonly described as learning a skill (e.g., programming) or as acquiring knowledge (e.g., how a compiler works) not as an activity where a sovereign subject obtains some kind of power that it can wield autonomously, but as a process of acculturation *into* a cultural technique that shapes and, in a certain sense, produces a 'new', composite subject that shares agency with the objects and concepts the technique implies (cf. Vismann, 2013). As Winthrop-Young argues (2013), '[i]f ideas, concepts, and in some cases the objects themselves emerge from basic operations, then it is only logical to assume that this also applies to the agent performing these operations' (p. 9).

That said, I would argue that the most concrete manifestation of technicity and knowledge in computer science and related disciplines is, in fact, the ever-growing archive of algorithmic techniques, ready-to-hand for integration into concrete technical artifacts. Simondon's philosophy emphasizes technical evolution to the point where 'the individual technical object is not this or that thing, given *hic et nunc*, but that of which there is genesis' (Simondon, 2017, p. 26). In this vein, I suggest that algorithmic techniques denote schemas that bind actual artifacts to the trajectories constituting technical evolution. Schemas run through stages of concretization and adaptation, and it is the schema, understood as technical essence, that gives identity to both the object and its trajectory, not the concrete physical manifestation at a given instance. From this perspective, we can see algorithmic techniques both as carriers of the technicity running through 'working structures' (Simondon, 2017, p. 18) and as the object or content of the 'sensitivity to technicity that allows for the discovery of possible assemblages' (Simondon, 2017, p. 74). As constitutive elements in computing, they are apprehended by technical imagination and thereby become units of knowledge. Layton, building on Koyré's work, sees 'technology as a spectrum, with ideas at one end and techniques and things at the other' (Layton, 1974, p. 37f.) and I conceive algorithmic techniques in similar terms, with the crucial provision that they are not on one side of a spectrum but rather spanning and connecting the domains of knowledge and operation.

In line with Simondon's framing of technology as a fundamental relationship with the world, I want to emphasize that technical knowledge, here, should not be merely understood as a collection of recipes for production, but as a deeper category that connects directly to Heidegger's interpretation of techne (τέχνη) as a form of knowing. In a lecture given to an assembly of vocational school teachers, 'Überlieferte Sprache und technische Sprache' ('Traditional language and technological language'), Heidegger (1998) argues that techne means 'to know one's way in something [*sichauskennen in etwas*], namely in the fabrication [*herstellen*] of something' (p. 135, translation amended), but that this '[k]nowing one's way is a kind of knowing [*erkennen*], having known and knowledge' (p. 135). Heidegger here describes 'technology' (*Technik*) as fundamentally entangled in *Erkennen*, a term often translated as 'perception' or 'recognition', but which, in this context, denotes 'knowing' in its full sense as a verb, as 'coming to know' or, more abstractly, as 'constituting knowledge'. Technology, in that sense, is not only something that can be known, but a means to know, a fundamental form of knowing. It is neither a simple application of science, nor a mere manifestation of social or economic forces, but a mode of revealing the world. Despite Heidegger's (1977, p. 19) assessment that modern technology knows in the form of *Gestell* ('enframing'), revealing or 'challenging' nature as mere resource, his notion of *sichauskennen* ('knowing one's way') echoes Simondon's 'sensitivity to technicity' and marks a space of knowing that has true epistemic substance, character, and content.

In his aptly named *What Engineers Know and How They Know It*, Vincenti (1990) also argues that engineering has a specific 'intellectual content' (p. vii) that cannot be adequately understood as applied science and needs to be treated as its own 'epistemological species', not least because of its status as 'a means to a utilitarian end' (p. 3). Although the OECD's (2013) assessment that software 'is essentially an expression of human expertise translated into code' (p. 49) does not capture the important technical and infrastructural qualities at play, the term 'expertise' is another way to address the intellectual dimension of the specific knowing and revealing computational forms engage in. One could argue that the articulations of software-making as 'realization of rule-based thinking' (Coy, 2007) or applications of 'computational thinking' (Wing, 2006) constitute the broadest frame for such an endeavor. While these general characterizations are certainly not wrong, they do not capture how far any kind of 'thinking' is always already entangled in webs woven by more specific techniques. A short example should be instructive.

Media theorists have been very interested in the notion of 'recursion' (e.g., Krämer, 1988, p. 165ff.), often discussing it as a property of software. But what if we consider recursion 'in action', as a technique that is available as a concrete means of functional expression? In the context of programming, recursion occurs when a subroutine – a series of instructions that can be addressed as a unit – calls itself, creating a potentially infinite chain or loop. The fact that such a thing can exist has to do with how processors function and how programming languages arrange that function into more abstract constructs. But this does not tell us why and when recursion is a useful way to construct the computer behavior able to perform some task. Take the example of Netvizz, an extractor for Facebook data I used to build and maintain (Rieder, 2013). One of its modules was a Page network crawler, a small program that started with a user-specified Facebook Page, got the Pages liked by that Page, and so forth, until it had either retrieved the whole network or reached a chosen 'depth' or distance from the starting point. The main element of this module was a recursive loop, a subroutine that received a Page ID as input, got the IDs of liked Pages, and then called itself for each 'discovered' Page with that ID as the new input, and so forth. There was a global data structure that collected all Page references, to make sure that the recursive loop crawled each Page only once and to create an output file with all the collected data. The fact that we do not know how many Pages there are going to be when we start the crawl is the reason why recursion is such a useful way to produce the desired function or behavior in this case. While 'normal' loops work through set lists of items, a recursive loop can forage through a tree or network for which we have no prior map or overview. Recursion thus constitutes an instance of technicity made available to developers to build a program that has certain operational properties or capabilities. Situated at the level of the element, however, its technicity is still 'pure' or 'unconstrained' because it is not yet bound into a functional whole. At this level, we also encounter contingency, redundancy, and overlap: one could easy produce the same general behavior of Netvizz's module without using recursion, for example, by creating a queue that Page IDs are added to and worked off one by one. This approach would draw on other technicities at hand and would have different characteristics, for example, in terms of memory use or performance. Making a program may be rule-based thinking, but it unfolds inside a technical domain that requires the sensitivity to technicity or *sichauskennen* that constitutes technical knowledge.

While algorithmic techniques are ultimately destined for implementation in a program, they often begin with ideas that have little to do with computation. For example, there is nothing intrinsically computational about the inkling that spam messages can be identified by inspecting their textual content (Chapter 6). But Paul Graham's (2002) proposal to create a statistical classifier that treats every single word in a message as an indicator for 'spamminess' moves the initial intuition firmly into computational territory, even if actual programs may enact the idea in a variety of ways. The term 'statistical classifier' points not only to the larger space of probability theory but also to a list of commonly used and well-documented algorithmic techniques for performing statistical classification. These techniques revolve around a general rationale, a number of central ideas forming a conceptual core that can be laid out in (a combination of) natural language, diagrams, mathematical notation, or code. They constitute both technicity and technical knowledge, even if their implementation in a working system requires many decisions to be made concerning the units to take into account, the parameters to specify, the tweaks to apply, the outputs to produce, and so forth. Algorithmic techniques are, at the same time, analytical (they involve descriptions of the world), procedural (they establish heuristics and actual computational behavior), and even normative (they define right and wrong ways of doing).

Technical knowledge, then, consists in large part of knowing techniques and how to use them. And algorithmic techniques are indeed central as part of the "intellectual furniture" (Dourish, 2016, p.1) of software-making. As Vismann argues, '[r]eproducibility and learnability are among the key features of cultural techniques' (Vismann, 2013, p. 87) and the question of both transmission and learning is thus unavoidable. My attempt to isolate the technical subject matter analytically is not meant to deny the social aspects involved in learning. If we consider learning new techniques as a process of acculturation rather than mere acquisition, it is important to emphasize 'that learners inevitably participate in communities of practitioners and that the mastery of knowledge and skill requires newcomers to move toward full participation in the sociocultural practices of a community' (Lave and Wenger, 1991, p. 29). Computing is full of such 'communities of practice' and even if computer science and neighboring disciplines represent the most systematic effort to invent, study, stabilize, document, and disseminate techniques, it is clearly not the only one. There is a large offer of schools and classes outside of university that propose structured training, including online environments such as MOOCs (Massive Open Online Courses) or step-by-step tutorials. But maybe more importantly, companies can and should be seen as hosting communities of practice that engage heavily in the production and circulation of technical knowledge. Open-source projects play a similar role. The enormous amounts of literature and documentation, coming in many shapes and forms, can also be seen as output from and input to communities of practice. Well-known algorithms like Quicksort or

PageRank (Chapter 7) have canonical formulations[13] that can be found in textbooks or on Wikipedia. Social media play an exceedingly important role in this context (cf. Storey et al., 2014). The most impressive example in this regard is certainly the StackExchange Network, a series of Q&A-style websites that cover a range of technical topics. In late 2017, the flagship community, Stack Overflow, which describes itself as 'Q&A for professional and enthusiast programmers', hosted 14 million questions and 23 million answers that cover the problem space of software-making to an uncanny degree. The experience that a Google search for almost any programming problem will directly lead to a relevant answer on Stack Overflow has become almost proverbial. Similar arguments could be made for GitHub, the leading platform for hosting software repositories, and these examples indeed raise questions concerning not only the distribution and standardization of technical knowledge, but also forms of commodification and capitalization (Mackenzie, 2017b).

Going back to Simondon's distinction between artisanal and industrial modes of producing technical objects, we can certainly see efforts in both academia and parts of the business sphere to put software-making on more structured, formalized, and scientific foundations. At the same time, movements like 'software craftsmanship' (Mancuso, 2015) explicitly focus on skill over process methodology and sites like Stack Overflow and GitHub represent and facilitate much more artisanal modes of learning and working with algorithmic techniques, where problem-solving is ad hoc, exploratory, and driven by the circumstances of time and place. The role of modularity is crucial in this context and needs to be addressed in more detail.

Abstraction, Infrastructure, Archive

A more robust and systematic analysis of the knowledge spheres evoked in the last section could follow McLure Wasko and Faraj (2000) in distinguishing between 'knowledge as object, knowledge embedded in individuals, and knowledge embedded in a community' (p. 157). While I have alluded to all three, I would like to start this section by expanding on the first perspective. The idea that knowledge can be 'codified and separated from the minds of

13   In this day and age, a good way to determine whether there is such a canonical formulation is to check an algorithm's Wikipedia page. The pages for Quicksort and PageRank, for example, propose not only extensive descriptions in natural language and mathematical notation, but also actual implementations in code, since these algorithms only repeat a small number of operations over many iterations.

people' (p. 157), and therefore be stored, searched, and retrieved, is clearly a relevant way to address the heaps of literature and documentation available to programmers, even if one remains hesitant about full disembodiment or reification. Still, the 'knowledge as object' perspective opens a pathway toward an even more radical interrogation that pushes beyond the idea of symbolic encoding, for example, in the form of written material, and asks how we can understand technical objects themselves as carriers and not just products or manifestations of knowledge. Such an interrogation seems to be particularly appropriate in the context of software, with its highly layered and modular character. This section will therefore address the question of how techniques and technical knowledge spread in ways that are not fully addressed by common conceptualization of knowledge. This requires a discussion of abstraction.

Abstraction and Modularity

It is certainly no exaggeration to say that abstraction is absolutely fundamental to computing. Colburn's acute account captures the notion in particularly vivid terms:

> Indeed, the foundational concepts of computer science are described in the language of binary arithmetic and logic gates, but it is a fascinating aspect of the discipline that the *levels of abstraction* that one can lay upon this foundational layer are limitless, and provide the ability to model familiar objects and processes of every day life entirely within a digital world. (Colburn, 2000, p. 174)

Abstraction, in computing, thus refers to layering and to the idea that many 'worlds' can be modeled upon computation in one way or another. The canonical example are high-level programming languages, such as C, Python, or the already mentioned JavaScript. The rationale behind these languages can be summarized in three steps:

> 1) *The problem*: Programming a computer by directly manipulating registers in binary code is really difficult and cumbersome. Even the most basic operations require several commands, it is easy to make mistakes, and it is hard to write programs that exceed a basic level of structural or functional complexity. Furthermore, actual computers can have different instruction sets and transposing a program written for one microarchitecture to another means rewriting it.

2) *The observation*: Despite these difficulties, it seems that programming consists of basic compound operations that are repeated over and over again. All programs seem to be made out of a relatively small number of such constantly recurring operations.

3) *The solution*: One can come up with a syntax that standardizes these common operations into a series of higher-level commands or functions and then write a program that translates them back into machine language. This makes programming easier and quicker, and we can focus on the broader functional aspects of the program. We can even translate our programs to different machines instead of rewriting them for every microarchitecture.

This somewhat cartoonish summary illustrates the rationale behind the development of high-level programming languages in the 1950s and 1960s. These languages were designed to capture computation in a syntax more adapted to humans and they rely on compilers – initially called 'autocoders' – to translate that syntax back into machine language. In Colburn's terms, a programming language represents a 'modeled world' that, in the case of general-purpose languages, has the same universal character as the underlying hardware,[14] but structures access to that full space of computation in specific ways. When programmers say that they prefer one language to another, what they mean is that they prefer a particular way of abstracting computation behind a particular syntax. But why is this important from a perspective concerned with techniques and technical knowledge?

Programming languages represent a major instance of entanglement between abstraction and knowledge. They can be seen as 'carriers' of 'objectified' knowledge because they are not simply transparent layers that make programming easier or more convenient; they already contain various functional building blocks, such as sorting mechanisms or generic data structures. Programming languages introduce concepts and techniques that imply ways of doing and, most importantly, they make complex or compound function available to their users. Contemporary programming languages do this in very comprehensive ways. While Dijkstra (1972) was critical of the 'baroque monstrosities' (p. 12) higher level programming languages had in his view become, he clearly recognized how abstraction

---

14 A language is called Turing-complete if it can compute all computable functions. Microsoft's Office programs, for example, are Turing-complete via their implementations of Visual Basic for Applications.

facilitates and plays a role in widening the space of what can be considered programmable:

> Programming will remain very difficult, because once we have freed ourselves from the circumstantial cumbersomeness, we will find ourselves free to tackle the problems that are now well beyond our programming capacity. (Dijkstra, 1972, p. 12)

For Dijkstra, development tools both influence and enhance human capacities, and, in a sense, they represent a material form of knowledge that can be built on and that continuously expands what software can do. Another example should make this argument clearer.

We want to make a program that gets some data from a remote web server. This means dealing with the HTTP protocol and the specific ways it structures machine communication. This is not easy and would require us to learn not only how HTTP works, but also how the operating system we are targeting handles network connections and other things. But we are using the PHP programming language, because it already comes preinstalled on our system and is well-suited to web tasks. And PHP comes with a predefined function called *file_get_contents*() that takes a URL as input and returns the data stored at that location. A single line of code launches a large series of instructions specified in the PHP interpreter[15] and in underlying procedures furnished by the operating system. Although using the PHP function does not imply any knowledge 'transfer', it grants the programmer the capacity to produce a particular operation, a complex behavior; there is thus an 'activation' of knowledge stored as 'fixed and crystallized gesture' (Simondon, 2017, p. 18) that the programmer can call upon via the PHP programming language. This is how technical elements in software can be seen as both means of injecting existing technicity into a new program and carriers of objectified knowledge. The specifics of how the URL's content is retrieved are hidden behind an abstraction layer and it is safe to assume that most PHP programmers ignore the more detailed technical operations executed in the background. What the programmer needs to know, however, is that such a function exists, what it does, namely that it 'reads entire file into a string' according to the PHP documentation,[16] and how it can be used,

15 An increasing number of programming languages are not compiled, but *interpreted*, which means that they are parsed and executed one line at a time by a special program, an interpreter, rather than directly translated into machine code.

16 http://php.net/manual/en/function.file-get-contents.php, accessed 12 December 2019.

that is, that it requires a parameter that is either a local file or an address on the web. Abstraction can generally be by-passed: if we require more control over the specificities of the file transfer, there are other modules that provide just that.[17]

Since PHP is a programming language specialized in web development, reading files from the web is a common operation and apparently common enough to justify making it a part of the core language. Different languages organize such integration differently. Python, for example, has the Python Standard Library, a collection of modules that are not part of the core language but distributed with it by default. To get a file from the web, we could use the urllib.request module, which 'defines functions and classes which help in opening URLs (mostly HTTP) in a complex world'.[18] Or we could download Requests, an external library that describes itself as 'HTTP for Humans'[19] and abstracts HTTP operations to a level of simplicity similar to PHP, taming the 'complex world' of Internet communication protocols into a small number of simple commands. Freed from the 'circumstantial cumbersomeness' of protocol management, we can move on to tackle other things. These different ways of providing packaged function constitute a vector next to learning in a more traditional sense for techniques to 'travel', for becoming parts of concrete programs and thereby of end-users' everyday practices.

This logic holds not only for externally provided function. Programmers use subroutines and similar constructs to abstract their own code into more manageable units: when we program, '[w]e control complexity by building abstractions that hide details when appropriate' (Abelson et al., 1996, p. xxii), which in practice means to 'hide concerns about the representation of data as collections of bits and the representation of programs as sequences of primitive instructions' (Abelson et al., 1996, p. 489). Dijkstra (1974) remarked that 'a large sophisticated program can only be made by a careful application of the rule "Divide and Conquer"' (p. 609) and there are different ways to design this kind of modularity. But how such functions are packaged, distributed, and rendered accessible to programmers is less important than to recognize that this allows for techniques of all levels of complexity and sophistication to become *elements* in larger systems of functioning, without actually having to be understood in any substantial way by the programmer integrating them. Rather than invest into a taxonomy of elements in software, we can

17   PHP, like many other programming languages, comes with an interface to the very powerful libcurl/cURL package.

18   https://docs.python.org/3/library/urllib.request.html, accessed 12 December 2019.

19   http://docs.python-requests.org/en/master/, accessed 12 December 2019.

appreciate the different means to *delineate* such units, both analytically and on the level of code. Contemporary programming languages indeed provide various means to make and stabilize elements by assembling instructions into larger building blocks such as subroutines, classes, or modules on a more elemental level and packages, libraries, or frameworks further up.

We again arrive at Krämer and Bredekamp's (2013) assessment that 'skill and knowledge are going their separate ways' (p. 26), but this time the externalization does not concern the end-user, but the developer, who, in a sense, becomes a *user* of a programming language. Since integrating packaged function into one's own program requires only comprehension of what an element does and how to address it though its API (application programming interface),[20] the 'mechanism of forgetting' at work concerns the specific principles and procedures that make function happen. While the term 'knowledge' is maybe not fully appropriate here, we have to recognize that learning the actual details of an algorithmic technique is only one way to draw on its intellectual content and to integrate its technicity into an operational setting, where it may serve as a means of production that enables specific forms of value generation.

We can think about this reification of knowledge by extending Mokyr's (2005) analysis of the 'knowledge revolution' that accompanied the Industrial Revolution, which involved not merely an increase in the production of knowledge but also meant that a 'great deal of knowledge that previously was tacit and oral was codified and described in scientific and technical writings and drawing' (p. 56). Spurred by printing and the growth in learning institutions, the 'Enlightenment began a process that dramatically lowered [...] access costs' (p. 73) to knowledge and stimulated forms of invention that relied on the variation and combination of elements, facilitating the emergence of technical schemas situated at higher levels of the constructive ladder, to speak with Simondon. Abstraction and modularity push this logic even further: if a developer seeks to integrate machine learning into an application, she can simply download a library like TensorFlow, follow one of many tutorials, consult the documentation, and modify the source code if needed. She can even move another step up and use the Keras package, which adds a layer of abstraction on top of TensorFlow, describing itself as 'an API designed for human beings, not machines' supporting 'easy and fast prototyping'.[21]

20   The term API is now often used more specifically for web-based data interfaces. But it actually denotes, broadly speaking, any structured means for communication between software components.
21   https://keras.io, accessed 12 December 2019.

Certainly, competent application to a specific problem requires experience and a significant investment of time, but the remarkable availability of such highly complex and concretized elements has important consequences for the spread of technicity and knowledge through the software landscape.

Looking at these different forms of transmission suggests the notion of 'stability' as analytical category. I propose to distinguish between two ends of a spectrum. 'Solid techniques' take the form of libraries, modules, (web) services, and other types of packaged function. Here, 'ways of carrying out a particular task' (OED) are specified and materialized in ready-made code that can accelerate development overall but also make difficult things easy, cumbersome things convenient, and boring things quick to get done with. This convenience may come at the price of performance or flexibility since packaged functionality implies an act of delegation to a technique already implemented as a technical element, which encapsulates a particular schema that may not be fully appropriate or optimized for the specific task at hand. There may be occasions where the sorting algorithm built into a programming language may not be the fastest or least memory-intensive way to sort a list. In many cases, however, available elements actually have performance advantages if they went through numerous cycles of optimization or concretization. 'Liquid techniques' are closer to knowledge in its more traditional form, that is, schemas that can be found in textbooks, classrooms, or minds. But even liquid techniques are constantly stabilized through the standardization of practices resulting from converging educational standards, dominant publications, corporate best practices, or – increasingly – the voting system on Stack Overflow.

Algorithmic techniques are solidified or 'frozen' when they are modular-ized, moved to a subroutine, or packaged in some other way. They may even 'sink down' into the bowels of computational infrastructure and become part of an operating system, programming language, or piece of hardware. As a case in point, the PHP programming language has gained many new functions over time, reducing standard operational chains in web programming to single lines of code. Instead of sorting lists by using one of the algorithms discussed by Knuth, programmers can simply select from the many preexisting functions, which actually rely on Hoare's Quicksort method internally.[22] One can, of course, still decide to implement another sorting technique oneself, but using the 'native' solution is the path of least

---

22   At the time of writing, the official PHP documentation lists thirteen different ready-made functions for sorting arrays. According to http://php.net/sort (accessed 12 December 2019), most of them rely on the Quicksort algorithm.

resistance. The language thus not only confers the capabilities of Quicksort to developers but elevates it to a de facto standard that becomes 'completely embedded in everyday tools of use' (Lampland and Star, 2009, p. 11), in this case in the specific functional reservoir provided by PHP. More advanced algorithmic techniques become 'infrastructural' in similar ways, making their use a realistic option for much larger groups of people and projects.

Another example for the way programming languages freeze specific concepts and techniques, thereby 'transferring' them to developers, concerns data structures. When Niklaus Wirth (1971) designed the Pascal programming language at the end of the 1960s on the basis of the earlier ALGOL 60, he argued that, compared to its predecessor, 'its range of applicability is considerably increased due to a variety of data structuring facilities' (p. 35). Certain conventions for structuring and addressing data in memory had already been emerging at the time and Wirth decided to solidify some of them as part of the language itself. In his classic *Algorithms + Data Structures = Programs*, he introduces what he calls the 'fundamental structures' already in the preface:

> We therefore postulate a number of basic building principles of data structures, called the *fundamental structures*. It is most important that they are constructs that are known to be quite easily implementable on actual computers, for only in this case can they be considered the true elements of an actual data representation, as the *molecules* emerging from the final step of refinements of the data description. They are the *record,* the *array* [...], and the *set.* (Wirth, 1976, p. xiv)

These fundamental structures have indeed become integral parts of almost any programming language; in Python, for example, they are referred to as 'dictionary', 'list', and 'set'. It is important to note that Wirth uses the terms 'postulate', highlighting the axiomatic and contingent nature of his design decision, and 'molecule', indicating that these constructs are, in fact, structures modeled from – or on top of – the 'atoms' of computation. While the specific designs of such abstractions are heatedly debated[23] and certainly not arbitrary, they are, ultimately, contingent conventions that are solidified and circulated by freezing them into influential programming languages like Pascal, but also through widely read publications such as Wirth's book,

---

23   Brian W. Kernighan, a contributor to the C programming language, famously published a paper called 'Why Pascal Is Not My Favorite Programming Language' in 1981 (https://www.lysator.liu.se/c/bwk-on-pascal.html, accessed 29 January 2020).

through integration into teaching curricula, or through effective lobbying work in some standards board.

As molecules or elements that can be integrated into a wide variety of functional contexts, algorithmic techniques function as boundary objects that 'are both plastic enough to adapt to local needs and constraints of the several parties employing them, yet robust enough to maintain a common identity across sites' (Star and Griesemer, 1989, p. 393). The actual work they perform is defined by their role in a concrete program operating at a specific site; but they also form a transversal vocabulary of possible function that transcends individual sites. This functional potential can be extremely broad: in later chapters I will show how certain techniques require little more than adherence to a specific data format to order basically any digital object.

The stability of techniques clearly varies. Freezing a technical schema into a module or giving it a canonical formulation can create a particularly stable boundary object, an 'immutable mobile' that remains fully consistent between sites but continues to be highly 'readable' and 'combinable' (cf. Latour, 1986). The Natural Language Toolkit for Python, for instance, offers modules that implement various (advanced) techniques for text-mining that developers can integrate into their programs, which includes researchers using these techniques as methods to generate new insights. As modules, they are indeed highly combinable with other code and the excellent documentation and close relationship with standards and conventions makes them as readable as any sophisticated technique can ever be. But stability in software can easily be reversed. Techniques can be 'liquefied' or 'heated up' when modules are reworked, optimized, extended, or replaced by custom code. Whereas freezing entails black-boxing and delegation, heating up can lead to concretization and adaptation, yielding enhancements or modifications that are again cooled into stable forms, often marked by a new version number. In practice, software-making almost always means combining more solid elements with more liquid ones. Modules are tied together, custom programming sits on top of system functions, legacy code is kept unchanged over decades as a system evolves around it, and so forth. Technical creation, in software more than anywhere else, 'consists of assembling a coherent system from disparate elements' (Chabot, 2013, p. 14).

In this context, conceptualization plays an important role but as outcome or accompaniment rather than foundation or origin. Indeed, if we consider algorithmic techniques as a specific kind of cultural technique, we can observe that they are, more often than not, 'older than the concepts that are generated from them' (Macho, 2003, p. 179). In many of the examples I will discuss in the second part of this book, we stray close to what Ramsay calls a 'hermeneutics of screwing around' (2010), where vaguely formulated ideas and practices follow meandering pathways of intuition and experimentation rather than straight lines of deductive reasoning. For example, Gerard Salton's canonical Vector Space Model for Information Retrieval, discussed in Chapter 5, receives its fully formalized formulation at a time when lists of word frequencies had already been widely used to represent text documents for almost two decades (cf. Dubin, 2004). Wirth's presentation of the Pascal language (1971) makes it amply clear that many of his ideas and decisions were developed in tight relationship with the practice of using, teaching, and extending ALGOL 60 and other languages. Likewise, his influential postulation of the three 'fundamental structures' for data representation was based on their extensive use as modules, testing and pushing them in concrete situations before making them part of the conceptual and technical infrastructure that is Pascal.

At the same time, we need to consider explicit conceptual formulation not just as varnish painted onto an already fully formed technique: conceptualization and formalization themselves can be seen as types of technique that change the status of what they describe. In the domain of information ordering, this often involves mathematization, which facilitates intellectual transfer in two ways: on the one side, well-formalized techniques travel more readily from one domain to another; on the other side, when 'placing' an idea into the conceptual space of mathematics, it becomes easier to import or connect to the wide range of existing mathematical techniques. The Vector Space Model provided not only a formal definition but also facilitated the practical and intellectual transfer of concepts and techniques from geometry and arithmetic into information retrieval. I would therefore argue that concepts, models, and theories should be seen as tied to techniques in a mutually reinforcing relationship, to the point where they become part of the techniques themselves. How a technique is conceptualized, narrated, formalized, documented, and stabilized is part of its character. Techniques define spaces of possibility that are both technical, in the sense that they provide actual schemas for producing function, and cognitive, in the sense that developers approach any problem from the vantage point of what they know to be achievable. They imply particular perspectives on what constitutes a problem and how it is to be solved; they incorporate definitions of good work and best practices; they tie the software-making occurring at a specific place and time to larger spheres and technical trajectories.

All of this does not mean that techniques travel through completely open spaces of circulation. Most programmers or companies freeze some of their own techniques into modules or libraries to code faster and to build more reliable programs but never share these elements. Copyright, patent law, and technical procedures such as compilation[24] or obfuscation constitute some of the strategies for limiting the circulation of techniques. Considerable amounts of software are simply built for internal use in some organization. Many large web companies, for example, do not rely on existing (relational) database packages such as MySQL or Oracle RDBMS but build custom tools that reflect their specific needs. Google's Bigtable, for example, only implements the database functions needed for the specific tasks the company primarily deals with and is heavily optimized for the load patterns these tasks produce. Bigtable is made available to external developers via the Google Cloud Platform, but not as a software package.

Infrastructure

Modules, libraries, and other forms of packaged function constitute an important part of the development infrastructures that serve as a base layer for concrete software projects. Although much more could be said about the deeply relational character of software-making, I want to briefly sketch two ways how development infrastructures could be analyzed further.

First, one could indeed venture deeper into the strata that sit below end-user applications. Here, one would find physical hardware coagulating around somewhat standardized device form factors (server, laptop, smartphone, embedded system, and so forth) that have particular computational capabilities, particular connections with the world, and a particular spectrum of common application types. One would also find operating systems that provide an increasingly large array of intermediary capabilities, ranging from graphical user interfaces to hardware abstraction layers and network stacks. Developers generally target combinations of device and operating system, for example, a smartphone running iOS or Android, but then also select a development environment and, if appropriate, a 'solution stack' that contains one or several programming languages, software that aids in the development process, such as code editors or versioning software, and components that provide some core functionality, such as database subsystems like MySQL. There are many possible combinations and concrete choices depend on numerous factors, from personal preference to task

---

24 Even libraries or modules are sometimes distributed as 'binary blobs' that can be integrated into other software but are not available as source code and therefore not amendable to adaptation.

specificity and cost. Hardware, operating system, and development environment together create a base layer of capabilities and functions to draw on. They form what we could call with Wirth (1976) an 'abstract computer' (p. 3) that, in most cases, is already full of operational opportunities to build on and that can be expanded further through modules, libraries, and so forth. Rather than instructing the hardware directly, the developer addresses this composite environment and what it affords in order to build a program. Technologies like Docker make it possible to 'freeze' concrete environments into 'containers' that can be easily transferred from one physical machine to another, reducing or eliminating the need to replicate and configure the environment locally. A deeper mechanological investigation of the many possibilities on offer would require another book but suffice to say that the information ordering techniques discussed in the second part have blended into the reservoirs of possible and easily accessible technicity.

Second, one could approach the question through the lens of control. In his astute discussion of the dichotomy between hardware and software, Moor (1978) suggests that we should move away from the problematic use of physicality as a criterion toward 'a pragmatic distinction', where 'the software will be those programs [...] which contain instructions the person can change, and the hardware will be that part of the computer system which is not software' (p. 215). This leads to a relational distinction that revolves around the infrastructural moment:

> For the systems programmer who programs the computer in machine language much of the circuitry will be hardware. For the average user who programs in an applications language, such as Fortran, Basic, or Algol, the machine language programs become hardware. For the person running an applications program an even larger portion of the computer is hardware. [...] What is considered hardware by one person can be regarded as software by another. (Moor, 1978, p. 215f.)

For the programmer using a high-level programming language, the compiler and the language design it imposes become the 'abstract computer' that cannot be changed. A developer working with a particular development environment and solution stack accepts these elements as hardware. Certainly, one can always decide to use a different language, a different environment, or even machine language directly. But that argument extends down to hardware as well. It is not impossible to rewrite the firmware configuring a piece of electronics, to use programmable logic arrays, or to manufacture one's own electronics. According to folklore, Alan Kay once said that '[p]eople who are really serious about software should make their own hardware' (Hertzfeld, 1982) and for a company like Apple, *everything* is software. Instead of trying to draw an ontological line, Moor's perspective highlights the moment when a software-maker herself draws that line for a given project, when she decides to use this or that device, language, or environment. At that moment, she decides – most likely bounded by her professional environment – on the specific layers of technology she will accept as hardware. Infrastructure, we are reminded, 'is a fundamentally relational concept' that needs to be thought 'in relation to organized practices' (Star and Ruhleder, 1996, p. 112).

How much leeway or control over the abstract computer developers have is not merely a question of available skills and resources, even if these elements are crucial. The environment a project targets may be imposed for various reasons, and the last years have seen clear tendencies toward a 'platformization' (Helmond, 2015) of software development. Cloud computing services like Amazon's AWS or Microsoft's Azure are not simply web-hosting facilities, but top-to-bottom technology providers that offer advanced computational capacities in areas such as data management, dynamic scaling, or machine learning, which would be very difficult to replicate without considerable investment. The reification of abstraction into tight, commodified infrastructures has maybe gone the furthest in the domain of mobile applications. Apple's integrated platform consists not only of hardware devices, iOS's many system functionalities, two programming languages (Objective-C and Swift), the XCode development environment, and a broad set[25] of frameworks and libraries but also ties software-making to an exclusive deployment and monetization model, the App Store. Apple provides various means of production as well as market access to hundreds of millions of users, taking a 30 percent cut on revenues in return. For developers, complex tasks like transnational app distribution and payment processing disappear behind an abstraction layer that has technical specificities as well as significant legal and commercial dimensions. Here, notions like abstraction and infrastructure fully intersect with economic platform models that 'redefine industrial architectures' (Gawer, 2010, p. 1).

In contrast, systems like GNU/Linux are attempts to profit from the constructive accumulation and labor sharing that abstraction enables and facilitates, without losing autonomy, flexibility, and control in a technical situation that necessarily requires dependence and delegation. One could argue that Apple radically extends what is hardware for its users and

25 https://developer.apple.com/documentation/, accessed 12 December 2019.

third-party developers, while GNU/Linux attempts to keep things soft and open to modification, at least for those with the desire, skill, and resources to shape their computational infrastructures. In both cases there remains a considerable space of plasticity when it comes to designing end-user functionality and one could argue that Apple's unyielding hand-holding actually facilitates artisanal modes of development, since many logistical constraints are taken care of. But the fact that these perks can be taken away at any moment shows how far platform power has penetrated into software-making.

The many different infrastructural components and techniques that define software-making inform *negotiations* between technicity and the world of social purposes and circumstances. With reference to Simondon one could argue that developers designing functionality for real or imagined end-users seek to tie the objective to the objectal in specific ways, even if one does not dissolve into the other. Considering that software is increasingly deployed as online service, where a new 'version' can be released at any time, we realize that these negotiations can become continuous processes that are increasingly empirical as changes and their effects on user can be evaluated almost instantly. Computerization can be seen as the cumulative outcome of the many individual instances where practices are mediated, constituted, or 'captured' (Agre, 1994) in software. These processes advance on the basis of the technical possibilities available at a given time and place. These possibilities are the outcome of technical evolution and one of the central vectors of this process is the continuous accumulation of algorithmic techniques that define and extend what computers can (be made to) do. But if we take a step back from the sprawling landscape of objects, techniques, and practices, we need to ask how much variation or variability there *really* is. Could it be that the many things that have been happening in and around computing are merely variations on a constant theme? How to conceive of commonality and variation?

Epistemological Pluralism

Over recent decades, scholars have increasingly recognized the material, operational, and functional dimension of computing – what Simondon calls 'objective' – but often in ways that boil technicity down to the computational operations performed by the logic gates in processors. This logical substrate is then regularly linked to forms of rationalism or instrumental reason. As already discussed, Golumbia (2009) identifies a computational universalism that includes 'a commitment to the view that a great deal, perhaps all, of human and social experience can be, explained via computational processes' (p. 8). This 'computationalism' is described as an expansive, invasive, and 'messianic' (p. 8) ideology that frames everything it comes upon in terms de-rived from computation. In this perspective, the possible variation between algorithmic techniques is epistemically and ideologically insignificant. Indeed, it can hardly be contested that the last 70 years have seen their fair share of instances where 'the computer boys take over' (Ensmenger, 2010) and information retrieval can be seen as yet another example.

But I want to ask whether computationalism's rationalist blueprint marks all of computing or, rather, a particular understanding of computing. The strong association Golumbia makes between computationalism and Chomsky's computational cognitivism leads me to believe that his legitimate critique of the rationalist ideologies found in many corners of computing is based on a partial apprehension of the actual landscape of algorithmic techniques and the conceptual spaces they connect with. Drawing on Derrida, Golumbia (2009) argues that '[l]ogical rules allow for no substantive ambiguity; either a proposition follows or it does not' (p. 194), an assessment that can be defended if one takes the immediate functioning of electronic logic gates to represent the essence of computing. But this view is clearly limited if one considers the many heuristics or techniques that implement, on top of the computational substrate, probabilistic, nonmonotonic, or fuzzy operations that can express and, indeed, calculate ideas such as partial truth, multivalued conclusions, tentative reasoning, or probabilistic class membership. This does not take away from Golumbia's broader argument concerning the various ways computer zealots have come to play important and ideologically tinted cultural roles. It should, however, remind us that a simple inference from the workings of logical gates and digital encoding to the vast domain of computing is not sustainable if one engages technicity as constructive enterprise.

The question whether there is a singular, uniform 'logic' inherent to computing that undergirds and unifies the sprawling mass of software has often been raised. Krämer (2006), for example, argues that for Kittler, 'the digital' constitutes a unifying code and that 'digitalization becomes the modern form of a universal language' (p. 108). I would argue, however, that this perspective mistakes an alphabet for a language; alphabets can encode different languages, and bits can stand for a an even larger variety of things. In his pioneering *La machine univers*, Pierre Lévy (1987) indeed argues that '[f]ar from evolving toward the definition of a universal language, as some had believed in the 1960s, informatics has multiplied its software dialects' (p. 33).

The dynamic domain of programming languages is only one of the areas where balkanization reigns. Accumulation, sedimentation, variation, and contestation are present almost anywhere in computing. One of the central arguments developed in this book holds that practices such as quantification, mathematization, digitization, or computerization not only imply forms of standardization, homogenization, and 'commensuration' (Espeland and Stevens, 1998) but also produce their own vectors of differentiation. As Simondon (2017) says, '[technical objects] are not deducted from a single principle' (p. 50) and this concerns computing specifically since it has become so pervasive that it connects to almost all human desires and struggles, integrating forms and techniques from a large number of domains, including art and political theory. As a particular way of producing operation, of shaping practices, and of drawing things together, computing has obviously provoked fundamental shifts in the fields it touches, but these shifts are much more complicated than a singular logic taking over.

It certainly makes sense to see capture and constitution of human practice in software as forms of reification that integrate technology ever more deeply into human practice. As Latour (1991) argues, 'technology is society made durable'. But, if we consider, with Simondon (2017), that technology is constructive and inductive, built up from an ever-growing archive of technicity that encounters a large diversity of uses, we have to consider – and demand – that there is 'technological pluralism' (p. 226, translation amended). This extends beyond technicity into technical practice. Studies like Turkle and Papert's (1990) classic observation of programmers in action points to forms of 'epistemological pluralism' that imply 'distinctive and varied styles of use' (p. 157) and significant variation in outlook, method, and practice. Similarly, Hjørland (2010) distinguishes between four sets of 'epistemological assumptions' (p. 74) in information science, leading to the competition between rationalist, empirical, hermeneutical, and critical theories of indexing and, by extension, of knowledge. I will come back to these distinctions in the second part of the book but suffice to say that computing can hardly be reduced to computationalism.

Does this mean that I consider every technical object to be a monad or every technical trajectory to form its own isolated path and set of rules? Most certainly not. First, I fully accept that the very fact of computation on the lowest mechanical level represents an a priori for software, even if I consider it to be broad enough to accommodate a large set of schemas and 'assumptions' in its fold. If we can acknowledge that language structures both what we can see and what we can say, yet allows for a considerable range of possible expression, we can do so for software as well. Second, it would be hard to argue that there are no sphere of commonality, dominant trends, or other instances of transversal consolidation. The various entanglements with contemporary capitalism, for instance, mean that software has come to serve rather streamlined modes of value production. But variation and standardization are not mutually exclusive, and they can coexist and intermingle in various ways (cf. Star and Ruhleder, 1996, p. 112). Indeed, Simondon's claim that the same technical elements are assembled into very different individuals and often travel from one trajectory to another opens interesting avenues for pondering how standardization, normalization, and other forms of commonality emerge over time. An analysis of algorithmic techniques must therefore proceed historically.

Historicizing Software

Historical work has, to a degree, come out of the computing disciplines themselves. But these accounts mostly list inventions on the path to the current state of the art and rarely attempt to address the contingent and embedded character of technical trajectories. Stonebraker and Hellerstein's introductory chapter in the fourth edition of *Readings in Database Systems* (2005), for example, provides a highly valuable historical account of the history of database systems, but refrains from any kind of cultural interpretation or positioning. The title of Astrachan's (2003) short paper 'Bubble Sort: An Archaeological Algorithmic Analysis' raises eyebrows, but despite tracing the algorithm's origins through a series of publications, it essentially remains a technical evaluation, combined with a lamentation of bubble sort's terrible performance, inexplicable popularity, and unfortunate persistence in educational materials (Astrachan, 2003, p. 4). Texts such as these provide excellent material for humanists to draw on, but they cannot be considered 'historiographical' in a more academic sense of the term, since they have little interest in understanding the past in its specific composition and coherence.

In contrast, the growing number of more traditional histories of computing, some of which explicitly focus on information processing and management (e.g., Campbell-Kelly and Aspray, 1996; Abbate, 1999; Aspray and Hayes, 2011; Cortada, 2016), combine large numbers of elements into multilayered narratives including people, places, institutions, practices, machines, ideas, and money. These works provide excellent cultural and economic contextualization of technical inventions, but they also hold the technicity and intellectual content of technical objects at arm's length and rarely consider technologies' impact on society at large. Their goal is to show how the objects emerged, developed, and became part of everyday life, not to theorize their status or role as *media*.

The growing body of theoretically ambitious historiographies of computing, such as works by Edwards (1996), Akera (2007), Ensmenger (2010), Abbate (2012), or Halpern (2014), dive even deeper into cultural imaginaries and ideological entanglements but reserve equally little space for the examination of the actual substances constituting computing as technical domain. Brunton's (2013) discussion of the Bayesian approach to spam filtering – which I will pick up in Chapter 6 – is a noticeable exception from the tendency to keep concrete techniques out of narrations that frame computing primarily as a cultural project. While such accounts have addressed broader political and ideological aspects, a dimension largely absent from traditional histories, they give us little insight into technical ideas and materialities, ignoring how they enable and define the actual behavior and work performed by computers. A clear apprehension of how cybernetic principles continue to inform 'Silicon Valley thinking', to use Internet critic Evgeny Morozov's term (2013), can help us understand why systems are built as they are; a clear apprehension of the technicities involved, however, can push back against only seemingly inevitable associations between technology and ideology by making clear that technicity's inner logics do not neatly align with cultural normativity and allow for the expression of a variety of aspirations.

One area where scholars have been able to integrate these dimensions is the history of statistics. The foundational work by Hacking (1990), Desrosières (1998), Porter (1995), and others (Gigerenzer et al., 1989) has shown how a complex mathematical subject matter can be embedded in a critical cultural reading that remains highly receptive to the technical details involved. The attention given to the entanglements between statistics and power has been particularly inspirational to my own project. At the same time, the field has not ventured too deeply into the various relationships between statistics and computing although algorithmic information ordering is one of several areas where probability theory and statistical methods have dominated since the early 1960s. Decades before a 'revolution' in artificial intelligence embraced statistical techniques (Russell and Norvig, 2010, p. 25), information retrieval began to frame the computer as a 'thinking machine' performing cognitive tasks, even if the rhetoric remained much more subdued than what we find in more well-known fields. Rather than situating information ordering merely in a longer history of statistics, however, my goal is to 'start in the middle – from the entanglement of past and present' (Parikka, 2012, p. 5) and to show how it forms a 'trading zone' (Galison, 1996) where various trajectories commingle and culminate in concrete artifacts that perform and (re)define tasks like searching and classifying documents.

At least since Friedrich Kittler's work (1990), which itself draws heavily on Foucault's *Archaeology of Knowledge* (2002), media archeology has emerged as a field that narrates cultural history from the perspective of technical operations, to the point where 'the model of history itself appears as a function of cultural (symbolic and signal-based) operations' (Ernst, 2013, p. 3). But despite the German tradition's often remarked interest in mathematical formalism and machinic operation, there has been relatively little interest in the substance of computing beyond Turing's universal machine and Shannon's theory of communication (cf. Geoghegan, 2013, p. 68). Kittler's predilection for discretization techniques such as the Fourier transform (cf. Krämer, 2006) and his emphasis on hardware – 'there is no software' (Kittler 1997a) – indicate an almost obsessive adherence to a type of foundationalism that ignores the vast spaces of accumulation and variation marking not only software but also the sprawling differentiation of hardware form factors and interfaces. Parikka (2012) thus rightfully observes that 'the past fifty years of emergence of software and hardware cultures is something that is still waiting for more thorough work' (p. 37f.). This book indeed inquires into spaces where memories of analog times begin to fade, and digital operations are becoming the new real. If the Fourier transform and its most well-known application in the numerical representation of sound waves epitomizes a particular moment in media history, information ordering comes into its own when digitization has already occurred, and masses of digital material are channeled through mature digital infrastructures. This is a story of computerization and mathematization that sits downstream of the birth of computing. Because a lot has happened since.

My account of mathematization therefore eschews the philosophers and mathematicians dealing with universal languages and logic, leaving aside the well-known portrayals of computers as the outcome of historical trajectories leading from Aristotle to Leibniz and further to Gödel and Turing. In a sense, this book resonates with the question Alt asks in his inspiring take on object orientation in programming, namely 'How did computers and computation come to be viewed as media in the first place?' (Alt, 2011, p. 279). While I share his focus on software-making, the produced end-user 'mediality', in my case, is not the graphical user interface and its applications but the 'logistical' techniques for information ordering serving 'to organize and orient, to arrange people and property' (Peters, 2015, p. 37).

Information ordering has certainly not been absent from what can be understood as broadly media historiographical work. Works by Rayward (1975),

Beniger (1986), Headrick (2000), Krajewski (2011), or Hartmann (2012) indeed deal with methods and mechanics head on and constitute important references for my own approach. But the historical and archeological work that delves into subjects like information processing or knowledge organization almost invariably stops at the invention of the computer or bridges the space between the card catalogue and web search engines with a quick reference to Vannevar Bush's Memex. While graphical user interfaces and the web have received much attention, algorithmic information ordering remains understudied. Marcus Burkhardt's *Digitale Datenbanken* (2015), a study of the relational model for database management currently only available in German, remains a rare example of historical media scholarship investigating an information ordering technique invented after WWII. Considering the pivotal place the relational model takes in contemporary computing, one could dedicate an entire subfield to its study and interpretation. But names like Hans Peter Luhn, Gerard Salton, Karen Spärck Jones, M. E. Maron, or Edgar F. Codd, to cite some of the pioneers of algorithmic information ordering, are almost entirely absent from media historical work. Certainly, the work of specialized historians[26] such as Thomas Haigh (2006, 2009) and studies like Bruillard and Blondel's (2007) history of the spreadsheet have begun to fill these large holes in scholarship from the bottom up, one subdomain at a time, but these examples are far too rare given the cultural importance and large variety of techniques and technologies that have come to define the substance of contemporary computing. My attempt to make sense of information ordering will indeed refer to library techniques and the great universalist projects of humanists like Melvil Dewey and Paul Otlet, broadly canonized 'pioneers of the information age', but only insofar as they form the backdrop algorithmic information ordering develops *against*. In that sense, it qualifies as an 'alternative history' (Parikka, 2012, p. 7), even if the widespread presence of the techniques I discuss makes this a somewhat alarming observation. The particular focus on technicity my inquiry espouses requires a last set of theoretical remarks concerning its historical dimension before diving into the subject matter head on.

Accumulation and Archive

The idea that technicity requires specific attention should not be seen as a concession to the totalizing tendencies in certain strands of media

---

26   There are specialized sections in historiography that deal with more technical subject matters, such as the Academy of Accounting Historians, but these communities rarely figure in more general accounts.

archeology where digitization is seen as some kind of 'end of media history' (cf. Gitelman, 2006, p. 3). Technicity should also not be understood as a secret substructure that determines all cultural development. Instead, I want to highlight the 'unconventional' (Huhtamo and Parikka, 2011, p. 11) perspective of Siegfried Zielinski, who proposes the term 'variantology' for an analysis of media that 'favors "local" explorations, refusing to develop them into overarching explanations' (Huhtamo and Parikka, 2011, p. 12). Zielinski's work draws heavily on Foucault but further emphasizes heterogeneity and variation:

> The history of the media is not the product of a predictable and necessary advance from primitive to complex apparatus. [...] Media are spaces of action for constructed attempts to connect what is separated. [...] Instead of looking for obligatory trends, master media, or imperative vanishing points, one should be able to discover individual variations. Possibly, one will discover fractures or turning points in historical master plans that provide useful ideas for navigating the labyrinth of what is currently firmly established. (Zielinski, 2006, p. 7)

Zielinski's approach builds on a reading of Foucault that deemphasizes the formation of broad *épistémè* we find in *The Order of Things* (2005) and his attentiveness to small and local variations, improbable encounters, and dead ends resonates with Simondon's view of technology as transversal and contingent. Foucault himself constructs the methodology laid out in *The Archaeology of Knowledge* (2002) around the notion of 'discursive formation', a term that addresses conceptual regularities in knowledge practices in ways that are more variable and open than the earlier *épistémè*. Discursive formations are composed of 'statements' (*énoncés*), units of expression that assemble into a 'system of dispersion' (Foucault, 2002, p. 41). The notion of statement certainly has to be stretched to accommodate technological forms of expression, but it is hardly against the spirit of what Foucault tries to achieve if one admits things such as blueprints, models, or methods and even programming languages, lines of code, modules, and executable binaries into the fold. But I want to suggest that algorithmic techniques make for better candidates for genuine technical statements, since they are not tied to a particular material support. For Foucault (2002), statements are the 'specific forms of accumulation' (p. 138) that make up and characterize what he calls the 'positivity' of a discursive formation. This positivity constitutes the substance of a knowledge practice: the entities to appear, the rules of transformation, the conceptual forms, the mechanisms of validation, the modes of exclusion, and so forth. These elements are not defined on a singular plane of identity but constitute a transversal regularity that connects the objects under investigation, the concepts and methods, and the modes of expression making up a specific formation. Interested in both commonality and variation, Foucault's goal is not to define a unifying principle:

> The horizon of archaeology, therefore, is not *a* science, *a* rationality, *a* mentality, *a* culture; it is a tangle of interpositivities whose limits and points of intersection cannot be fixed in a single operation. Archaeology is a comparative analysis that is not intended to reduce the diversity of discourses, and to outline the unity that must totalize them, but is intended to divide up their diversity into different figures. Archaeological comparison does not have a unifying, but a multiplying, effect. (Foucault, 2002, p. 177, translation amended)

Foucault's perspective does allow for regularities to emerge, but the way these regularities are conceived is not akin to stricter notions like 'structure' or 'paradigm' in the sense of Kuhn (1962). Instead, the first underlying principle is that of rarity and I want to suggest that compared to the seemingly endless proliferation of technical objects that assemble well-known elements in myriad ways, the emergence of genuinely new technical schemas is essentially rare, even if the marketing chorus professes otherwise. Much like the statements in Foucault's (2002) *Archaeology*, algorithmic techniques are characterized by a 'law of rarity' (p. 134). The following passage applies with almost uncanny perfection:

> This rarity of statements, the incomplete, fragmented form of the enunciative field, the fact that few things, in all, can be said, explain that statements are not, like the air we breathe, an infinite transparency; but things that are transmitted and preserved, that have value, and which one tries to appropriate; that are repeated, reproduced, and transformed; to which pre-established networks are adapted, and to which a status is given in the institution; things that are duplicated not only by copy or translation, but by exegesis, commentary, and the internal proliferation of meaning. Because statements are rare, they are collected in unifying totalities, and the meanings to be found in them are multiplied. (Foucault, 2002, p. 135)

The quote evokes the enormous *care* algorithmic techniques receive in computer science and adjacent fields, for example, when Knuth describes, classifies, discusses, and interprets each algorithm in his massive collection in meticulous detail. These attempts to 'singularize' or demarcate techniques while multiplying their domains of application defines their richness and allows them to be repeated thousands of times in thousands of programs, adapted, transformed, and embedded in myriad ways. Fundamental technical elements are rare compared to the seemingly endless series of objects they inform.

The evolution of computing is characterized by both pivotal incursions, such as the microprocessor and the graphical user interface, and a steady stream of smaller inventions that, in the domain of software, represent new ways of making machines behave in certain ways. But more often than not, the making of a technical object does not involve anything that could be qualified as technical 'invention', that is, the creation of a new schema. Most programming is an adaptation of existing objective capacities to objectal circumstances, which certainly has the potential to produce its own forms of novelty but does not constitute a new technical positivity. Since most pieces of software draw together many elements, there is always technical imagination, creativity, and plasticity at work. And programmers regularly invent schemas that are new *to them*, since they did not know of or chose to ignore existing techniques. But the inception of something like the relational model for database management (Chapter 4) – not only a genuinely new schema but an almost complete replacement for its antecedents – does not happen very often. The more recent emergence of deep learning with neural networks is another example that shows how techniques enabling new machine behaviors can ripple through many different application domains in relatively short time when the necessary conditions fall into place.

In media archeological accounts, media are often thought to provide certain grids of possibility to society as a whole. As Wolfgang Ernst (2015) argues, 'the media-archeological index names the indispensable and invariable conditions of what can then become culturally effective as thinkable' (p. 196). In line with my focus on software-making, I more modestly propose to consider how computing, as discursive formation, defines an archive of statements that serves as an a priori for software developers, informing and orienting their technical practice. Connecting back to Simondon's constructive understanding of technology, this a priori should not be seen as a filter that only lets certain statements through but as the nonteleological condition of possibility for statements that would not be 'sayable' otherwise. In 1972, Dijkstra (1972) himself explicitly recognized the influence of the software archive and of programming languages in particular, arguing 'that the tools we are trying to use and the language or notation we are using to express or record our thoughts, are the major factors determining what we can think or express at all' (p. 11). While deeply caught up in questions of power, contemporary development infrastructures represent rich domains of knowledge and technicity to build on. Seen as an archive, both in the common sense as a collection of something and in Foucault's understanding as 'the law of what can be said' (Foucault, 2002, p. 145), there are certainly vectors pointing toward restriction and control, but there is also a widening of possible function and programmable behavior.

Even if Foucault would probably protest the analogy, we could argue that techniques, understood as statements, form a *langue* ('language') that manifests through the boundless sprawling of *parole* ('speaking'). In this sense I posit that a large, growing, but ultimately limited archive of technical schemas and techniques pervades the vast mass of software that exists in the world. Parikka's (2012) assertion that 'new technologies grow obsolete increasingly fast' (p. 3) therefore applies to a *parole* perspective that captures objectal variations but needs to be nuanced if we consider a *langue* dimension focusing on objective evolution: the latter evolves in a 'temporality of the technical' that forms 'its own genuine temporal figures' (Ernst, 2015, p. 190), which are often slower that the crest of concrete applications and artifacts. Despite the seemingly obvious velocity of technological change and renewal, many of the schemas and elements that make up the 'skeleton' of an archive of computing have proven to be remarkably persistent: Tony Hoare's Quicksort from 1959 is executed every time a PHP programmer calls the *sort()* function; E. F. Codd's relational model from 1970 still dominates most information handling practices; Dennis Ritchie's C, developed between 1969 and 1973, continues to set the standard for how the syntax of a programming language is supposed to look like and variants of the Unix operating system he developed with Ken Thompson and others power virtually every smartphone in use. In fact, although Richard Stallman would probably not approve, his GNU Emacs text editor, developed since 1976, runs on Android without too much trouble. The release of Apple's iPhone was a defining moment in the history of computing, but even a superficial look reveals how deeply caught up in historical trajectories this apparently revolutionary product necessarily is. iOS, Apple's operating system for mobile phones and tablets, was released in 2007, but the system itself is based on Mac OS X (2001), which, in turn, is built on a BSD kernel (1978), a Unix (~1973) derivative. It runs on an ARM processor core (1985) and still relies to a large extent on the Objective-C programming language, which was first introduced in 1983 and makes heavy use of concepts imported from C (1971) and Smalltalk (1969). This list could be continued almost indefinitely, and any piece of software could be submitted to such a form of genealogical analysis.

But this should not mean that there is 'nothing new under the sun', that all innovation has already happened, and that everything new is, in fact, old. This attitude would be similarly ahistorical as a perspective emphasizing novelty in every small variation of a known schema. While the historical 'overhead' is never too far away, there is certainly an ongoing movement of innovation that builds on existing technicity and leads, at times, to real instances of discontinuity. Even if the objective dimension of technology determines the fundamental range of possible function and behavior, the objectal adventure adds layers of variation that are highly significant in terms of actual outcomes. Indeed, the *parole* of software should not be seen as merely derivative or inconsequential since techniques can only ever become part of actual circumstances by becoming *parole*, by being spoken in the form of a textbook, module, or concrete program. And the real-world effects these programs can have cannot be deductively derived from the *langue* they instantiate. On the contrary, the cumulative and modular character of software does not reduce its plasticity or 'generativity' (Zittrain, 2008), but constantly adds new possibilities to a space that allows for a wide range of expression.

We should also not downplay the significance of what Simondon calls concretization and adaptation. The application of known techniques to new domains can yield surprising results. The current revolution in machine learning, for example, can be seen as the result of both invention and optimization: without the demonstration by Raina, Madhavan, and Ng (2009) that some of the most powerful machine learning techniques can be distributed onto the massively parallel processors in consumer graphics cards, it would have been infeasible to apply them to any large-scale applications. The Unix of 1973 is not the Unix of 2019. Swift, the programming language Apple introduced in 2014 as an eventual replacement for Objective-C, does certainly not mark a revolution, having 'benefited from the experiences hard-won by many other languages in the field, drawing ideas from Objective-C, Rust, Haskell, Ruby, Python, C#, CLU, and far too many others to list',[27] but the way it simplifies development for Apple devices may well have real consequences. Easier access for programmers used to similar object-oriented languages, for example, changes the resource equation and makes Apple's platforms – including the restrictive App Store model – more attractive to developers. While I would argue that Swift should be seen as another chapter in a story of concretization rather than brimming with genuine invention, it certainly is one *more* programming language, one further addition to the archive of computing.

27   http://nondot.org/sabre/, accessed 12 December 2019.

The proliferation and functional diversification of programming languages is indeed an area where the larger movement of accumulation becomes particularly visible: Bill Kinnersley's Language List[28] counts no less than 2500 languages that appeared in the decades since *Plankalkül* – generally considered the first high-level programming language – was conceived by Konrad Zuse in the early 1940s. While most of these languages have never found a significant audience, they contribute to the continuous proliferation of technical forms that constitute the field and substance of computing.

The emphasis on the presence of long-standing trajectories must therefore be balanced with a perspective that recognizes how, at least on a certain temporal scale, even the most stable 'arrangements are at best temporary consolidations until emergent practices and technologies displace and rearrange the constituent parts' (Geoghegan, 2013, p. 6). This appreciation of technical evolution as complex and contingent raises the question of how to assess 'true' novelty in the cacophony of techniques and objects. Is blockchain technology a new schema or simply a specific orchestration of well-known cryptographic techniques? There is no way around nuanced and conceptually informed investigation when trying to answer such questions.

Path, Technical System, *Épistémè*

Computing needs to be analyzed through concepts that acknowledge its contingency and diversity, not as manifestation of instrumental rationality or cybernetic teleology, set in motion with Babbage's analytical machine and bound to develop more or less the way it did. Technical evolution is never the unfolding of singular principles. And the processes of accumulation and sedimentation in software clearly go beyond Darwinian competition to include strange couplings, cross-fertilization, conceptual transfer, mono- or bidirectional inspiration, as well as rejection, stonewalling, sabotage, conflict, and mutual indifference. While many techniques can be generalized or transferred from one setting to another, some work well in one domain and badly in others; and some may be so specific that they only make sense in a single field of application. And even if the end goal is the formulation of a program that runs on a digital computer, software constantly invokes forms of reasoning that are inspired and justified by ideas that have little to do with logic or other fields of mathematics. The current state of computing can thus be seen as the situated outcome of technical evolution, understood as the nonteleological and cumulative unfolding of myriad processes of invention,

---

28   http://www.info.univ-angers.fr/~gh/hilapr/langlist/langlist.htm, accessed 12 December 2019.

concretization, and adaptation. Thinking technology in such inductive terms, however, does not mean that there is no room for broader trends, tendencies, and shifts; variation and consolidation and not mutually exclusive.

One conceptual vehicle for conceptualizing the emergence of larger zones of stability is the notion of 'path dependence', which highlights how existing technologies can exert a gravitational pull that makes it hard to switch from one trajectory to another. This comes, for example, in the form of user resistance: having already invested considerable time into learning the QWERTY keyboard layout, people are reluctant to switch to the apparently more efficient Dworak keyboard (David, 1985). But there is also a broad infrastructure of software and hardware in place that is organized around the incumbent design and moving from one path to another would thus mean changing much more than just user habits. Computing is full of similar examples and the remarkable persistence of programming languages like C and operating systems like Unix show how consolidation and standardization can occur in the absence of a singular, overarching logic or telos.

Bertrand Gille (1986) introduced the notion of 'technical system' (*système technique*) to think consolidation in similar, yet even broader terms. A technical system delineates a historical state of technological development and represents 'a coherent ensemble of compatible structures' (p. viii) defined by interoperability, common standards, mutual dependence, and synergies between technical elements, as well as a certain measure of coherence with forms of social organization. The technical system of the Renaissance, for example, is characterized by the systematic synergies between hydraulic power, the newly invented crankshaft, innovations in mining, and new metallurgic techniques, which enable early forms of mass production and lead to a social system that marks the end of feudal organization and the emergence of capitalism. Although the notion of technical system is much more general and less stringent than Kuhn's (1962) 'paradigm', it has similar infrastructural effects: it stabilizes, orients research and development, and potentially blocks the exploration of alternative routes. Not by rendering them impossible, but by making it that much easier to follow or extend existing paths. The concept extends the notion of path dependence to the level of larger ensembles and, ultimately, to civilizational development but also allows for the possibility of real heterogeneity or 'technological pluralism' since variation remains possible and systemic closure is never absolute.

Path dependence and the emergence of technical systems of compatibility are ways to think the emergence of larger zones of commonality from the bottom up and help us imagine how something like an *épistémè* could develop inductively. The commitment to variation and contingency notwithstanding, one could speculate about a 'fini-unlimited' *épistémè*, where 'a finite number of components yields a practically unlimited diversity of combinations' (Deleuze, 1988, p. 131), along these lines. This would frame computerization more generally as the drive toward a technical system built around computing and make room for economic explanations in the emergence of commonalities, synergies, and zones of domination. Algorithmic information ordering, more specifically, then appears as the preferred technique for 'distinction-making' in this environment, as a means to generate both knowledge and economic surplus.

Relying on concepts like discursive formation, technical system, and even *épistémè* safeguards against the temptation to conceive technical evolution as the simple embodiment or deployment of instrumental rationality. Foucault writes:

> I think that the word 'rationalization' is dangerous. What we have to do is to analyze specific rationalities rather than forever invoke the progress of rationalization in general. (Foucault, 1982, p. 779f.)

As we will see in the next chapter, the two sides in what Bowles (1999) termed the 'information wars' – librarians and information scientists – represent such 'specific rationalities'. They develop from substantially different 'problematizations' and define their own specific ideas, techniques, and 'truth criteria' (Foucault, 1990, p. 10f.). Their respective positivities yield different operational and epistemological practices. Algorithmic information ordering indeed develops from an opposition to library traditions and over the course of several decades, the 'disruptive' new techniques have become available to software-makers everywhere. The second part of this book dives deep into a set of technical trajectories that begin by putting text documents into sequence and end up ordering almost anything that can be brought into the fold of computing.

Bibliography

Abbate, J. (1999). *Inventing the Internet*. Cambridge, MA: MIT Press.

Abbate, J. (2012). *Recoding Gender: Women's Changing Participation in Computing*. Cambridge, MA: MIT Press.

Abelson, H., Sussman, G. J., and Sussman, J. (1996). *Structure and Interpretation of Computer Programs* (2nd ed.). Cambridge, MA: MIT Press.

Agre, P. E. (1994). Surveillance and Capture: Two Models of Privacy. *The Information Society 10*(2), 101-127.

Agre, P. E. (1997a). *Computation and Human Experience*. Cambridge: Cambridge University Press.

Akera, A. (2007). *Calculating a Natural World*. Cambridge, MA: MIT Press.

Alt, C. (2011). Objects of Our Affection: How Object Orientation Made Computers a Medium. In J. Parikka and E. Huhtamo (eds.), *Media Archaeology: Approaches, Applications, and Implications* (pp. 278-301). Berkeley: University of California Press.

Aspray, W., and Hayes, B. M. (eds.). (2011). *Everyday Information: The Evolution of Information Seeking in America*. Cambridge, MA: MIT Press.

Astrachan, O. (2003). Bubble Sort: An Archaeological Algorithmic Analysis. In S. Grissom (ed.), *SIGCSE '03 Proceedings of the 34th SIGCSE Technical Symposium on Computer Science Education* (pp. 1-5). New York: ACM.

Beniger, J. (1986). *The Control Revolution: Technological and Economic Origins of the Information Society*. Cambridge, MA: Harvard University Press.

Bjerknes, G., Ehn, P., and Kyng, M. (eds.). (1987). *Computers and Democracy: A Scandinavian Challenge*, Aldershot: Avebury.

Bowles, M. D. (1999). The Information Wars: Two Cultures and the Conflict in Information Retrieval, 1945-1999. In M. E. Bowden, T. Bellardo Hahn, and R. V. Williams (eds.), *Proceedings of the 1998 Conference on the History and Heritage of Science Information Systems* (pp. 156-166). Medford: Information Today.

Brooks, F. P., Jr. (1975). *The Mythical Man-Month*. Reading: Addison-Wesley.

Brooks, F. P., Jr. (1996). The Computer Scientist as Toolsmith II. *Communications of the ACM 39*, (3): 61-68.

Bruillard, E., and Blondel, F.-M. (2007). Histoire de la construction de l'objet tableur. Retrieved from https://hal.archives-ouvertes.fr/hal-00180912.

Brunton, F. (2013). *Spam: A Shadow History of the Internet*. Cambridge, MA: MIT Press.

Burkhardt, M. (2015). *Digitale Datenbanken. Eine Medientheorie im Zeitalter von Big Data*. Bielefeld: transcript Verlag.

Buxton, J. N. (1978). Software Engineering. In D. Gries (ed.), *Programming Methodology: A Collection of Articles by Members of IFIP WG2.3* (pp. 23-28). New York: Springer.

Campbell-Kelly, M., and Aspray, W. (1996). *Computer: History of an Information Machine*. New York: Basic Books.

Chabot, P. (2013). *The Philosophy of Simondon: Between Technology and Individuation* (A. Krefetz, trans.). London: Bloomsbury.

Chen, P. P. (1976). The Entity-Relationship Model – Toward a Unified View of Data. *ACM Transactions on Database Systems 1*(1), 9-36.

Colburn, T. R. (2000). *Philosophy and Computer Science*. Armonk: M. E. Sharpe.

Cortada, J. W. (2016). *All the Facts: A History of Information in the United States since 1870*. Oxford: Oxford University Press.

Coy, W. (2001). Was ist Informatik? In J. Desel (ed.), *Das ist Informatik* (pp. 1-22). Berlin: Springer.

Coy, W. (2007). Kulturen – Nicht Betreten? Anmerkungen zur 'Kulturtechnik Informatik'. *Informatik-Spektrum 31*(1), 30-34.

David, P. A. (1985). Clio and the Economics of QWERTY. *American Economic Review 75*(2), 332-337.

Deleuze, G. (1988). *Foucault* (S. Hand, trans.). Minneapolis: University of Minnesota Press.

Denning, P. J. (2007). Computing Is a Natural Science. *Communications of the ACM 50*(7), 13-18.

Desrosières, A. (1998). *The Politics of Large Numbers: A History of Statistical Reasoning* (C. Naish, trans.). Cambridge, MA: Harvard University Press.

Dijkstra, E. W. (1972). The Humble Programmer. *Communications of the ACM 15*(10), 859-866.

Dijkstra, E. W. (1974). Programming as a Discipline of Mathematical Nature. *American Mathematical Monthly 81*(6), 608-612.

Dourish, P. (2016). Algorithms and Their Others: Algorithmic Culture in Context. *Big Data & Society 3*(2), 1-11.

Dreyfus, H. (1972). *What Computers Can't Do*. New York: Harper & Row.

Dubin, D. (2004). The Most Influential Paper Gerard Salton Never Wrote. *Library Trends 52*(4), 748-764.

Dyck, A., Penners, R., and Lichter, H. (2015). Towards Definitions for Release Engineering and DevOps. In *Proceedings of the 2015 IEEE/ACM 3rd International Workshop on Release Engineering* (pp. 3-3). Los Alamitos: IEEE Conference Publishing Service.

Edwards, P. N. (1996). *The Closed World: Computers and the Politics of Discourse in Cold War America*. Cambridge, MA: MIT Press.

Ensmenger, N. L. (2010). *The Computer Boys Take Over: Computers, Programmers, and the Politics of Technical Expertise*. Cambridge, MA: MIT Press.

Ernst, W. (2013). From Media History to Zeitkritik. *Theory, Culture & Society 30*(6), 132-146.

Ernst, W. (2015). Technophysikalische and Symbolische Medienoperationen als Herausforderung der Historischen Zeit. In S. Haas and C. Wischermann (eds.), *Die Wirklichkeit der Geschichte* (pp. 185-204). Stuttgart: Franz Steiner Verlag.

Espeland, W. N., and Stevens, M. L. (1998). Commensuration as a Social Process. *Annual Review of Sociology 24*, 313-343.

Foucault, M. (1982). The Subject and Power. *Critical Inquiry 8*(4), 777-795.

Foucault, M. (1990). *The Use of Pleasure: Volume 2 of the History of Sexuality* (R. Hurley, trans.). New York: Vintage Books.

Foucault, M. (2002). *Archaeology of Knowledge* (A. M. Sheridan, trans.). London: Routledge.

Foucault, M. (2005). *The Order of Things: An Archaeology of the Human Sciences.* London: Routledge.

Foucault, M. (2008). *The Birth of Biopolitics: Lectures at the Collège de France, 1978-79* (G. Burchell, trans.). Basingstoke: Palgrave Macmillan.

Fuller, M. (ed.). (2008). *Software Studies: A Lexicon.* Cambridge, MA: MIT Press.

Galison, P. (1996). Computer Simulations and the Trading Zone. In P. Galison and D. J. Stump (eds.), *The Disunity of Science: Boundaries, Contexts, and Power* (pp. 118-157). Stanford: Stanford University Press.

Gawer, A. (2010). Platforms, Markets and Innovation: An Introduction. In A. Gawer (ed.). *Platforms, Markets and Innovation* (pp. 1-16). Cheltenham: Edward Elgar.

Geoghegan, B. D. (2013). After Kittler: On the Cultural Techniques of Recent German Media Theory. *Theory, Culture & Society 30*(6), 66-82.

Gigerenzer, G., Swijtnik, Z., Porter, T., Daston, L., Beatty, J., and Krüger, L. (1989). *The Empire of Chance: How Probability Changed Science and Everyday Life.* Cambridge: Cambridge University Press.

Gille, B. (ed.). (1986). *The History of Techniques, Volume 1: Techniques and Civilizations* (P. Southgate and T. Williamson, trans.). Montreux: Gordon and Breach.

Gitelman, L. (2006). *Always Already New: Media, History, and the Data of Culture.* Cambridge, MIT Press.

Golumbia, D. (2009). *The Cultural Logic of Computation.* Cambridge, MA: Harvard University Press.

Goody, J. (1977). *The Domestication of the Savage Mind.* Cambridge: Cambridge University Press.

Graham, P. (2002). A Plan for Spam, August. Retrieved from http://www.paulgraham.com/spam.html.

Gürses, S., and Van Hoboken, J. (2018). Privacy after the Agile Turn. In E. Selinger, J. Polonetsky, and O. Tene (eds.), *The Cambridge Handbook of Consumer Privacy* (pp. 579-601). Cambridge: Cambridge University Press.

Hacking, I. (1990). *The Taming of Chance.* Cambridge: Cambridge University Press.

Haigh, T. (2006). 'A Veritable Bucket of Facts': Origins of the Data Base Management System. *ACM SIGMOD Record 35*(2), 33-49.

Haigh, T. (2009). How Data Got Its Base: Information Storage Software in the 1950s and 1960s. *IEEE Annals of the History of Computing 31*(4), 6-25.

Halpern, O. (2014). *Beautiful Data.* Durham: Duke University Press.

Hartmann, F. (2012). Die Logik der Datenbank. In F. Hartmann (ed.), *Vom Buch zur Datenbank. Paul Otlets Utopie der Wissensvisualisierung* (pp. 11-61). Berlin: Avinus.

Headrick, D. R. (2000). *When Information Came of Age.* New York: Oxford University Press.

Heidegger, M. (1977). *The Question Concerning Technology, and Other Essays* (W. Lovitt, trans.). New York: Garland.

Heidegger, M. (1998). Traditional Language and Technological Language. *Journal of Philosophical Research 23*, 129-145.

Helmond, A. (2015). The Platformization of the Web: Making Web Data Platform Ready. *Social Media + Society 1*(2), 1-11.

Hertzfeld, A. (1982) Creative Think. Retrieved from https://www.folklore.org/StoryView.py?project=Macintosh&story=Creative_Think.txt.

Hjørland, B. (2010). The Importance of Theories of Knowledge: Indexing and Information Retrieval as an Example. *Journal of the American Society for Information Science and Technology 62*(1), 72-77.

Huhtamo, E., and Parikka, J. (2011). Introduction: An Archaeology of Media Archaeology. In J. Parikka and E. Huhtamo (eds.), *Media Archaeology: Approaches, Applications, and Implications* (pp. 1-24). Berkeley: University of California Press.

IEEE. (1999) *IEEE Standard Glossary of Software Engineering Terminology* (Standard No. 610.12-1990). Retrieved from https://standards.ieee.org/standard/610_12-1990.html.

Kittler, F. A. (1990). *Discourse Networks, 1800/1900* (M. Metteer, trans.). Stanford: Stanford University Press.

Kittler, F. A. (1997a). There Is No Software. In J. Johnston (ed.), *Literature, Media, Information Systems: Essays* (pp. 147-155). Amsterdam: Overseas Publishers Association.

Kittler, F. A. (1997b). The World of the Symbolic – A World of the Machine. In J. Johnston (ed.), *Literature, Media, Information Systems: Essays* (pp. 130-146). Amsterdam: Overseas Publishers Association.

Kittler, F. A. (1999). *Gramophone, Film, Typewriter* (G. Winthrop-Young and M. Wutz, trans.). Stanford: Stanford University Press.

Knuth, D. (1997). *The Art of Computer Programming, Volume 1: Fundamental Algorithms* (3rd ed.). Reading: Addison-Wesley.

Knuth, D. (1998). *The Art of Computer Programming, Volume 3: Sorting and Searching* (2nd ed.). Reading: Addison-Wesley.

Krajewski, M. (2011). *Paper Machines: About Cards & Catalogs, 1548-1929* (P. Krapp, trans.) Cambridge, MA: MIT Press.

Krämer, S. (1988). *Symbolische Maschinen. Die Idee der Formalisierung im Geschichtlichen Abriß*. Darmstadt: Wissenschaftliche Buchgesellschaft.

Krämer, S. (2006). The Cultural Techniques of Time Axis Manipulation: On Friedrich Kittler's Conception of Media. *Theory, Culture & Society 23*(7-8), 93-109.

Krämer, S., and Bredekamp H. (2013). Culture, Technology, Cultural Techniques – Moving beyond Text. *Theory, Culture & Society 30*(6), 20-29.

Kuhn, T. (1962). *The Structure of Scientific Revolutions*. Chicago: University of Chicago Press.

Lampland, M., and Star, S. L. (eds.). (2009). *Standards and Their Stories*. Ithaca: Cornell University Press.

Laplante, P. A. (2007). *What Every Engineer Should Know about Software Engineering*. Boca Raton: CRC Press.

Latour, B. (1986). Visualization and Cognition: Thinking with Eyes and Hands. *Knowledge and Society: Studies in the Sociology of Culture Past and Present 6*, 1-40.

Latour, B. (1991). Technology Is Society Made Durable. In J. Law (ed.), *A Sociology of Monsters: Essays on Power, Technology and Domination* (pp. 103-131). London: Routledge.

Lave, J., and Wenger, E. (1991). *Situated Learning*. Cambridge: Cambridge University Press.

Layton, E. T., Jr. (1974). Technology as Knowledge. *Technology and Culture 15*(1), 31-41.

Lévy, P. (1987) *La Machine univers. Création, cognition et culture informatique*. Paris: La Découverte.

Macho, T. (2003). Zeit und Zahl: Kalender- und Zeitrechnung als Kulturtechniken. In S. Krämer and H. Bredekamp (eds.), *Schrift, Zahl: Wider die Diskursivierung der Kultur* (pp. 179-192). München: Wilhelm Fink Verlag.

Mackenzie, A. (2017a). *Machine Learners: Archaeology of a Data Practice*. Cambridge, MA: MIT Press.

Mackenzie, A. (2017b). 48 Million Configurations and Counting: Platform Numbers and Their Capitalization. *Journal of Cultural Economy 11*(1), 36-53.

Mancuso, S. (2015). *The Software Craftsman: Professionalism, Pragmatism, Pride*. Upper Saddle River: Prentice Hall.

Manovich, L. (2001). *The Language of New Media*. Cambridge, MA: MIT Press.

Manovich, L. (2013c). *Software Takes Command*. New York: Bloomsbury.

Marino, M. C. (2006). Critical Code Studies. *Electronic Book Review*, 4 December. Retrieved from http://www.electronicbookreview.com.

Maron, M. E. (1963). A Logician's View of Language-Data Processing. In P. L. Garvin (ed.), *Natural Language and the Computer* (pp. 128-151). New York: McGraw-Hill.

McLuhan, M. (1962). *The Gutenberg Galaxy*. Toronto: University of Toronto Press.

McLure Wasko, M., and Faraj, S. (2000). 'It Is What One Does': Why People Participate and Help Others in Electronic Communities of Practice. *Journal of Strategic Information Systems 9*(2-3), 155-173.

Mokyr, J. (2005). *The Gifts of Athena: Historical Origins of the Knowledge Economy*. Princeton: Princeton University Press.

Moor, J. H. (1978). Three Myths of Computer Science. *British Journal for the Philosophy of Science 29*(3), 213-222.

Morozov, E. (2013). *To Save Everything, Click Here*. New York: Public Affairs.

Newell, A., and Simon, H. A. (1976). Computer Science as Empirical Inquiry: Symbols and Search. *Communications of the ACM 19*(3), 113-126.

Nontrivial. (n.d.). ComputerLanguage.com. Retrieved from https://www.compu-terlanguage.com/results.php?definition=nontrivial.

OECD. (2013). *Supporting Investment in Knowledge Capital, Growth and In-novation*. OECD Publishing. Retrieved from http://www.oecd.org/sti/inno/newsourcesofgrowthknowledge-basedcapital.htm.

Parikka, J. (2012). *What Is Media Archaeology?* Cambridge: Polity Press.

Parikka, J. (2013). Afterword: Cultural Techniques and Media Studies. *Theory, Culture & Society 30*(6), 147-159.

Peters, J. D. (2015). *The Marvelous Clouds: Toward a Philosophy of Elemental Media*. Chicago: University of Chicago Press.

Porter, T. (1995). *Trust in Numbers: The Pursuit of Objectivity in Science and Public Life*. Princeton: Princeton University Press.

Raina, R., Madhavan, A., and Ng, A. Y. (2009). Large-Scale Deep Unsupervised Learning Using Graphics Processors. In A. Danyluk, L. Bottou, and M. Litt-man (eds.), *ICML '09 Proceedings of the 26th Annual International Conference on Machine Learning* (pp. 873-880). New York: ACM.

Ramsay, S. (2010). The Hermeneutics of Screwing Around; or What You Do with a Million Books. In K. Kee (ed.), *Pastplay: Teaching and Learning History with Technology* (pp. 111-120). Ann Arbor: University of Michigan Press.

Raymond, E. (1999). The Cathedral and the Bazaar. *Knowledge, Technology & Policy 12*(3), 23-49.

Rayward, W. B. (1975). *The Universe of Information: The Work of Paul Otlet for Docu-mentation and International Organization*. Moscow: VINITI for the International Federation for Documentation.

Resnick, P., Iacovou, N., Suchak, M., Bergstrom, P., and Riedl, J. (1994). GroupLens: An Open Architecture for Collaborative Filtering of Netnews. In J. B. Smith, F. D. Smith, and T. W. Malone (eds.), *CSCW '94 Proceedings of the 1994 International ACM Conference on Computer Supported Cooperative Work* (pp. 175-186). New York: ACM.

Rieder, B. (2006). *Métatechnologies et délégation: pour un design orienté-société dans l'ère du Web 2.0*. PhD dissertation, Université Paris 8. Retrieved from https://tel.archives-ouvertes.fr/tel-00179980/.

Rieder, B. (2013) Studying Facebook via Data Extraction: The Netvizz Application. In H. Davis, H. Halpin, and A. Pentland (eds.), *WebSci '13 Proceedings of the 5th Annual ACM Web Science Conference* (pp. 346-355). New York: ACM.

Russell, S., and Norvig, P. (2010). *Artificial Intelligence* (3rd ed.). Upper Saddle River: Pearson Education.

Sedgewick, R. (1983). *Algorithms*. Reading: Addison-Wesley.

Siegert, B. (2007). Cacography or Communication? Cultural Techniques in German Media Studies. *Grey Room 29*, 26-47.

Siegert, B. (2013). Cultural Techniques; or The End of the Intellectual Postwar Era in German Media Theory. *Theory, Culture & Society 30*(6), 48-65.

Simon, H. A. (1996). *The Sciences of the Artificial* (3rd ed.). Cambridge, MA: MIT Press.

Simondon, G. (2017). *On the Mode of Existence of Technical Objects* (C. Malaspina and J. Rogove, trans.). Minneapolis: Univocal Publishing.

Star, S. L., and Griesemer, J. R. (1989). Institutional Ecology, 'Translations' and Boundary Objects: Amateurs and Professionals in Berkeley's Museum of Vertebrate Zoology, 1907-39. *Social Studies of Science 19*(3), 387-420.

Star, S. L., and Ruhleder, K. (1996). Steps toward an Ecology of Infrastructure: Design and Access for Large Information Spaces. *Information Systems Research 7*(1), 111-134.

Stonebraker, M., and Hellerstein, J. M. (eds.). (2005). *Readings in Database Systems* (4th ed.). Cambridge, MA: MIT Press.

Storey, M.-A., Singer, L., Cleary, B., Figueira Filho, F., and Zagalsky, A. (2014). The (R) Evolution of Social Media in Software Engineering. In J. Herbsleb (ed.), *FOSE 2014 Proceedings of the on Future of Software Engineering* (pp. 100-116). New York: ACM.

Swanson, D. R. (1988). Historical Note: Information Retrieval and the Future of an Illusion. *Journal of the American Society for Information Science 39*(2), 92-98.

Tedre, M. (2011). Computing as a Science: A Survey of Competing Viewpoints. *Minds and Machines 21*(3), 361-387.

Turkle, S. and Papert, S. (1990). Epistemological Pluralism: Styles and Voices within the Computer Culture. *Signs 16*(1), 128-157.

Vincenti, W. G. (1990). *What Engineers Know and How They Know It*. Baltimore: Johns Hopkins University Press.

Vismann, C. (2013). Cultural Techniques and Sovereignty. *Theory, Culture & Society 30*(6), 83-93.

Wing, J. M. (2006). Computational Thinking. *Communications of the ACM 49*(3), 33-35.

Winthrop-Young, G. (2013). Cultural Techniques: Preliminary Remarks. *Theory, Culture & Society 30*(6), 3-19.

Winthrop-Young, G. (2014). The *Kultur* of Cultural Techniques: Conceptual Inertia and the Parasitic Materialities of Ontologization. *Cultural Politics 10*(3), 376-388.

Wirth, N. (1971). The Programming Language Pascal. *Acta Informatica 1*(1), 35-63.

Wirth, N. (1976). *Algorithms + Data Structures = Programs*. Englewood Cliffs: Prentice-Hall.

Zielinski, S. (2006). *Deep Time of the Media*. Cambridge, MA: MIT Press.

Zimmer, M. (2010). Web Search Studies: Multidisciplinary Perspectives on Web Search Engines. In J. Hunsinger, L. Klastrup, and M. Allen (eds.), *International Handbook of Internet Research* (pp. 507-521). Dordrecht: Springer.

Zittrain, J. (2008). *The Future of the Internet and How to Stop It*. New Haven: Yale University Press.

Part II

4. From Universal Classification to a Postcoordinated Universe

Abstract

This chapter starts off from standard takes on knowledge organization and classification in libraries and encyclopedias, but then zeros in on the field of information retrieval, which develops in fundamental opposition to even the most visionary of library techniques. Coordinate indexing, the first technique in this lineage, is explicitly designed to eliminate the influence of librarians and other knowledge mediators by shifting expressive power from the classification system to the query and, by extension, to the information seeker. Order is no longer understood as a stable map to the universe of knowledge but increasingly as the outcome of a dynamic and purpose-driven process of ordering. The chapter closes by discussing coordinate indexing as a precursor of the relational model for database management.

Keywords: bibliographic organization, coordinate indexing, information wars, relational model for database management

This chapter delves into the question of information order and ordering through an investigation that leads from the library, long the principal institution dedicated to the organization of knowledge, to the first widely used technique in information retrieval, coordinate indexing, and its much more elaborate cousin, the relational model for database management. The goal is not to establish a narrative of progress that inevitably leads to our contemporary situation, but to highlight certain fault lines emerging around the closely related issues of knowledge organization and access, and how they relate to specific techniques. A significant part of contemporary information ordering indeed develops from attempts to fundamentally restructure how text documents are to be cataloged and retrieved. While the library tradition sees organization as a prerequisite for access, information

Rieder, B., *Engines of Order: A Mechanology of Algorithmic Techniques*. Amsterdam: Amsterdam University Press, 2020

DOI 10.5117/9789462986190_CH04

retrieval rejects this idea and turns the sequence around: organization is to follow the specific needs expressed when accessing information. The order of knowledge is no longer a universal map, but a pathway defined by a momentary purpose.

The concepts and techniques involved in this story rely on different forms of physical machinery, but my account will not be another story of punched card machines, or at least not primarily. What I am interested in are the specific schemas that combine disparate material and symbolic elements into coherent systems. Specific ways of doing are clearly more compatible with specific mechanical trajectories and may rely on the availability of certain operational capabilities. But coordinate indexing finds expression in at least three material manifestations and there are good reasons to consider it more abstractly as an algorithmic technique that delineates its own technical specificity across different implementations. The arrival of the computer marks a clear incision, but, as we will see, it becomes the 'stage' (cf. Laurel, 1993) for a variety of techniques rather than being tied to a single operational logic or arrangement.

Following Siegert (2007), I consider these techniques as 'media that process the observation, displacement, and differentiation of distinctions' (p. 31) since ordering, here, usually means arranging documents in relation to each other, physically or in a catalog, in classes or as a sequence. Knowledge organization is a practice of 'distinction-making' where different traditions draw not only on different techniques but pursue different objectives and incorporate different ideas about the world. While my focus, in this chapter and beyond, is squarely on the lineages that form and develop in conjunction with the computer, a broader historical perspective allows me to articulate more clearly how this is a much more complex transformation than the move from 'analog' to 'digital' suggests.

The question of how words and things are to be organized is by no means a new one and since the dawn of writing as a form of material inscription, practical answers entail a tight connection between conceptual and material elements. Scholars of literacy like Jack Goody have long argued that writing itself is instrumental to the 'process of dissection into abstract categories' (Goody and Watt, 1963, p. 331) that dominates Western culture to this day. The earliest surviving texts, written in the fourth millennium BCE in Mesopotamia, were, indeed, mostly administrative documents in list form (Casson, 2001, p. 2), efforts to record – and thereby control – things by externalizing them onto a material surface. The list, Goody (1977) argues, is not just a memory aid, but a device that 'enables [speech] to be inspected, manipulated and re-ordered in a variety of ways' (p. 76) and thereby allows for the question of *how* things should be arranged to become explicit. The list has no natural order, no authoritative narrative, but instead 'encourages the ordering of the items, by number, by initial sound, by category' (p. 81) or by other schemes, according to the specific purpose it would serve. But once the list is made, its material presence and cognitive substance, backed by the social authority of the writer, can produce effects that have far-reaching consequences for how the 'listed' domain is perceived and acted upon. The list facilitates both the process of ordering and the imposition of order onto the world (cf. Young, 2017).

In this chapter, I will not venture into the fundamental question of how human beings discern and distinguish the world they inhabit, how they make it cognitively and practically apprehensible through gestures like classification and hierarchization. Instead, I will trace a lineage dedicated to a highly explicit form of ordering, namely the arranging of written knowledge. My use of that term should certainly not be read as a commitment to a theory of knowledge that considers it to be something that can be fully externalized and stored in a scroll or a codex. Rather, the techniques I will discuss are themselves caught up in defining how written material can be made to serve learning and knowing, how its *value* can be understood and exploited. Indeed, writings of all kinds were collected and preserved from the beginning, testifying to their perceived importance and raising the question of how these potential knowledge reservoirs should be arranged.

Libraries and Knowledge Ordering

The earliest way to impose a certain order on collections of clay tables probably did not involve written lists, but simply spatial arrangement by shelf or by room. And spatial arrangement remains a central element in various forms of ordering to this day – including in the list itself, which can be seen as a specific way of arranging items on a writing surface. As far as we know, lists of written works appeared roughly around 2000 BCE, when collections began to grow beyond a certain size. These early inventories did not follow any particular order, but the mere fact that there was an easy way to consult the holdings of a library should be considered a first step toward systematization (Casson, 2001, p. 4). The roughly 30,000 tablets in Assyrian king Ashurbanipal's library, created in the seventh century BCE and archeologically preserved due to its destruction during the fall of Nineveh in 612 BCE, were arranged by subject matter, but the catalogs seem to have served mainly as inventories and vanguards against theft (Harris, 1999, p. 19; Casson, 2001, p. 13f.).

The most remarkable step toward a more deliberate approach to cataloging happened at the Library of Alexandria in the third century BCE, where Callimachus's famous bibliographic work *Pinakes* (Tables) employed different techniques to aid the finding of individual texts, inaugurating an order of knowledge in the process. This monumental catalog of the library's 490,000 scrolls was divided into ten subject matters that contained further subcategories. Authors were, for the first time in history, listed in alphabetical order to facilitate retrieval. The *Pinakes* has not survived, but we know that the catalog divided authors into poetry and prose, and the latter into subject domains such as philosophy, history, and medicine. Individual works could be retrieved with the help of a shelf list (Casson, 2001, p. 39ff.). Systematic organization and broad access had direct consequences for the use of the library as an institution of knowledge management and acquisition, making it 'possible for the student to plan for himself a rational course of reading in whatever subject interested him, offering opportunities for independent learning' (Lerner, 2009, p. 17). The arrangement in subject matters projected a specific division of knowledge domains onto the most important library of antiquity, and thus onto a large zone of influence, but the enumeration of authors following the letters of the Greek alphabet stands out even further. For Goody, this mode of arrangement is a particularly powerful feature of the combination between the list form and the phonetic alphabet:

> [T]he value of alphabetic listings is that each word is automatically assigned a specific but logically arbitrary place in the system, a space that only that item can fill. It is thus of immense value in retrieval systems dealing with masses of disordered information, such as subscriptions for the telephone or students in a class. (Goody, 1977, p. 110)

While the subject catalog requires considerable intellectual effort and can be considered a genuine work of metaphysics, the alphabetical list appears as the first 'mechanical' ordering device. Libraries had grouped works by 'objective' properties such as type of support, size, or language before, but none of these allowed for the same precision, speed, and convenience. The technique only works because the (Greek) alphabet is itself an *ordered* list of letters and those who learn to read also learn the specific sequence of letters. This arbitrary ordering – there is no specific reason that α should come first – represents a resource for the mechanical sorting of any set of words, providing more granularity when moving from the first letter to the second and so forth. The alphabet assigns a place to every thing through its name and remains one of the most common ordering devices in use – every programming language 'knows' the sequence of letters and PHP's *sort*() function will readily apply that sequence when presented with a list of character strings.

After the partial destruction of the Library of Alexandria in 48 BCE, it took almost two millennia before any institution could match the cataloging achievements of the Ptolemies. Roman libraries were much smaller in size, less systematically organized, and in large part privately owned (Casson, 2001, p. 8off.). Libraries in the Islamic world, such as the ones in Baghdad, Cairo, or Cordoba, had book collections counting in the hundreds of thousands, but we know little about the exact details of cataloging (Harris, 1999, p. 79f.) used in them other than that knowledge organization followed a logic of 'nobility first', evaluated in religious terms (Lerner, 2009, p. 62). This reminds us that classification often involves the attribution of value and significance to items.

Further to the east, the Chinese assigned great importance to well-ordered libraries and catalogs, dividing subjects into classics, histories, philosophers, and collected works following Chinese scholarly tradition (Lerner, 2009, p. 41f.). In the West, the monastic libraries of the Middle Ages were small, focused on theological texts, and were mainly driven by the concerns of education and preservation. Since collections were so small – the library of the Vatican held a mere 1209 volumes as late as 1455 (Lerner, 2009, p. 89) – catalogs were mostly inventories of highly valuable objects and not attempts to systematize knowledge (Svenonius, 2000, p. 29; Lerner, 2009, p. 35). As monasteries prospered and expanded their educational role, ordering volumes by subject, generally following the *trivium* and *quadrivium*, became a common practice. Mostly implemented via spatial placing in library rooms, librarians ran into logistical problems as titles were added (Harris, 1999, p. 110; Lerner 2009, p. 70). Only at the end of the Middle Ages and in particular when printing started to significantly expand the number of books in circulation did catalogs become more methodical, again mostly by registering volumes alphabetically. However, as books collections grew and covered broader fields, organizational principles multiplied (Murray, 2009, p. 205), typically following the specific ideas of a head librarian who held almost exclusive power over cataloging.

Until the late eighteenth century, catalogs were themselves books that simply listed works according to one of several available ordering schemes. While librarians would leave some space between entries for new arrivals, these would eventually fill up and require notes on the margins, the addition of new pages, supplementary volumes and, sooner or later, a full – and thus very costly – retranscription of the entire catalog. But the increase in printed volumes in the late eighteenth century and the steady stream of innovations in mechanical printing during the nineteenth century set the stage for a new material substrate that solved many of the basic limitations of the book form and stimulated interest in more systematic organization: the card catalog.

The Card Catalog

Until the Enlightenment period, state-owned libraries in the West were assembled for the purpose of representation rather than the efficient management of knowledge. The many problems cataloging and shelfing encountered mattered less to the limited audiences that had access in the first place. During the eighteenth and nineteenth centuries, however, this conception of the library came under attack from democratic reformers that requested public admission to what was increasingly perceived as a valuable resource for learning and social reform (Harris, 1999, p. 243f.). Librarians fully embraced the democratic ethos of the Enlightenment and began to see themselves as stewards of knowledge that should guide seekers through ever larger collections. The transformation of the library into an institution of public education and a 'temple of reason' defines its mission to this day.[1] But making access for wider audiences a reality was not only a political but also a logistical struggle. As Mortimer Taube, one of the information retrieval pioneers of the 1940s and 1950s, argues, classification became an essential part of the solution:

> The patron of the public library was the 'common man,' the citizen of the republic of letters to whom all knowledge was to be made available. To be sure, there have always been attempts to classify knowledge; but library classification became a major factor in bibliographic organization only when it became a specialized tool for the modern public library. (Taube, 1951, p. 64)

If the new patrons were to be served well, a uniform, systematic, and up-to-date catalog was required, not only to help with orientation and book retrieval but also with management tasks such as inventory handling or lending. The card catalog greatly facilitated all of these functions.

---

1   As Carla Hayden, the current Librarian of Congress, writes in her welcome message: 'The Library preserves and provides access to a rich, diverse and enduring source of knowledge to inform, inspire and engage you in your intellectual and creative endeavors' (Hayden, n.d.).

Although the Swiss naturalist and bibliographer Conrad Gessner had already used a complex system of paper slips to compile his *Bibliotheca Universalis* in the sixteenth century, the first real card catalog was introduced by diplomat, politician, and librarian Gottfried van Swieten in 1780 in the Hofbibliothek in Vienna (cf. Krajewski, 2011). In this quite revolutionary system, pioneered in parallel in revolutionary France, works were no longer listed in bound volumes, but each title received a card and these cards would be stored in adapted cabinets, ordered by alphabet or subject. The system greatly facilitated the creation, handling, and maintenance of catalogs, in particular for larger collections. When a new title arrived, the corresponding card could be lodged between two others; if space became scarce, the cards would simply be transferred to a larger cabinet. Leaving blank space for future additions or scribbling new titles on margins was no longer necessary. While the card catalog was not directly related to any specific ordering system, it transformed the very act of cataloguing from a special project that would take place at the initiative of a particularly ambitious librarian at a specific moment in time and then slowly deteriorate into an ongoing process that could infiltrate much more deeply into library practices. The importance of the new approach is hard to overstate.

But the card catalog is not only a practical tool that facilitates the life of both librarian and library patron; it is a critical step toward mobility and abstraction, that is, toward 'the process of considering something independently of its associations or attributes' (OED). Catalogs in book form had already made it possible to move beyond the crucial limitation of ordering by physical placement on shelves, namely that there could only ever be a single arrangement. Creating lists of references pointing to physical locations allowed for alphabetical, subject-based, and other ordering rationales to coexist in the context of a single collection. Catalogs are essentially collections of metadata that decontextualize individual items and encourage experimentation with different forms or order. Even if card catalogs were still mostly ordered by author or subject (Harris, 1999, p. 147), the mobility of individual references further enhanced organizational possibilities. While physical books could always be rearranged but only into a single order at a time, written list could be easily multiplied but were hard to expand or adapt. Moving to cards, the reference entries themselves became movable and what held them together was no longer a list, but a cabinet. In a sense, the card catalog still follows the list form, but the drawer replaces the page and the sides of the cabinet the outer binding of the book. The major difference is that the items on the list become 'atoms' that are suddenly able to move, giving a boost to the reordering function highlighted by Goody (1977, p. 76), even if the card catalog mostly served to uphold existing ordering schemes as the mass of items to manage grew at increasing speed and the mandate of the library had begun to transform.

Although Simondon's work focuses on more industrial forms of technology, I would argue that a card catalog is a technical individual that combines various elements – one of them being an ordering scheme – into a working system. The specific technicity of the card and cabinet had important consequences: the card catalog played a central role in transforming the library into a knowledge resource and learning tool open, at least in theory, to an entire population. The change in materiality from the book form to the card form contributed to a shift of attention from the cumbersome logistical work of cataloging to more conceptual aspects of organization and arrangement. The logistical 'unburdening' kept collection growth manageable and meant that ordering principles, seen as means to make collections more accessible, could come more strongly into view. Although the adoption of card catalogs was relatively slow and required the greater part of the nineteenth century, it is no surprise that their diffusion coincides with the period where the great knowledge systematizations that structure library collections to this day took form. These attempts to create stable and all-encompassing orders of knowledge were greatly inspired by the universalist outlook of Enlightenment philosophers, even if the realities of library management meant that concessions had to be made.

Toward Universalism

Next to serving as objects of prestige, state-owned libraries before the nineteenth century were (sometimes) to assist 'persons of merit and knowledge' (Lerner, 2009, p. 91) in their intellectual endeavors. Hiring a scholar of renown as the librarian could further both of these objectives. For someone like the philosopher and polymath Gottfried Leibniz, who served as librarian for many years, such an assignment was an excellent opportunity to think about and experiment with the organization of knowledge. His work on the catalog in Wolfenbüttel followed in large part the 21 subject categories laid out by Conrad Gessner and his own recommendations for library classification systems favored pragmatic schemes based on university faculties (cf. Schulte-Albert, 1971). He did, however, introduce a decimal extension to distinguish between the volumes of an ongoing series (Schulte-Albert, 1971, p. 140). But Leibniz was not just interested in the systematization and accessibility of the works in the institutions he headed. The ambition to devise a more perfect form of reasoning than natural language with its many ambiguities echoes though Leibniz's designs for an 'alphabet of human thought' (*alphabetum cogitationum humanarum*), a system combining a universal language (*characteristica universalis*) and a universal framework for logical calculation (*calculus ratiocinator*). These elements amount to 'not just a theory of classification [...], nor just a general theory of philosophical method [...], but a formalism for the representation and for the generation of all knowledge' (Mittelstrass, 1979, p. 604). Here, we find the most explicit expression of the idea that calculation can be a means for producing (philosophical) knowledge (Krämer, 1988, p. 100f.). The attempt to develop not merely an inventory of knowledge, but a thorough formalization of both semantic representation and logical inference opens a direct lineage toward efforts in areas such as symbolic artificial intelligence or the Semantic Web. We will come back to such intersections between calculation and meaning, but Leibniz's work can already illustrate the interest in the organization and formalization of knowledge philosophers began to take in the seventeenth century. This interest funnels into a second lineage next to the library that was concerned with collecting and organizing human knowledge: the Encyclopedia.

Here, Francis Bacon's *Of the Proficience and Advancement of Learning* from 1605 is worth mentioning since its classification of all knowledge into a tree with three main branches – memory, imagination, and reason – became highly influential (Darnton, 1999). Among others, Diderot and D'Alembert's *Encyclopédie*, a highly ambitious attempt to collect and systematize all available knowledge, drew on Bacon's system for its own hierarchical taxonomy. While encyclopedias and libraries differ in fundamental ways, they follow a similar mission and their histories intersect frequently. The *Discours préliminaraire* from 1751 defines the task Diderot and D'Alembert set out for themselves, and it is worth quoting a particularly instructive passage in full:

[The encyclopedic arrangement of our knowledge] consists of collecting knowledge into the smallest area possible and of placing the philosopher at a vantage point, so to speak, high above this vast labyrinth, whence he can perceive the principal sciences and the arts simultaneously. From there he can see at a glance the objects of their speculations and the operations which can be made on these objects; he can discern the general branches of human knowledge, the points that separate or unite them; and sometimes he can even glimpse the secrets that relate them to one another. It is a kind of world map which is to show the principal countries, their position and their mutual dependence, the road that leads directly from one to the other. (D'Alembert, 1995, p. 47)

For Diderot and D'Alembert, the tree of knowledge could be drawn in different ways, but the task of the *philosophes* was not to merely produce an arbitrary arrangement supporting the pragmatic goal of making the 70,000 articles in the *Encyclopédie* accessible. In line with Foucault's description of the classic *épistémè*, they were confident that rigorous analysis would be able to adequately and accurately account for a world 'offered to representation without interruption' (Foucault, 2005, p. 224). But as Darnton (1999, p. 191ff.) argues, the specific way categories were chosen was in itself a statement designed to promote secular and antiauthoritarian ideals. The universalism of the French Enlightenment is thus first a commitment to the universal values and natural rights[2] that find their most widely disseminated expression in the *Déclaration des droits de l'homme et du citoyen* of 1789. The adherence to these ideals, however, also had a 'universalizing' effect in epistemological terms, in the sense that those who reject the authoritarian impulses of religious or political despotism and allow themselves to be guided by their desire for truth would be able to come to a shared understanding concerning the systematization of knowledge, even if an element of arbitrariness remains. The argument the *philosophes* made was twofold: on the one side, nature itself possesses a structure, which we are able to perceive through our senses and to represent adequately; on the other side, the practical task of diffusing knowledge to everyone requires a certain coherence and unity. The *Encyclopédie*, a colossal effort that drew on the contributions of 140 individuals, should thus be seen as a socio-epistemological project that attempts to produce not only a collection of all human knowledge but also the adherence to a shared understanding concerning its systematization. Epistemological and political universalism go hand in hand in this endeavor.

Modern Library Classification Techniques

Although libraries had to deal with logistical problems that did not affect the creators of the *Encyclopédie*, the public library movement of the nineteenth century embraced a similar set of beliefs. The objective to cover all areas of knowledge and to provide access to everyone required enormous effort and provoked increased interest in systematization, commonality, and standardization. While the librarians of the Middle Ages and Renaissance

---

2   For the encyclopedists, it is the 'cry of Nature' against injustice that compels an understanding of good and bad, creating the moral imperative to use knowledge as a means for emancipation (D'Alembert, 1995, p. 12).

had begun to create union catalogs that covered more than one institution and wrote manuals for library organization that were instrumental for developing a set of shared ideas, these undertakings deepened in the nineteenth century. Anthony Panizzi's 92 bibliographical rules for the British Museum (1841) and Charles Coffin Jewett's 39 rules for the library at the Smithsonian Institution (1853) were not only much more detailed than earlier recommendations but were also taken up in many other locations (Lerner, 2009, p. 177). These efforts culminated in Charles Ammi Cutter's *Rules for a Printed Dictionary Catalog* (1876), 'likely the most cited text in the bibliographic literature' (Svenonius, 2000, p. 16), which built its rules and recommendations on three explicitly stated objectives for catalogs: to help find a specific book; to show what a library has on offer, for example, on a specific subject; to 'assist in the choice of a book' (Cutter, 1876, p. 10).

Such attempts to formulate explicit rules and guidelines were part of a larger conversation that led to the emergence of library science as an academic discipline and to librarianship as a profession. A crucial question was how to best realize the shared objectives Cutter synthesized into paradigmatic form and systematization was to play an important role. Other than basic author lists, the two central lines of development for cataloging were the structured subject heading list and the hierarchical classification scheme, both of which endure until today. Building on a long line of precursors, some of them already mentioned, they received their modern form in the second half of the nineteenth century.

The formulation and standardization of modern subject headings is generally attributed (Kilgour, 1969, p. 31; Wiegand and Davis, 1994, p. 605), at least in the American context, to Jewett, still working at Brown University in the early 1840s, and later to Cutter's (1876) canonical formulation. The modern form generally contains three elements that are combined into a single, alphabetically ordered list: broad subjects, specific subjects, and so-called subject-word entries that take the word judged most important from a book's title. The first two are taken from a controlled, uniform vocabulary and are the most important part of the system. Cutter's version already contained the 'see' (for linking nonuniform terms to the corresponding uniform terms) and 'see also' (for linking to related or more specific headings) type references that continue to exist, for example, in the Library of Congress Subject Headings (LCSH), prepared since 1898. LCSH entries are strictly controlled expressions containing a main heading and, possibly, a subdivision (e.g., 'Classification--Books'). As Svenonius (2000, p. 179) remarks, the LCSH is a largely enumerative language, where all allowable expressions are given in a centrally controlled list, even if more 'synthetic' features were added after 1974, allowing 'free-floating' subdivisions, for example, for time or geography (e.g., 'Art--Censorship--Europe--Twentieth century').

While the preparation of an actual catalog requires consistency and thus an authoritative thesaurus of subject headings, such thesauri are generally not based on a structured, philosophical vision concerning the order of knowledge (Wiegand and Davis, 1994, p. 606). Their specific brand of universalism is conventional rather than Hegelian. Despite continuous criticism stemming from the extreme reluctance to adapt existing vocabulary (Wiegand and Davis, 1994, p. 606; Drabinski, 2013, p. 97), the ongoing use of the LCSH in the US, the Répertoire d'autorité-matière encyclopédique et alphabétique unifié (RAMEAU) in France, or the Schlagwortnormdatei (SWD) in Germany shows that the adherence to a shared standard remains highly attractive to librarians committed to the practical unification of knowledge promoted by the *philosophes*. Subject headings also work very well with the logistics of the card catalog: subjects are written on the top of taller cards and individual titles are ranged alphabetically behind them. But they largely leave open another problem that the creators of the *Encyclopédie* did not have to deal with: the placement of titles in a library.

While systematic classifications based on hierarchical category trees can be used for cataloging and indexing, their enduring success in libraries mostly concerns the physical arrangement of books. Despite the affinity between Enlightenment thinking and the library movement, it was not the Bacon-*Encyclopédie* lineage that became dominant but a much more utilitarian system that took some inspiration from Leibniz's decimal numbering system. As its name implies, the Dewey Decimal Classification (DDC), first introduced by Melvil Dewey in 1876, is based on a nested tree structure where ten main categories are subdivided into ten subcategories, and so forth. Although the initial version only proposed a depth of three, there is no theoretical limit. Dewey, who insisted on copyrighting his invention, argued that 'philosophical theory and accuracy have been made to yield to practical usefulness' and conceded that 'the division of every subject into just nine heads is absurd' (Dewey, 1876, p. 4). But his invention allowed for a very convenient numbering scheme: Bacon's work would be found in the main class 'Philosophy' (100) and the subclasses 'Modern Philosophies' (190) and 'English' (192). Although there was, from the beginning, an alphabetical index of all classes, the system's decimal requirement introduced all kinds of conceptual difficulties that made it less suitable for cataloguing than the 'flat' structure of subject headings. Its hierarchical organization was more useful for the physical placement of books, which was previously based on fixed rather than 'logical' locations. The decimal system provided a practical means to organize and locate books in a way that titles treating a similar subject would be placed together on the shelf, encouraging browsing and discovery. The capacity to move from the more general to the more specific traded the greater flexibility of subject headings for easier navigation. Since both systems have their respective strengths and weaknesses, many libraries employ both in conjunction.

To complete this short overview of the backdrop against which algorithmic ordering techniques develop, the work of two other pioneers is worth mentioning: Paul Otlet and Siyali Ranganathan. Although Paul Otlet's contributions are often mentioned as precursors to contemporary forms of information access, his work can be seen as the culmination of the nineteenth century when it comes to knowledge organization. Working with international lawyer Henri La Fontaine in Belgium, Otlet founded the discipline of 'documentation' as a direct response to the proliferation of publications of all kind, ranging from scientific journals to audiovisual contents. The challenge to the book as the primary support of knowledge justified their highly systematic approach. In the 1890s, they founded the Office international de bibliographie and started to work on the Répertoire bibliographique universel, a 'universal catalog' (Otlet, 1934, p. 241) that would cover *all* document types. To give structure to this immense edifice, a modified version of the DDC was used. The Classification decimale universelle (CDU), still in use today, extended Dewey's classes to account for certain particularities of the European context and introduced a syntax for cross-referencing between classes, similar to the 'see also' connections used in subject headings.

But Otlet was dissatisfied with mere bibliography. While recorded knowledge obviously had to have some kind of support, books and other documents contain many different 'facts' that are not easily accessible through a catalog. Otlet therefore also imagined an encyclopedia, a 'universal book', that would be based on a repertoire of facts, extracted and retranscribed on index cards and classed into the universal systematization of the UDC (Otlet, 1934, p. 7). The Mundaneum, which housed the different card collections and was to be at the heart of a network of information centers, could indeed be described as an 'analog search engine' (Wright, 2008) that responded to 1500 information queries per year during its heyday. Otlet indeed combined the basic principles of the card catalog with the encyclopedic impulse inherited from the Enlightenment to produce a collection of knowledge closer to the 'logic of the database' than the monographic form (Hartmann, 2015, n.p.). He also shared with many of his successors the idea that books were now only one support among many and that the sheer mass of publications required creative solutions, including technical innovations such as microfilm and electronic data transmission (cf. Hartmann, 2012).

Where Otlet remains largely attached to the nineteenth century is the strong emphasis on systematization, standardization, synthesis, unity, and '*universalism*, that is, a system that would embrace all things' (Otlet, 1934, p. 430). Trained as a lawyer rather than a scientist or librarian, he espoused a deeply positivistic vision of science that, as Hartmann (2012, p. 56) remarks, tends toward an almost Hegelian totalization, where the stock of knowledge forms a coherent, unambiguous set of laws that can be captured in a singular structure. Knowledge, broken up into atoms collected on index cards, would be put together again, not by the king's horses and men, but through universal classification 'conform to the order intelligence discovers in things' (Otlet, 1934, p. 41). Although Otlet showed a certain pragmatism when it came to logistical solutions, he shunned the alphabetical subject-heading approach as 'too empirical' (Otlet, 1934, p. 381) and too scattered to capture the complex expressions of contemporary science. Ironically, Otlet was heavily criticized by one of his contemporaries, Henry E. Bliss (1935), for his decision to adopt a modified version of the DDC which, 'disregarded, or ignored, the principles of logical classification and the systems of science and education' (p. 100). For Bliss, the UDC was not positivistic enough: if '[o]rganizations of knowledge [...] become organizations for thought' (p. 87) the microcosm of mental organization needs to correlate with the 'intrinsic physical organization of the *cosmos*, the *macrocosm*' (p. 102).

In fact, the philosophical structure of classification was not at the center of Otlet's interests. Rayward (1994) rightly remarks that his objectives were ultimately more ambitious and classification 'was simply the first step in a more general system of what might be called documentary processing' (p. 237), a practice that would go deeply into the content of a document. His ideas concerning techniques for establishing connections between excavated facts are sometimes presented as precursors to hypertext and the web (Hartmann, 2006), but despite clear similarities, I would argue that his vision more accurately amounts to a centralized and fully systematized version of Wikipedia, a universally accessible, navigable repository of all 'factual' knowledge.

In contrast, a system that focused explicitly on pushing the mechanisms of classification beyond their nineteenth-century formulations was introduced in 1933, a year before Otlet published his magnum opus, the *Traité de la documentation*. Invented by S. R. Ranganathan, a mathematician who somewhat accidentally became librarian at the University of Madras in 1923, the 'colon classification', named for the prominent use of the colon sign in its syntax, was 'designed to overcome the difficulty enumerative languages have in keeping pace with knowledge' (Svenonius, 2000, p. 175). Enumerative languages, like the DDC or the LCSH, are based on the principle that all classes have to be listed in a main thesaurus; synthetic classifications – of which the colon classification was the first fully developed example – instead define a syntax for combining 'aspects' into a classificatory expression, 'reducing the vast universe of knowledge to a set of atomic concepts and certain basic relations among them' (Svenonius, 2000, p. 175). This meant that indexers did not have to wait for a central authority, like the Library of Congress, to update their category listings. Star argues that the colon classification thus frames 'the universe(s) of knowledge as potentially infinite, open, and evolving' (Star, 1998, p. 226), even if the basic ordering into disciplines does not stray very far from the Baconian tradition. Ranganathan's system is based on a list of main classes (e.g., B Mathematics, R Philosophy) that are complemented by five 'facets', each marked by a specific sign: ',' for personality, ';' for matter, ':' for energy, '.' for space, and "'" for time. While both the DDC and the CDU have known facets in some sense from their inception, for example, to distinguish between types of publication or to indicate period and geography, the colon classification fully embraces the synthetic principle (Satija, 2002). Facets are independent from each other and can be combined into compound classificatory expressions. The technique does not, however, define a singular abstracted system of semantic coordinates. For example, personality in the context of library science means the kind of library, while in the context of chemistry it describes elements or compounds. But the different components can form complex phrases, such as the commonly given example 'research in the cure of the tuberculosis of lungs by x-ray conducted in India in 1950s' (Chan, 1994, p. 39), which is noted as L,45;421:6;253:f.44'N5 and translates, from left to right, into 'Medicine' (main category), ',Lungs' (personality, the specific subject), ';Tuberculosis' (matter, the property), ':Treatment' (energy, the intend to cure the tuberculosis), ';X-ray' (matter, the means to cure), ':research' (energy, this concerns research into this specific treatment), '.India' (space), and "'1950' (time). This system allows for extremely fine-grained descriptions and makes it easy to add new elements to different facets, for example, a new treatment. In certain respects, Ranganathan's system is closer to Leibniz's *characteristica universalis* than to traditional classification systems. While the colon classification has remained in active use, in particular in the Indian context, its enormous complexity makes it hard to use beyond special cases. It does, however, point into the broad direction algorithmic information ordering was taking.

Toward Computation: Documentation and Coordinate Indexing

At the eve of WWII, two techniques for organizing documents by subject dominated: subject headings, generally based on increasingly long lists of increasingly specific topics (e.g., 'Classification--Dewey decimal' in the LCSH), and classification trees, often used for physical placement, where each book is supposed to sit at a specific place in the hierarchy.[3] This is the backdrop against which the field of information retrieval developed a set of ideas, concepts, and – most importantly – techniques that broke with the library tradition in fundamental ways. Often relying on statistical approaches, information retrieval became one of the fundamental *ancestral communities of probabilization*' (Mackenzie, 2017a, p. 118) and its contributions continue to define contemporary information ordering. The rest of this book can thus be understood as an attempt to 'excavate the present' (Parikka, 2011, p. 214) by following a series of inventions that sought to transform knowledge organization into a dynamic, machine-supported process of ordering.

Documentation Centers

Even though catalogs, classification schemes, and other aspects of library logistics had become quite elaborate in the first half of the twentieth century, the degree of mechanization remained low. Herman Hollerith had begun to commercialize his punched card tabulators in the 1890s, but as Williams (2002, p. 16) notes, the earliest reports of uses in libraries came in the mid-1930s and concerned management tasks such as circulation control and the statistical analysis of book use to inform future buying decisions. Existing catalogs relied heavily on trained librarians as 'knowledge mediators', both for bibliographic control when new titles arrived and to guide visitor through standardized vocabularies and intricately organized floor plans. Even university libraries, catering to more specialized audiences than their public cousins, were organized in similar ways and run by professional librarians rather than academics. Their broad outlook and public mandate meant that the mechanization of information ordering did not happen in these institutions, and neither did the upheaval of conventional ordering schemes.

The emergence of technical and intellectual innovations – or disruptions – in knowledge ordering are closely linked to so called 'special libraries' and 'documentation centers' (Williams, 2002; Varlejs, 2004). Special libraries

---

3   Some libraries had also begun to use alphabetical lists mixing authors, titles, and subjects into a single catalog.

had existed at least since the early 1800s and they had generally been more concerned with matters of classification than their less specialized cousins (Shera, 1952, p. 189f.). But the emphasis on public education had marginalized these more focused institutions, with 'the disastrous effect of diverting librarianship from its proper concern with the analysis and organization of recorded knowledge' (Shera, 1952, p. 191). In the US, documentation services had not received the same amount of attention as in Europe, where Paul Otlet was promoting the idea of information centers, and were mostly concerned with new methods for photographic reproduction (Shera, 1952, p. 193). However, these traditions 'received a new vitality when the Second World War brought into existence a need for greater and more efficient access to information than traditional library methods were able to give' (Shera, 1952, p. 195). Varlejs gives a concise summary of the background to the substantial change in perspective and approach about to happen:

> Hundreds of thousands of reports generated by wartime and postwar scientific and technical research, together with several hundred tons of captured enemy documents, challenged traditional methods of information organization, dissemination, and retrieval. In the interests of maintaining military superiority and jump-starting the economy, U.S. government policy favored maximum declassification and speedy dissemination of information to business and industry. The urgent need to carry out this policy fostered new techniques and adaptations of old methods in the 1940s and 1950s, some of which have had a lasting impact. (Varlejs, 2004, p. 89)

Existing as well as newly founded centers quickly became the practical and intellectual locus of a movement of 'modernization' that would concern all aspects of handling documents and, by extension, of handling information and knowledge. While the tasks at hand were still often referred to as 'library problems' (Mooers, 1950, p. 2; Maron, 1963, p. 144; Rau, 2007, p. 159), their main object was not so much the traditional book, but rather technical and scientific literature, generally published in the form of research papers or reports; the real and imagined audience was not the 'common man', but scientists and engineers in academia, government, and business; and the political mandate was not public education, but scientific, economic, and military development[4] in the context of the Cold War, which affected the development of computing more broadly (cf. Edwards, 1996).

---

4   In his foreword to the Weinberg Report, US president Johnson writes: 'One of the major opportunities for enhancing the effectiveness of our national scientific and technical effort and

The already mentioned idea that there is a 'problem of too much information' (Bowles, 1999, p. 156), a 'growing mountain of research' (Bush, 1945, p. 112) or simply a 'scientific information crisis' (Weinberg, 1963, p. 15) is virtually everywhere in the hundreds of papers and reports published in the wake of WWII that begin to flesh out a technical and conceptual domain that was initially referred to as 'machine documentation' (Wasserman, 1965, p. 19) but ultimately consolidated around the productively vague concept of 'information'.[5] The idea that too much information is detrimental to efficiency and progress became the founding myth of what Calvin Mooers (1950), one of the central figures of the emerging field, canonically named 'information retrieval' in 1950. If the operational goals of libraries since the eighteenth century were closely tied to the ideals of the Enlightenment, the explicit objective of special libraries and documentation centers was to make knowledge productive and 'actionable' in a direct and measurable sense and as quickly as possible.[6] In a climate of technological optimism, this inevitably meant that machines were to play a central role.

The centers and institutions dedicated to what a much-regarded presidential report in 1963 called the 'transfer of information' (Weinberg, 1963) often collaborated with academics and with startups that developed in close physical, social, and intellectual proximity to universities and other research bodies. The initial conviction that solving the information crisis would be beneficial to development in just about all sectors of society meant that considerable amounts of money were made available through government agencies. And these funds were often distributed in the form of grants promoting experimentation and fundamental research. While the effects of the concerted governmental support on the emergence of computing post-WWII is generally well-known (cf. Campbell-Kelly and Aspray, 1996), backing from direct funders, such as the Office of Naval Research, and intragovernmental institutions for the promotion and coordination of research, such as the Research and Development Board, also benefited the

the efficiency of Government management of research and development lies in the improvement of our ability to communicate information about current research efforts and the results of past efforts' (Weinberg, 1963, p. iii).

5   This shift is completed on an institutional level when the American Documentation Institute, founded in 1937, changed its name to American Society for Information Science in 1968. In 2000, it finally became the American Society for Information Science & Technology.

6   'The true concern of the special library is the information that its clientele will need today and tomorrow. If the special library is doing its work effectively, its clients' needs will change rapidly, in response to the ever-changing environment that it has helped to create' (Lerner, 2009, p. 156).

wider field of documentation and information retrieval, whether it aimed directly at mechanization or not.

The role of Vannevar Bush merits specific mention in this context. Bush, a pioneer in analog computing, became a prominent science administrator during the war, heading the Office of Scientific Research and Development, which oversaw the Manhattan Project. Both his research in computing and his work in science management prompted an interest in the use of machines to support the organization of and access to knowledge, with the goal of facilitating the generation of new knowledge. In an often-cited article from 1945, he described a machine, the Memex, that would allow its users to retrieve and connect documents, stored on microfilm, via 'associative trails', networks of connections that evoke the subsequent notion of hypertext. While the Memex, a personal information device rather than a retrieval system, probably had little actual influence on concrete research in the field (cf. Buckland, 1992), Bush's considerable clout, as both the 'engineer of the American century' (Zachary, 1999) and influential figure in research funding, contributed to securing public interest, recognition, and financial support for everything having to do with mechanical information processing.

Taken together, these elements led to an environment where special libraries and documentation centers with higher budgets and smaller, more specialized audiences than their publicly minded counterparts were in a position to experiment with a variety of technical innovations (Williams, 2002, p. 16). These institutional differences were accompanied by a fundamental divergence in outlook that led to what Bowles (1999) termed the 'information wars', a rift that can be traced up to the present. To understand this divergence within a broader historical frame, we have to examine the role calculation and mechanical reasoning have played in business and government long before digital computers were invented.

Mechanical Reasoning, Statistics, and Decision-Making

In the introduction to their seminal *Computer: History of an Information Machine*, Campbell-Kelly and Aspray argue that the 'canonical' story of the invention of the computer as a calculating device born out of the encounter between centuries of mathematical innovation and America's WWII efforts is incomplete. They point out that 'research scientists and atomic weapons designers still use computers extensively, but the vast majority of computers are employed for other purposes, such as word processing and keeping business records' (Campbell-Kelly and Aspray, 1996, p. 2) and propose to incorporate the mechanization of office work and data processing into the history of computing, for example, the famous application of Hollerith machines to the 1890 US census.

Although there are clear connections between information retrieval and tasks like data processing and document management, there are even broader traditions of applied mechanical reasoning situated at the intersection of calculation and decision-making that are largely absent from the (pre)history of computing. Editors Becker and Hayes (1963) indeed introduce their influential Information Sciences Series, published by Wiley & Sons from 1963 onwards, with the statement that '[i]nformation is the essential ingredient in decision making' (p. v), connecting the newly established 'resource' directly to management practices in business and government.

Decision-making assisted by calculation has a long history, and the development of capitalism, in particular, is closely related to the use of arithmetic as a means to take on size, complexity, and uncertainty. The fifteenth century is particularly rich in this respect: Luca Pacioli's *Summa de arithmetica, geometria, proportioni et proportionalità* standardized and disseminated double-entry bookkeeping while popular *algorismi*, manuals for learning arithmetic, proposed practical methods that were both enabling and responding to the needs of increasingly complex forms of trade, such as dealing with logistics and planning, with diverse units and currencies, and with the distribution of risks and profits. The requirements of long-distance trade, the emergence of larger commercial entities, and a general rise in organizational complexity 'elevated computation to the status of an empirical science' (Swetz, 1987, p. 295). This science provided precise tools to control and to decide, which stabilized, standardized, and systematized how merchants managed their businesses and interacted with their peers. While these methods were not (yet) the scientific management that emerges in the late 1800s, the considerable risks that characterized early capitalism inspired new forms of control relying on data collection and calculation (cf. Beniger, 1986).

These techniques – listing and tabulating, applied arithmetic with Arabic numerals, bookkeeping – subsequently spread to other domains. William Petty's *Political Arithmetik*, developed over the second half of the seventeenth century, is of particular interest as it systematically applied quantitative reasoning to matters of government and produced concrete recommendations concerning public investment and economic policy. Rather than (merely) appealing to moral principles, to the authority of great individuals, or to 'evident' truths, Petty's mode of argumentation amounted to what we would nowadays call cost-benefit analysis. As the following problem from one of Petty's essays (1655, p. 63ff.) shows, the discussed topics ring eerily familiar, even if the details of the calculation certainly seem peculiar: given the worth of a human being, based on the price of a slave at the market in Algiers, would additional spending on certain Parisian hospitals to lower mortality rates represent a good investment for the king of France? Answer: yes.

It is symptomatic of our somewhat lopsided historical perspective, which puts abstract and seemingly disinterested pursuits over practical and profitable ones, that Charles Babbage is now mostly remembered for his work on mechanical calculation, although his considerable contributions to statistics, economics, insurance, and management – the foundations of the considerable fame he won during his lifetime – could be considered as equally important to the history of computing. After all, one of the main uses of his difference engine would have been the calculation of life expectancy tables for the purpose of setting the price of life insurance annuities (cf. Babbage, 1864). Certainly, these fields were not directly related to the mathematical theory of computation and its mechanization in modern computers, but they provided a space beyond science and engineering where such machines could find an objectal embedding through some form of practical or imaginary utility. This tension between the fundamental and the applied is characteristic and the history of statistics is of particular relevance in this context, since it arguably represents the most pervasive application of calculation to governance and decision-making.

To this day, the term 'statistics' has kept a double meaning. First, it refers to the collection of facts or *data*, which, in the nineteenth century, turned into a true 'avalanche' (Hacking, 1990, p. 2) or 'deluge' (Cohen, 2005, p. 113) of tabulated numbers covering every conceivable subject. This kind of description by numbers is what we mean when we talk about 'accident statistics' or 'employment statistics' and it directly connects to various technical inventions and organizational practices emerging after 1800 (cf. Gardey, 2008). Second, '[b]y 1889, users of statistics [...] had become discontent with the mere presentation of numerical facts, and were looking for more refined methods of analysis' (Gigerenzer et al., 1989, p. 58), which led to the development of statistics as a series of mathematical concepts and techniques used to find and analyze patterns in collected data, for example, dependencies between variables. Both meanings refer to 'epistemic practices', that is, practices caught up in the production and definition of knowledge, but the second indeed mobilizes mechanical reasoning in its fullest sense, as a purely formal transformation of symbols that nonetheless produces an epistemic surplus. The detection of a significant level of correlation between two variables is not simply a 'presentation of numerical fact'; it must be considered a 'cognitive'[7] operation that generates an interpretation of the world behind the numbers, an interpretation that consistently lays claim to being both true and enlightening, and thus to a legitimate role in orienting ideas and actions. In the words of economist and engineer Jules Dupuit (1995), written in 1844, 'mathematics [...] are machines that, in a certain sense, can think for us' (p. 92). Whether we fully accept this claim is secondary here; what counts is that 'in the operations of government, the conduct of business and finance, the activities of science and engineering, and even in some aspects of daily life' (Cohen, 2005, p. 17), mechanical reasoning involving complex calculations has become an accepted form of relating to a world seen as complex, uncertain, and wrought with struggles for power. As Porter argues, 'quantification is a social technology' (Porter, 1995, p. 48), a 'technology of trust' (Porter, 1995, p. 15), that purports to reduce subjectivity, individual discretion, and, ultimately, the arbitrariness of the powerful, by instating 'rules of discourse so constraining that the desires and biases of individuals are screened out' (Porter, 1995, p. 74). Even if associated techniques and practices have come to know widespread application and acceptance, claims to objectivity and impartiality have certainly been contested. Tensions manifest particularly clearly in contemporary critiques of 'big data', where '*trust* in the objectivity of quantified methods as well as in the *independence* and *integrity* of institutions deploying these methods' (p. 204) is embattled from different sides. Such manifestations of a much larger 'legitimation crisis' (Habermas, 1975) can be observed in many domains and 'library problems' are certainly one area where the question of *how* decisions are made and *who* makes them have been at the heart of arduous debates.

Independently from contestations of legitimacy, statistics constitutes the most pervasive example of machines 'thinking for us' that is not based on forms of logical inference, like Leibniz's *calculus ratiocinator*, but on the collection and analysis of (quantitative) empirical data. The idea that diligent counting and mathematical examination of what is counted allow for a particularly performant coupling of knowing and managing is the point where statistics intersects with Foucault's work on power. In the context of 'bio-politics', a 'technology of power' that concerns itself with the management of life and thus with birth and mortality rates, public hygiene, or urban living conditions, Foucault sees statistics as a 'technique

---

7   The term is used here in connection with its etymological root in the Latin *cognoscere*, 'to know', and should not be read as a commitment to any particular theory of (human) cognition.

of observation' (Foucault, 2007, p. 161) that plays a central role in the regulation of a population. The objective of bio-politics is not merely to keep the
population in a state of submissive docility, but rather to optimize output
and to 'turn society into a machine of production' (Foucault, 2007, p. 194).
Foucault frames statistics in line with the etymological origins of the term
as 'the state's knowledge of the state' (Foucault, 2009, p. 162) and puts it at
the center of a 'governmental rationality' (Foucault, 2008, p. 56) that is no
longer an art of government, but a 'political science' (Foucault, 2009, p. 106)
intrinsically tied to political economy as its dominant way of thinking
society. While these associations point beyond the subject matter treated
in this book, they should remind us that information ordering techniques
under conditions of pervasive computerization have come to serve similar
governmental functions.

The application of statistics to decision-making provided a model when
it came to framing the library problem and, by extension, the problem of
knowledge organization and access as a *technical* problem that could be
solved with the proper scientific attitude and methodology. WWII certainly
played a crucial role in more than one respect, but it crucially 'strengthened
the decision theoretic approach to statistical problems, and accustomed
people to the idea that reasonable decisions can be made on the basis of
formal, mechanized reasoning combined with measurements' (Gigerenzer et
al., 1989, p. 120). Operations research, which developed a largely probabilistic
approach to military decisions during the war,[8] left deep impressions on
the individuals and institutions that set out to transform the handling of
published material into a science of information. This included a broad
ethos carrying 'a novel blend of pessimism about the scope and quality
of human reason and optimism about the power of social and technical
mechanisms for producing rational choices' (Heyck, 2012, p. 100). As we
shall see, the mission to remove or at least rearrange 'human reason' in
information ordering did not sway toward the universalist classifications of
the nineteenth century. Espousing a probabilistic outlook that recognized
uncertainty as a fundamental fact of life, it turned to statistics as a means
to 'tame chance' (Hacking, 1990) in a way that combines the imperatives
of rationalism and pragmatism.

Desrosières addresses what I mean by 'pragmatism' when he discusses how
statistics allows for different attitudes toward the world it means to describe,
'metrological realism', the correspondence or equivalence theory of truth,

---

8   Operations research itself connects to a long prehistory in scientific management. See, for
example, Chandler (1977) or Yates (1989).

being just one of several 'orchestrations of reality' (Desrosières, 2001, p. 346). What we find in commerce and government is in fact 'accounting realism', where the '"equivalence space" is composed not of physical quantities (space and time), but of a general equivalent: money' (Desrosières, 2001, p. 342). Here, the benchmark for validity is no longer disinterested correspondence between reality and representation but effectiveness when it comes to attaining specific goals. The notion of accounting realism thus echoes Lyotard's (1984) assessment that the contemporary knowledge regime seeks 'no longer truth, but performativity – that is, the best possible input/output equation' (p. 46). Subscribing neither to the 'high rationalism' epitomized by Chomsky's computationalism, nor to the epistemological and political universalism that characterizes the public library, information retrieval evolves in an intellectual environment and institutional context that espouses accounting realism as its dominant epistemological attitude.

Information Wars

Coming back to the main thread of the story, we can indeed appreciate how the early literature on information retrieval frames the 'library problem' as the question of how to make recorded knowledge *useful*. At least in the 1940s and 1950s, this debate still occurs in large parts around institutions, publications, and conferences that remain connected to a library science tradition marked by Enlightenment values such as public education and philosophical universalism. But what is underway is a full-frontal assault on this tradition. In the paper where Mooers first introduces the term 'information retrieval', he makes a programmatic declaration that could hardly be any clearer:

> In order to approach this slippery problem with any hope of success or efficiency of thought, it will be necessary for us to put aside almost all the ideas, doctrines, and symbolic or metaphysical superstructure about libraries and library methods that we have learned or otherwise picked up in the past. It can be said – and demonstrated – that almost everything that librarians hold dear in classification is absolutely wrong for information retrieval. (Mooers, 1950, p. 4)

While these are not the first shots fired in the 'information wars', 'the professional battle between scientists (documentalists) and humanists (librarians) over information retrieval' (Bowles, 1999, p. 156), Mooers himself epitomizes certain fault lines characterizing the dispute. Trained in mathematics and physics rather than library science, he considered the library methods of the time to be positively archaic, 'stalled for two millennia' (Mooers, 1950, p. 17), and 'incapable of information retrieval' (Mooers, 1950, p. 4). He saw a need for a completely different approach 'guided by the principles of engineering and the scientific method instead of the outworn metaphysics' (Mooers, 1950, p. 17). To Mooers and his colleagues, the term 'scientific method' implied not just mathematization and measurement but included the commitment to ideas related to scientific management and, in particular, to operations research and applications of analytical methods to process optimization and decision-making (cf. Rau, 2013).

Even if Mooers was particularly vocal, the dismissive attitude toward traditional library ideas was widespread. Together with the 'information overload' hypothesis, the idea that there was preciously little to learn from cataloging principles and techniques like the DCC or the LCSH became the point of departure for the emergent discipline. Mortimer Taube, another central figure in the field, indeed argued that 'rebels' like himself 'invaded the holy of holies of sanctified library practice' with radical new ideas (Taube, 1952, p. 167). In an article published in 1982 in the influential Advances in Computing series, James E. Rush looks back at these early days with little modesty:

> [T]he automation revolution has resulted in much greater technological innovation in libraries during the past 20 years than had been achieved during the entire history of librarianship up to about 1960. (Rush, 1982, p. 334)

Contrary to most libraries, the people staffing documentation centers were indeed mostly scientists, not librarians (Williams, 2002, p. 20). And the tensions between the two 'sides' were palpable.[9] In his book *The Librarian and the Machine*, published in 1965, Paul Wasserman euphemistically remarked that 'there seemed now to be a number of members of the academic community who were prepared to suggest that they knew a great deal more about the way in which the technology of modern times could be applied to library processes than did the librarians themselves' (p. 10). Dismissive attitudes were reflected in the fact that almost none of the early retrieval systems attempted to support, mimic, or even acknowledge existing classification

9   'Today we seem to be on the brink of startling new developments in the field of high-speed manipulation of large masses of bibliographic data, and already the emotional responses are becoming apparent' (Shera, 1952, p. 15).

systems, such as the DCC.[10] The ideas of non-American thinkers like Otlet or Ranganathan were discussed even less.

Similar to the statisticians of the nineteenth and twentieth century and subsequent 'method experts', the 'information scientists' of the 1950s and 1960s who pioneered many of the algorithmic ordering techniques at work today presented themselves as modernizers and rationalizers. Their story fits neatly into the picture drawn in Ensmenger's (2010) *The Computer Boys Take Over*, which details the intricate connections between the nascent and expansive discipline of computer science on the one side and the ideological and methodological nexus forming around business administration, operations research, systems analysis, cybernetics, efficiency consulting, and associated techniques. The task information retrieval set for itself was not merely to introduce new machinery and techniques into an existing setting but to redesign the library on the whole as an information system.[11] And while much of the concrete work revolved around automation and mechanization, the systems perspective always lingered in the background, becoming particularly noticeable whenever new performance measurements sought to quantify the effectiveness of provided services.

These elements for a social history of the information wars can provide crucial context, but I am specifically interested in the actual techniques transforming knowledge organization into information ordering. The information wars can indeed be narrated in terms of machinery (computers vs. manual methods) or socialization (scientists vs. humanists), but the actual 'epistemological operators' (Young, 2017, p. 45) put forward crystallize around a specific document retrieval technique that lays the foundations for many further developments: coordinate indexing.

Coordinate Indexing

As already mentioned, the objective of special libraries and documentation centers was not to support public education but to facilitate access

10   This is what Mooers has to say about Dewey's system: 'The postulates of the Dewey system are incompatible among themselves, and the system can never be readjusted so as to perform the task set for it' (Mooers 1950, p. 8).
11   A 1965 survey on the state of automation in libraries, porting the ominous subtitle *A Study in Reluctant Leadership*, criticizes the lack of systems thinking: 'The preceding survey shows that none of the libraries which have adopted mechanization or automation to any extent has attempted seriously to consider a whole library as a total information system which is to be integrated so far as possible in its concepts, design, provision of equipment, and daily operations' (Gull, 1965, p. 5).

to relevant information for the 'knowledge worker': the research scientist pushing for new findings and the engineer requiring a particular detail about a specific process, but also the manager having to make a quick decision and the public administrator planning the details of a specific policy. With Foucault, we should hesitate to see this shift as another step in a general movement of rationalization. As we have seen, traditional library methods were certainly not immune to rationalist universalism and if we 'analyze specific rationalities rather than forever invoke the progress of rationalization in general' (Foucault, 1982, p. 779f.), we realize that this is indeed a matter of competing claims to rationality.

The most fundamental difference, in fact, concerns the framing of the library problem. The information specialists were not concerned with lofty ideals of emancipation through knowledge but saw themselves as contributors to professional environments where information was a central resource. Information retrieval's purpose was thus to satisfy specific 'information needs', a concept that has remained at the heart of information retrieval ever since.[12] These needs were seen as not being met by existing methods and techniques:

> What is required is the recognition that the Library of Congress system, for all its complexity and detail, is not a tool for specialists but a general system for the non-specialist's approach to knowledge as a whole. (Taube, 1951, p. 63)

Specialists required specialized means to access specialized knowledge and coordinate indexing was one of the earliest techniques built on this very premise.[13] It developed, at least indirectly, from earlier applications of document processing techniques by scientists using edge-notched punched cards to analyze categorical research data in the 1930s. The McBee Keysort system was probably the most used commercial variant. These were 'almost entirely "term on item" systems' (Kilgour, 1997, p. 340) where a card would register various characteristics (terms) of a chemical compound, animal species, or plant (items). A notched card could encode as many binary variables as the

---

12   The definition of information retrieval given by one of the most well-known textbooks reads: 'Information retrieval (IR) is finding material (usually documents) of an unstructured nature (usually text) that satisfy an information need from within large collections (usually stored on computers)' (Manning et al., 2008, p. 1).

13   This statement requires some qualification since special services like abstracting or 'current awareness' publications can be seen as fulfilling retrieval functions and such services had been around since the nineteenth century.

These photos show the use of the McBee Keysort system in the context of the famous Experiments in Art and Technology, launched by engineers Billy Klüver and Fred Waldhauer and artists Robert Rauschenberg and Robert Whitman in 1967. Here, the coordinate indexing logic was applied to a contact database of collaborators, encoding their specific skills and interests. Photos courtesy of Klüver/Martin Archive.

space on the cards' edges permitted. The card would 'describe' a particular entity by marking the value for each field with either a hole or a notch.

A card for 'dog', for example, would have a hole in the 'carnivore' field and a notch for 'retractable claws'. The card for 'cat' would have a hole for both. When using a so-called sorting needle on a stack of cards along a particular characteristic, the cards with holes would get lifted while the cards with notches would stay put. If we were to apply the needle to the 'carnivore' field, both dog and cat would be pulled, but the needle would not get the dog card when fishing for retractable claws. While actual implementations of this system could be entirely manual, the simple logic based on items (objects) and terms (properties) was well-suited to mechanization. And despite its simplicity, the system allowed for Boolean operators in queries: using two needles would constitute an OR; using a needle sequentially to first get items with characteristic A and then lift cards with characteristic B from those results would constitute an AND. The outcome would be a *selection*, following no particular order, of documents satisfying the specified logical condition. Even the NOT operator could be applied by removing cards with certain properties from the results (Kilgour, 1997, p. 341). Although the cats and dogs example may seem trivial, such a system was able to query thousands of items along up to around a hundred binary variables, the physical limit of the cards, which meant that it was capable of 'operationalizing distinctions' (Siegert, 2013, p. 14) dynamically in relatively large and complex datasets. This simple principle constitutes the operational schema in what was to become the first and, for a considerable time, the dominant framework for the computerization of document retrieval.

The technique was applied to bibliographic indexing in several places at roughly the same time, most prominently by Mortimer Taube, even if his approach favored a somewhat different implementation than the one just described. Taube's system, for which he invented the term 'coordinate indexing', solved one of the problems related to a major limitation of notched cards, which could deal with fairly large collections of items but were only able to accommodate a relatively small number of terms, limiting the size of the indexing vocabulary. Taube thus decided to use cards not only for listing the documents to be searched but also for what he called 'uniterms', simple keywords describing catalogued works (Wasserman, 1965, p. 57f.; Kilgour, 1997). While the procedure for selecting and attributing uniterms to documents was a matter of debate, the general idea was to eschew complex categories or subject headings in favor of single words (Doyle, 1975, p. 174). Every uniterm received a card which listed the reference numbers for the works tagged with that term. A card could, in principle, list hundreds of titles and a title described by ten terms would therefore appear on ten cards. To make queries, searchers would combine or 'coordinate' the terms they were looking for and then search for the numbers appearing on all of the cards. Partial matches could be taken into account and counting the number of query terms a document would match constituted a simply ranking mechanism.

In the beginning, the system relied on manual use, facilitated only by the rather ingenious use of ordered columns for reference numbers to facilitate lookup. In this setting, the numbers of terms and items were mainly limited by the searcher's capacity (or willingness) to drudge through lists and lists of entries. What would appear completely impractical for the large stocks of public libraries, which covered many different areas of knowledge, was much more workable in the context of specialized collections. Coordinate indexing became a widespread and popular technique (Wasserman, 1965, p. 62; Salton, 1987, p. 376) and the introduction of Boolean operators continues to resonate through electronic catalogs and other search systems. Compared to traditional classifications or subject headings, coordinate indexing had two perceived clusters of advantages that each connect to larger debates about knowledge organization and access.

First, compared to existing indexing practices, the attribution of uniterms or descriptors was seen as easier, faster, cheaper and more adapted to the needs of searchers. The mandate to serve the professional knowledge worker meant that special libraries and documentation centers were not limited to books but included the quickly growing mass of journal publications and reports. Together with the desire for fast distribution of the latest findings, often termed 'current awareness' (Svenonius, 2000, p. 28), and thus for fast bibliographic attribution, this meant that the person tasked with indexing would have little time to spend on individual items. Much of the early literature on coordinate indexing thus builds its criticism of library techniques on the central role complex classification and subject heading systems confer to those who develop these controlled knowledge structures and those who assign records to specific places in the system. The 'bibliographic power' (Wilson, 1968) these knowledge mediators hold is not seen as a guarantor of neutrality but as a source of subjectivity, arbitrariness, and conservativism, which is particularly problematic in emerging and cutting-edge fields of knowledge. Since standardization and continuity were considered essential by librarians, the structures and vocabularies of systems like the DDC or LCSH were somewhat extended but never substantially reorganized. While coordinate indexing did not necessarily do away with the idea of a predefined or controlled vocabulary, since institutions often developed their own thesaurus, it opened the door for thinking about ways to eliminate the expert indexer trained in the arcane details of the indexing system.

Explicitly framed as a technique for creating any number of bibliographic systems, coordinate indexing never had any universalist pretentions.[14] From the beginning, it embraced local perspectivism not only in the sense

14   'I think that in this matter librarians have been misled by the universal acceptance of the elements of descriptive bibliography and have concluded erroneously that it is possible to create a universal system of subjects which will be satisfactory to all specialists' (Taube, 1951, p. 61).

that uniterm vocabularies were only meant to cover specific fields but also by empowering the expert searcher. This was accomplished by moving from static and complex 'precoordinated' systems to a 'postcoordinated' perspective, where compound, multipart concepts were no longer attributed by a librarian at the moment of indexing, but *constructed* by the searcher at 'retrieval time' through the combination of simple terms using Boolean operators.[15] The complex precoordinated entry 'Spain--History--Civil War, 1936-1939--Literature and the war' from the LCSH would become an unordered list of keywords such as 'Spain, Civil War, Literature' in the postcoordinated logic. Luhn summarizes the difference in particularly clear language:

> The introduction of discriminating terms, such as key words, has brought about a new degree of freedom. Instead of applying a static set of categories or subject headings beforehand, such categories or subject headings may be formulated dynamically at the instant of inquiry by a tailor-made assembly of such key words. (Luhn, 1968a, p. 126)

Keywords or uniterms could be attributed much more easily, disregarding order and syntax. The already mentioned Weinberg report (1963), for example, stressed the role of scientists in the process, asking them to 'self-index' their papers through relevant keywords. Providing well-written abstracts should help indexers with 'emergent' coding where keywords would be taken from the document itself. This, indeed, became the recommended method (Doyle, 1975, p. 176) and anyone who has ever submitted a paper to an academic journal should be familiar with these practices. Moving away from controlled vocabularies meant that librarians were not only besieged on the side of indexing but also on the side of searching, since users could employ terms they were familiar with rather than a predefined syntax and semantics (Lerner, 2009, p. 190). Overall, the measured efficiency of coordinate indexing was similar to more elaborate methods, while being faster and cheaper (Salton, 1987, p. 3).

   Second, coordinate indexing was seen as ideally suited for mechanization and computerization. Since Alonzo Church and Alan Turing had shown 'that numbers were an inessential aspect of computation – they were just one way

---

15 'Pre and post reference the time at which terms are concatenated into large expressions. In a precoordinate language, this is done prior to retrieval by a professional in a manner defined by the syntax rules of the language. In a postcoordinate language, it is done at the time of retrieval by a user using a Boolean-based syntax' (Svenonius, 2000, p. 178).

of interpreting the internal states of the machine' (Barr and Feigenbaum, 1981, p. 4), the 'digital handling of non-numerical information' (Mooers, 1950) had become a plausible endeavor. While early computers were much too costly for practical use, Wasserman (1965) argues already in 1965 that 'an almost morbid fascination with the latest form of technology' (p. 9) had contributed to a climate where the computerization of library functions started to look like both an imperative and an inevitability.[16] Coordinate indexing played a central role in this context, because '[i]t was the only system for retrieving bibliographic information that was compatible with computers of the mid-1950s' (Segesta and Reid-Green, 2002, p. 28). The formulation 'compatible with' highlights the fact that coordinate indexing is not bound to a particular material substrate. It plays the role of a technical element that needs to be articulated in conjunction with other elements to become a working system. While coordinate indexing represents a departure from the library tradition, its success relied on the straightforward compatibility with existing technical trajectories, including manual list comparison, punched cards, film, and early computing hardware. This compatibility can be attributed to its practical and conceptual simplicity, especially compared to Ranganathan's similarly flexible but much more complicated colon classification. In the early 1950s, information processing machinery was both an incipient reality and a future promise, but Taube and others fully invested this emerging technological space, arguing that 'bibliographic coordination is designed for machine sorting and collating' (Taube, 1951, p. 70), even if it was not clear which technical trajectory would eventually dominate.

The limited space for terms on edge-notched cards prompted Mortimer Taube to develop his list-based approach, which allowed for the creation of what we would today call 'high-dimensional datasets', where each item can have a large number of variables or properties. The very same limitation led Mooers to develop a system that was relying on similar principles but used a different implementation. At a time when Taube, a trained librarian, was promoting his manual technique using concepts and terms familiar to librarians, the mathematician Mooers was not only pondering similar ideas, but building actual machines.[17] In a paper titled 'Zatocoding Applied

16   As Segesta and Reid-Green argue, asking 'if the computer could help' had become 'a natural question' (2002, p. 28) by 1953 already.
17   In an oral history interview, Mooers himself claims primacy for the general idea and argues that Taube's success came because '[h]e was a great salesman and a smooth talker and he charmed the librarians' (Mooers and Mooers, 1993, p. 13).

to Mechanical Organization of Knowledge' (Mooers, 1951), he described a system using punched cards and the postcoordination logic of independent 'descriptors' that could be combined to create complex queries. Interestingly, Mooers's presentation did not focus on the question of classification but on solving the limitations of punched card systems. Zatocoding was a form of superimposed coding that drew heavily on Shannon's statistical theory of information to encode a much larger number of terms onto the limited number of fields available on a card. This allowed him to build a system using the well-mastered and thus relatively cheap punched card technology, which became 'the first broadly marketed system that did not use precoordinated (like Library of Congress subject headings) subject terms' (Williams, 2002, p. 22). While Mooers's implementation of coordinate indexing worked well with existing equipment, Taube's combination of reference numbers and lists was almost perfectly suited for the operating principles of digital computers. Experiments with IBM's first commercial scientific computer, the IBM 701, clearly showed the workability of the method in 1954 (Bracken and Tillitt, 1957; Segesta and Reid-Green, 2002). After all, comparing lists is something that computers do very well indeed.

Overall, coordinate indexing funneled into quite different working systems that could be demonstrated, evaluated, and experimented with. These systems, understood as technical individuals combining coordinate indexing principles with other elements, promised to deliver what Charles Baggage already identified as the machine's 'one great advantage', namely 'the check which it affords against the inattention, the idleness, or the dishonesty of human agents' (Babbage, 1832, p. 54). This both resonates with the 'pessimism about the scope and quality of human reason' (Heyck, 2012, p. 100) underpinning the overt distrust in librarians and highlights the computer's capacity to take over simple tasks like finding the same numbers in long lists, which become infeasible for humans beyond a certain point due their repetitive nature and mind-numbing dullness. Coordinate indexing thus reveals how Peters's (1988) assertion that '[t]he computer existed as a practice before it existed as a machine' (p. 15) is both enlightening and insufficient. The technique shows how older and more elementary principles can find expression in contemporary practices, traveling through different technical trajectories, in this case from notched cards to manual list comparison to digital computers. But coordinate indexing also sits at the precise point where these continuities begin to dissolve into a technical universe where a machine can perform a range of simple operations so quickly and competently that it 'has outgrown its basic triviality by several orders of magnitude' (Dijkstra, 1974, p. 608).

A Postcoordinated Universe

The introduction of coordinate indexing is not a story of traditional analog approaches being swept away by the digital computer. The various applications built around it find a certain success, but even in 1975, Van Rijsbergen still emphasizes that '[m]any automatic information retrieval systems are *experimental*' (Van Rijsbergen, 1975, p. 1). Public libraries have long remained unaffected by information retrieval: when they finally begin computerization in the 1970s, they focus on digitizing existing card catalogs and on making them more easily available as OPACs (Online Public Access Catalogs) (cf. Husain and Ansari, 2006). Boolean operators have certainly found their way into more recent bibliographic systems and simple keyword indexing coexists with more elaborate techniques like subject headings and hierarchical classification. Computerization and digitization can lead to standardization and normalization, but they also provide margins of plasticity, with the effect that actual working systems are often hybrids fusing seemingly contradictory techniques into productive arrangements.

Rather than follow coordinate indexing through historical instances of adoption and adaptation, I want to develop two different lines of interpretation. In Chapters 5 and 6, I will show how the basic 'term on item' setup becomes the starting point for a variety of statistical techniques that seek to deepen its *empirical* dimension, in particular regarding automated indexing and ranking. In the last section of this chapter, however, I want to dive further into the notion of postcoordination. This will lead me beyond coordinate indexing to one of the most influential techniques in all of computing, the relational model for database management.

Postcoordination

The question of how knowledge should be arranged has never been innocent. Darnton (1999, p. 191ff.) explains how Diderot and D'Alembert's seemingly minor modifications to the tree of knowledge inherited from Francis Bacon was in fact a risky political move that reshuffled the place of secular and religious ideas, and, in doing so, installed the philosophers of the Enlightenment as the supreme guardians of knowledge. Scholars such as Sanford Berman (1980, 1989) have repeatedly argued that traditional but still heavily used classification systems such as the DDC have strong biases, sidelining not only non-Western cultures on the whole but also marginalized groups in Western societies. As Bowker and Star have shown in their influential *Sorting Things Out* (1999), classification systems have infrastructural qualities that organize and orient important aspects of our lives. The epistemic character of particular knowledge ordering schemes is an imminently political issue, even without taking computers into account.

But the rejection of library principles by early information scientists is not so much a rejection of a particular classification or thesaurus. It is not a battle pitting one taxonomy against another but a fundamental contestation of two thousand years of knowledge organization en bloc. The pioneers mentioned in this chapter never pursued the mechanization of established practices and principles. What they developed and promoted was a new way of conceiving order as 'ordering', a dynamic process and practice that was fundamentally different from the creation and application of stable, universal systems. While the information wars have sometimes been framed as pitting 'people' against 'machines', this narrative obfuscates a more conceptual and indeed more political disagreement about where one should turn when looking for order and organization. What the information scientists propose – and this may sound familiar to readers versed in Silicon Valley disruption talk – is that knowledge ordering no longer needs stewards that guarantee the coherence and adequacy of a tree or 'world map'. Diderot and D'Alembert's philosopher, acting as cartographer of knowledge 'at a vantage point, so to speak, high above this vast labyrinth' (D'Alembert, 1995, p. 47), is no longer seen as the guarantor of impartiality, but as a problem: overreaching, slow, and subjective. The very 'image of objectivity', to speak with Daston and Galison (1992), is under attack.

On a very general level, we find the charge that traditional ordering schemes serve the needs of the library rather than its patrons (Lerner, 2009, p. 189), going back to Thomas Carlyle calling Anthony Panizzi's catalog 'a vanity of bibliographical display' (Svenonius, 2000, p. 10). But the change in perspective is more concretely tied to the real and imagined audiences for catalogs and retrieval systems: the library traditionally adheres to an inclusive mandate emphasizing public education and universal access while the special libraries and documentation centers embrace the specialist looking for actionable answers rather than broad knowledge. If the librarians following the Enlightenment tradition emphasize the creation of a shared, systematic, and stable map of all knowledge that functions as an institutional gateway to a well-tended garden of knowledge, the early information scientists see a growing rift between the 'finished schemes of the nineteenth century' (Taube, 1952, p. 167), such as the DDC and LCSH, and a twentieth-century witness to 'the swirling rush of new literature and new forms of literature' (Taube, 1952, p. 167). Where the former value the universality of classification schemes as an asset, the latter see it as a liability that risks cementing outdated worldviews and missing the realities of modern science. Positivist universalists like Otlet and Bliss regarded science and knowledge as singular and unified whereas the actual scientists involved in information retrieval saw a complex, dynamic, and highly specialized research landscape, where established knowledge is constantly questioned and disciplinary boundaries shift. While Otlet (1934) shunned even subject headings as 'too empirical' and 'scattered' (p. 381) to provide the synthetical and well-ordered perspective the CDU epitomizes, empiricism and fragmentation are precisely what information retrieval pioneers championed, at least to a certain degree. The 'grand narrative' of the Enlightenment, emancipation through universal education in a shared space of knowledge, had not so much lost its 'credibility' (Lyotard, 1984, p. 37) in this context, but rather its relevance to an application space that defined itself in more directly utilitarian terms. Most of the complicated details of bibliographic control were seen as neither necessary nor helpful to exploit information as a resource for knowledge creation and decision-making. On the contrary, debating whether two editions of a book constitute the same work, to name a common example from library theory, was deemed a frivolous waste of time.

Early information science literature thus brims with doubts about the capacity of librarians (or any other nonscientist) to adequately deal not only with the mass of material but also with the subject matter. The struggle for what Wilson (1968) calls 'descriptive control' – the 'ability to line up a population of writings in any arbitrary order, to make the population march to one's command' (p. 25) – was real and (information) scientists sought to wrestle it away from human(ist) knowledge mediators. If we understand the bibliographic chain as composed of source material, ordering scheme (or simply 'library system'), and searcher, traditional librarianship argued that a lot of expertise was required in the middle to assure the tasks of indexing, organizing, and guiding patrons. The new perspective, however, tried to 'disintermediate' the process by buttressing expertise at the two ends of the chain: the specialists writing and self-indexing the material and the decision-makers querying the material were the actual experts and the middle suddenly appeared as a source of delay, incompetence, and subjectivity. Coordinate indexing achieved this goal by two means: on the one end, simple 'uniterms' (Taube's term) or 'descriptors' (Mooers's term) were attributed without order or preconceived relationship (precoordination) and could even be taken directly from the text, eliminating dependence on the expertise of catalogers and indexers (Lerner, 2009, p. 189); and on the other end, postcoordination allowed searchers to create elaborate queries by combining multiple words in Boolean sequences. The central element, here, is the shift of syntactic and semantic expressivity from the bibliographic language to the query language, meaning that 'the vocabulary control hitherto deemed essential for indexing purposes could be replaced by additional controls introduced during the search formulation and retrieval processes' (Salton, 1987, p. 3). The map is replaced by a system laying dynamic pathways into a multidimensional information space. Knowledge organization is reframed as a function of knowledge access. Long before the term 'disintermediation' becomes a Silicon Valley favorite and 'postmodern theorists and artists embrace hyperlinks as a way of freeing us from anonymous specialists organizing our databases and deciding for us what is relevant to what' (Dreyfus, 2009, p. 12f.), information scientists developed coordinate indexing as a means to orchestrate knowledge organization around an algorithmic technique.

This technique indeed relies on highly queryable information grids that index atomized items with a vocabulary that is itself analytically disassembled into singular terms. The use of Boolean operators already points to the role of calculation as a means for synthetical reassembly. The standard model uses set theory to capture these processes in mathematical terms but coordinate indexing can be conceptualized in more than one way. Although 'coordination' refers to the combination of search terms (Varlejs, 2004, p. 96), it evokes a formal or conceptual understanding of a bibliographic system as a 'coordinate system', a geometric construct that assigns a place to each item in a multidimensional 'document space' lacking a clear navigational form like a list or tree structure (cf. Luhn, 1953). A coordinate index, that is, a space constituted and populated by items and associated terms, represents what I will call throughout the book an 'intermediate form',[18] an abstract representation that results from a process of formalization into a normalized structure. Intermediate forms both enable and require calculation to generate specific outputs like result lists or visual diagrams. Creating such outputs represents an act of ordering that is distributed over two components: data adhering to an intermediate form, for example, a coordinate index covering a specific collection of documents, and a technique for algorithmic inference, for example, a system that implements Boolean querying.

---

18   I am generalizing this notion from Tan (1999), who argues that text mining has two broad components. The first, text refinement, basically contains the transformations that yield a 'purified' representation of a text, that the second step, knowledge distillation, will then process. This purified representation is referred to as intermediate form.

Whether we think about the search process as intersecting sets of terms or already as a geometric operation is less important, at this point, than the idea that the query indeed defines the category or conceptual 'location' of objects to be retrieved. A logical condition – keywords coordinated with the help of Boolean operators – is submitted into a document space defined by an indexing vocabulary and the system returns a specific *selection* of items that meet the condition as the result. Order, here, is no longer a stable representation, but the momentary outcome of a calculative process that combines indexed items into ad hoc categories. While the card catalogue already introduced a form of mobility that, in practice, 'rescued' the stable organization of knowledge by allowing the universalist systems of the nineteenth century to integrate new works into their folds without too much trouble, the mobility of the coordinate index is more fundamental. Unlike the knowledge maps of the DDC or CDU, coordinate indexing is no longer a system of order but a postuniversalist ordering technique that folds knowledge into a specific and temporary arrangement upon request.

This is a first step into a computational universe, even if the technical simplicity and widespread use of what boils down to a combination of tagging and Boolean search makes it difficult to think of coordinate indexing as a particularly powerful algorithmic technique. But Mortimer Taube, although not a mathematician himself, already observed that the mechanical transformations at hand have the potential to provide a genuine epistemic surplus:

> [T]he system of bibliographic coordination would, if properly set up, disclose to the searcher more information than had been put into the system. It has become fashionable to state that we can get nothing more out of machines than we put into them. This is like saying that since mathematics is tautological there is never any more in the conclusion than there is in the premises. It is certainly true that when we add a column of figures with an adding machine we get an answer that we did not know even though the answer was implicit in the column of figures. Similarly, in the system of bibliographic coordination, by combining various categories, we may get information which, although implicit in the system, was never explicitly recognized. (Taube, 1951, p. 71)

Although Taube mainly thought about the enhanced potential for information retrieval afforded by Boolean operators, we can easily imagine forms of calculation that describe the document collection on the whole, for example, in terms of 'co-tagging' patterns: if we consider two terms to be 'related' if they are applied to the same item, we can generate a network that shows the relationships between all tags used in a collection, providing a conceptual map that could be used as overview or means of navigation. Much of algorithmic information ordering indeed relies on techniques that make 'implicit' information explicit in the way Taube describes, often by harvesting expressions of 'latent human judgment' (Kleinberg, 1999, p. 606), in this case patterns in term attribution.

The epistemic surplus an algorithmic ordering technique is able to deliver usually springs from the combination of many small instances of counting or calculation, that is, from 'methods of buying originality with plodding' that depend on the existence 'of slaves which are [...] persistent plodders' (Wang, 1960, p. 3). Computerization has made such persistent plodders universally available and datafication has multiplied the 'items' available in digital form. Early uses in scientific data processing already indicate that Boolean operators can be applied to any set of entities that can be captured into the intermediate form of a coordinate index. If this requirement is met, the full set of algorithmic manipulations becomes readily available. The considerable possibilities for adaptation and extension become clearer if we consider, for example, the use of the basic 'term on item' principle in websites implementing collaborative indexing. While the word 'folksonomy', a portmanteau of 'folk' and 'taxonomy' (Vander Wal, 2007), no longer raises eyebrows, the proponents of free, user-driven keyword attribution, popularized by sites like Flickr or Delicious, not only reiterated many of the arguments[19] made in favor of coordinate indexing in the 1950s but showed how multiuser tagging can be processed in multiple ways to produce rankings, recommendations, or semantic enrichment.

With an eye on Simondon's theoretical apparatus, one could argue that information ordering has developed around trajectories that combine basic principles such as keyword tagging, intermediate forms promoting calculability, and algorithmic ordering techniques into working systems, each element providing ample opportunity for variation. Coordinate indexing constitutes such a sprawling lineage, even if the genealogical connections between contemporary variants and the fundamental propositions by pioneers like Mooers and Taube have largely faded.

But much like the complicated trajectories that constitute what I have called, somewhat callously, 'traditional' library techniques, this is not a

---

19   Mathes (2004), for example, explicitly presents Folksonomies as an alternative to the DCC, LCSH, and other forms of controlled or hierarchical classification system.

linear journey toward some real or imaginary telos. Interestingly, Taube himself tempered expectations concerning the mechanization of coordinate indexing and later became a vocal critic of mathematization, in particular regarding measures of relevance (Taube, 1965). But Taube's version of coordinate indexing became a (commercial) success[20] and represents an early manifestation of the resolutely perspectivist direction the field had taken. Shera gives a particularly vivid depiction of that vision:

> [T]he classification of knowledge will not be a fixed and unalterable pattern, based on a priori assumptions regarding the most neatly logical arrangement of books on the shelves, but a series of quite widely varying schematisms, each constructed for a specific purpose, or purposes, in accordance with a particular point of view or philosophic orientation. (Shera, 1952, p. 17)

But does information retrieval really subscribe to epistemological pluralism? Is it a harbinger of a postmodern reservation toward 'grand narratives' (Lyotard, 1984)? I would suggest a somewhat different interpretation. Taking Hjørland's (2010) classification of indexing approaches based on 'epistemological assumptions' (p. 74) as reference, there is little reason to belief that the perspectivism manifest in coordinate indexing is based on serious hermeneutical or critical doubts about the very possibility of knowledge independent from interpretation. What we find, at this stage, is either a pragmatic empiricism that holds that the world is knowable, even if knowledge necessarily remains partial and guided by interest, or a form of rationalism that suggests 'that subjects are constructed logically from a fundamental set of categories' (Hjørland, 2010, p. 74) that can be permutated at will. Even if the practice of keyword attribution relied mostly on empirical principles, controlled vocabularies could tend in the direction of Ranganathan's analytico-synthetic method which sought to reduce 'the vast universe of knowledge to a set of atomic concepts and certain basic relations among them' (Svenonius, 2000, p. 175). While the historical configuration is more complicated, one could argue that coordinate indexing bifurcates into the largely empiricist tradition of information retrieval, which relies predominantly on statistical techniques, and a more rationalistic, logic-based trajectory that is most clearly epitomized by the relational model for database management.

---

20   Maybe unsurprisingly, Taube's first customers were the US military and, later, NASA.

The Relational Database Model

Although the relational model for database management, one of the most pervasive technical ideas in all of computing, would easily merit a full chapter or book, even a shorter discussion can help us understand how postcoordination principles have found their way into techniques that define contemporary information ordering more broadly. This is not so much a straightforward case of idea transfer from coordinate indexing to the world of databases but a parallel invention that highlights the contingent character of technical evolution.

The 'library problems' information retrieval set out to tackle were certainly seen as pressing issues, but questions concerning information organization were virulent in other areas of computing, in particular around the different bureaucratic tasks performed in companies and governmental organizations. In areas like accounting, inventory and employee management, payroll handling, or airline reservations, the problem was not to find some document that would respond to a (possibly vague) information need but the precise creation, access, and manipulation of data entries and the generation of reports from the analysis of clearly defined sets of records. Early file management systems placed a first abstraction layer for file manipulation on top of physical storage in the late 1940s and report generators created the kind of aggregate data overviews management decisions could be based on (cf. Haigh, 2006). In the 1960s, we see the emergence of the first Database Management Systems (DBMS) that were not designed for a single task but 'general-purpose' in the sense that users could create their own data models, that is, the semantic structures that would define and organize the files in their databases. These DBMS implemented either a hierarchical (e.g., IBM's Information Management System) or a networked (e.g., GE's Integrated Data Store) database model that defined how users could design their specific data models and interact with the data (cf. Haigh, 2009). Also referred to as 'navigational' database systems, these systems relied on pointers linking one record to the next, making it possible to fast-forward to the correct location on magnetic tape and turning the programmer writing applications on top of a DBMS into a 'mobile navigator who is able to probe and traverse a database at will' (Bachman, 1973, p. 654). Navigational systems were designed to deal with some of the central problems DBMS were facing, namely the speed of data access and the assurance of integrity and coherence when data were modified. But although the pointer system constituted a layer of abstraction on top of the physical storage, the logical representation of data was still largely tied to its physical organization and programmers had to find pathways through trees or networks of records to get to the desired information. This is precisely the problem that Edgar F. Codd's famous introduction of the relational model starts off with:

> Future users of large data banks must be protected from having to know how the data is organized in the machine (the internal representation). (Codd, 1970, p. 377)

To achieve a situation where only the 'natural structure' (p. 377) of data is visible, that is, the logical or informational structure as specified in the data model, 'physical data independence' was a first requirement. But decoupling the logical structure of the data from the idiosyncrasies of the underlying hardware was far from trivial. Coordinate indexing for bibliographic control was adequately served by early computing machinery because it implied little more than intersecting lists of reference numbers and hardly any data modification. Handling large sets of critical company files and frequent, possibly complex updates was an entirely different matter. The first commercially available Relational Database Management System (RDBMS), Oracle, thus only came to market in 1979, nine years after Codd's initial proposal. Sequential storage such as magnetic tape was not well-suited for the level of detachment the relational model sought to realize and hard disk storage had to become more common to practically succeed in 'hiding away' (most) concerns with physical representation from users.

The considerable difficulties in implementing the relational model are in stark contrast to its simplicity on the user side. All data are stored in an intermediate form called 'relation' – 'basically just a mathematical term for table' (Date, 2004, p. 26) – that has the familiar shape of rows of records sharing the same fields or columns. As Dourish (2017) explains, what is being 'related' here are the data items or fields in a row so that 'one row expresses the relationship between the name "John Smith" and the social security number 123-45-6789' (p. 117). Unlike coordinate indexing, where all items were covered by the same vocabulary, the relational model allows for the creation of many different tables, each defining its own variables. The requirement that row and column order in a table should be irrelevant (Date, 2004, p. 148) reminds us that relations are again abstract data structures waiting to be queried rather than visual representations already carrying a particular sequence. In coordinate indexing, the terms attributed to an item constitute a *set* rather than a list, because their sequence carries no importance or meaning. The first indexing term is not more significant

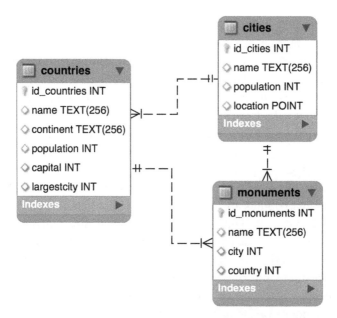

A mock-up data model, visualized with MySQL Workbench, consisting of three relations (tables): 'countries', 'cities', and 'monuments'. Note that the city information is not stored directly in the two other tables: the fields 'capital' and 'largestcity' on the table 'countries' are *foreign keys* that link to the field 'id_cities', the *primary key* of the 'cities' table. The table 'monuments' is connected to both of the other tables in the same way. In a 'real' database, each table would be filled with actual records.

than the last one. Likewise, in the relational model, the grid of rows and columns is a *relation* rather than a table because the order of rows should not carry any information.

Fields can have a number of predefined types, such as INT (integer), TEXT, BOOLEAN, or DATETIME in the case of the popular MySQL RDBMS. Although the relational model is clearly much richer than a simple term on item system, critics still consider it 'semantically impoverished' (Stonebraker and Hellerstein, 2005, p. 19) because complex data structures, such as classes, are not native to the model and have to be (awkwardly) modeled out of tables. Indeed, to create more elaborate semantic constructs at the data-modeling stage, database designers use primary key/foreign key relationships to connect tables to each other.

Looking at the mock-up data model shown above, one can imagine that cities may appear in all kinds of contexts, for example, as capitals of countries or as locations for monuments. In this case, the table for countries stores two links (foreign keys) to another table, which holds the actual information about cities and attributes a unique identifier (primary key) to each city. The table recording monuments links to both 'countries' and 'cities' in the same way. If some information about a city changes, it is not necessary to modify each table where city information appears, only the specific row in the 'cities' table. This avoids one of the cardinal sins in relational database design, redundancy, and makes data manipulation much less cumbersome. The process of chopping up the world into information atoms without redundancy is called 'normalization' and it is part of the data-modeling stage, where the application domain (e.g., cities and their monuments) is captured into a set of tables. Job titles like 'database architect' indicate that there is a real body of professional knowledge that informs these practices.

Normalization entails analytical disaggregation to make sure dependencies between attributes are arranged in ways that database integrity and maximum expressivity at query time are guaranteed. Although the relational model provides a richer semantic vocabulary of data types and the possibility to specify precoordinated relationships between tables, modeling practices follow coordinate indexing in refraining, as much as possible, from using composite elements.[21] All information should be distributed over separate and independent variables or 'coordinates'. The more fine-grained the decomposition, the greater the potential for recomposition at query time. If, for example, an address is properly decomposed into postal code, city, district, street name, and house number, each of these elements can become a means for making distinctions between informational items and, by extension, the things they stand for. One cannot easily list the inhabitants of a city in a database where city names in addresses have not been isolated into a separate field. Normalization is an 'elimination procedure' (Codd, 1970, p. 381) that seeks to find and decompose all such instances.

It should thus come as no surprise that the second main ingredient of the relational model, next to the relation as universal intermediate form, is a powerful query language that incorporates further possibilities for postcoordinated *selection* of items, but also for aggregate *description* and different forms of *ranking* or *grouping*. Here, the main difference with earlier database models is that data is not retrieved by writing a program that forages through a tree or network of records (record-at-a-time principle) but by making a declarative statement (query) that demarcates a group or class of records fitting the statement (set-at-a-time principle), much like in coordinate indexing. Similar to the move from the elaborate structures of the LCSH and DDC to simple keyword combinations, we switch from navigating complex prearranged trees or networks to logical declarations

---

21   'A relation is *in first normal form* if ... none of its domains has elements which are themselves sets' (Codd, cit. in Date, 2006, p. 109).

using a grid of attributes. Based on more advanced predicate logic rather than the basic Boolean logic used in coordinate indexing, query languages such as SQL (Structured Query Language) have considerable 'linguistic power' (p. 381) in the sense that they make it possible to submit complex 'questions' to a database. Here are some examples in MySQL syntax, the SQL dialect used by the MySQL RDBMS:

SELECT * FROM table_name WHERE condition ORDER BY field_name;

The basic schema of a MySQL query. In natural language, it would read: select the records, showing all fields ('*'), from the table 'table_name' that satisfy a certain condition and order the result table by the field 'field_name'.

SELECT name FROM countries WHERE population > 1000000 ORDER BY population DESC;

Here, we are using the basic query schema to select the names of countries with more than one million inhabitants, ordering the results from largest to smallest.

SELECT * FROM cities WHERE name LIKE "new%";

This query retrieves all cities with names beginning with 'new'.

These examples show how different field types allow for modes of selection that go substantially beyond the binary presence/absence condition coordinate indexing is built on. Text search, numerical cutoffs, or, in more recent systems, geographical queries are some of the examples for the richer semantics and much more developed calculative expressivity RDBMS allow for. Since the result of a query is also a table, queries can be stacked on top of each other and stabilized into virtual tables, called 'views'. Queries can also cover several tables at once, using for instance primary/foreign key relationships to draw data together.

There would be much more to say about the relational model, but I hope that my short presentation shows how the principles of atomization (disassembly) and postcoordination (reassembly) have found expression in other areas of computing. While recent years have seen both extensions to the relational model and the proliferation of alternatives for certain task profiles, in particular in areas where retrieval speed primes over query power, it is hard to overstate the importance of RDBMS in the context of almost any bureaucratic process. In line with the postuniversalist perspective outlined above, the relational model emphasizes a local approach to the modeling of databases and 'gives no indication about the way in which the world is to be represented by a collection of relations' (Schmid and Swenson, 1975, p. 212). As a general-purpose technique, it provides no classification systems itself, merely the building blocks for modeling data into atomized units with disassembled properties and the query engine as a means for flexible postcoordination. The goal is 'application-independent design' emphasizing decomposition into the smallest logical components in order to remain open for future uses: 'we are primarily concerned with what the data *is*, rather than how it will be *used*' (Date, 2004, p. 330). Data modeling with an RDBMS has indeed stronger affinities with Ranganathan's analytico-synthetic and 'rationalist' (Hjørland, 2010, p. 74) technique, which seeks to disassemble the world into its smallest logical components, than with the more empirical, pragmatic, and purpose-oriented approach to uniterm selection in coordinate indexing. The difference in broad 'philosophical' outlook is one of the ways we can recognize how 'each kind of information technology embeds its own definition of information' (Haigh, 2009, p. 20).

From the start, the relational model emphasized combinatorial analysis, that is, the creation of *new* information through querying, over mere storage and access. Indeed, it explicitly carried the hope that hiding the technical complexities of data storage behind a simple, yet powerful model would turn managers and other nonprogrammers into direct users of database systems, allowing them to model and query the databases that support their daily practices themselves.[22] Even if the SQL-fluent business executive probably remains an exception, the relational model has certainly facilitated the integration of databases into organizational processes, supporting informational control not only through much greater ease for storing and accessing information but also through the creation of knowledge layers that establish, examine, and process distinctions in various ways. While terms like 'knowledge discovery' or 'data mining' point toward processes of examination and 'exploitation' that are not necessarily limited to relational data pools, RDBMS have rapidly integrated various types of calculation and analysis, for example, statistical techniques.

SELECT AVG(population) FROM cities WHERE Y(location) < 0;

This example calculates the average population of cities in the southern hemisphere.

---

22   Driscoll (2012) even argues that RDBMS were central to a wider interest in personal databases and 'database populism' in the 1980s.

This MySQL query shows how easily selection and statistical description can be combined, yielding rich and malleable analytical possibilities that allow for complex forms of interrogation and aggregate description that may not have been anticipated when the initial data model was created. These capabilities are particularly interesting in settings where databases store transactional data, for example, sales records or inventory movement. Here, the discovery of patterns or trends can directly inform managerial decisions. This opens onto the vast field of practices and techniques often addressed as 'business intelligence', which rely heavily on the exploitation of atomized data stored in RDBMS. An exploration of the various direct and indirect relationships between the relational model and a 'new spirit of capitalism' (Boltanski and Chiapello, 2005) emphasizing flexibility, autonomy, and the capacity to adapt to change is beyond the scope of this book, but it is hardly far-fetched to claim that there has been no technology more central in helping 'giants learn to dance' (Kanter, 1989).

This highlights a major difference between coordinate indexing and the relational model: the former was initially applied to 'a population of writings' (Wilson, 1968, p. 25), whereas the latter hoped to capture many different kinds of population from the beginning, most significantly populations of human beings. In this context, neither the standardizing and normalizing effects of database practices should be left unmentioned, nor their potential to impose 'an impoverished, limited language, one that uses the norm to constitute individuals and define deviants' (Poster, 1990, p. 94). But such forms of bureaucratic and informational control can be exerted with the help of almost any database system. What distinguishes the relational model is its flexibility, which makes it useful for totalitarian modes of power as well as supportive of Deleuzian models of control where real-time modulation primes over static attribution (Deleuze, 1992). It vividly reminds us that customization and standardization are not opposites but form complicated relationships (cf. Star and Ruhleder, 1996). If anything, the relational model makes if particularly easy to move from the individual to the population and back again, allowing for modes of grouping that are only limited by the granularity of the data. If a process of formalization is articulated around atomization, it increases the potential for subtle modes of differentiation and 'soft' bio-politics (Cheney-Lippold, 2011, p. 165) where identity and difference are established dynamically and not as hard cuts along preestablished categories.

I will come back to these questions, but to build a broader perspective on the technicity of contemporary information ordering, I want to caution against a perspective that sees databases, and RDBMS in particular, exclusively through a bureaucratic or administrative lens. Their application space has become much more general. Today, RDBMS form the information storage backends for many different programs and services. Running as server software that application programs can access for their own purposes or distributed in the form of programming modules ready for direct integration, they function as constitutive elements in myriad systems, forming a central core between interfaces for data collection and output facilities. The popular content management system WordPress, for example, has at its center a MySQL database that is fed through an administrative interface. An infinite number of navigable views on the stored contents can be generated with the help of a powerful and flexible template engine that draws directly on the combinatorial possibilities of the underlying database system. Many of the adaptive capacities of web interfaces I have highlighted in the introduction are made possible by the presence of an RDBMS running in the background. Information ordering algorithms, such as ranking or recommendation engines, are performing calculations that decide which story to bring to the top or which video to play next, but this requires that data are ready-to-hand in the form of information atoms that can be accessed and grouped at will. Facebook, to name one of the most impressive examples, uses a complex and heavily optimized data infrastructure to handle the petabytes of information fragments it assembles into familiar interfaces. But this infrastructure still runs MySQL at its core, producing granular and highly queryable repositories of data that ranking and recommendation – including personalized advertisement – can then draw on (Matsunobu, 2016).

Following these operative chains, the next chapter turns to a second tradition building on the coordinate indexing model. Espousing an empiricist rather than rationalist perspective, this tradition makes heavy use of statistical techniques to count a world cut into pieces.

Bibliography

Babbage, C. (1832). *On the Economy of Machinery and Manufactures* (3rd ed.). London: Charles Knight.

Babbage, C. (1864). *Passages from the Life of a Philosopher*. London: Longman.

Bachman, C. W. (1973). The Programmer as Navigator. *Communications of the ACM 16*(11), 653-658.

Barr, A., and Feigenbaum, E. A. (eds.). (1981). *The Handbook of Artificial Intelligence, Volume I*. Los Altos: William Kaufmann.

Becker, J., and Hayes, R. M. (1963). *Information Storage and Retrieval: Tools, Elements, Theories*. New York: John Wiley.

Beniger, J. (1986). *The Control Revolution: Technological and Economic Origins of the Information Society*. Cambridge, MA: Harvard University Press.

Berman, S. (1980). DDC 19: An Indictment. *Library Journal 105*(5), 585-589.

Berman, S. (1989). DDC 20: The Scam Continues. *Library Journal 114*(15), 45-48.

Bliss, H. E. (1935). The System of the Sciences and the Organization of Knowledge. *Philosophy of Science 2*(1): 86-103.

Boltanski, L., and Chiapello, E. (2005). *The New Spirit of Capitalism* (G. Elliott, trans.). London: Verso.

Bowker, G. C., and Star, S. L. (1999). *Sorting Things Out*. Cambridge, MA: MIT Press.

Bowles, M. D. (1999). The Information Wars: Two Cultures and the Conflict in Information Retrieval, 1945-1999. In M. E. Bowden, T. Bellardo Hahn, and R. V. Williams (eds.), *Proceedings of the 1998 Conference on the History and Heritage of Science Information Systems* (pp. 156-166). Medford: Information Today.

Bracken, R. H., and Tillitt, H. E. (1957). Information Searching with the 701 Calculator. *Journal of the ACM 4*(2), 131-136.

Buckland, M. (1992). Emanuel Goldberg, Electronic Document Retrieval, and Vannevar Bush's Memex. *Journal of the American Society for Information Science 43*(4), 284-294.

Bush, V. (1945). As We May Think. *Life Magazine*, 9 October, 112-124.

Campbell-Kelly, M., and Aspray, W. (1996). *Computer: History of an Information Machine*. New York: Basic Books.

Casson, L. (2001). *Libraries in the Ancient World*. New Haven: Yale University Press.

Chan, L. M. (1994). *Cataloging and Classification: An Introduction* (2nd ed.). New York: McGraw-Hill.

Chandler, A. D., Jr. (1977). *The Visible Hand*. Cambridge, MA: Harvard University Press.

Cheney-Lippold, J. (2011). A New Algorithmic Identity: Soft Biopolitics and the Modulation of Control. *Theory, Culture & Society 28*(6), 164-181.

Codd, E. F. (1970). A Relational Model of Data for Large Shared Data Banks. *Communications of the ACM 13*(6), 377-387.

Cohen, I. B. (2005). *The Triumph of Numbers: How Counting Shaped Modern Life*. New York: W. W. Norton & Company.

Cutter, C. A. (1876). *Rules for a Printed Dictionary Catalogue*. Washington, DC: Government Printing Office.

D'Alembert, J. (1995). *Preliminary Discourse to the Encyclopedia of Diderot* (R. N. Schwab, trans.). Chicago: University of Chicago Press.

Darnton, R. (1999). *The Great Cat Massacre and Other Episodes in French Cultural History*. New York: Basic Books.

Daston, L., and Galison, P. (1992). The Image of Objectivity. *Representations 40*, 81-128.

Date, C. J. (2004). *An Introduction to Database Systems* (8th ed.). London: Pearson Education.

Date, C. J. (2006). *Date on Database: Writings 2000-2006*. Berkeley CA: Apress.

Deleuze, G. (1992). Postscript on the Societies of Control. *October 59*(Winter), 3-7.

Desrosières, A. (2001). How Real Are Statistics? Four Possible Attitudes. *Social Research 68*(2), 339-355.

Dewey, M. (1876). *A Classification and Subject Index for Cataloguing and Arranging the Books and Pamphlets of a Library*. Hartford: Case, Lockwood & Brainard.

Dijkstra, E. W. (1974). Programming as a Discipline of Mathematical Nature. *American Mathematical Monthly 81*(6), 608-612.

Dourish, P. (2017). *The Stuff of Bits: An Essay on the Materialities of Information*. Cambridge, MA: MIT Press.

Doyle, L. B. (1975). *Information Retrieval and Processing*. New York: John Wiley & Sons.

Drabinski, E. (2013). Queering the Catalog: Queer Theory and the Politics of Correction. *The Library Quarterly 83*(2), 94-111.

Dreyfus, H. (2009). *On the Internet* (2nd ed.). London: Routledge.

Driscoll, K. (2012). From Punched Cards to 'Big Data': A Social History of Database Populism. *Communication+1 1*, 2-33.

Dupuit, J. (1995). De la mesure de l'utilité des travaux publics. *Revue Française d'Économie 10*(2), 55-94.

Edwards, P. N. (1996). *The Closed World: Computers and the Politics of Discourse in Cold War America*. Cambridge, MA: MIT Press.

Ensmenger, N. L. (2010). *The Computer Boys Take Over: Computers, Programmers, and the Politics of Technical Expertise*. Cambridge, MA: MIT Press.

Foucault, M. (1982). The Subject and Power. *Critical Inquiry 8*(4), 777-795.

Foucault, M. (2005). *The Order of Things: An Archaeology of the Human Sciences*. London: Routledge.

Foucault, M. (2007). The Meshes of Power. In J. W. Crampton and S. Elden (eds.), *Space, Knowledge and Power: Foucault and Geography* (pp. 153-162). Aldershot: Ashgate.

Foucault, M. (2008). *The Birth of Biopolitics: Lectures at the Collège de France, 1978-79* (G. Burchell, trans.). Basingstoke: Palgrave Macmillan.

Foucault, M. (2009). *Security, Territory, Population: Lectures at the Collège de France, 1977-78* (G. Burchell, trans.). Basingstoke: Palgrave Macmillan.

Gardey, D. (2008). *Écrire, calculer, classer. Comment une evolution de papier a transformé les sociétés contemporaines (1800-1940)*. Paris: La Decouverte.

Gigerenzer, G., Swijtnik, Z., Porter, T., Daston, L., Beatty, J., and Krüger, L. (1989). *The Empire of Chance: How Probability Changed Science and Everyday Life*. Cambridge: Cambridge University Press.

Goody, J. (1977). *The Domestication of the Savage Mind*. Cambridge: Cambridge University Press.

Goody, J., and Watt, I. (1963). The Consequences of Literacy. *Comparative Studies in Society and History 5*(3), 304-345.

Gull, C. D. (1965). The Present State of Library Automation. In F. B. Jenkins (ed.), *Proceedings of the Clinic on Library Applications of Data Processing* (pp. 1-14). Urbana: Graduate School of Library Science, University of Illinois at Urbana-Champaign.

Habermas, J. (1975). *Legitimation Crisis*. Boston: Beacon Press.

Hacking, I. (1990). *The Taming of Chance*. Cambridge: Cambridge University Press.

Haigh, T. (2006). 'A Veritable Bucket of Facts': Origins of the Data Base Management System. *ACM SIGMOD Record 35*(2), 33-49.

Haigh, T. (2009). How Data Got Its Base: Information Storage Software in the 1950s and 1960s. *IEEE Annals of the History of Computing 31*(4), 6-25.

Harris, M. H. (1999). *History of Libraries in the Western World* (4th ed.). Metuchen: Scarecrow Press.

Hartmann, F. (2006). Von Karteikarten zum vernetzten Hypertext-System. *Telepolis*, 29 October. Retrieved from https://www.heise.de/tp/.

Hartmann, F. (2012). Die Logik der Datenbank. In F. Hartmann (ed.), *Vom Buch zur Datenbank. Paul Otlets Utopie der Wissensvisualisierung* (pp. 11-61). Berlin: Avinus.

Hartmann, F. (2015). Paul Otlets Hypermedium. Dokumentation als Gegenidee zur Bibliothek. *LIBREAS Library Ideas 28*, n.p.

Hayden, C. (n.d.) Welcome Message from Carla Hayden, 14th Librarian of Congress. Retrieved from https://www.loc.gov/about/.

Heyck, H. (2012). Producing Reason. In M. Solovey and H. Cravens (eds.), *Cold War Social Science* (pp. 99-116). New York: Palgrave Macmillan.

Hjørland, B. (2010). The Importance of Theories of Knowledge: Indexing and Information Retrieval as an Example. *Journal of the American Society for Information Science and Technology 62*(1), 72-77.

Husain, R., and Ansari, M. A. (2006). From Card Catalog to Web OPACs. *DESIDOC Bulletin of Information Technology 26*(2), 41-47.

Kanter, R. M. (1989). *When Giants Learn to Dance: Mastering the Challenges of Strategy, Management, and Careers in the 1990s*. New York: Simon & Schuster.

Kilgour, F. G. (1969). Computerization: The Advent of Humanization in the College Library. *Library Trends 18*(1), 29-36.

Kilgour, F. G. (1997). Origins of Coordinate Searching. *Journal of the American Society for Information Science 48*(4), 340-348.

Kleinberg, J. M. (1999). Authoritative Sources in a Hyperlinked Environment. *Journal of the ACM 46*(5), 604-632.

Krajewski, M. (2011). *Paper Machines: About Cards & Catalogs, 1548-1929* (P. Krapp, trans.) Cambridge, MA: MIT Press.

Krämer, S. (1988). *Symbolische Maschinen. Die Idee der Formalisierung im Geschichtlichen Abriß*. Darmstadt: Wissenschaftliche Buchgesellschaft.

Laurel, B. (1993). *Computers as Theatre*. Boston: Addison-Wesley.

Lerner, F. (2009). *The Story of Libraries: From the Invention of Writing to the Computer Age* (2nd ed.). New York: Continuum.

Luhn, H. P. (1953). A New Method of Recording and Searching Information. *American Documentation 4*(1), 14-16.

Luhn, H. P. (1968a). Auto-Encoding of Documents for Information Retrieval Systems. In C. K. Schultz (ed.), *H. P. Luhn: Pioneer of Information Science: Selected Works* (pp. 126-131). New York: Spartan Books.

Lyotard, J.-F. (1984). *The Postmodern Condition: A Report on Knowledge* (G. Bennington and B. Massumi, trans.). Manchester: Manchester University Press.

Mackenzie, A. (2017a). *Machine Learners: Archaeology of a Data Practice.* Cambridge, MA: MIT Press.

Manning, C. D., Schütze, H., and Raghavan, P. (2008). *Introduction to Information Retrieval.* Cambridge: Cambridge University Press.

Maron, M. E. (1963). A Logician's View of Language-Data Processing. In P. L. Garvin (ed.), *Natural Language and the Computer* (pp. 128-151). New York: McGraw-Hill.

Mathes, A. (2004). Folksonomies – Cooperative Classification and Communication through Shared Metadata. Graduate School of Library and Information Science, University of Illinois Urbana-Champaign, December. Retrieved from http://adammathes.com/academic/computer-mediated-communication/folksonomies.html.

Matsunobu, Y. (2016). MyRocks: A Space- and Write-Optimized MySQL Database [blog post], 3 August. Retrieved from https://code.facebook.com/posts/190251048047090/myrocks-a-space-and-write-optimized-mysql-database/.

Mittelstrass, J. (1979). The Philosopher's Conception of *Mathesis Universalis* from Descartes to Leibniz. *Annals of Science 36*(6), 593-610.

Mooers, C. N. (1950). *The Theory of Digital Handling of Non-Numerical Information and Its Implications to Machine Economics* (Zator Technical Bulletin, no. 48). Retrieved from https://babel.hathitrust.org/cgi/pt?id=mdp.39015034570583.

Mooers, C. N. (1951). Zatocoding Applied to Mechanical Organization of Knowledge. *American Documentation 2*(1), 20-32.

Mooers, C. D., and Mooers, C. N. (1993). Oral history interview by K. D. Corbitt [tape recording]. Minneapolis: Charles Babbage Institute, 22 June. Retrieved from https://conservancy.umn.edu/handle/11299/107510.

Murray, S. A. P. (2009). *The Library: An Illustrated History.* New York: Skyhorse Publishing.

Otlet, P. (1934). *Traité de documentation. Le Livre sur le livre.* Bruxelles: Editiones Mundaneum.

Parikka, J. (ed.). (2011). *Medianatures: The Materiality of Information Technology and Electronic Waste.* Ann Arbor: Open Humanities Press.

Peters, J. D. (1988). Information: Notes toward a Critical History. *Journal of Communication Inquiry 12*(2), 9-23.

Petty, W. (1655). *Several Essays in Political Arithmetik* (4th ed.). London: D. Browne, J. Shuckburgh, J. Wiston, B. White.

Porter, T. (1995). *Trust in Numbers: The Pursuit of Objectivity in Science and Public Life*. Princeton: Princeton University Press.

Poster, M. (1990). *The Mode of Information: Poststructuralism and Social Context*. Chicago: University of Chicago Press.

Rau, E. P. (2007). Managing the Machine in the Stacks: Operations Research, Bibliographic Control and Library Computerization, 1950-2000. *Library History* 23(2), 151-168.

Rayward, W. B. (1994). Visions of Xanadu: Paul Otlet (1868-1944) and Hypertext. *Journal of the American Society for Information Science 45*(4), 235-250.

Rush, J. E. (1982). Library Automation Systems and Networks. In M. C. Yovits (ed.), *Advances in Computers, Volume 21* (pp. 333-422). New York: Academic Press.

Salton, G. (1987). Historical Note: The Past Thirty Years in Information Retrieval. *Journal of the American Society for Information Science 38*(5), 375-380.

Satija, M. P. (2002). *Manual of Practical Colon Classification* (4th ed.). New Delhi: Concept Publishing.

Schmid, H. A., and Swenson, J. R. (1975). On the Semantics of the Relational Data Model. In J. P. Fry (ed.), *SIGMOD '75: Proceedings of the 1975 ACM SIGMOD International Conference on Management of Data* (pp. 211-223). New York: ACM.

Schulte-Albert, H. G. (1971). Gottfried Wilhelm Leibniz and Library Classification. *Journal of Library History 6*(2), 133-152.

Segesta, J., and Reid-Green, K. (2002). Harley Tillitt and Computerized Library Searching. *IEEE Annals of the History of Computing 24*(3), 23-34.

Shera, J. H. (1952). Special Librarianship and Documentation. *Library Trends 1*(2), 189-199.

Siegert, B. (2007). Cacography or Communication? Cultural Techniques in German Media Studies. *Grey Room 29*, 26-47.

Siegert, B. (2013). Cultural Techniques; or The End of the Intellectual Postwar Era in German Media Theory. *Theory, Culture & Society 30*(6), 48-65.

Star, S. L. (1998). Grounded Classification: Grounded Theory and Faceted Classification. *Library Trends 47*(2), 218-232.

Star, S. L., and Ruhleder, K. (1996). Steps toward an Ecology of Infrastructure: Design and Access for Large Information Spaces. *Information Systems Research 7*(1), 111-134.

Stonebraker, M., and Hellerstein, J. M. (eds.). (2005). *Readings in Database Systems* (4th ed.). Cambridge, MA: MIT Press.

Svenonius, E. (2000). *The Intellectual Foundation of Information Ordering*. Cambridge, MA: MIT Press.

Swetz, F. J. (1987). *Capitalism and Arithmetic: The New Math of the 15th Century*. La Salle: Open Court.

Tan, A.-H. (1999). Text Mining: The State of the Art and the Challenges. In *Proceedings of the PAKDD Workshop on Knowledge Discovery from Advanced Databases* (pp. 65-70). Retrieved from https://pdfs.semanticscholar.org/9a80/ec16880ae43dc20c792ea3734862d85ba4d7.pdf.

Taube, M. (1951). Functional Approach to Bibliographic Organization: A Critique and a Proposal. In J. H. Shera and M. E. Egan (eds.), *Bibliographic Organization* (pp. 57-71). Chicago: University of Chicago Press.

Taube, M. (1952). Special Librarianship and Documentation. *American Documentation 3*(3), 166-167.

Taube, M. (1965). A Note on the Pseudo-Mathematics of Relevance. *American Documentation 16*(2), 69-72.

Vander Wal, T. (2007) Folksonomy Coinage and Definition, 2 February. Retrieved from http://vanderwal.net/folksonomy.html.

Van Rijsbergen, C. J. (1975). *Information Retrieval*. London: Butterworths.

Varlejs, J. (2004). The Technical Report and Its Impact on Post-World War II Information Systems. In M. E. Bowden, T. Bellardo Hahn, and R. V. Williams (eds.), *Proceedings of the 1998 Conference on the History and Heritage of Science Information Systems* (pp. 89-99). Medford: Information Today.

Wang, H. (1960). Toward Mechanical Mathematics. *IBM Journal of Research and Development 4*(1), 2-21.

Wasserman, P. (1965). *The Librarian and the Machine*. Detroit: Gale Research.

Weinberg, A. M. (1963). *Science, Government, and Information: The Responsibilities of the Technical Community and the Government in the Transfer of Information: A Report of the President's Science Advisory Committee*, Washington, DC: The White House. Retrieved from https://files.eric.ed.gov/fulltext/ED048894.pdf.

Wiegand, W. A., and Davis, Jr., D. G. (eds.). (1994). *Encyclopedia of Library History*. New York: Garland Publishing.

Williams, R. V. (2002). The Use of Punched Cards in US Libraries and Documentation Centers, 1936-1965. *IEEE Annals of the History of Computing 24*(2), 16-33.

Wilson, P. (1968). *Two Kinds of Power: An Essay on Bibliographical Control*. Berkeley: University of California Press.

Wright, A. (2008). The Web Time Forgot. *New York Times*, 17 June.

Yates, J. (1989). *Control through Communication*. Baltimore: Johns Hopkins University Press.

Young, L. C. (2017). *List Cultures: Knowledge and Poetics from Mesopotamia to BuzzFeed*. Amsterdam: Amsterdam University Press.

Zachary, G. P. (1999). *Endless Frontier: Vannevar Bush, Engineer of the American Century*. Cambridge, MA: MIT Press.

5. From Frequencies to Vectors

Abstract

This chapter investigates early attempts in information retrieval to tackle the full text of document collections. Underpinning a large number of contemporary applications, from search to sentiment analysis, the concepts and techniques pioneered by Hans Peter Luhn, Gerard Salton, Karen Spärck Jones, and others involve particular framings of language, meaning, and knowledge. They also introduce some of the fundamental mathematical formalisms and methods running through information ordering, preparing the extension to digital objects other than text documents. The chapter discusses the considerable technical expressivity that comes out of the sprawling landscape of research and experimentation that characterizes the early decades of information retrieval. This includes the emergence of the conceptual construct and intermediate data structure that is fundamental to most algorithmic information ordering: the feature vector.

Keywords: information retrieval, text mining, vector space model, feature vector

While the potential of digital computers is recognized early on, the 1950s, 1960s, and even 1970s were marked by physical hardware that was either forbiddingly expensive or limited in terms of its computational capacity – and often both. The computer plays the role of an omnipresent 'evocative object' (Turkle, 1985) that stimulates (technical) imagination, but often remains practically inadequate or financially out of reach. In the context of information retrieval, the 1950s were mainly dedicated to exploring the concrete possibilities of novel hardware for document search, while the conceptual side revolved in large parts around coordinate indexing (Salton, 1987, p. 375). But toward the end of the decade and more so in the 1960s, there was a growing interest in more computational – including more heavily mathematized – approaches to information processing. While these attempts remain largely experimental, they yield new techniques

Rieder, B., *Engines of Order: A Mechanology of Algorithmic Techniques*. Amsterdam: Amsterdam University Press, 2020

DOI 10.5117/9789462986190_CH05

that form empirical, statistics-driven trajectories setting off from the basic coordinate indexing setup. If the relational model for database management has become the main technique for storing and accessing large pools of structured data through logical manipulation, techniques revolving around the measurement of frequencies in various 'real-world' datasets underpin contemporary search applications as well as areas like machine learning, recommender systems, or personalization. These techniques remained largely confined to academic research and specialized task domains until the 1990s, when computer hardware became sufficiently powerful and the web pushed information ordering into the limelight in spectacular fashion.

The following two chapters investigate the inception of statistical information ordering by discussing early attempts to move from manual indexing to the automatic processing of text documents. While Chapter 6 is mostly dedicated to M. E. Maron's work in automatic classification based on Bayesian filtering, a prototypical example for machine learning, this chapter explores the foundations for the statistical processing of text and, by extension, of any data that can be made to conform to the intermediate forms introduced in this context. After a short discussion of Roberto Busa's attempt to create an index to the work of Thomas Aquinas, I focus on the work of two German-born pioneers: Hans Peter Luhn, who laid the groundwork for the application of statistical methods to automatic indexing, and Gerard Salton, one of the central figures in the creation and development of the field of information retrieval. Salton was the director of the influential SMART project, where many fundamental techniques were developed and experimented with, and constitutes a direct link to the present: his work spans four decades and his doctoral students include influential figures such as Amit Singhal, Google's employee no. 176 and former Head of Search (Hardy, 2016). While I cannot fully account for the various technical trajectories leading from the 1960s to our current moment, I will show how certain technical schemas continue to underpin algorithmic information ordering today.

Text as Raw Material: Roberto Busa

The earliest use of information machinery to process the content of text documents can be attributed to a Jesuit monk from Italy, Roberto Busa, and his project of creating an index to the work of the scholastic philosopher and theologian Thomas Aquinas. At the center of this project was to be a file listing every word used in Aquinas's massive oeuvre (~11 million words), where it appears, and the sentence it appears in. Specific indexes and concordances[1] would then be generated from that file (Winter, 1999, p. 6). Busa thought that these resources would be highly useful to Aquinas scholars like himself, since '[e]ach writer expresses his conceptual system in and through his verbal system' (Busa, 1980, p. 83) and this system could be analyzed in great detail with the help of indexes. As part of his dissertation, defended in 1946, Busa had already made a manual but complete concordance index of the single word 'in', using 10,000 handwritten cards (Busa, 1980, p. 83). Producing a full *Index Thomisticus* with the same technique would have been unfeasible and Busa began looking for mechanical aides. An extensive visit in 1949 to 25 universities in the US – 'asking about any gadget that might help in producing the type of concordance I had in mind' (Busa, 1980, p. 83) – ultimately led him to the office of Thomas Watson, Sr., the legendary head of IBM and, at the time, the world's most powerful 'information mechanizer'. Initially hesitant, Watson ultimately decided to assign an engineer, Paul Tasman, to the task and provided extensive support to Busa's project through IBM's offices in Milan (Burton, 1981, p. 139).

Since IBM's punched card systems were mainly built for accounting purposes, the processing of text for Busa's project required the invention of a complex tool chain – or a technical ensemble in Simondon's terminology – that combined several machines, beginning with a typewriter-like punching machine for digitizing the full text and ending with a card sorter (Winter, 1999). With the support of IBM and the resources of the Catholic Church at his disposal, Busa constructed a hybrid technical schema or 'program', combining single-task data processing machinery with the manual labor of (female) typists and (male) clergy (Birnbaum et al., 2017; Busa, 1980). What is actually possible in technology depends, in no small part, on the available means and Busa could compensate for the technical limitations of the time with an early version of Amazon's Mechanical Turk. In 1951, a proof of concept using four of Aquinas's hymns was published under the title *S. Thomae Aquinatis Hymnorum Ritualium: Varia Specimina Concordantiarum: A First Example of a Word Index. Automatically Compiled and Printed by IBM Punched Card Machine.* This work already demonstrated the considerable computational expressivity afforded by a digitized text corpus, even if the actual processing was performed through human/machine teamwork. The system was able to isolate individual words by running over the blanks on each sentence card, the basic data structure all text was transcribed into.

---

1   A concordance lists all occurrences of a word in a corpus and provides some context, in most cases the immediately preceding and following words.

Most contemporary programming languages contain functions to split character strings in this way and the one in Python, *str.split*(), even separates on white space by default. Cutting up longer documents or data sequences into chunks creates the discrete units further (statistical) processing commonly operates on. In this case, atomizing literary works into sentences and further into words allowed Busa's program to create an alphabetical list of all words and their frequencies, a list sorted by occurrence count, and the concordance itself, which embedded each word in its immediate context and pointed to the hymn and verse number (Burton, 1981).

The project highlights the particular status high-quality manual labor has kept to this day: with the help of ten priests working over two years, Busa created the *Lexicon Electronicum Latinum* that provided the linguistic knowledge for machine lemmatization, that is, for the grouping together of inflected word forms ('badly', 'worse') under a single dictionary form ('bad') (Busa, 1980, p. 86; Winter, 1999, p. 12). This allowed for the compilation of frequency lists of lemmas to supplement words lists and to link words to their lemmas in various ways. Since language is notoriously unruly, lemmatization can generally not be reduced to a set of simple rules and is therefore hard to perform automatically, as anyone working in text-mining knows all too well. For many tasks, manual work still sets the gold standard and the human workforce Busa had at his disposal makes certain parts of his project hard to emulate over 60 years later. The central role such 'propositional' or 'declarative' knowledge – facts, descriptions, or rules generated or at least verified by human agents – continues to play in many areas testifies to the value of manual labor in computational processes. The synonym database WordNet, the collection of location names GeoNames, or the eminently machine-readable knowledge repository that is Wikipedia are just three examples for heavily used knowledge repositories that, like Busa's *Lexicon*, can be used to enrich algorithmic work. Indeed, Google's capacity to create, compile, and verify propositional knowledge in various ways, from crowdsourcing to an internal labor force, is one of the main reasons why it is far from trivial to emulate the performance of the company's search engine. Rather than seeing such manual labor in opposition to pure statistical processing, we have to appreciate how the former can inject (semantic) detail into the latter and vice versa. Computing is always an assembly of different techniques into a coherent system and output performance easily trumps epistemological purity in concrete application settings.

We have to understand, however, that Busa's process remained painfully slow, even if the use of machinery certainly sped up the work. Punched card machines were overwhelmed by the colossal task at hand and even when computers began to replace the single-task data processing hardware, editing and proofreading still had to be done manually. The first volumes of the full *Index Thomisticus*[2] therefore only appeared in 1974 (Burton, 1981). And the computational component was rather modest: while the project introduced word frequency lists and lemmatization, two fundamental techniques in contemporary text processing, Busa's goal was to produce practical tools for Aquinas scholars, not to 'understand' the text through deeper statistical analysis. He knew, from the beginning, which outputs he wanted to generate, and his use of information processing hardware was ultimately a largely logistical venture that drew little of its epistemological imagination from the new technicities at hand.

That being said, we need to be weary of a perspective that is merely looking for straight lines leading to the present. The process of technical accumulation is no stranger to continuity, dispersion, and divergence, but also riddled with parallelism, side-stepping, transfer, convergence, saturation, standardization, and a good number of dead ends. Simondon's thinking indeed guides us to resist the temptation to apply rigid principles to the contingent trajectories technical objects delineate. These trajectories unfold in and contribute to the medium of technicity, where the capacity to arrange stable forms of causality is bounded by technicity itself; technical objects are not the visible result of some invisible law of technological progress, but the exact opposite: technological evolution is the result of the genesis of technical objects and schemas as they appear, evolve, and perish. If one favors 'empirical historical objects' over 'philosophical idealization' (Siegert, 2013, p. 10), the record is necessarily jagged and muddled.

Toward a Statistics of Text: Hans Peter Luhn

While Busa's work remains well-known and is often singled out as the founding moment of the digital humanities, the rest of this chapter is dedicated to a more 'computationally involved' lineage that can, remarkably, be traced to the same office of Thomas Watson, Sr., at IBM. In 1948, a year before Busa, James W. Perry and G. Malcolm Dyson, two chemists and leading advocates of punched cards, petitioned Watson to dedicate additional research and development efforts to finding mechanical solutions for scientists' specific information problems (Williams, 2002, p. 21; Schultz, 1968, p. 6). As a result of that meeting, IBM assigned Hans Peter Luhn, a prolific creator and one of

2   The current version can be found at: http://www.corpusthomisticum.org, accessed 12 December 2019.

the company's top engineers, to the task. Over the following fifteen years, Luhn developed an impressive number of new techniques and ideas, some of them in the form of working systems, others far ahead of what could be considered practical at the time (cf. Moore, 1968). His official status as 'inventor' inside of IBM gave him the freedom to pursue various directions with little regard to commercial viability (Moore, 1968, p. 16).

Initial contributions to mechanical documentation, such as the Luhn Scanner, were directly based on his substantial experience with the design of electronic relays and other information processing equipment. But as large electronic computers and magnetic tape became available in the 1950s, his work shifted toward techniques that could be implemented in digital machinery (Moore, 1968, p. 19). The 80 patents Luhn received over his career testify to his rich technical imagination and bind back to Simondon's notion that 'sensitivity to technicity [...] allows for the discovery of possible assemblages' (Simondon, 2017, p. 74), which holds particularly true at a time when the spaces of both formal conceptualization and mechanical realization were in a fundamental state of flux. The part of Luhn's work I am most interested in clearly profited from his broad familiarity with various technical domains and his competence in applied mathematics: there was a wide reservoir of technicity to draw on. Salton summarizes Luhn's work in a succinct passage:

> Between 1957 and 1959, at a time when the documentation literature was still largely preoccupied with the use of punched card and film equipment, a remarkable series of papers appeared by H. P. Luhn that actually formed the beginning of the computer age in the text processing field. Before Luhn, most experts were convinced that the terms and keywords attached to the information items would have to be chosen by trained indexers, or by persons with special insight in the subject areas under consideration. Luhn was the first to propose that the computer could handle not only the keyword matching and sorting tasks, but also the intellectual work related to the content analysis of written texts. (Salton, 1987, p. 376)

Much like Mooers and Taube, Luhn's work in information retrieval developed in directions that differed fundamentally and explicitly from traditional library techniques and set out from arguments that should sound familiar at this point:

> The essential purpose of literature searching is to find those documents within a collection which have a bearing on a given topic. Many of the systems and devices, such as classifications and subject-heading lists, that

have been developed in the past to solve the problems encountered in this searching process are proving inadequate. The need for new solutions is at present being intensified by the rapid growth of literature and the demand for higher levels of searching efficiency. [...] Rather than subtilize the artful classificatory schemes now in use, new systems would replace them in large part by mechanical routines based on rather elementary reasoning. (Luhn, 1957, p. 309)

The focus on 'rather elementary reasoning' and simplicity is shared with coordinate indexing and these principles are clearly visible in Luhn's most well-known invention, the Key Word in Context (KWIC) technique. Addressing the desire for quick processing and dissemination (Wasserman, 1965, p. 63), often captured in the term 'current awareness', a KWIC index is simply a machine-generated concordance, generally applied to lists of titles taken from scientific journals. Luhn did not take credit for the much older idea of concordance indexing itself but proposed a fully automated system 'affording speed of compilation, accuracy and completeness' (Luhn, cit. in Stevens, 1968, p. 28). To make this a reality, certain hardware requirements had to be met, but, more importantly, there had to be some heuristic to decide which words to use as index terms in the first place, which means that 'rules have to be established for differentiating between what is significant and nonsignificant' (Luhn, 1960, p. 289). Luhn proposed two approaches to the problem, which still play an imminently important role today. The first one simply specifies lists of words to ignore, now often referred to as 'stop words' collected in so-called 'droplists'. These manually created lists are another way of bringing explicit, propositional knowledge into algorithmic processing, not unlike Busa's *Lexicon Electronicum Latinum*, even if the purpose is exclusion rather than lemmatization.[3]

The second approach requires some background: Human language had first become object of explicit statistical examination in the 1930s when American linguist George Kingsley Zipf and others discovered that word use frequencies followed a power law probability distribution, meaning that 'there are a few very common words, a middling number of medium frequency words, and many low frequency words' (Manning and Schütze, 1999, p. 24). For Luhn, and basically everyone else in information retrieval, this opened the door toward a statistical approach to keyword selection and exclusion. The argument holds

---

3   'A list of nonsignificant words would include articles, conjunctions, prepositions, auxiliary verbs, certain adjectives and words such as "report," "analysis," "theory," and the like. It would become the task of an editor to extend this list as required' (Luhn, 1960, p. 161).

that the words that appear most frequently in the English language – articles, conjunctions, and so forth – are also the ones that carry the least amount of meaning and can therefore be eliminated (Luhn, 1968a, p. 127). The same could be done for the very rare words making up the long tail of the frequency curve. Luhn was reluctant, however, to give a strong answer to the heatedly debated question which precise statistical measures would identify the most significant terms (Fairthorne, 1968). For both the manual and the statistical approach to keyword exclusion, he took an explicitly empiricist and perspectivist stance that characterizes large parts of the information ordering field: concrete exclusion lists or cutoff points should be set by the users of a system in the context of their specific requirements and experiences.

Luhn's work broadly resonates with the postuniversalist perspective I have described in the last chapter but ads a nuance to the distinction between precoordinated (a priori) and postcoordinated (a posteriori) bibliographic systems. He called systems like the DDC or LCSH 'adopted' (Luhn, 1968b, p. 167) since they are compiled by experts independently from any concrete site of application. But he further divided postcoordinated approaches into two separate categories: the 'synthetic' type, epitomized by coordinate indexing, is manually 'created by reasoning, judgement and experience with regard to the field covered by a given document collection' (Luhn, 1968b, p. 168); the 'native' type, however, 'is derived from the individual collection it is to serve by statistical analysis' (Luhn, 1968b, p. 168). Both types are inductive and empirical, but the first type relies on specifically human faculties while the second is the work not merely of a machine, but of a system that implements a particular technique or method to make the material 'speak'. This technique serves as a means to 'harvest' the latent meaning present in the text and the resulting index is thus 'born of the collection' (Luhn, 1968b, p. 168). These formulations evoke contemporary tropes, for example, the idea that algorithmic techniques herald ways of 'listening to the world' (Lynch, cit. in Silberman, 2000, n.p.), processes more akin to 'farming' (Domingos, 2012, p. 81) than to programming, or even an 'end of theory' where we 'view data mathematically first and establish a context for it later' (Anderson, 2008, n.p.).

Luhn's work in this and other areas can be described as a series of attempts to close the distance between information processing machinery, concrete scenarios of use, and applied mathematics. The KWIC system was the most successful outcome in terms of adoption, constituting a second pillar of computer use in information retrieval besides coordinate indexing (cf. Wasserman, 1965, p. 49ff.), but Luhn's desire to further mathematize a wide variety of 'library problems' is clearly visible from his very first paper (Luhn, 1953), where he suggests seeing coordinate indexes as multidimensional geometric spaces. This idea, already alluded to in the last chapter, later becomes one of the fundamental paradigms in information retrieval though Salton's canonical formulation. Luhn's most far-reaching contribution, however, concerned the application of statistical reasoning to the full text of documents.

Much of the (early) work in information retrieval starts from the idea that the expertise required to classify a document is already present in the text itself, putting the question of how to extract it at the center. Authors suggesting their own keywords, emergent classification based on manual attribution, and automatic extraction from titles or abstracts were all but steps toward the holy grail of mechanical documentation, namely the processing of the full contents of documents. Concrete objectives were less ambitious than Otlet's plan to extract atomic 'facts' from documents, but the direction was broadly similar. Even if information retrieval has come to use terms like 'knowledge' or 'meaning' quite prudently, Luhn leaves little doubt that this is what he wants to tackle. And, indeed, we should consider these efforts to mechanize a particular kind of 'intellectual effort' (Luhn, 1957, p. 313) as a form of machine intelligence that extends the practical space of what computers can do. While the field of artificial intelligence emerges at roughly the same time around attempts to use either logical inference or connectionist models to simulate 'general' intelligence, the work of Luhn and others epitomizes the 'task-specific' intelligence that has come to drive the resurgence of the field over the last two decades. Having developed in parallel for most of their history, there has been a 'process of reintegration' (Russell and Norvig, 2010, p. 26), fueled by the practical and commercial conditions created by computerization, where information retrieval, artificial intelligence, and other areas now appear as a tightly connected disciplinary cluster. If Judea Pearl's *Probabilistic Reasoning in Intelligent Systems* (1988) marks the final rehabilitation of probabilistic reasoning in artificial intelligence, Luhn's work should be seen as one of its beginnings.

What stands out from 'A Statistical Approach to Mechanized Encoding and Searching of Literary Information', the 1957 paper one could consider the founding document of the field now called 'text mining', is that Luhn embeds the application of statistical techniques to textual material in a theoretical frame that describes human communication as a probabilistic process relying on shared experience (Luhn, 1957, p. 310). Although the theory of symbolic interaction is not mentioned explicitly, Luhn's conceptual starting point evokes the work of George Herbert Mead and, in particular, of Herbert Blumer, who holds that meaning is constructed through individual and collective processes of interpretation and interaction (cf. Blumer, 1962). In Luhn's perspective, shared experience and semantic 'overlap' receive a statistical interpretation, in the sense that '[t]he fewer experiences we have in common, the more words we must use' (Luhn, 1957, p. 310). The understanding that text is not a self-contained encoding of meaning and that communication requires commonality thus renders propositional, logic-based approaches infeasible[4] and also constitutes an important caveat for statistical text processing. Extracting notions or ideas from 'free-style renderings of information' (Luhn, 1957, p. 312) with any confidence would only be possible in areas that have a coherent 'syntax of notions' or 'technese' (Luhn, 1957, p. 312), such as technical or academic disciplines. A hierarchical mapping of such fields, further divided into 'age classes' to account for changes in substance and vocabulary over time, would demarcate zones with sufficient internal coherence and would speed up the search process by targeting only specific sections of the index. These considerations testify both to Luhn's prudent attitude and to the enormous technical limitations that characterized early experiments.

Interestingly, the idea that an index should be a syntax of notions rather than mere words is embedded in this rudimentary theory of communication and it becomes a central vehicle for arriving at a reduced vocabulary of 'high quality' index terms. Indeed, what Luhn proposes is not an index based on brute word frequencies, but a technique that uses not only the manual and statistical cutoff principles described above, but also a thesaurus, manually assembled by experts in the field, that normalizes the 'words of similar or related meaning into "notional" families' (Luhn, 1957, p. 314) identified by a single keyword. Just like Busa's *Lexicon* reduces word forms into single lemmas, an idea that Luhn integrates as well (Luhn, 1968a), the thesaurus serves to connect the different words authors may use to describe an idea to the more standardized syntax of notions used for actual indexing.

The proposal is thus still quite close to coordinate indexing since notional descriptors are selected by human experts, even if automated concordances would help with vocabulary decisions. But there are two important deviations or extensions. First, with the help of normalization and 'data cleaning', another contemporary term somewhat applicable here, the machine attributes the chosen set of notions/keywords automatically. This is what

---

4   'The very nature of free-style renderings of information seems to preclude any system based on precise relationships and values, such as has been developed in the field of mathematics. Only by treatment of this problem as a statistical proposition is a systematic approach possible' (Luhn, 1957, p. 312). Interestingly, the logician M. E. Maron (1963) makes a very similar argument.

'mechanized encoding' refers to: the system runs through the full text of a document, eliminates 'irrelevant words', lemmatizes where possible, and uses the thesaurus to translate words to notions. That way, '[t]he ideas of an author would not be narrowed, biased, or distorted through the intervention of an interpreter' (Luhn, 1957, p. 316). In one experiment, this resulted in 10 to 24 keywords describing each document (Luhn, 1968a, p. 129). The process amounts to the first stage in what is generally considered to be a two-stage process in more contemporary formulations: '[t]*ext refining* that transforms unstructured text documents into an *intermediate form*; and *knowledge distillation* that deduces patterns or knowledge from the *intermediate form*' (Tan, 1999, p. 65). The term 'unstructured', here, is misleading: text quite obviously has some kind of structure; what is happening is a projection of certain *aspects* of that structure into the intermediate data structure further processing will be based on. In most cases, at least in information retrieval, this involves atomization and reduction of syntactic salience, similar to what we have seen with coordinate indexing.

Second, the resulting intermediate form in Luhn's experiment is not a binary coordinate index, where a descriptor either applies or not for a given document, but a 'frequency list' that records the occurrence counts for each keyword. This 'weighting' of keywords not only allows for a more differentiated appreciation of keyword significance (Luhn, 1968a, p. 127) but also opens up a space for search and retrieval that goes beyond Boolean queries and enables more fine-grained matching through the pivotal notion of *statistical similarity*:

> The more two representations agreed in given elements and their distribution, the higher would be the probability of their representing similar information. (Luhn, 1957, p. 313)

Mathematical notions of similarity, which I will discuss in more detail further down, are now regularly used for all kinds of tasks, from clustering to classification, but Luhn's application setting is less far-reaching. His system would ask users to formulate a query 'in the form of an essay describing reasons for searching information, giving as many details as possible concerning the problem, objectives, assumed, speculated or planned approaches to solutions, references to other authors and subjects' (Luhn, 1957, p. 315f.). The essay was then to be encoded using the same indexing technique in order to compare its statistical keyword profile to the profiles of the documents in the collection. The degree of similarity between the 'query essay' and each document is then used for both retrieving and ranking results.

While I do not want to make a causal explanation here, an investigation concerned with technical objects as beings that function needs to consider that Luhn operates in a technical space where the limited speed and memory of computing machinery mean that anything beyond index search can hardly be imagined. The real-time searching of full text we have become so used to is at least 20 years away and the statistical approach Luhn proposes is still very much focused on the creation of an index that fits into existing coordinate indexing systems and remains useful for manual retrieval.

But Luhn nonetheless thinks about directions for further development. Long passages on 'the special care taken by the author in wording titles, headings, and resumes' (Luhn, 1957, p. 315) highlight possibilities for (semantic) differentiation and enrichment we know well from search engines, where specific structural elements, for example, text appearing in titles or subheadings, are given higher weight in a document representation. This points beyond the common treatment of documents as mere 'bags of words', a common formulation that goes back to a 1954 paper by Zellig Harris (1954), who argued, somewhat ironically, that language should *not* be treated as an assembly of words without order or structure. Luhn's attention to the structural properties of documents yields two other statistical techniques that have become part of the canon. While I only want to allude to the first, a method for text summarization referred to as 'automatic generation of literature abstracts' (Luhn, 1958), the second concerns an analytical technique that was taken up in the field of science studies in the early 1980s as 'co-word analysis' (Callon et al., 1983) and has since become a common method for the study of textual contents (Danowski, 1993). If we do not discard all structural features of documents, we find that words do not randomly appear in the vicinity of other words, but show a 'degree of association' (Luhn, 1968a, p. 129) that carries meaning.[5] Luhn uses the physical proximity of words in a text to establish a network of branching structures where links are created when two words co-occur at least twice (Luhn, 1968a, p. 130). Setting such explicit cutoff points manually is a common practice in the implementation of algorithmic techniques and a major moment of discretion. But Luhn also uses frequency to make distinctions between first and second order 'significant words'. His graphical representation makes the analytical principle particularly clear.

5   The same intuition has prompted many different approaches and techniques, maybe most prominently 'topic modeling' through Latent Dirichlet Allocation (LDA), first introduced in Blei, Ng, and Jordan (2003). This (Bayesian) technique frames a dataset as a series of 'topics' and attempts to find groups of units (e.g., words) that characterize these topics in an optimal way. In early 2018, the paper had almost 22,500 citations on Google Scholar.

LATTICE OF WORD-PAIR LINKAGES

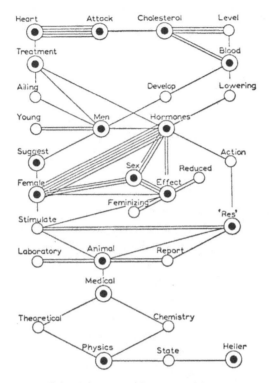

Nodes designate word frequency as follows:
1st order ◉ = 5 and over; 2nd order ○ = 2, 3, 4
Frequency of word pairs is indicated by number of intervening links

Luhn's representation of a medical text discussing heart attacks. Nodes are differentiated as first and second order significant words and link thickness indicates frequency of co-occurrence. Reprinted from Luhn, H. P. (1959) Auto-Encoding of Documents for Information Retrieval Systems. In M. Boaz (ed.), *Modern Trends in Documentation* (pp. 45-58). New York: Pergamon Press.

The diagram relies on the thesaurus approach and the network is arranged manually and not by a layout algorithm, but the selection of terms and their co-occurrence is based on the automated processes I have just described. Until this point, a manual 'simulation' of algorithmic processing has never been too far removed, but Luhn breaks from his exceptionally sober style to make clear that this is no longer the case here:

It is only due to the speeds and logical capabilities of electronic machines that such methods become practical in the first place and no sane person would recommend that such extensive operations be applied manually. (Luhn, 1968a, p. 131)

This has in part to do with the number of documents and index terms he hoped to cover, but also with the type of processing required for the identification of word-pairs. Even a relatively small number n of index terms gives rise to $n*(n-1)/2$ possible word combinations if we discount the order of their association, removing manual compilation from the realm of possibility. This procedure thus fleshes out what I mean by terms such as 'nonanthropomorphic' information ordering or 'compound behavior'. Individual gestures remain traceable but repeating them over and over again produces an effect of 'buying originality with plodding' (Wang, 1960, p. 3). If, as Swanson (1988) argues, 'the goal of much advanced IR is to make computers do humanlike things' (p. 97), this does not happen in ways that neatly emulate human practice. Although the 'rather elementary reasoning' (Luhn, 1957, p. 309) each processing step is based on remains clearly accessible to human understanding, its epistemic surplus emerges, progressively, over many cycles of iteration and aggregation. The computer produces an appreciation of the texts it parses that is not a simulation of human understanding but a different breed of cognition that enables different ordering practices. While pondering whether machines could ever think like humans remains riveting, we may indeed want to invest greater effort in making sense of techniques that produce genuine forms of machine intelligence.

I will come back to these issues at the end of the chapter but to throw a larger net into the field, I now turn to a body of work that develops Luhn's statistical experiments further into a canonical model for information retrieval and introduces the notion of statistical normalization. To better understand the significance of these developments, however, we need to pay at least some attention to information retrieval's formation as a discipline.

Evaluation and Epistemology

Even if Luhn is certainly not the only person experimenting with statistical measures in the 1950s, his work becomes a reference and starting point for a coagulation of the emerging field around statistical principles. During the 1960s, researchers like Cyril W. Cleverdon, Lauren B. Doyle, Gerard Salton, Karen Spärck Jones, H. Edmund Stiles, Don R. Swanson, and others transform information retrieval into an identifiable discipline distinct from both library and computer science through the elaboration of a theoretical apparatus, a set of common techniques, and the continuous construction, experimentation, and evaluation of concrete systems.

Evaluation, which generally meant comparing systems to each other and to attributions of topic relevance by human experts, became a particularly important pillar of the field's epistemological makeup: the system that retrieves the largest number of documents manually tagged as relevant for a series of questions wins. Such competitions continue to structure information retrieval and adjacent fields like machine learning, where algorithms compete on already tagged data sets. One would have to make a different argument for the history of 'traditional' or 'good old-fashioned' artificial intelligence (Haugeland, 1985), which pursues and builds on a true theory of reasoning, but even here, one should not underestimate the enormous evocative power and persuasiveness of a working system. The ability to *show* that a technique can produce a certain output or behavior has a similar effect to the 'matters of fact' Shapin and Schaffer locate in the history of experimental science: because the program works, the underlying ideas and assumptions appear as self-evident. The process rests 'upon the acceptance of certain social and discursive conventions' (Shapin and Schaffer, 2011, p. 22) that involve, among other things, 'a multiplication of the witnessing experience' (Shapin and Schaffer, 2011, p. 25). As Peter Norvig (2015), one of the central figures in artificial intelligence, states, 'engineering success shows that something is working right, and so is evidence (but not proof) of a scientifically successful model' (n.p.). The standardized corpora for testing, the elaborate evaluation setups, and the regular competitions we find in information retrieval and beyond indeed serve to establish that 'something is working right' in a public arena, and they are of particular importance for disciplines and practices that regularly venture into domains that are ambiguous and contested. If the logical rationalism that marks 'computationalism' (Golumbia, 2009) attempts to fully model the inner laws of thought or language, fields like information retrieval radically reduce their ambition to understand the application domain in any substantive way and move the definition of scientific success to a form of 'epistemological audit'. Proof is replaced by benchmark.

This overly simplistic opposition is problematic in more than one way, but it explains, to a certain degree, why the application of algorithmic techniques to governmental or commercial ends generally goes over smoothly and why the leading academics can move in and out of the commercial sector without losing their scientific credentials: surprisingly little actually changes. Engineering success is defined by an evaluative apparatus in both cases and the very purpose of the technique, namely, to order information according to a user-defined (information) need or desire, remains unchanged. Both configurations favor a pragmatic, empiricist ethos and epistemology that profit from the aura of mathematization and the respectability of quantitative evaluation.

The Cranfield experiments (Cleverdon, 1967), conducted by Cyril Cleverdon at Cranfield University in the UK, were the most famous of a long series of experimental assessments that animated not only the continuing rivalry with traditional library techniques but also the more theoretical question what it means to evaluate contested and context-dependent notions such as 'relevance' in the first place (cf. Swanson, 1988; Spärck Jones, 1981). The first large-scale competition, which pitted Mortimer Taube's coordinate indexing against the Armed Services Technical Information Agency (ASTIA) subject heading system in 1953, already brought the fundamental conundrum to the front: out of the 15,000 documents under consideration, the two teams could agree that 1390 documents were relevant to at least one of the 98 questions, but a full 1577 documents were considered relevant by only one of the groups (Swanson, 1988, p. 92). Why would this be any different for the much more diverse population of actual searchers working in a wide variety of settings? Even if the discipline developed concepts such as 'recall' (which percentage of relevant documents are retrieved?) and 'precision' (which percentage of the retrieved documents are relevant?) to reason about relevance in quantitative terms (Kent et al., 1955), none of the attempts to define fully formal criteria for retrieval performance became widely accepted.

Systems that retrieve and rank documents in response to a query are, fundamentally, engines of order that govern the visibility of ideas, perspectives, and associated actors. This observation indeed undergirds the contemporary debates concerning algorithmic work in domains such as web search ranking or social media message filtering. In the context of information retrieval, which remains committed to its postuniversalist roots, this 'dilemma' (Grimmelmann, 2009) has not been resolved through a shared normative theory but is most commonly tackled in one of two directions: on the one side, there are techniques for automated personalization and interfaces allowing searchers to either express their interests more explicitly or to navigate through result sets; on the other side, we find the empirical evaluations just discussed as well as user studies[6] and similar efforts to gain a better understanding of the 'human factors' involved. This second direction, in particular, constitutes a bridge to more traditional library studies and the public education perspective.

---

6   One of the central texts in this area is Wilson (1981).

Together, these elements constitute a broad epistemological context for the emerging discipline of information retrieval. The focus on empirical evaluation serves as a means to lower the requirements for theory-building and opens a space for technical experimentation that is relatively unburdened by the fundamental interrogations we find in fields like artificial intelligence. This does not mean that information retrieval has no conceptual core, but that its core is built around the accumulation of techniques rather than the formulation of theory. Indeed, while coordinate indexing with Boolean queries becomes the de facto standard for computer-supported literature search, the statistical work pioneered by Luhn constitutes the beginning of a broad cluster of technical trajectories that define much of information retrieval and inform algorithmic information ordering to this day. They represent a vector for computerization that complements the machine's capabilities as calculator, filing cabinet, and communication medium with the capacity to *differentiate* on a semantic level and to *act* based on these interpretations. The forms of appreciation that emerge follow specific 'styles of reasoning' (Hacking, 1985, 1992) and produce 'statements' about the world that have real-world consequences, in particular if they become part of infrastructural modulations.

To better understand how the operational epistemology of information retrieval proceeds, we need to consider different levels and forms of expression. What we can observe, throughout the history of the broader field, are quite different manifestations of thought that include intuitions, ideas, and experiments, as well as more explicit frameworks and well-defined formal models. They all constitute forms of technical imagination that capture some aspect of technicity, but they do so quite differently. There is also real divergence concerning the penetration of computation into the epistemological horizon. Roberto Busa's project, for example, mobilized the available hardware to its fullest to speed up a rather traditional indexing project that never attempted to view the corpus through the lens of statistics as a 'population of words'. As information retrieval moves toward mathematization, however, it begins to develop a more refined epistemological substance that involves new commitments and decisions.

The term 'frequency list', which Luhn uses to describe his 'encoding' of a document into a set of notions, is an example for a seemingly straightforward idea that unveils considerable depth when probed further. On a first level, it points to a rudimentary theory of language and, in particular, a theory of the relationship between word frequency and meaning, even if things remain fairly vague. But the idea that word frequencies capture some part of the content of a document is sufficiently intuitive that it authorizes, on a second level, a formalization into an intermediate form, namely the representation of a document as a list of keywords (or notions) and how often they occur. This formalization has not only a technical component but institutes a model that frames the frequency *list* as a frequency *distribution*, thereby linking it to probability theory. On a third level, this association authorizes the application of common techniques from the field of statistics, which may have been developed at very different times and places but can easily be imported once the formalization as frequency distribution has been realized. These techniques can produce various kinds of outputs that, if all goes well, will capture and manipulate some aspect of the meaning of a document, however skewed or partial.

Each of the three levels allows for variation affecting the other two. First, the move from a 'bag of words' representation of language to an appreciation of document structure and word distance can yield new possibilities for formalization that open onto other forms of processing. Second, a probabilistic model is not the only mathematical way to look at words in documents. Luhn himself points, at least implicitly, toward set-theoretical and geometric interpretations and scholars like Chomsky (1975) have favored perspectives grounded in logic. These models open onto their own sets of associated techniques. Third, the available toolkit for distilling 'patterns or knowledge from the intermediate form' (Tan, 1999, p. 65) is constantly growing, both through internal development of proper information retrieval techniques and through import from other areas. Techniques, understood as elements, move from one trajectory to another if the formal compatibility requirement, that is, the adherence to an intermediate form, are met.

Each broad articulation of the three level affords and requires many specific commitments. For example, the notion of 'collocation' that we find in Luhn's map of notions connects to ongoing debates about what co-occurrences of two words (can) mean and which statistical techniques and parameters are best suited to establish and rank such co-occurrences.[7] When it comes to the construction of actual working systems, these technique-specific considerations are, of course, confronted with a whole range of other issues, such as task particularities, hardware limitations, costs, social norms and values, and so forth. Mathematization multiplies moments of discretion and choice during the development of an information system, even if the system serves to reduce discretion and choice when in use.

7   See Manning and Schütze (1999), Chapter 5.

From Lists to Vectors and Beyond

While information retrieval is often hesitant to elaborate or commit to firm theoretical formulations concerning language, meaning, or knowledge, there are certainly attempts at stabilization, often through formal models that are already detached from domain specificities. One of the most well-known examples is the so-called 'vector space model' (VSM), which develops from Luhn's work on word frequencies and allows for a more concrete discussion of both technical and epistemological substance. The VSM is generally attributed to Gerald Salton, a trained mathematician, (early) computer scientist, and preeminent figure in information retrieval. Born Gerhard Anton Sahlmann in 1927 in Nuremberg, he fled Germany during WWII and ultimately received his PhD in 1958 as one of the last doctoral students of Howard Aiken, the designer of the Harvard Mark I and important pioneer in the history of computing (Stout, 1995). Salton himself developed and tested most of his ideas in the context of a concrete technical prototype, the SMART Automatic Document Retrieval System,[8] which his research group worked on continuously, first at Harvard and later at Cornell, where he cofounded the computer science department.[9] SMART was designed as a series of modules that could be combined to assure that 'several hundred different methods are available to analyze documents and search requests' (Salton and Lesk, 1965, p. 391), producing its own practical variantology of technical elements. But even if Salton shared Luhn's experimental outlook, his formal education meant that information retrieval was approached, from the beginning, through an even more focused mathematical lens. This becomes evident in 1963, when Salton published one of his central contributions. The paper added little to Luhn's lay theory of language but proposed to think of word frequency lists not as probability distributions but as 'document vectors', opening a different pathway for mathematical imagination and technique.

A vector is a mathematical construct used, for example, in Euclidian geometry, where it has a magnitude (or length) and a direction. In a two-dimensional Cartesian coordinate system, a vector may, for example, start at point (0,0) and go to point (2,5). This basic setup then allows for the

8   'More than just an IR system, SMART was the working expression of Salton's theories and the experimental environment in which those theories were evaluated and tested' (Dubin, 2004, p. 752).
9   While Salton published a paper in *American Documentation* early on, most of his work appears in journals published by the Association of Computing Machinery (ACM). He anchors information retrieval as a subfield of computer science, which implies a transfer of concepts, techniques, and perspectives – but also application domains – in both directions.

application of linear algebra to geometry. Salton decides to represent a document as a vector of 'terms', which, at this point, means that words and their frequencies are treated like spatial coordinates. We end up with something along these lines: {word1: 5, word2: 8, word3: 3, ...}. This may seem no different from a frequency distribution, but now, each word is considered to constitute a 'dimension' and the n words appearing in a document collection form a vector space that has n dimensions. In a later publication (Salton, Wong, and Yang, 1975), the authors explicitly use an image of a Cartesian coordinate system to illustrate the analogy, which we can further simplify:

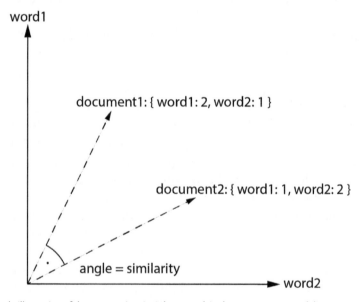

A simple illustration of the geometric principles at work in the vector space model.

Taking a set of documents as a series of document vectors, Salton then represents the entire collection as a term-document matrix that indexes the relationship between each word and each document:

	word 1	word 2	word 3	...
document 1	5	8	3	
document 2	2	5	0	
...				

A generic term-document matrix using numerical values for word frequencies. In many cases, only binary values are used, similar to the coordinate indexing logic.

It is important to understand that these are not just visual representations of documents, but conceptual models that authorize and enable, much like in geometry, the application of linear algebra. The computational possibilities are immense, and Salton proposes three techniques that are based on the capacity to calculate the similarity between two vectors using, in this case, the cosine of their angle (Salton, 1963, p. 443). First, following Luhn, he specifies a system for search ranking based on the similarity between a query and the documents in a collection, where documents with high frequencies for the searched terms are ranked higher. This becomes the basis for a formal definition – not a domain theory – of *relevance*. Second, he suggests an alternative to Luhn's thesaurus of notions to compensate for authors' diverging vocabularies. From the term-document matrix, one can calculate the 'association' between terms, based on the idea that terms coappearing in the same documents are similar in meaning. This allows for 'associative searching' where similar terms are added automatically to a query in order to retrieve a larger number of documents. Third, he proposes a comparable procedure to widen the result set with documents that are similar to the ones initially retrieved. This opens the door for broader attempts to process collections in terms of relationships between documents and not merely in response to a query.

Today, information retrieval systems can choose from a series of computations to generate similarity coefficients (Salton, 1979) and vector similarities are used for various purposes, such as document classification or clustering.[10] A rather basic technique is again the starting point of almost endless technical permutation. Two lines of interpretation are particularly important for my overall argument and the two following section discuss them in turn.

Computation and Generalization

First, the early work by Salton and others (e.g., Switzer, 1965) on vector models shows how the broader field of computing – including information retrieval – discovers possibilities to connect spheres previously considered to be the exclusive domain of humans to established mathematical concepts and techniques. Seemingly straightforward quantifications of language make it possible to draw on reservoirs of existing knowledge and technique that can be used to create an entirely new domain of technicity. Formalization involves a movement of analysis that implies reduction or atomization when it comes to representing the 'real world', for example, language

---

10   See Salton (1989), Chapter 10.

and meaning, but it also affords considerable expressivity, plasticity, and capacity for synthesis on the level of algorithmic transformation. This brings us back to the syntactic reduction we have seen in the shifts from subject headings to coordinate indexing and from navigational databases to the relational model. Each time, disassembly prepares the terrain for algorithmic reassembly. This also holds for the VSM and the other major models in the field.[11] These models do not require stifling commitments to paradigmatic purity but can be mixed and matched, often providing different roads to similar destinations. Probabilistic models, for example, offer calculations of similarity that resemble those proposed by the VSM. Borko in fact uses Pearson's correlation coefficient in 1962 for his 'method for developing an empirically based, computer derived classification system' (Borko, 1962, p. 279). The specific way different computations actually differ is a subject of debate and, more importantly, an object of study, since effects on outcomes are often not straightforward and may heavily depend on context. This is why algorithmic techniques constitute a domain of research *after* their inception; they introduce complex mechanisms into already complex settings, and even fully deterministic principles can yield results that are not easily accounted for. As statements in the discursive formations of information retrieval, they become subject to 'exegesis, commentary, and the internal proliferation of meaning' (Foucault, 2002, p. 135). When Allen Newell and Herbert Simon (1976) argue that 'the phenomena surrounding computers are deep and obscure' (p. 114), this is what they mean.

The calculative power afforded by the possibility to freely apply mathematical techniques to both numerical and nonnumerical information creates a space of experimentation where even highly simplistic representations of language such as word frequency counts can yield spectacular results, at least in well-controlled experimental settings. And the potential for generalizability seems almost limitless. In his 1963 paper, Salton proposes to use citations between papers as another type of 'content indicator' (Salton, 1963, p. 446) that can be formalized in the familiar way as lists or vectors, using cited papers instead of words as properties or dimensions, to be then submitted to the same similarity calculations. Since citations constitute networks, the resulting frequency lists can be enriched further using citation chains and not only direct mentions. Here, Salton connects

---

11   Amit Singhal (2001), Google's former Chief of Search and one of Salton's doctoral students, distinguishes three main groups: The VSM, probabilistic models, and the Inference Network Model. One could add the set-theoretic/Boolean model used in coordinate indexing to that list.

to the graph theoretical approaches discussed in Chapter 7 and feeds them, without little hesitation, into his own model. In 1975, he generalizes even further:

> Although we speak of documents and index terms, the present development applies to any set of entities identified by weighted property vectors. (Salton, Wong, and Yang, 1975, p. 613)

This means, concretely, that the techniques for ranking, filtering, clustering, and so forth, that stem from the VSM and other models, can be applied to any domain that can be formalized into the basic intermediate form of a 'feature vector', to use the term most commonly used today. If we consider user profiles on Facebook as documents and liked items as features or properties, we can use similarity calculations and other methods to operate on people in myriad ways. In the context of contemporary online environments, user profiles are indeed a common type of feature vector. As Ertzscheid (2009) provocatively quips, social networking sites turn human beings into 'documents like any other'.

In a more recent paper, Karen Spärck Jones, another pioneer of information retrieval, discusses the relationship between her own field and AI, suggesting that the willingness to work with unsophisticated formalizations may well be the best strategy to approach domains that are, by definition, imprecise:

> Weak, but model-based, methods have demonstrated their value for one form of information management, namely document retrieval, and have begun to be explored, in promising directions, for others. The claim here is that they work because, in situations where information demand, and hence supply, is underspecified, the right strategy is to be broadly indicative, rather than aggressively analytic [...]; and, further, that the appropriate way of being indicative is to allow many small and individually ambiguous clues to combine and interact within whatever match of document to query is found. [...] [T]here are important tasks that can be labelled 'information management' – finding, recovering, reminding, sorting, grouping, tagging, etc., arising in very different contexts, that are quite crude and can often be done in mode because they are fundamentally inexact. (Spärck Jones, 1999, p. 227f.)

This passage, initially published in 1989, is highly prescient both of the 'statistical turn' in AI and of the widespread application of ordering techniques in domains where large numbers of entities or participants yield such 'many small and individually ambiguous clues' in ways that algorithmic distinctions can yield considerable (economic) benefits. If we think of user interfaces, tracking techniques, and – increasingly – sensors as devices that channel aspects of human practice into data structures that serve as intermediate forms, it is no wonder that many of the techniques pioneered in information retrieval from the 1950s on have seen a second spring in recent years. The more we do with digital appliances involved, the greater the number of entities and phenomena that can be formalized as feature vectors, that is, as sets of objects described by their properties. The ensuing proliferation of problems that mirror the 'information overload' diagnosis makes algorithmic solutions highly attractive and seemingly inevitable.

Technicity and Concept

Second, one can use the concrete example of the VSM to declare with Macho (2003) that cultural techniques are indeed 'always older than the concepts that are generated from them' (p. 179). Even if it is difficult to substantiate such a broad claim in a space that, even in the 1960s, is already overflowing with both concepts and techniques, it is clear that many of the early formalizations one finds in the works of authors like Luhn and Salton are conceptually underdeveloped and either not justified at all or through vague intuitions. As I have argued earlier, this vagueness is not resolved through a more stringent conceptual corset, for example, a Chomskyan theory of language, but merely bounded through the deference to empirical evaluations. This does not mean that there is no progression toward formalization, but rather that formalization limits its ambitions, glosses over application domains, and emphasizes the description of algorithmic techniques, trying to avoid as much as possible to venture too deeply into hazardous concepts like 'meaning' and 'relevance'. Experimentation and evaluation remain the focus and conceptual construction is slow. As Dubin argues, the VSM is not 'invented' in 1963, but develops over several decades:

> What began as a growing comfort in using vector spaces to explain computations led to the use of language that suggested the VSM was a retrieval model in its own right. (Dubin, 2004, p. 761)

Dubin (2004) indeed argues that the VSM only receives a fully explicit formulation in 1989 (Salton, 1989), after being used heavily in practice and as a conceptual reference point for 25 years. I nonetheless want to break out of the temporal order Macho suggest. Conceptualization may indeed follow the technique, but there is clearly a bootstrapping relationship: as the VSM progressively becomes more explicit as a substantial model and not only a series of ad hoc computations, it begins to lay the ground both for further innovation in its core domain and for a 'detachment' into new fields, an 'open adventure' in the sense of Simondon. Through progressive formalization, experimentation, and critical commentary, the VSM gains paradigmatic status. It becomes not only more teachable to newcomers but stabilizes into an immutable mobile that sheds the complicated story of its inception and the memories of incongruence and ambiguity, to become applicable as technique to any information ordering tasks that fits the canonical intermediary form. However, what we see over the history of information retrieval is not a coagulation around a single approach but the development of clearly identifiable trajectories that stabilize and continue to branch out at the same time, forming the rich reservoirs of knowledge and technicity I have theorized in Chapter 3. A variantology of only the VSM could easily fill another volume.

Before closing this chapter, I want to discuss a specific extension to the VSM that exemplifies another fundamental principle in algorithmic information ordering and again demonstrates how plasticity is a defining characteristic of technicity in computing.

Specificity

When attempting to understand how even largely stabilized techniques can afford significant discretion and variation, one can point to refining or cleaning operations such as elimination lists, cutoffs, or word transformations, but also to decisions regarding what to count and how to count. For example, are pure frequency counts of word occurrences workable indicators for subject matter? Such interrogations have prompted semantic strategies like the thesaurus approaches discussed above, where words are linked to a reduced set of notions or concepts in order to capture and structure meaning more explicitly. These efforts establish direct connections with the field of knowledge representation, which plays an important role in areas like expert systems or the Semantic Web. But there have also been many statistical approaches that use keyword 'weighting' as a quantitative means to enhance semantic salience.

Certainly, frequency counts themselves are already a way to differentiate between terms, but there are various ways to think about this question from a more involved statistical perspective, following at least three broad directions. The first direction concerns the level of the document itself, where the variable length of texts raised doubts about pure frequency counts early on. If one ranks documents by the number of times a query term appears in them, it seems obvious that longer documents would be privileged. In the early days of the web, spammers would indeed fill pages with invisible text to trick frequency counting search engines. One way to deal with this is a form of normalization that uses percentages rather than absolute numbers. The cosine similarity coefficient that Salton uses in 1963 already includes such an operation. Second, at the other end of the spectrum, one could use information about the frequency of word occurrences in overall language use, based on some corpus, and calculate for each word in a document whether it is used more or less frequently than expected. There are many word frequency lists available online, one of the most well-known coming from Google's Ngram Viewer project. Third, and most interesting in the context of information retrieval, one can situate words – or any other feature for that matter – within the context of the document collection under scrutiny. The early literature on information retrieval contains many attempts taking that direction. M. E. Maron, whose work on the Bayes classifier I will discuss in the next chapter, already noted in 1961 that a good 'clue word' or indicator for a subject category should not simply be a word appearing frequently in that category, but one that 'peaked' for it, in the sense that it appears more rarely in *other* categories (Maron, 1961, p. 408). Building on this idea, one could use the distribution of keywords over a document collection to define and calculate the *specificity* of each term.

In her often-referenced paper from 1972, Spärck Jones (2004) argued that almost any 'real' document collection will have to deal with the fact that some keywords have low specificity in the sense that they apply to a large percentage of documents and are therefore not very good for retrieval purposes. If a search query and a document have a very frequent word in common in a basic coordinate indexing setup, this match would count as much as a match of an infrequent word, even if the latter is likely to be more 'semantically focussed' (Manning and Schütze, 1999, p. 542). Since throwing out frequent terms would create problems for searchers using broad queries, one should rather 'exploit the good features of very frequent and non-frequent terms, while minimizing their bad ones' (Spärck Jones, 2004, p. 498). This could be achieved through a weighting scheme that captures the significance and specificity of individual keywords by situating them within the overall collection. Spärck Jones discusses two strategies: one could adjust the weight given to a term by counting how often it appears in the overall collection (collection frequency), but since this may not be feasible for many indexing situations where full frequency numbers are not available, one could simply consider the number of documents (document frequency) a term appears in at least once. The following passage argues that choosing between these two strategies is not merely a matter of feasibility and shows how a simply counting decision can raise deeper epistemological concerns:

> Weighting by collection frequency as opposed to document frequency is quite different. It places greater emphasis on the value of a term as a means of distinguishing one document from another than on its value as an indication of the content of the document itself. The relation between the two forms of weighting is not obvious. In some cases a term may be common in a document and rare in the collection, so that it would be heavily weighted in both schemes. But the reverse may also apply. It is really that the emphasis is on different properties of terms. (Spärck Jones, 2004, p. 499)

While Spärck Jones certainly makes claims about the general thrust of each counting method, she quickly adds that the semantic and pragmatic performativity of each measure will, *in fine*, depend on the specific collection and task it is applied to. Since collection frequency required considerably greater logistical effort, her experiments focused on document frequency as a means to attribute higher weight to less common search terms. This work lays the foundation for the notion of 'inverse document frequency', where the specificity of a term is understood as a function of its rarity in a collection. If each keyword is adjusted accordingly,[12] matches for more rare or 'specific' keywords will thus receive a higher value in the ranking of search results. Salton later expands the idea, creating what is certainly the most well-known term-weighting scheme in information retrieval and beyond, tf-idf (term frequency-inverse document frequency), where both the frequency of a term in a document and its rarity in the collection are used to calculate its weight (Salton, Wong, and Yang, 1975, p. 616). Once the weighting scheme is applied, all other calculations – for example, to establish similarity – can proceed as they did before.

12   Inverse document frequency is normally calculated by dividing the overall number of documents by the number of documents a term appears in and taking the logarithm of the result. If a collection has 100 documents and a term appears in 5, its weight will be 1.3. If a term appears in 50 documents, its weight is 0.3.

226 ENGINES OF ORDER

Compared to the above-mentioned frequency cutoffs and dictionary transformations, tf-idf and similar weighting schemes represent genuinely statistical attempts to differentiate between the individual properties present in a feature vector. These processes of 'distinction-making' revolve around articulations between local and global properties or between individual and population. Instead of singling out this or that property of an item as more or less significant, based on a theory or a hunch, the statistical tradition in information retrieval seeks to attribute significance to the signal that has the highest capacity to discern or to differentiate. The construction of overall distributions, here, does not serve to establish a norm to follow, a *homme moyen* ('average man') to speak with Quetelet (1835) but constitutes a horizon that makes the individual item stand out and identifies the features that make it different.

Algorithmic Plasticity

The operations discussed in this chapter were generally based on some form of counting, but their goal was not to create aggregate assessments of datasets or populations. Unlike many other quantitative techniques, such as averages, the objective was to order, not merely to describe. Similarity calculations between a query and each item in a collection were, at least initially, mainly used to rank a list of search results. A high value means that the semantic 'distance' is small, and documents can be put in sequence accordingly. But Salton (1963) showed early on that such distances can also be established between the documents themselves. In the first case, which reflects the standard setup of information retrieval, statistical or geometric similarity takes a concrete reference point and orders the data pool from that perspective, resulting in a navigational form such as a ranked result list, a recommendation, or a filtered stream. The second case, however, opens onto a set of techniques that perform something more akin to aggregate description, at least if we consider that ordering items into clusters or classes without query or other reference points can be called a description.

Given a collection of documents stored in VSM-type intermediary forms, one may not want to find the answer to a particular question but gain an overview of the collection itself or divide it into distinct groups. Techniques from the field of 'unsupervised' machine learning use similarity calculations between items to create groups without having to learn a model from 'supervision', that is, from already classified data. The popular *k*-means clustering technique, for example, requires users to select the desired number of clusters (k), assigns entities randomly to clusters, and then modifies cluster composition until some optimal distribution is found or a specified number of iterations is reached.[13] While the underlying math problem is far from trivial, the goal is basically to distribute items in such a way that the combined distances inside of each cluster are as small as possible. Clustering not only stands for a set of techniques that connect directly with the VSM but also demonstrates how information ordering articulates the relationships between individual and population and between individuals themselves to manipulate 'scale' in various ways. Clusters or classes are means to differentiate and – potentially – to act differently on ad hoc groups that sit between individual and population. This capacity may or may not be 'useful' depending on operational context, but it adds another lever to the arsenal of possibilities for projecting and manipulating digital items and what they represent. The notion of 'plasticity' should thus include both the fundamental malleability of software and the continuous accumulation of algorithmic techniques that add expressive capabilities.

Depending on the actual collection and the specific way language has been formalized, transformed, and filtered (Single word frequencies? Co-occurrences? Lemmatization? Dictionary enrichment? Frequency cutoffs? Term weighting?), clusters of items may or may not reflect cultural categories such as topics, and 'fiddling around' with parameters is a common practice in areas where the constitution of outputs can be hard to anticipate and even harder to explain. This is one of the many instances where copious amounts of judgment flow into the domain of calculation, turning these processes into forms of 'qualculation' (Cochoy, 2008), where quantitative measures combine with situated qualification, technical experience, reasoning by plausibility, and empirical evaluation.

How underlying computations are expressed at the interface level, however, is yet another question. While the difference between these two broad uses of similarity calculations, ranking and clustering, does not map fully onto the common distinction between searching and browsing in information retrieval (cf. Chu, 2003, p. 81ff.), information ordering techniques inform the range of possible navigational outputs. The possibilities for design and variable 'orchestration', that is, the arrangement of forms and functions, are multiplied as the archive of techniques grows. A model like the VSM catapults developers into a space where many different techniques are ready-to-hand for implementation and creative combination.

13   The basic idea goes back to the work of Polish mathematician Hugo Steinhaus (1956).

The broad uptake the VSM and weighting schemes like tf-idf have found beyond the 'classic' information retrieval setup – keyword index, search query, ranked result list – supports these arguments. Whenever we hear about 'algorithms' making decisions with socially relevant repercussions, there is a good chance that items are represented as weighted feature vectors and arranged according to some computational appreciation of their differences and similarities. In a recent survey of 200 research articles about recommender systems, for example, Beel et al., (2015) found that 64 percent used VSM feature vectors to store item representations and user models, and 70 percent relied on tf-idf as weighting scheme. While the two techniques certainly do have canonical, frozen formulations, they also point toward a space of variation that covers parametrization, implementation in concrete systems, and derivation into similar-but-not-identical models and metrics. Indeed, tf-idf is often used as part of the VSM, replacing pure frequency counts with weighted numbers, both to achieve better semantic differentiation between documents and to reduce the number of features and dimensions to make calculations less 'expensive' in computational terms. These kinds of decisions and their consequences are a subject of research in computing disciplines and often lead to much experimentation and optimization in concrete application settings, where the specifics of the domain will affect how different techniques and parameters perform. As Agre points out:

> Technical methods do not simply 'work' or 'fail to work.' The picture is always mixed. Every method has its strengths and weaknesses, its elegance and its clumsiness, its subtle patterns of success and failure. (Agre, 1997a, p. 14)

Software-makers implementing techniques into concrete systems sit precisely at the point where objective capacities and objectal embeddings enter into negotiation to define what success or failure would actually mean, creating the relationships and dependencies that bind the 'free' technicity of the element into operational commitments. The creation of a technical object, with Simondon, is not the declination of a singular principle or 'logic' but the assembly of a functioning whole out of heterogeneous elements that enter into relations of reciprocal causality. The plasticity and artisanal character of software-making means that local forces may have strong effects on actual arrangements.

When it comes to the particularities of information ordering, the techniques discussed so far demonstrate the variety of approaches to similar problems, or rather, to problems that can be framed and formalized in similar ways. Requiring little more than compliance with a basic intermediate form or data structure, they have introduced a number of broad principles that resonate through the field and its many applications. Coordinate indexing establishes the idea of an information space constituted by (manually) assigned, binary index terms that either apply to an item or not, a space that can then be manipulated with the help of a query language based on set theory and Boolean operators. The relational model for database management builds on this basic idea but introduces much richer means for semantic differentiation and expressivity, on the level of both the data model and the query language. These two frameworks envision information ordering as the deliberate construction of a multidimensional address space that lays a disjointed semantic grid over an atomized world, making it queryable in endless combinations of a finite vocabulary.

The frequency-driven explorations of Luhn, Salton, and Spärck Jones, however, take a more dynamic approach to the material under consideration. Documents and many other items one 'finds' in the world seem to have structural properties that appear as straightforward enough to do *something* with them. Texts themselves are full of words that stand out as identifiable units, they have a frequency, they are arranged in a sequence, they are distributed over different documents, and so forth. One can count these atoms in various ways, either to funnel them back into a stable vocabulary of notions, as Luhn did, or to deal with them more or less directly, as most full-text search engines do. This is not a binary choice, but rather a continuum that includes operations like data cleaning, lemmatization, or term weighting. The outcome is always a specific form of mediation, even if the process of funneling the world into intermediary forms can be ad hoc and driven by experimentation rather than theorization.

While one could argue that coordinate indexing and the relational model epitomize a rationalistic, deductive, and logic-based route to information ordering and the techniques discussed in this chapter an empiricist, inductive, and statistical direction, their opposition should not be exaggerated. Statistical techniques forage through relational databases and declarative knowledge enhances statistical techniques' capacity to differentiate. There have certainly been many debates, in academia and beyond, about the best ways to handle information and what it stands for, but technical and conceptual trajectories are brought together, on the one side, by the medium of technicity, which only knows the promiscuity of function, and, on the other, by the medium of human purposes, where outcomes matter more than intellectual and methodological purity.

Bibliography

Agre, P. E. (1997a). *Computation and Human Experience.* Cambridge: Cambridge University Press.

Anderson, C. (2008). The End of Theory: The Data Deluge Makes the Scientific Method Obsolete. *Wired*, 23 June. Retrieved from https://www.wired.com.

Beel, J., Gipp, B., Langer, S., and Breitinger, C. (2015). Research-Paper Recommender Systems: A Literature Survey. *International Journal on Digital Libraries 17*(4), 305-338.

Birnbaum, D. J., Bonde. S., and Kestemont, M. (2017). The Digital Middle Ages: An Introduction. *Speculum 92*(S1), S1-S38.

Blei, D. M., Ng, A. Y., and Jordan, M. I. (2003). Latent Dirichlet Allocation. *Journal of Machine Learning Research 3*, 993-1022.

Blumer, H. (1962). Society as Symbolic Interaction. In A. M. Rose (ed.), *Human Behavior and Social Processes* (pp. 179-192). Boston: Houghton Mifflin.

Borko, H. (1962). The Construction of an Empirically Based Mathematically Derived Classification System. In G. A. Barnard (ed.), *AIEE-IRE '62 (Spring) Proceedings of the May 1-3, 1962, Spring Joint Computer Conference* (pp. 279-289). New York: ACM.

Burton, D. M. (1981). Automated Concordances and Word Indexes: The Process, the Programs, and the Products. *Computers and the Humanities 15*(3), 139-154.

Busa, R. (1980). The Annals of Humanities Computing: The Index Thomisticus. *Computers and the Humanities 14*(2), 83-90.

Callon, M., Courtial, J.-P., Turner, W. A., and Bauin, S. (1983). From Translations to Problematic Networks: An Introduction to Co-Word Analysis. *Social Science Information 22*(2), 191-235.

Chomsky, N. (1975). *The Logical Structure of Linguistic Theory.* New York: Plenum Press.

Chu, H. (2003). *Information Representation and Retrieval in the Digital Age.* Medford: Information Today.

Cleverdon, C. W. (1967). The Cranfield Tests on Index Language Devices. *Aslib Proceedings 19*(6), 173-194.

Cochoy, F. (2008). Calculation, Qualculation, Calqulation: Shopping Cart Arithmetic, Equipped Cognition and the Clustered Consumer. *Marketing Theory 8*(1), 15-44.

Danowski, J. A. (1993). Network Analysis of Message Content. In W. D. Richards and G. Barnett (eds.), *Progress in Communication Sciences, Volume XII* (pp. 197-222). Norwood: Ablex.

Domingos, P. (2012). A Few Useful Things to Know about Machine Learning. *Communications of the ACM 55*(10), 78-87.

Dubin, D. (2004). The Most Influential Paper Gerard Salton Never Wrote. *Library Trends 52*(4), 748-764.

Ertzscheid, O. (2009). L'Homme, un document comme les autres. *Hermès 53*(1), 33-40.

Fairthorne, R. A. (1968). H. P. Luhn, Applied Mathematician. In C. K. Schultz (ed.), *H. P. Luhn: Pioneer of Information Science: Selected Works* (pp. 21-23). New York: Spartan Books.

Foucault, M. (2002). *Archaeology of Knowledge* (A. M. Sheridan Smith, trans.). London: Routledge.

Golumbia, D. (2009). *The Cultural Logic of Computation.* Cambridge, MA: Harvard University Press.

Grimmelmann, J. (2009). The Google Dilemma. *New York Law School Law Review* 53, 939-950.

Hacking, I. (1985). Styles of Scientific Reasoning. In J. Rajchman and C. West (eds.), *Post-Analytic Philosophy* (pp. 145-163). New York: Columbia University Press.

Hacking, I. (1992). Statistical Language, Statistical Truth and Statistical Reason: The Self-Authentification of a Style of Scientific Reasoning. In E. McMullin (ed.), *The Social Dimensions of Science* (pp. 130-157). Notre Dame: University of Notre Dame Press.

Hardy, Q. (2016). Amit Singhal, an Influential Engineer at Google, Will Retire. *New York Times,* 3 February.

Harris, Z. S. (1954). Distributional Structure. *Word* 10(2-3), 146-162.

Haugeland, J. (1985). *Artificial Intelligence: The Very Idea.* Cambridge, MA: MIT Press.

Kent, A., Berry, M. M., Luehrs, Jr., F. U., and Perry J. W. (1955). Machine Literature Searching VIII: Operational Criteria for Designing Information Retrieval Systems. *Journal of the Association for Information Science and Technology* 6(2), 93-101.

Luhn, H. P. (1953). A New Method of Recording and Searching Information. *American Documentation* 4(1), 14-16.

Luhn, H. P. (1957). A Statistical Approach to Mechanized Encoding and Searching of Literary Information. *IBM Journal of Research and Development* 1(4), 309-317.

Luhn, H. P. (1958). The Automatic Creation of Literature Abstracts. *IBM Journal of Research and Development* 2(2), 159-165.

Luhn, H. P. (1960). Keyword-in-Context Index for Technical Literature. *American Documentation* 11(4), 288-295.

Luhn, H. P. (1968a). Auto-Encoding of Documents for Information Retrieval Systems. In C. K. Schultz (ed.), *H. P. Luhn: Pioneer of Information Science: Selected Works* (pp. 126-131). New York: Spartan Books.

Luhn, H. P. (1968b). Indexing, Language, and Meaning. In C. K. Schultz (ed.), *H. P. Luhn: Pioneer of Information Science: Selected Works* (pp. 166-170). New York: Spartan Books.

Macho, T. (2003). Zeit und Zahl: Kalender- und Zeitrechnung als Kulturtechniken. In S. Krämer and H. Bredekamp (eds.), *Schrift, Zahl: Wider die Diskursivierung der Kultur* (pp. 179-192). München: Wilhelm Fink Verlag.

Manning, C. D., and Schütze, H. (1999). *Foundations of Statistical Natural Language Processing*. Cambridge, MA: MIT Press.

Maron, M. E. (1961). Automatic Indexing: An Experimental Inquiry. *Journal of the ACM 8*(3), 404-417.

Maron, M. E. (1963). A Logician's View of Language-Data Processing. In P. L. Garvin (ed.), *Natural Language and the Computer* (pp. 128-151). New York: McGraw-Hill.

Moore, H. (1968). H. P. Luhn, Engineer. In C. K. Schultz (ed.), *H. P. Luhn: Pioneer of Information Science: Selected Works* (pp. 16-20). New York: Spartan Books.

Newell, A., and Simon, H. A. (1976). Computer Science as Empirical Inquiry: Symbols and Search. *Communications of the ACM 19*(3), 113-126.

Norvig, P. (2015). *On Chomsky and the Two Cultures of Statistical Learning*. Retrieved from http://norvig.com/chomsky.html.

Pearl, J. (1988). *Probabilistic Reasoning in Intelligent Systems: Networks of Plausible Inference*. San Mateo: Morgan Kaufmann.

Quetelet, A. (1835). *Sur l'homme et le développement de ses facultés: ou, Essai de physique sociale*. Paris: Bachelier.

Russell, S., and Norvig, P. (2010). *Artificial Intelligence* (3rd ed.). Upper Saddle River: Pearson Education.

Salton, G. (1963). Associative Document Retrieval Techniques Using Bibliographic Information. *Journal of the ACM 10*(4), 440-457.

Salton, G. (1979). Mathematics and Information Retrieval. *Journal of Documentation 35*(1), 1-29.

Salton, G. (1987). Historical Note: The Past Thirty Years in Information Retrieval. *Journal of the American Society for Information Science 38*(5), 375-380.

Salton, G. (1989). *Automatic Text Processing*. Reading: Addison-Wesley.

Salton, G., and Lesk, M. E. (1965). The SMART Automatic Document Retrieval System: An Illustration. *Communications of the ACM 8*(6), 391-398.

Salton, G., Wong, A., and Yang, C.-S. (1975). A Vector Space Model for Automatic Indexing. *Communications of the ACM 18*(11), 613-620.

Schultz, C. K. (1968). H. P. Luhn, The Man. In C. K. Schultz (ed.), *H. P. Luhn: Pioneer of Information Science: Selected Works* (pp. 3-15). New York: Spartan Books.

Shapin, S., and Schaffer, S. (2011). *Leviathan and the Air-Pump* (2nd ed.). Princeton: Princeton University Press.

Siegert, B. (2013). Cultural Techniques; or The End of the Intellectual Postwar Era in German Media Theory. *Theory, Culture & Society 30*(6), 48-65.

Silberman, S. (2000). The Quest for Meaning. *Wired*, 1 February. Retrieved from https://www.wired.com.

Simondon, G. (2017). *On the Mode of Existence of Technical Objects* (C. Malaspina and J. Rogove, trans.). Minneapolis: Univocal Publishing.

Singhal, A. (2001). Modern Information Retrieval: A Brief Overview. *Bulletin of the Technical Committee on Data Engineering* 24(4), 35-43.

Spärck Jones, K. (1981). Retrieval System Tests 1958-1978. In K. Spärck Jones (ed.), *Information Retrieval Experiment* (pp. 213-255). Newton: Butterworth.

Spärck Jones, K. (1999). Information Retrieval and Artificial Intelligence. *Artificial Intelligence* 114, 257-281.

Spärck Jones, K. (2004). A Statistical Interpretation of Term Specificity and Its Application in Retrieval. *Journal of Documentation* 60(5), 493-502.

Steinhaus, H. (1956). Sur la division des corps matériels en parties. *Bulletin de l'Académie Polonaise des Sciences Classe III* 4(12), 801-804.

Stevens, M. E. (1968). H. P. Luhn, Information Scientist. In C. K. Schultz (ed.), *H. P. Luhn: Pioneer of Information Science: Selected Works* (pp. 24-30). New York: Spartan Books.

Stout, D. (1995). Gerard Salton, 68, an Authority on Computer Retrieval Systems. *New York Times*, 8 September.

Swanson, D. R. (1988). Historical Note: Information Retrieval and the Future of an Illusion. *Journal of the American Society for Information Science* 39(2), 92-98.

Switzer, P. (1965). Vector Images in Document Retrieval. In E. Stevens, V. E. Guiliano, and L. B. Heilprin (eds.), *Statistical Association Methods for Mechanized Documentation* (pp. 163-171). Washington, DC: National Bureau of Standards.

Tan, A.-H. (1999). Text Mining: The State of the Art and the Challenges. In *Proceedings of the PAKDD Workshop on Knowledge Discovery from Advanced Databases* (pp. 65-70). Retrieved from https://pdfs.semanticscholar.org/9a80/ec16880ae43dc20c792ea3734862d85ba4d7.pdf.

Turkle, S. (1985). *The Second Self: Computers and the Human Spirit*. New York: Simon and Schuster.

Wang, H. (1960). Toward Mechanical Mathematics. *IBM Journal of Research and Development* 4(1), 2-21.

Wasserman, P. (1965). *The Librarian and the Machine*. Detroit: Gale Research.

Williams, R. V. (2002). The Use of Punched Cards in US Libraries and Documentation Centers, 1936-1965. *IEEE Annals of the History of Computing* 24(2), 16-33.

Wilson, T. D. (1981). On User Studies and Information Needs. *Journal of Documentation* 37(1), 3-15.

Winter, T. N. (1999). Roberto Busa, S.J., and the Invention of the Machine-Generated Concordance. *The Classical Bulletin* 75(1), 3-20.

6. Interested Learning

Abstract

This chapter examines one of the most active areas where feature vectors play a central role: machine learning. The Bayes classifier is used as an entry point into the field, showing how a simple statistical technique introduced in the early 1960s is surprisingly instructive for understanding how machine learning operates more broadly. The goal is to shed light on the core principles at work and to explain how they are tweaked, adapted, and developed further into different directions. This chapter also develops the idea that contemporary information ordering represents an epistemological practice that can be described and analyzed as 'interested reading of reality', a particular kind of inductive empiricism.

Keywords: machine learning, Bayes classifier, optimization, interested readings of reality

Coordinate indexing and its relational database cousin constitute a technique for laying a disjoint, atomized, and therefore highly queryable grid over the world. Ordering becomes a particular operationalization of disassembly and reassembly in a multidimensional coordinate system that affords purpose-driven grouping and ordering through logical declaration. The query specifies the coordinates or properties one is interested in and matching items are retrieved. The statistical techniques discussed in the last chapter, which often describe their work as automatic encoding or indexing, can be seen as attempts to build such a grid from the world itself, not necessarily by grammatization, 'the process whereby the currents and continuities shaping our lives become discrete elements' (Stiegler, 2010, p. 70), but by counting what already appears as discrete units. In the case of information retrieval, this mainly concerned the words appearing in a text document, but one could easily imagine users as items and elements like posts, songs, or products they interacted with in some way as properties to begin clustering or recommending on the base of similarity calculations. The various techniques grouping around the VSM

Rieder, B., *Engines of Order: A Mechanology of Algorithmic Techniques*. Amsterdam: Amsterdam University Press, 2020
DOI 10.5117/9789462986190_CH06

measure similarity or distance, rank, cluster, or otherwise arrange items in the already discretized environments computerization multiplies. The notion of specificity, as it appears, for example, in tf-idf, shows how these processes can draw on the relationships between individuals and populations in (high-dimensional) data spaces to glean additional semantic salience.

The space of investigation, experimentation, and steady accumulation of concepts and techniques opened up by Luhn and others quickly develops in a number of directions. One of them points toward an epistemological posture emblematically expressed in an interview with Michael Richard Lynch, the cofounder of Autonomy Corporation, a company now owned by HP that specializes in mining large amounts of 'unstructured' data:

> 'Rules-based, Boolean computing assumes that we know best how to solve a problem,' he says. 'My background comes completely the other way. The problem tells you how to solve the problem. That's what the next generation of computing is going to be about: listening to the world.'[1]

In a sense, 'listening to the world' is what statistical techniques broadly set out to do, but this process can be enacted and orchestrated in different ways. With the exception of a short excursion into unsupervised machine learning used for clustering, the techniques discussed in the last chapter were either used for document indexing or created with the expectation that actual searching and ranking of items would be performed in relation to a query, for example, by measuring the similarity between a search vector and any number of document vectors. A contemporary adaptation of the same principle for purposes of personalization or recommendation would be to treat a user profile as an 'indirect' query – there is still an individual reference point that serves to line up the population.

In this chapter, however, I want to explore a technical lineage, again incepted in the 1960s in the context of information retrieval, which uses similar principles to order information not in response to some explicitly formulated need or desire for information, but to orchestrate a more implicit and potentially autonomous classificatory process that enacts a form of continuous and adaptive observation to derive decision-making principles. No less ambiguous than notions like meaning or relevance, this highlights the question of how techniques can make machines 'learn'.

In this context, the Bayes classifier constitutes an ideal example. First, it connects directly to the nexus of techniques already discussed, both

---

1   Lynch, cit. in Silberman (2000, n.p.).

historically and conceptually. The Bayes classifier builds on principles already familiar from previous chapters and can be understood without a deeper dive into probability mathematics. Second, since it constitutes a technique that is probabilistic (classifications are not binary but with degrees of certainty), adaptive (it 'learns' from experience), and well suited for personalization, it allows for a discussion of broader aspects of machine learning and its role in contemporary information ordering. Even if many new and much more complex techniques have appeared in recent decades, the Bayes classifier is still one of the 'most efficient and effective inductive learning algorithms for machine learning and data mining' (Zhang, 2004, p. 1) and has 'remained popular over the years' (Hastie, Tibshirani, and Friedman, 2009, p. 211). In very general terms, it provides a specific method for making use of statistical inference to sort a new element, for example, an incoming email, on the basis of a decision model derived from previously categorized elements, for example, messages already marked as spam. This canonical example can provide a guiding rationale through the more detailed historical and technical presentation that follows.

From Probabilistic Coordinate Indexing to the Bayes Classifier

The story begins in the late 1950s when M. E. Maron,[2] a physicist turned analytical philosopher and cybernetician working at the Ramo-Wooldridge Corporation and the Rand Corporation before becoming a full professor at Berkeley's School of Information in 1966, 'was thinking hard about the problem of information retrieval' (Maron, 2008, p. 971). He was particularly unsatisfied with a fundamental aspect of coordinate indexing, namely that assigning a tag (or keyword, uniterm, descriptor, etc.) to an item in order to describe its subject was 'a two-valued affair' (Maron, 2008, p. 971): a term is either attributed or not, nothing in between. In Maron's view, this makes the system too 'primitive' since it cannot express 'degrees of aboutness' (Maron, 2008, p. 971), an obvious limitation for the representation of document content itself and a problem for retrieval and ranking. Pure Boolean

2   This presentation focuses on the work of M. E. Maron, although a fuller account of the use of Bayes's theorem for classification and learning would have to include Solomonoff's experiments on 'a machine which is designed to learn to work problems in mathematics' (1957, p. 56), but this would stray too much from the focus on document classification. Another interesting addition would be the work of Borko (1962) and, in particular, Borko and Bernick (1963). The latter repeats Maron's earlier experiments, but uses factor analysis instead of Bayes's theorem, with similar results.

matching certainly constitutes a powerful way to manipulate an information space through postcoordination, but it lacks nuance and provides no
means to weight keywords or index terms. This becomes problematic as
collections grow and queries return large numbers of documents, without
much possibility for additional differentiation other than the number of
search terms matched.

The first improvement Maron and colleague J. L. Kuhns proposed was
not to count word occurrences in documents like Luhn did but for indexers
to specify a value somewhere between 0 and 1 to indicate the relevance of
a tag for a document. This method, named 'probabilistic indexing', made
it possible, through inverse statistical inference via Bayes's theorem, to
generate a probabilistically ranked result list for a subject query instead of
merely an unordered set of documents (Maron and Kuhns, 1960). Leaving
aside its complicated history (Stigler, 1983) and various interpretations,
Bayes's theorem basically provides a simple method for calculating the
probability of a hypothesis being true (or an event occurring) based on
existing knowledge. For example, if we know the percentage of women in
a population and the a priori percentages of women and men with long
hair, we can calculate the probability of the hypothesis that a person with
long hair we see only from behind is a woman.[3] If we add other variables
to the equation, such as height or clothing style, the assessment becomes
increasingly specific. Bayes's theorem thus provides a means to reason in
a space of uncertainty where we have some prior knowledge that can be
used to assess a particular case. My example already shows that this kind of
reasoning implies not only potentially problematic forms of categorization,
such as the division of people into women and men, but also raises the
question of how 'prior knowledge' is constructed and operationalized.

In the case of information retrieval, the 'hypothesis' under investigation concerns the probability that a document (tagged with a number
of weighted terms) is relevant for a query (represented by a number of
search terms that could also be weighted). The indexers provide 'prior
knowledge' by establishing probability relationships between keywords
and documents. Interestingly, Maron proposed from the outset to replace
the a priori probability of a document (the equivalent of the 'percentage

3   To calculate this example, let us consider that half of the population is female and that 75%
of all women have long hair and 15% of all men. The probability that a person with long hair is
a woman would then be calculated as:

$$P(F|L) = \frac{0.75 * 0.50}{0.75 * 0.50 + 0.15 * 0.50} = 0.83333$$

of women in a population'), which would normally be one divided by the number of documents in the collection, with statistics on document use. In the end, Maron's formula for relevance looked like this, using a dot product[4] to calculate the 'closeness' between query terms ('WordsQuery') and the document terms ('WordsDoc'):

$$P(DocumentIsRelevant) = (WordsQuery \cdot WordsDoc) * P(DocumentUse)$$

A simplified version of Maron's relevance formula, which would be calculated for each document that has at least one term in common with the query.

We again encounter the familiar representation of documents and queries as term frequency lists or feature vectors and the closeness calculation between the two is comparable to the similarity coefficients discussed in the last chapter. When searching for [hydraulics], a document tagged with 0.7 for that term would thus have a higher 'relevance number' than a document tagged with a value of 0.3. Documents accessed more often would also receive a higher value. Results were then ranked according to their relevance number. Term combinations and weighted search terms were possible as well. The method was still based on manual indexing and manual weighting but represented nonetheless 'a theoretical attack which replaced traditional two-valued indexing and matching with a statistical approach [...] to make predictions about the relevance of documents in the collection' (Thompson, 2008, p. 964). While indexing with manual term weighting never became a common practice, the idea explicitly framed information retrieval as an operation under uncertainty and thus not sufficiently well served by Boolean logic.

The indexing and ranking technique I just outlined is not a Bayes classifier, however. It introduced Bayes's theorem into information retrieval, but the actual classifier emerged only through a second experiment, which attempted to do away with the human indexer, who Maron described, in line with other information scientists of the time, as slow, unreliable, and biased (Maron, 1961). Although he did not reference Luhn's work, the chosen strategy was to tackle the full text of the document itself. Based on the assertion that 'statistics on kind, frequency, location, order, etc., of

---

4   A dot product is the sum of the products of two sequences of numbers. For example, the dot product between the query { hydraulics: 0.7, car: 0.5 } and the document terms { hydraulics: 0.6, car: 0.8 } would be 0.7 * 0.6 + 0.5 * 0.8, thus 0.82. The more terms overlap between a query and a document and the higher the weight of the terms, the more 'relevant' the document.

selected words are adequate to make reasonably good predictions about the subject matter of documents containing those words' (Maron, 1961, p. 405), Maron devised a technique for the automatic classification of documents. His approach to meaning remained prudent yet pragmatic: considering words as isolated atoms – the only practically feasible formalization at the time – was certainly not ideal but said at least *something* about the subject matter a document discusses, 'reasonably good' for the task at hand. The technique thus again conceived text documents as 'objects' (or items) having certain 'properties' (or terms, features, etc.), but this time Maron decided to represent each text by the words it actually contained rather than sets of manually chosen descriptors (Maron 1961, p. 406). We end up with a feature vector in both cases, but the former implies a higher degree of automation and echoes Luhn's (1968b) empiricist notion of a 'native' thesaurus or classification that is 'born of the collection' (p. 168).

Classification, in terms of the probabilistic approach proposed by Maron, meant that text documents were to be sorted into user-specified subject categories: '[b]ased on some more or less clear notion of the category, we must decide whether or not an arbitrary document should be assigned to it' (Maron 1961, p. 404). A simple contemporary example is indeed spam filtering: emails are documents and categories are 'spam' and 'not-spam' (or 'legitimate'). The task is to sort incoming emails into these categories. As Rish (2001) summarizes, 'Bayesian classifiers assign the most likely class to a given example described by its feature vector' (p. 41).

The first step in Maron's setup, which used a collection of 405 scientific abstracts in digital form, was to select a number of characteristic 'training' documents for each one of the subject categories. Human intervention was thus rearranged, not eliminated: while 'prior knowledge' in probabilistic indexing came from the explicit attribution of terms, it now shifted to the less explicit act of labeling or sorting example documents into categories. A combined word list for each category was generated from the initially classified documents. Not all words were retained. Just like in Luhn's experiments and based on the same intuitions, very frequent words and very rare words were discarded. The resulting selection was submitted to a technique similar in spirit to the tf-idf metric introduced by Spärck Jones and Salton: words that were evenly distributed over all categories and did not 'peak' anywhere were considered inadequate 'clues' and thus rejected (Maron, 1961, p. 408). The statistical horizon was again used to single out the most specific signals.

An index where each retained word received a relevance value for each category was then generated, determining 'certain probability relationships between individual content-bearing words and subject categories' (Maron, 1961, p. 405). In a nutshell: if a word appears very often in the training documents assigned to a certain category but rarely in others, it becomes a strong clue or indicator for that category. Once the training phase was complete, human intervention was no longer required: based on the general idea that a document should be attributed to a category if it contains many good indicators for that category and few for others, new documents could be automatically classified in the same way as documents were matched with queries in the earlier experiment. In fact, there were now as many 'queries' as categories, and the task was to decide for each document which query it was 'closest' to. The method was therefore very similar to the ranking procedure in Maron and Kuhn's first experiment, but instead of determining the fit between query terms and document terms, the fit between the word list for each category and the word list for each incoming document was calculated by adding up the probability relationships for all of the 'clue words'. The technique again follows the logic that Spärck Jones advocates as the most appropriate for many tasks that are 'underspecified' or 'fundamentally inexact', namely 'to allow many small and individually ambiguous clues to combine and interact' (Spärck Jones, 1999, p. 414).

Since many words[5] were taken into account, every document was likely to receive a relevance number (or 'posterior probability') for several categories, for example, document n is 0.4 relevant for category i, 0.2 for category j, and so forth, resulting in probabilistic rather than binary classification. In the case of Maron's experiment, the categories would actually represent subject descriptors and the final output of the system would be an automatically generated probabilistic index that could be used to search and rank in the same way as the manually created index used in the first experiment. The basic coordinate indexing setup remains the reference point. Unlike a manually generated index, however, the system was dynamic by design in the sense that it incorporated a pathway for learning beyond the initial training phase: if new documents were classified or a user decided to reclassify a document, the word lists for each category could be recalculated, adding new 'knowledge' to the statistical model.

This is the basic outline of a Bayes classifier and a surprisingly representative illustration of the larger field of supervised machine learning, where techniques require classified or 'labeled' data from which a model

---

5   Although Maron's first experiment used only 90 'clue words' to cover 405 research paper abstracts (including both the training set and the documents to classify), his method was explicitly aimed at much larger sets (cf. Maron, 1961 p. 414).

representing relationships between inputs (feature vectors) and outputs (class attributions) can be derived. This model can then be applied to new inputs. There are a number of important aspects to consider.

The Technicity of Learning

Bayes classifiers connect back to the previous chapters in various ways, but they also raise specific questions that are crucial for an appreciation of the larger space of contemporary information ordering. In this section, I want to address some of these questions from the angle of technicity before addressing the epistemological dimension in more depth in the following section. Five points stand out.

Understanding Choice

First, I want to stress that the outlined procedure constitutes precisely what the term 'algorithmic technique' attempts to thematize. What I have laid out in plain English and some basic formulas is not yet an algorithm in a more restrictive understanding of the term, but it outlines a method for classification that entails a way of both looking at and acting on the world. It frames and formalizes text documents as word frequency lists, formulates a sequence of stages from training to classification to adjustment, and specifies a number of proto-mathematical functions for weighting and calculating. Any software developer would be able to create a working program from my description, but every implementation would be different since many details remain underspecified and require decisions. Should words be reduced to their lemmas or stems? Where to cut off frequent and infrequent words? How to calculate word specificity? How to calculate closeness? Should document use become part of relevancy assessments? How to embed all of this in interface and activity flows? These and other questions need to be answered when an algorithmic technique is brought to bear on a specific task in a specific operating environment.

The consequences of these decisions are hard to estimate beforehand, due to the potentially large number of items, properties, and iterations. And there are not only technical reasons why the design process should not be understood as a selection from straightforward options: a working system is the outcome of a complex process of negotiation that can have far-reaching, unanticipated consequences when becoming part of concrete practices. Maron's decision to integrate document use statistics, for example, may indeed improve some empirical measure of retrieval performance or user satisfaction, but it also introduces the principle of cumulative advantage or 'Matthew effect' (Merton, 1968) into ranking dynamics, since documents with greater use will end up further up on the result list, leading to even higher use as a consequence.

This again highlights that the study of algorithmic techniques is not enough to make sense of actual systems, their behavior, the many specific commitments they imply, and the actual connections and dynamics they enter into. But a robust apprehension of common techniques can both embed more general forms of theorizing in a better understanding of software-making and inform more concrete forms of empirical analysis. It can lay the groundwork for comparison between different implementations by proving analytical categories, for example, selected units and features, intermediate forms, training and feedback setup, decision modalities, and so forth. The notion of algorithmic technique describes a pathway for asking 'how the machine "thinks"' (Burrell, 2016) and, by extension, how software-makers embedded in concrete circumstances think through or with the machine, in the sense that instances of technicity provide means of expression in the form of function that reflect both technical trajectories and local purposes and specificities.

Dramaturgy

Second, Maron follows Luhn's path in framing meaning as 'aboutness' and relies on the same reduction to word frequencies as language model. Although techniques using more involved formalizations of language both can and do exist, any running system requires and relies in some way on formalization, selection, and reduction. This more often than not implies the already familiar distillation into a common intermediate form, a gesture that enables and explains the wide applicability of algorithmic techniques. Bayes classifiers, much like other classification techniques, can be used to produce groupings of any class of objects represented by feature lists, that is, of 'any set of entities identified by weighted property vectors' (Salton, Wong, and Yang, 1975, p. 613).

What is being introduced into the arsenal of information ordering, however, is not so much the capacity to group, which is already realized through queries in the coordinate indexing setup or through some optimal arrangement of similarities and differences in unsupervised learning, but the idea that we can 'show' the machine *how* to group. Whereas Boolean or SQL queries specify logical selection criteria and unsupervised techniques look for 'natural' zones of density, the supervised approach implies a different orchestration: the 'correct' interpretation of the data is provided for a set of training items, the machine derives a model (or function) that maps inputs (feature vectors) to outputs ('target variables', i.e., classes), and that model is then applied to data that has not yet been classified. Based on the same underlying intermediate form, the ordering process thus follows a different dramaturgy. Crucially, the setup revolves around forms of supervision or 'labeling' and the move to integrated online environments, which I have addressed as 'computerization' in Chapter 1, provides not only the opportunity to normalize almost anything to the common form of the feature vector but also constant streams of feedback that function as signals for continuous supervision and training. Schäfer (2011, p. 51) refers to situations where 'users are actually not aware that they contribute to an application simply through using it' as 'implicit participation', a value-generating mechanism that is sunk into the design of the system. Voting, rating, or liking are only the most obvious ways to train the Bayesian engines: every click, every interaction, every emoji, every act of paying attention to something can be formalized as an instance of labeling and flow into the classifier. These techniques thus 'feed' on digital media environments on both ends: they receive both masses of data to classify and constant feedback regarding how well they did and how they can further improve. Optimization for specific classificatory goals becomes part of adaptive infrastructures as it is '"sunk" into' (Star and Ruhleder, 1996, p. 115) technological base layers.

Statistics

Third, evoking the name of Thomas Bayes points toward long-standing debates in statistics[6] concerning the interpretation of probability itself. Are we dealing with actual properties of nature or varying degrees of certainty? These epistemological debates are certainly important, but both beyond the ambitions of this book and hardly acknowledged[7] when statistics is used in computer and information science. If a technique can be shown to perform well, allegiances to frequentist or Bayesian interpretations of statistics are rarely considered relevant and, in line with the previous

---

6   See Russell and Norvig (2010, p. 491) for a pedagogical overview and Hacking (1990) or Stigler (1999) for a historical perspective.

7   Hastie, Tibshirani, and Friedman's influential *The Elements of Statistical Learning* (2009), for example, is completely silent on the matter.

examples of variability, one can actually develop Bayes classifiers that do not rely on Bayesian methods.[8]

It should be noted, however, that a Bayesian outlook that thinks in terms of degrees of certainty is ideally suited for situations where one might want to begin calculating probabilities for different hypotheses (e.g., concerning class membership) even if very few observations are available, continuously updating and refining prior probabilities as more evidence comes in. A spam filter starts building its model from the very first classified email and every additional act of labeling will produce an imprint while leaving room for future adaptation. The outlook also suggests and justifies 'greediness' when it comes to evidence: the more features, the better. Does an email contain images? How many? Does the image contain text? Does the email use HTML formatting? What kind of HTML features are used and how many times? What about the sender? The sending route? The time of day the message was sent? All of these elements – and many others – can become part of always larger feature vectors and develop their own probability relationships with the output categories.

This example also highlights another aspect that differentiates the use of statistics in information retrieval from more traditional settings. Whereas 'standard' datasets, for example, data on human individuals, generally contain potentially large populations characterized by a limited and stable number of variables or dimensions, the number of documents in a collection (or similar data) may easily be smaller than the number of properties in a feature vector based on word statistics. As a consequence, much research in computational statistics has been dedicated to techniques for dimensionality reduction. The various differences in application context and data characteristics, in combination with an engineering ethos that privileges output performance and (computational) cost over scientific purity, means that contemporary uses of statistics in the context of information ordering have spawned processes of 'disciplinarization' into academic and industry fields that have developed their own character and epistemological substance, even if they remain in conversation with traditional techniques and concepts.

Beyond the Basics

Fourth, the technique that Maron laid out in the 1960s is generally referred to as a 'naive' Bayes classifier, because it treats features as statistically

---

8   Russell and Norvig (2010, p. 499) argue that the naive Bayes model need not be considered Bayesian at all. For a deeper discussion of the issue, see Hand and Yu (2001).

independent from each other. Most commentators consider this to be a 'poor' or 'unrealistic' assumption (Rish, 2001, p. 41), since features such as word frequencies taken from text documents tend to correlate. Taking correlation patterns into account could be potentially useful for improving classification performance because the fact that, for example, two words tend to co-occur could help sieve another dose of meaning from the documents under scrutiny. It is certainly not difficult to explain why Maron chose to assume independence: its simplicity made naive Bayes the obvious starting point from a conceptual perspective and well-suited to the computational capacities of available hardware. One could also argue that the larger context of information retrieval, very much dominated by coordinate indexing, provided a setting that suggested and valued the compositional capacities independence between atomized dimensions affords. Still, few commentators fail to mention the 'surprisingly good classification performance' (Zhang, 2004, p. 2) demonstrated by the fact that 'the Bayesian classifier outperforms several more sophisticated approaches on a large number of data sets' (Domingos and Pazzani, 1997, p. 105) in empirical studies.

It may seem strange that 'the reasons for the Bayesian classifier's good performance were not clearly understood' (Domingos and Pazzani, 1997, p. 105) in settings were all the used data, the full specifications, and even the source code of used algorithms are available, but there are at least two good reasons for this. On the one side, there is an increasingly well-known opacity stemming from the 'mismatch' between algorithms that process large collections of high-dimensional data inductively through many cycles of iteration and 'the demands of human-scale reasoning and styles of semantic interpretation' (Burrell, 2016, p. 2). On the other side, there are simply no means to appreciate the actual statistical relationships latent in specific data other than statistical techniques themselves, which means that there is no privileged, a priori knowledge of the territory the algorithm maps, other than the initial classification of training documents. This leads to the curious situation that algorithmic techniques in machine learning and other domains become objects of study in ways evoking the observation of natural phenomena in the laboratory or 'in the wild'. As Mackenzie stresses, machine learning involves a constant stream of measures that communicate the internal states of the classifier, such as levels of precision or error rates, as well as a whole array of observational devices, including 'a striking mixture of network diagrams, scatterplots, barcharts, histograms, heatmaps, boxplots, maps, contour plots, dendrograms, and 3D plots' (Mackenzie, 2017a, p. 86) that attempt to make operation observable and more clearly understandable. This also involves efforts 'to understand the data characteristics which affect the performance of naïve Bayes' (Rish, 2001, p. 41) in order to be able to define the 'complete set of necessary and sufficient conditions for the optimality of the Bayesian classifier' (Domingos and Pazzani, 1997, p. 127). The capacity of algorithmic techniques to move between application domains, which I have emphasized a number of times, is indeed bounded: there are 'habitats' – data sets and classification characteristics – where one set of technique thrives and another withers.

And invention and adaptation of techniques continue. In fact, the seemingly obvious insufficiency of the independence assumption has led to the development of techniques that seek to model dependencies. Bayesian networks,[9] for example, provide a broader framework for reasoning with probabilities and powerful – but computationally demanding – means 'for augmenting the Naive Bayes classifier with limited interactions between the feature variables' (Koller and Sahami, 1997, p. 173). There are also many nonprobabilistic learning techniques, such as logistic regression or support-vector machines, that handle dependency differently. Deep neural networks' very raison d'être is to model complex nonlinear relationships between input variables and output classes. From here, branches lead off in various directions, many of them boasting ever more complex mathematics. The problem with many of these techniques is not just their conceptual and technical complexity, which widely available modules hide behind layers of abstraction, but their quickly increasing computational cost as the number of features grows. There are many tricks and techniques for dimensionality reduction (e.g., using weighting with tf-idf to select the most salient features) and considerable research goes into finding more efficient ways of implementing specific techniques. These investments in concretization can have enormous consequences in terms of real-world applicability. The recent rise of convolutional neural networks for deep learning, which has transformed task domains like image recognition, cannot be imagined without forms of implementation that distribute calculations over the massively parallel hardware of graphics processors (Raina, Madhavan, and Ng, 2009).

But a deeper appreciation of the substance present in many datasets can begin, much more modestly, at the level of the atoms turned into features. In the context of human language, I have already discussed dictionary- or

---

9   Bayesian networks are acyclical, directed graphs, where nodes are connected through probabilities. The canonical formulation comes from Pearl (1988), the text that Russell and Norvig (2010, p. 557) identify as the single most important publication of the 'resurgence of probability' in artificial intelligence research.

thesaurus-based transformations or enrichments that anchor heftier hooks in the meat of meaning. And moving from taking single terms as features to co-occurring word-pairs, often referred to as 'bi-grams', can introduce relative word location into the mix without explicit dependency modeling on the level of the classification technique. There rarely is a singular technical locus in software, and the spaces of possible variation are considerable.

Personalization and Recommendation

Fifth, as already mentioned, Bayes classifiers are ideal for personalization, since they can easily turn user interactions into acts of labeling to construct or adapt a decision model specifically for that user. It should come as no surprise that one of the first attempts to personalize information retrieval for individuals and not just categories of 'typical' users (novice, expert, etc.) relied on a probabilistic method close to the one described above. Drawing on explicit input in the form of initial self-descriptions and on implicit feedback based on the idea that '[o]ne of the simplest ways to derive information about a user is to look at the way he uses the system' (Rich, 1983, p. 205), Elaine Rich's personalized fiction literature recommender system built a 'user model' along a number of culturally and psychologically salient facets, such as 'interests' (e.g., 'sports'), 'politics' (e.g., 'liberal'), or 'tolerate-violence' (expressed as numerical value). These facets served as the features of a user vector that was then compared to the manually attributed book vectors in the collection.[10] As the system begins to suggest book titles and users provide feedback on recommendations, their profiles are updated accordingly. While Rich's use of probabilistic inference spans different stages, this last step can be understood as a single-class Bayes classifier, where the relevance number (or posterior probability) for that class is used to rank the books to recommend.

Personalization, understood as the process of adapting a service to individual users, is not an algorithmic technique, but a gesture or application that may draw on very different technical procedures. One such technique, often used in recommender systems, eschews actual content features altogether[11] and relies on 'collaborative filtering', an approach that operates on the intuition that 'a good way to find interesting content is to find other people who have

10   Rich's system is actually a little more complicated since it uses 'stereotypes', such as 'intellectual' or 'feminist', as intermediate categories.
11   Many systems use hybrid approaches that combine both content-based and collaborative filtering. For an early example, see Balabanović and Shoham (1997).

similar interests, and then recommend titles that those similar users like' (Breese, Heckerman, and Kadie, 1998, p. 43). This idea can inform a technique that starts from user models in the form of feature vectors taking songs 'liked' or listened to as dimensions. Similarity between users is then computed exactly the same way as described in the previous chapter, using, for example, cosine similarity or the Pearson correlation coefficient. The system can then suggest new songs listened to by similar users. User profiles and content features are simply two types of entities that can be funneled into a vector space and gestures like 'personalization', 'recommendation', or 'retrieval' are merely different ways of arranging similar operations into interface outputs.

While a system based on collaborative filtering could work for spam triage to a certain degree, emails have too much variation and are too specific to individual users to work as dimensions in a vector. Here, the specific features of the machine learning approach come as an advantage. Using content features as input for a Bayes classifier and user feedback as learning mechanism allows for the creation of fully individualized decision models that take the features of an incoming item as carriers of meaning and interpret them from the vantage point of past interactions. This highlights a crucial aspect that holds for most supervised machine learning techniques: the learning algorithm orchestrates and governs the construction of a decision model, but the actual mapping between input and output is based on the encounter between data and supervision. This has far-reaching consequences, which I will address in more depth in the next section.

Interested Readings

Bayes classifiers and other machine learning techniques arrange information ordering and decision-making in ways that are profoundly different from the common framing of algorithms as set formulas executing a stable sequence of operations. Even in academic publications, a common conception still seems to imagine a group of developers enumerating variables to take into account and specifying how to couple and weight them. The makers of Facebook, for example, would brood over the criteria for News Feed filtering, meticulously arranging metrics such as affinity between users, post engagement, and some function of time to produce a clear decision recipe that is guarded like a precious secret. Intense reflection about the application domain is certainly part of the practice, but this conception is increasingly outdated. Supervised machine learning techniques such as Bayes classifiers constitute means to derive decision models from the encounter between a purpose, data, and a mechanism that provides the 'correct' interpretation for at least some of these data, for example, through initial labeling or continuous feedback. This echoes Shera's vision from 1952 that 'classification of knowledge will not be a fixed and unalterable pattern, [...] but a series of quite widely varying schematisms, each constructed for a specific purpose' (Shera, 1952, p. 17). What changes here is the way classification and purpose come together. In coordinate indexing, the technique serving as the backdrop to Shera's argument, purpose guides the process of creating and attributing an indexing vocabulary and informs every act of searching. In the case of Bayesian spam filtering, nobody has to manually compile a list of 'spammy' words and there is also no query. The purpose is expressed through the definition of classes, for example, 'spam' and 'not-spam' for sorting emails. When a user begins to label messages, the probability relationships between words and classes are generated automatically from the message content, producing a basis for distinction- and decision-making that is not a clear-cut formula, but an adaptive statistical model containing potentially millions of features. If the word 'Viagra' appears often in mails marked as spam and rarely in others, it will become a strong indicator or clue. But every word that has not been discarded by filtering or weighting will acquire meaning that way, and the final score for an incoming message is based on all of these 'small and individually ambiguous clues' (Spärck Jones, 1999, p. 227f.), making it hard to create a simple causal narrative.

The assessment that machine '[l]earning is more like farming, which lets nature do most of the work' (Domingos, 2012, p. 81) is clearly incomplete. Even if it is certainly not wrong to say that '[m]achine learning systems automatically learn programs from data' (Domingos, 2012, p. 81), this 'program' – or decision model – sits among a whole range of other programs, that is, things that are not 'nature' or 'the world'. Machine learning systems themselves have two essential technical components, a training engine that learns from examples and an inference engine that applies the learned model (the mapping between input features and output categories or target variables) to incoming data. But further upstream we have other interfaces, infrastructures, programs, or manual gestures like data cleaning that formalize and filter the world into a neat queue of well-behaved feature vectors and submit them to a labeling process.[12] Techniques like A/B/N testing, where two or more versions of the same content or application are submitted

---

12   While Mackenzie (2017a) dives deep into the mathematical dimension of machine learning, he remains remarkably silent on the origin of training data, on the role and orchestration of labeling, and on the embedding of both of these things into the vast digital infrastructures I have addressed with the term 'computerization'.

to random samples of users, create such feedback situations as part of an ongoing process of development and optimization. Google's Experiments architecture, part of Google Analytics, describes its purpose as providing a framework that 'enables you to test almost any change or variation to a website or app to see how it performs in optimizing for a specific goal'.[13] Such goals may range from product design and improvement to the more specific forms of behavior modification Zuboff (2019) describes as 'surveillance capitalism'. Built on a Bayesian statistical engine,[14] Google's framework permits developers unfamiliar with statistical learning to integrate empirical decision processes into their design and development methodology. But even if the practice draws on actual user behavior, the whole setup of these experimental situations is clearly not accidental or 'natural' in any sense of the word. When Domingos states that machine learning is like farming, he wants to stress its inductive character, but – inadvertently or not – positions it as an activity that is not a 'disinterestedness' pursuit. Agriculture is not biology and its goal is to grow crops, not to understand the world.

And, indeed, no deep understanding of the application domain is required to produce a model. When a payday lender uses Facebook data to decide whether an applicant is likely to pay back a loan (cf. Deville, 2013), there is no need for a Bourdieusian sociologist who tags every possible profile element as an indicator of class or socioeconomic potential. This is precisely why Andrejevic (2013) calls data mining a 'post-comprehension' (p. 41) strategy: no 'theory' of the social needs to intervene, no framework that ties the myriad data traces associated with 'the "diversification" and individualization of lifestyles and ways of life' (Beck, 1992, p. 91) back into a neat description of society. It is enough to have some users who have already labeled their own profiles by the act of paying back or defaulting on their loans to generate a model where every single profile item becomes first a feature in a vector and then an indicator for 'creditworthiness'. This is what 'generalizing from examples' (Domingos, 2012, p. 78) means and it should give us an idea how engines of order can 'automate inequality' (Eubanks, 2018) if every small act or preference can be examined in relation to its economic significance. This goes beyond the encoding of 'human prejudice, misunderstanding, and bias into the software systems that increasingly [manage] our lives' (O'Neil, 2016, p. 3) toward an ever-expanding capacity to read and assess the world in relation to a purpose (Rieder, 2016).

13   https://developers.google.com/analytics/solutions/experiments, accessed 11 January 2019.
14   https://support.google.com/analytics/answer/2844870?hl=en&ref_topic=1745207, accessed 11 January 2019.

Bayes classifiers and similar techniques are neither static recipes for decision-making nor theories engaged in ontological attribution; they are methods for making data signify in relation to a particular desire to distinguish, to establish differences, and to operate on them; they are devices for the automated production of *interested readings of empirical reality*.[15] Maron's goal was not to say anything deep about the relationship between text and meaning but to design a system that produces 'good' results in the domain of its application. I thus use the term 'interested' to emphasize that the epistemic process is not just tainted by some unavowed bias[16] but fully designed around an explicit goal or purpose that trumps any epistemological or ontological qualms one may have. Just as Desrosières's (2001) notion of accounting realism suggests and Lyotard (1984) emphasizes further, 'the goal is no longer truth, but performativity – that is, the best possible input/output equation' (p. 46). This means that the definition of the desired outcome becomes the central locus of normativity.

One of the central narratives that – often implicitly – informs and justifies the empiricist organization of information ordering around behavioral feedback and clickstream data is the notion of 'revealed preference'. In 1938, the economist Paul Samuelson was voicing his dissatisfaction with recent developments around the notion of 'utility', which was central to the idea of consumer choice, he argued, but had been complicated to the point of removing 'the assumption of the measurability of utility' (p. 61). It could therefore no longer support forms of economic theory revolving mostly around mathematical modeling. In its place, Samuelson (1948) put what was to become the idea of 'revealed preference', which basically anchors the notion of utility or preference not in some elaborate psychological theory but in the observable fact that a purchase has been made: 'the individual guinea-pig, by his market behaviour, reveals his preference pattern' (p. 243). This conceptual gesture 'opened up the way for empirical studies of preferences based on observed market behaviour' (Sen, 1973, p. 242). The process of purification at work here is similar to other empirical definitions that do not really provide an actual critique of what they seek to replace but axiomatically bind the concept to a particular form of measurement rather than a theoretical construct. This is precisely what makes the notion of revealed preference so

---

15   Berry (2008, p. 365) talks about network models as constituting particular 'readings of reality'.

16   Although it may very well be. This is not the focus of the more conceptual approach taken in this book, but there is much research on bias and discrimination in data mining, for example, Custers et al. (2013). More explicitly on the technique discussed here, see Calders and Verwer (2010).

attractive in the context of information ordering. If behavior reveals preference and preference is the guiding principle for designing systems that espouse dynamic perspectivism to liberate 'the territory subjugated by classification' (Weinberger, 2008, p. 92), behavioral data can simply become another form of query, another expression of an information need or desire. From this perspective, everything falls into place, since optimization criteria such as time on site or click rate become expressions of user preference. What users do is what they want and what they want is what they shall receive. How could it be otherwise? Incidentally, this also justifies the quest to increase click rates and time on site, framing the process as a win-win situation: in the context of a music-streaming service, for example, a recommendation is doubly 'successful' if a user actually listens to the track, because it both satisfies the user's revealed preference and increases the use of the service. Machine learning, in particular, thrives on this circular logic. Grammatized infrastructures facilitate disassembly into intermediary forms and algorithmic techniques instantiate dynamic reassembly through learning or optimization processes designed around operational goals.

In the battle for users' time, attention, and money, such forms of optimization move to the center of business processes. Plasticity and modularity in software may imply creativity and expression, but they also enable companies driven by profit motives to constantly analyze, optimize, and experiment with orderings and their effects on the bottom line. Engaged in both representing and intervening, algorithmic techniques become both 'machineries of knowing' (Knorr Cetina, 1999, p. 5) and engines of order that create direct and indirect feedback loops between knowledge and power in ways that are hard to overstate. Facebook can tune its Newsfeed filtering engine in a way that something like 'time on site' or 'ad click probability' becomes the target variable for determining the optimal traits of content items for each user, individually. Instead of selecting and weighting variables manually, the classifier derives – or 'learns' – the relevant features from the relationship between data (posts and their different properties), feedback (users' engagement with these posts), and purpose (to increase engagement). The system is then able to execute the following command: 'show to the user the posts similar to those that previously led to high engagement'. In a recent interview (Klein, 2018), Mark Zuckerberg describes a setup that shows how easily the technical principles can be arranged to accommodate different value narratives. Responding to ambient criticism, the company apparently decided to move away from directly monetizable target variables and invited panels of users to rank actual contents in terms of what seemed most 'meaningful' to them. We can thus imagine an arrangement where the feedback gathered this way becomes the labeling input for a classifier that is then generalized to the entire user population. 'Meaningfulness' is submitted to the vague and empiricist treatment we are already familiar with. In an earlier post, Zuckerberg had already announced that Facebook would increasingly seek to optimize for 'time well spent', which may have the effect that 'the time people spend on Facebook and some measures of engagement will go down'. But shareholders should not worry, since this 'will be good for our community and our business over the long term too' (Zuckerberg, 2018, n.p.). Similarly, YouTube argues that they are not simply optimizing for watchtime but for user 'satisfaction' (Lewis, 2018). And the different content-flagging tools on social media sites clearly serve as input for classifiers seeking to identify illegal, harmful, or other 'unwanted' content or behavior. The question, then, is how these 'target values' are being decided on, how they are being operationalized, and how they find expression in technical terms. Any working system is a practical answer to these questions and normative commitments are being made at each step of the way.

This does not mean that machine learning is not an academic discipline, but rather that most of its operational reality occurs outside of institutional settings subscribing to Mertonian norms of science. Merton argues that 'disinterestedness' is a central tenet of scientific inquiry and that 'disinterestedness has a firm basis in the public and testable character of science' (Merton, 1973, p. 276). But the work some of machine learning's most famous scholars do at Baidu (Andrew Ng), Facebook (Yann LeCun), or Google (Geoffrey Hinton, Peter Norvig) gets sucked into infrastructures of operation that are far removed from public scrutiny. This tension characterizes, at least to a degree, any discipline that produce highly applicable knowledge. And it is certainly true that algorithmic techniques do not determine the specific performativity of the resulting algorithm. The Bayes classifier provides the capacity for making interested readings and decisions but specifies neither the purpose nor the way an engine of order projects its output back into the world. Facebook can decide to train its News Feed engine based on any criterion the company could come up with. It may not be easy to find measures for concepts like diversity, plurality, or 'meaningfulness', which are heavily context-dependent and contested when pressed a little harder. But this is a question worthy of additional research and one that would, more broadly, benefit from a perspective more hesitant to locate political salience in singular instances of technicity rather than the larger systems or infrastructures technology forms. 'Implementation' of complex human values are not *problems* to be *solved* but ongoing struggles that require forms of 'cooperative responsibility' engaging multiple actors and institutions into forms of 'dynamic interaction' (Helberger et al., 2018).

Does the emphasis on optimization targets make Bayes classifiers neutral tools that could be used to further any kind of cause? The problem is more complicated than terms like 'neutrality' and 'objectivity' suggest. Mackenzie (2015) argues that 'as machine learning is generalized, the forms of value that circulate in the form of commodities alter' (p. 444), emphasizing that the different technical 'styles' of processing 'entail different kinds of value' (p. 436). In his most recent take on the subject, he further describes machine learning as 'a new enunciative mode that disperses patterns as the visible form of difference into a less visible but highly operational space', where algorithmic techniques 'define possibilities of grouping and assembling differences' (Mackenzie, 2017a, p. 149). To better understand what this means, one can appreciate how the spaces constituted by coordinate indexing, the relational model for database management, vectorization, and other modes of formalization into intermediate forms indeed give rise to what Deleuze described as the 'fini-unlimited', where a 'finite number of components yields a practically unlimited diversity of combinations' (Deleuze, 1988, p. 131). Any sufficiently complex dataset – and especially sets with high numbers of dimensions – can be cut, sliced, and put into sequence in many, many different ways, whether this is done through a set of search results, a statistical description, or an inductive learning process. This enables new forms of knowing that enter into complex relationships with existing practices and, in particular, with the goal-oriented processes we find in management and governance. My point, here, is that we need to take Mackenzie's (2017a) assessment that the 'optics' of machine learning are always 'partial' (p. 80) in both senses of the word: partial as incomplete or fragmentary; and partial as skewed, biased, or – preferably – interested.

One could argue that data mining techniques embody forms of cognition or enunciation that are, on the one side, nonanthropomorphic in the sense that they consist of procedures that can only be enacted by fast computing machinery and, on the other side, thoroughly entangled in operational arrangements. To speak with Virilio (1994), we could say that they are 'vision machines' to which we are 'delegating the analysis of objective reality' (p. 59) and argue that there is 'a "subjective" optical interpretation of observed phenomena and not just "objective" information' (p. 75). On the level of signification, machine learning and other techniques attribute meaning to every variable in relation to a purpose; on the level of performativity, the move to increasingly integrated digital infrastructures means that every classificatory decision can be pushed back into the world instantly, showing a specific ad, hiding a specific post, refusing a loan to a specific applicant, setting the price of a product to a specific level, and so forth. No data point remains innocent. Standing in for the wider category of information ordering techniques, Bayes classifiers entangle meaning – and not just the meaning of texts – in complex and often very direct ways with decision-making informed by specific objectives and purposes. In a sense, Bacon's famous distinction between 'is' and 'ought' disappears into a form of description that is built, from the ground up, on a prescriptive horizon. We no longer decide based on what we know; we know based on the decision we want to make.

What makes algorithmic techniques far from 'neutral', then, is not some intrinsic bias or allegiance to a specific political model but the fact that these new 'levers on "reality"' (Goody, 1977, p. 109) are distributed throughout social domains in specific ways, which has the potential to profoundly reconfigure power in contemporary societies. When looking at power as 'techniques' or 'functionings', as a 'network of relations, always in tension' (Foucault, 1995, p. 26), we can appreciate how algorithmic information ordering delivers specific ways to continuously establish, organize, and modulate the relationships between datafied entities in service of strategic goals. And if the 'exercise of power consists in "conducting conduct" and in adjusting the probabilities of possible outcomes' (Foucault, 1982, p. 789, translation amended), machine learning indeed provides concrete technical means to do so, informing the varieties of 'automated management' Kitchin and Dodge discuss in *Code/Space* (2011). Although Bayes classifiers do not determine how their results are used at the interface level and beyond, they stand for a new set of techniques that have the capacity to generate interested forms of knowledge used to make myriad of small and large decisions with concrete effects. They introduce a 'micro-physics'[17] that may well affect how power operates in significant ways. And the term 'operate' needs to be taken seriously, here. The computerized infrastructures human activities are increasingly entangled with imply forms of semiosis that take effect not like signs, but also, with loose reference to Lessig (1999), like *walls*, encroaching on conduct through modifications of the visible and navigable environment.

Information Retrieval as Trading Zone

This chapter discussed the Bayes classifier both as an example for the broad category of machine learning techniques and as a means to demonstrate how

17   Foucault (1995, p. 26) introduces the term to address the many subtle, diffuse, and productive technologies of power that operate on bodies in various ways.

the intermediate forms presented in previous chapters open onto spaces of technical expression and plasticity that introduce different epistemological and operational gestures into the arsenal of software-makers and, by extension, into the professional and institutional settings they are embedded in. While the field of machine learning comprises a whole range of historical trajectories, Maron's experiments in information retrieval again show that text documents are ideal test cases for techniques that, on the one side, deal with the complexity, ambiguity, and uncertainty of human endeavors and, on the other, set out to produce operationally viable results rather than scientific models of language or deep emulations of human thinking. The use of statistical techniques implies forms of cognition and learning that are fundamentally caught up in the utility equations of specific task domains.

The Bayes classifier demonstrates how, in Maron's (1963) own terms, 'methods, approaches, clues, tricks, heuristics' (p. 141) can inform intricate epistemological and operational engines functioning on top of basic computation. We again observe how algorithmic techniques enable complex and compound behavior based on the computer's capacity to perform very large numbers of simple operations. Maron's collection of 405 scientific abstracts, tiny by today's standards, already contained thousands of individual words and not even Roberto Busa's Jesuit colleagues would have been easily convinced to perform the mindless counting and calculating work necessary to classify even a single document.

The entanglement with operational concerns and the willingness to combine approaches from different fields make it problematic to consider these techniques simply as 'applied statistics' and we should not overestimate their relationship with disciplinary developments in statistics.[18] While I do not want to generalize too far from the small group of individuals I have mentioned by name over the last chapters, it bears mentioning that the educational background and thematic interest of early information retrieval researchers was not very close to the fields and preoccupations 'traditional' statistics were concerned with, such as the study of biological patterns of inheritance or 'the measurement of people and populations' (Beer, 2016, p. 9). Luhn was an engineer, Maron a physicist turned philosopher of science, and Salton one of the earliest 'genuine' computer scientists. Spärck Jones came to information retrieval through her PhD research in linguistics. They all had the education and capacity to use statistical techniques with ease but were

---

18 'Despite the obvious connections between data mining and statistical data analysis, most of the methodologies used in Data Mining have so far originated in fields other than Statistics' (Friedman, 1998, p. 3).

hardly interested in disciplinary debates around the nature of probability or the difference between its Bayesian and frequentist interpretations. And unlike Codd, who constructed the relational model on the basis of a strong mathematical formalism, even Salton was more concerned with in situ experimentation and testing than theoretical elaboration.

The point I want to make is that statistical concepts and techniques enter information retrieval as technical elements, detached from their origins and ready-to-hand for integration into techniques that draw on a variety of trajectories and, crucially, enter into ongoing dialog with the computational machinery of the day. The information retrieval setting and its pragmatic, output- and performance-focused attitude encouraged and justified experimentation, supporting an epistemological outlook that, at least to one commentator, yielded only 'relatively disappointing progress [...] to develop as a coherent and firmly based empirical discipline' (Ellis, 1998, p. 225) and favored approaches that 'lack a full paradigmatic identity' (Ellis, 1998, p. 239). Salton himself lamented the 'absence of basic theories, and the largely experimental nature of the information science field' (Salton, 1973, p. 220). This should not minimize achievements but rather emphasize that information retrieval and, by extension, the larger space of contemporary information ordering is best understood as a 'trading zone' (Galison, 1996), where statistics and other areas of mathematics intermingle with ideas about language, information, and knowledge as well as computing machinery, systems design, and the concrete and imaginary requirements of 'knowledge workers' and 'decision-makers'. Certainly, similar to what Galison finds in his analysis of Monte Carlo simulations, the pidgin languages we encounter in the earliest texts solidify into 'a full-fledged Creole: the language of a self-supporting subculture with enough structure and interest to support a research life without being an annex of another discipline' (Galison, 1996, p. 153). This stabilization is achieved through metanarratives concerning information needs and information overload, through concepts and metrics like recall and precision, through formal models such as the VSM, and through accepted knowledge rituals coming in the form of comparative experiments and competitions. Yet there is no common paradigm, no firm ontology, and not even a shared diagnosis what the 'library problem' really consists of. But again with Galison (1996), the different epistemological cultures begin to develop a 'common activity centered around the computer' (p. 153), despite serious internal doubts (cf. Taube, 1965) and despite the general reluctance of librarians, who felt like victims of colonization rather than partners (cf. Wasserman, 1965, p. 10) and retain an ambiguous relationship with the information retrieval trading zone to this day. The way the computer serves as a center should not be understood primarily through notions like quantification, formalization, or unification around a central paradigmatic reference like Shannon's information theory or logic-based computationalism. These elements are far from irrelevant, but, as the history of information retrieval shows, the computer's capacity to connect and to compel stems primarily from its capacity to *function*.

As mentioned earlier, Agre (1997b) build his critique of artificial intelligence on the assessment that 'AI people, by and large, insist that nothing is understood until it has been made into a working computer system' (p. 12) and argues that this constrains the space of ideas and styles of reasoning that are admitted into the discipline, hampering its creative and intellectual potential. Seen from another side, however, we can speculate that the normative force of a running system also *relaxes*, at least to a point, the demand for actual understanding. The Bayes classifier becomes a viable technique because it can be shown to work and, indeed, to work well. Knowing *why* a technique works well is not a fundamental requirement, even if the question prompts intense follow-up research that has the potential to push the discipline forward in terms of genuine understanding. The testing of classification performance on preclassified corpora is therefore not an entertaining sideshow but lies at the center of information retrieval and adjacent fields. For Spärck Jones, this has a profound effect on their epistemological makeup:

> [T]he role of experiments in AI is to try out designs for engineering artefacts, to see how well some system will meet some need. [...] This implies a performance measure related to the system's purpose, which may be more or less easy to find. But it is a measure of acceptability not of truth. (Spärck Jones, 1990, p. 281)

Experiments and competitions establish the working system and at least a partial appreciation of its capacities in the public arena, but they also frame the terms of what constitutes 'acceptability'. We can see a similar logic play out more recently around neural networks. The famous ImageNet corpus and the annual ImageNet Large Scale Visual Recognition Challenge, to name a concrete example, take part in defining what 'visual recognition' actually means, what constitutes 'success', 'failure', and so forth. The epistemological logic that drives the focus on the running system and its purpose-driven performance indeed constitutes an 'attitude to reality' (Desrosières, 2001, p. 339) that prepares and facilitates the transfer of techniques into the operational domains of business and government.

Machine learning, taken together with the techniques discussed in the previous two chapters, demonstrates how a variety of algorithmic techniques can build on the same intermediate forms and these are not simply different approaches to doing the same thing: the canonical query-response situation we know from coordinate indexing does not imply the same epistemological and operational setup as document clustering with the help of unsupervised machine learning, as item recommendation via collaborative filtering, or as training a classifier through examples and feedback. The difference between an explicit request for information and the implicit observation of use patterns that drives much of personalization captures only part of these variations. In the following chapter, I will initially leave the domain of information retrieval only to come back with new 'material' to integrate into algorithmic information ordering. Looking at the long and illustrious prehistory of the PageRank algorithm, which I take as a stand-in for the larger field of network analysis, I want to widen the perspective and show how contemporary information ordering draws on domains beyond document processing, encountering different modes of valuation and building on intermediate forms other than feature vectors.

Bibliography

Agre, P. E. (1997b). Toward a Critical Technical Practice: Lessons Learned in Trying to Reform AI. In G. C. Bowker, S. L. Star, W. Turner, and L. Gasser (eds.), *Social Science, Technical Systems, and Cooperative Work: Beyond the Great Divide* (pp. 131-158). New York: Psychology Press.

Andrejevic, M. (2013). *Infoglut: How Too Much Information Is Changing the Way We Think and Know.* New York: Routledge.

Balabanović, M., and Shoham, Y. (1997). Fab: Content-Based, Collaborative Recommendation. *Communications of the ACM 40*(3), 66-72.

Beck, U. (1992). *Risk Society: Towards a New Modernity* (M. Ritter, trans.). London: Sage.

Beer, D. (2016). How Should We Do the History of Big Data? *Big Data & Society 3*(1), 1-10.

Berry, D. M. (2008). The Poverty of Networks. *Theory, Culture and Society 25*(7-8), 364-372.

Borko, H. (1962). The Construction of an Empirically Based Mathematically Derived Classification System. In G. A. Barnard (ed.), *AIEE-IRE '62 (Spring) Proceedings of the May 1-3, 1962, Spring Joint Computer Conference* (pp. 279-289). New York: ACM.

Borko, H., and Bernick, M. (1963). Automatic Document Classification. *Journal of the ACM 10*(2), 151-162.

Breese, J. S., Heckerman, D., and Kadie, C. (1998). Empirical Analysis of Predictive Algorithms for Collaborative Filtering. In G. F. Cooper and S. Moral (eds.), *UAI '98 Proceedings of the Fourteenth Conference on Uncertainty in Artificial Intelligence* (pp. 43-52). San Francisco: Morgan Kaufmann.

Burrell, J. (2016). How the Machine 'Thinks': Understanding Opacity in Machine Learning Algorithms. *Big Data & Society 3*(1), 1-12.

Calders, T., and Verwer, S. (2010). Three Naive Bayes Approaches for Discrimination-Free Classification. *Data Mining and Knowledge Discovery 21*(2), 277-292.

Custers, B., Calders, T., Schermer, B., and Zarsky, T. (eds.). (2013). *Discrimination and Privacy in the Information Society: Data Mining and Profiling in Large Databases.* Berlin: Springer.

Deleuze, G. (1988). *Foucault* (S. Hand, trans.). Minneapolis: University of Minnesota Press.

Desrosières, A. (2001). How Real Are Statistics? Four Possible Attitudes. *Social Research 68*(2), 339-355.

Deville, J. (2013). Leaky Data: How Wonga Makes Lending Decisions. *Charisma Consumer Market Studies*, 20 May. Retrieved from http://www.charisma-network.net.

Domingos, P. (2012). A Few Useful Things to Know about Machine Learning. *Communications of the ACM 55*(10), 78-87.

Domingos, P., and Pazzani, M. J. (1997). On the Optimality of the Simple Bayesian Classifier Under Zero-One Loss. *Machine Learning 29*(2-3), 103-130.

Ellis, D. (1998). Paradigms and Research Traditions in Information Retrieval Research. *Information Services Use 18*(4), 225-241.

Eubanks, V. (2018). *Automating Inequality: How High-Tech Tools Profile, Police, and Punish the Poor.* New York: St. Martin's Press.

Foucault, M. (1982). The Subject and Power. *Critical Inquiry 8*(4), 777-795.

Foucault, M. (1995). *Discipline and Punish: The Birth of the Prison* (A. Sheridan, trans.). New York: Vintage Books.

Friedman, J. H. (1998). Data Mining and Statistics: What's the Connection? *Computing Science and Statistics 29*(1), 3-9.

Galison, P. (1996). Computer Simulations and the Trading Zone. In P. Galison and D. J. Stump (eds.), *The Disunity of Science: Boundaries, Contexts, and Power* (pp. 118-157). Stanford: Stanford University Press.

Goody, J. (1977). *The Domestication of the Savage Mind.* Cambridge: Cambridge University Press.

Hacking, I. (1990). *The Taming of Chance.* Cambridge: Cambridge University Press.

Hand, D. J., and Yu, K. (2001). Idiot's Bayes: Not So Stupid after All? *International Statistical Review 69*(3), 385-398.

Hastie, T., Tibshirani, R., and Friedman, J. H. (2009). *The Elements of Statistical Learning: Data Mining, Inference, and Prediction* (2nd ed.). New York: Springer.

Helberger, N., Pierson, J., and Poell, T. (2018). Governing Online Platforms: From Contested to Cooperative Responsibility. *The Information Society 34*(1), 1-14.

Kitchin, R., and Dodge, M. (2011). *Code/Space: Software and Everyday Life.* Cambridge, MA: MIT Press.

Klein, E. (2018). Mark Zuckerberg on Facebook's Hardest Year, and What Comes Next. *Vox*, 2 April. Retrieved from https://www.vox.com.

Knorr Cetina, K. (1999). *Epistemic Cultures: How the Sciences Make Knowledge.* Harvard: Harvard University Press.

Koller, D., and Sahami, M. (1997). Hierarchically Classifying Documents Using Very Few Words. In D. H. Fisher (ed.), *ICML-97 Proceedings of the Fourteenth International Conference on Machine Learning* (pp. 170-178). San Francisco: Morgan Kaufmann.

Lessig, L. (1999). *Code and Other Laws of Cyberspace.* New York: Basic Books.

Lewis, P. (2018). 'Fiction Is Outperforming Reality': How YouTube's Algorithm Distorts Truth. *The Guardian*, 2 February. Retrieved from https://www.theguardian.com.

Luhn, H. P. (1968a). Auto-Encoding of Documents for Information Retrieval Systems. In C. K. Schultz (ed.), *H. P. Luhn: Pioneer of Information Science: Selected Works* (pp. 126-131). New York: Spartan Books.

Lyotard, J.-F. (1984). *The Postmodern Condition: A Report on Knowledge* (G. Bennington and B. Massumi, trans.). Manchester: Manchester University Press.

Mackenzie, A. (2015). The Production of Prediction: What Does Machine Learning Want? *European Journal of Cultural Studies 18*(4-5), 429-445.

Mackenzie, A. (2017a). *Machine Learners: Archaeology of a Data Practice.* Cambridge, MA: MIT Press.

Maron, M. E. (1961). Automatic Indexing: An Experimental Inquiry. *Journal of the ACM 8*(3) 404-417.

Maron, M. E. (1963). A Logician's View of Language-Data Processing. In P. L. Garvin (ed.), *Natural Language and the Computer* (pp. 128-151). New York: McGraw-Hill.

Maron, M. E. (2008). An Historical Note on the Origins of Probabilistic Indexing. *Information Processing & Management 44*(2), 971-972.

Maron, M. E., and Kuhns, J. L. (1960). On Relevance, Probabilistic Indexing and Information Retrieval. *Journal of the ACM 7*(3), 216-244.

Merton, R. K. (1968). The Matthew Effect in Science. *Science 159*(3810), 56-63.

Merton, R. K. (1973). *The Sociology of Science: Theoretical and Empirical Investigations.* Chicago: University of Chicago Press.

O'Neil, C. (2016). *Weapons of Math Destruction: How Big Data Increases Inequality and Threatens Democracy.* New York: Crown.

Pearl, J. (1988). *Probabilistic Reasoning in Intelligent Systems: Networks of Plausible Inference*. San Mateo: Morgan Kaufmann.

Raina, R., Madhavan, A., and Ng, A. Y. (2009). Large-Scale Deep Unsupervised Learning Using Graphics Processors. In A. Danyluk, L. Bottou, and M. Littman (eds.), *ICML '09 Proceedings of the 26th Annual International Conference on Machine Learning* (pp. 873-880). New York: ACM.

Rich, E. (1983). Users Are Individuals: Individualizing User Models. *International Journal of Man-Machine Studies 18*(3), 199-214.

Rieder, B. (2016). Big Data and the Paradox of Diversity. *Digital Culture & Society 2*(2): 1-16.

Rish, I. (2001). An Empirical Study of the Naive Bayes Classifier. *IJCAI Workshop on Empirical Methods in Artificial Intelligence 3*(22), 41-46.

Russell, S., and Norvig, P. (2010). *Artificial Intelligence* (3rd ed.). Upper Saddle River: Pearson Education.

Salton, G. (1973). On the Development of Information Science. *Journal of the American Society for Information Science 24*(3), 218-220.

Salton, G., Wong, A., and Yang, C.-S. (1975). A Vector Space Model for Automatic Indexing. *Communications of the ACM 18*(11), 613-620.

Samuelson, P. A. (1938). A Note on the Pure Theory of Consumer's Behaviour. *Economica 5*(17), 61-71.

Samuelson, P. A. (1948). Consumption Theory in Terms of Revealed Preference. *Economica 15*(60), 243-253.

Schäfer, M. T. (2011). *Bastard Culture! How User Participation Transforms Cultural Production*. Amsterdam: Amsterdam University Press.

Sen, A. (1973). Behaviour and the Concept of Preference. *Economica 40*(159), 241-259.

Shera, J. H. (1952). Special Librarianship and Documentation. *Library Trends 1*(2), 189-199.

Silberman, S. (2000). The Quest for Meaning. *Wired*, 1 February. Retrieved from https://www.wired.com.

Solomonoff, R. J. (1957). An Inductive Inference Machine. *IRE Convention Record, Section on Information Theory 2*, 56-62.

Spärck Jones, K. (1990). What Sort of a Thing Is an AI Experiment? In D. Partridge and Y. Wilks (eds.), *The Foundations of Artificial Intelligence* (pp. 276-281). Cambridge: Cambridge University Press.

Spärck Jones, K. (1999). Information Retrieval and Artificial Intelligence. *Artificial Intelligence 114*, 257-281.

Star, S. L., and Ruhleder, K. (1996). Steps toward an Ecology of Infrastructure: Design and Access for Large Information Spaces. *Information Systems Research 7*(1), 111-134.

Stiegler, B. (2010). Memory. In W. J. T. Mitchell and M. Hansen (eds.), *Critical Terms for Media Studies* (pp. 64-87). Chicago: University of Chicago Press.

Stigler, S. M. (1983). Who Discovered Bayes's Theorem? *American Statistician 37*(4), 290-296.

Stigler, S. M. (1999). *Statistics on the Table: The History of Statistical Concepts and Methods*. Cambridge, MA: Harvard University Press.

Taube, M. (1965). A Note on the Pseudo-Mathematics of Relevance. *American Documentation 16*(2), 69-72.

Thompson, P. (2008). Looking Back: On Relevance, Probabilistic Indexing and Information Retrieval. *Information Processing and Management 44*, 963-970.

Virilio, P. (1994). *The Vision Machine* (J. Rose, trans.). Bloomington: Indiana University Press.

Wasserman, P. (1965). *The Librarian and the Machine*. Detroit: Gale Research.

Weinberger, D. (2008). *Everything Is Miscellaneous*. New York: Henry Holt.

Zhang, H. (2004). The Optimality of Naive Bayes. In V. Barr and Z. Markov (eds.), *Proceedings of the Seventeenth International FLAIRS Conference* (pp. 1-6). Menlo Park: AAAI Press.

Zuboff, S. (2019). *The Age of Surveillance Capitalism: The Fight for a Human Future at the New Frontier of Power*. New York: PublicAffairs.

Zuckerberg, M. (2018). No title [Facebook message], 12 January. Retrieved from https://www.facebook.com/zuck/posts/10104413015393571.

7. Calculating Networks: From Sociometry to PageRank

Abstract

This chapter ventures into the field of network algorithms, using the prehistory of Google's PageRank algorithm to discuss yet another way to think about information ordering. The chapter shows how algorithmic ordering techniques exploit and integrate knowledge from areas other than information retrieval – in particular the social sciences and citation analysis – and demonstrates how the 'politics' of an algorithm can depend on small variations that lead to radically different outcomes. The context of web search means that the various techniques covered in the second part of the book are brought together into a shared application space, allowing for a more concrete return to earlier discussions of variation and combination in software.

Keywords: PageRank, recursive status index, graph theory, sociometry, citation analysis

While many of the algorithmic techniques behind ordering gestures such as ranking, filtering, or recommending have indeed been pioneered in the context of information retrieval, there are other sites of inception that inform technical and conceptual trajectories. This chapter traces the development of network algorithms and the application of graph theory to information ordering through the fields of sociometry and citation analysis and then explains how these elements made their way into information retrieval, becoming part of Google's emblematic search engine.

Network analysis has seen a stellar rise over the last two decades: network visualizations have become a common sight in and beyond academia, social network analysis has found its way into the core curriculum of the social sciences, and certain scholars have gone as far as to declare the advent of a 'new science of networks' (Barabási, 2002; Watts, 2004). Powerful but

Rieder, B., *Engines of Order: A Mechanology of Algorithmic Techniques*. Amsterdam: Amsterdam University Press, 2020

DOI 10.5117/9789462986190_CH07

easy-to-use software packages such as Gephi (Bastian, Heymann, and Jacomy, 2009) have been highly successful in promoting network analysis, making the approach a mainstay in areas ranging from epidemiology to marketing. These tools incorporate sophisticated forms of calculation and visualization, and they have popularized concepts and techniques from graph theory beyond specialist circles. They enable and facilitate the analysis and mapping of relationships between websites using hyperlinks, between user accounts or content items on social media, or between words that co-occur in the same tweet or sentence. This popularity of network analysis as analytical tool has made it easier to talk about other domains where algorithmic techniques based on graph theory have proliferated.

Indeed, online platforms and services employ similar techniques to differentiate, rank, filter, connect, or group information items. A social scientist may use a network metric to identify 'opinion leaders' or to investigate power structures in a population of human beings more generally, but a social media site may use the exact same technique to decide which accounts to promote or which messages to discard from a content stream. While machine learning techniques are particularly competent at performing fast and self-adapting classification tasks and the relational database model is well suited for making complex and precise enquiries into data collections, network algorithms are especially apt when it comes to differentiating entities and ensembles in large-scale interaction systems. Unlike the empirical techniques discussed in the previous two chapters, which establish and operate on distributions or vectors describing objects and their properties, they channel descriptions and formalizations of pairwise relations between objects into another important intermediate form. In the context of web search, for example, a network perspective moves the focus of attention from the content of documents to the hyperlinks between them. This precise shift sits at the heart of the story behind Google Search, the company's web search engine, whose success is often attributed to PageRank, the most famous of all network algorithms and the focus of this chapter.

Using the algorithm's prehistory as an entry point into the large and complex field of network analysis, I will focus on what could be called 'evaluative metrics', techniques that, once again, seek to assess culturally embedded notions such as importance, relevance, authority, or quality through iterative calculations that attribute a value to each of the items under consideration. These metrics have come to play a significant role in a growing number of settings, and Google Search is just the tip of a much larger iceberg.

Even if this chapter takes a particular algorithm and its self-proclaimed mission of 'bringing order to the web' (Page et al., 1999) as its telos and spends more time on conceptual embeddings, I will still emphasize variation and technical coupling over singular logics and paradigmatic purity. Focusing on PageRank has the advantage of dealing with a contemporary algorithm that is well documented in two research papers (Brin and Page, 1998; Page et al., 1999) as well as two US patents (Page 2001, 2004) that, remarkably, are more thorough in their citation practices than the academic publications. Additionally, RageRank is one of the few algorithms venturing into deeply mathematical territory that has not only been studied extensively by mathematicians and computer scientists (Langville and Meyer, 2004; Bianchini, Gori, and Scarselli, 2005), but is also regularly commented on by scholars in the humanities and social sciences (Introna, 2007; Diaz, 2008; Rieder, 2009). This relative familiarity with the concept and its application in web search will hopefully make certain aspects of my argument more vivid and provide grounding material for the more abstract technicities I will address.

This chapter relates more explicitly to contemporary fields such as 'web search studies' (Zimmer, 2010) than earlier ones, but the intellectual genealogy of the models and techniques in question here can be traced back to at least the 1930s. It leads to another important trading zone, one that primarily involves mathematics and the social sciences but remains largely distinct from the well-documented history of statistics (Hacking, 1990; Stigler, 1999). In the first part of this chapter, I will reconstruct the historical context, focusing on the particular idea that one can measure the 'authority' of a node in a (social) network recursively, that is, by taking into account not only the number of connected nodes but also their respective status.[1] This idea has often been presented as a core innovation in PageRank: when calculating the 'importance' of a web page, a link from a highly ranked site is 'worth' more than a link from a site with a low rank. The second part of the chapter examines PageRank more concretely, first by comparing it to the very similar HITS algorithm (Kleinberg, 1999), and second by closely scrutinizing the damping factor α with the help of the sociometric texts that first introduced such a parameter into recursive status calculations. The argument begins with a closer look at the history of graph theory and its close relationship with the social sciences.

---

1   For the wider historical and conceptual background of the methods discussed here, see Mayer (2009).

Social Theory, Graph Theory

In the introduction to his *Theorie der endlichen und unendlichen Graphen* (Theory of finite and infinite graphs) from 1936, the first textbook on graph theory, the Hungarian mathematician Dénes Kőnig (1936) wrote that '[p]erhaps even more than to the contact between mankind and nature, graph theory owes to the contact of human beings between each other' (n.p.), pointing to the often overlooked fact that modern graph theory developed, perhaps even more so than statistics, in close contact with the social sciences. Rather than being imported into these disciplines as a ready-made mathematical toolkit, graph theory was shaped in no small part by the measuring fever in the field of 'small group' research, founded by Kurt Lewin and Jacob L. Moreno. Even the mathematician Frank Harary, the central figure in the development, application, and standardization of graph theory in the second half of the twentieth century, first came into contact with his future field of specialization at the Research Center for Group Dynamics, established by Lewin in 1948 at the University of Michigan (Harary, 1969, p. 6). This close relationship warrants further investigation.

The Development of Graph Theory in Relation to the Social Sciences

Despite its enormous success in recent decades, graph theory – 'a mathematical model for any system involving a binary[2] relation' (Harary, 1969, p. v) – has historically not been considered a noble endeavor. Although prominent names such as Leonhard Euler, Gustav Kirchhoff, Arthur Cayley, and William Hamilton are attached to its history, it is only in the second half of the twentieth century that graph theory emerges from what J. H. C. Whitehead called the 'slums of topology' (cit. in Erdős, 1977, p. 3). The *Journal of Graph Theory* was founded only in 1977, which further testifies to a lack of interest from (pure) mathematicians. But besides the growing number of practical applications in chemistry, physics, and engineering, it is in the social sciences, and specifically in social psychology, that a problem space appears that proves particularly fertile for the development of a mathematics concerned with *structure*. Unlike the 'library problem', which is intrinsically tied to the pragmatics of institutions having a clear utilitarian mission, whether that mission is public education or the support for knowledge

---

2   In graph theory, a connection always runs between exactly two individual elements, with the exception of a 'loop', that is, a node that links to itself.

work and decision-making, this particular space revolves around the more open-ended problems of scientific inquiry.

A first line of development can be traced to Jacob L. Moreno's (1934) book *Who Shall Survive?*, an original and idiosyncratic volume that launched the field of sociometry as 'the mathematical study of psychological properties of populations' (p. 432). Developed out of group psychotherapy, sociometry was essentially organized around the sociometric test, a questionnaire distributed in small- and mid-sized groups – schools, factories, etc. – that asked people to choose the individuals they liked best, admired most, had the most contact with, or similar questions. The resulting pairwise (network) data was thought to reveal the 'psychological structure of society' (p. 9) and was displayed and analyzed as a sociogram, a manually ar-ranged point-and-line diagram that would nowadays be called a 'network visualization'. But while Moreno indeed spearheaded the visual display of the network data produced by the sociometric test, his 'mathematical study' was underdeveloped in terms of actual mathematical method, which prompted criticism 'for lack of the methodological stringency appropriate to science' (Mayer, 2009, p. 60). Moreno's work still garnered significant interest and the journal *Sociometry*, founded in 1937, attracted a number of contributors with mathematical skill, who started to work on the peculiarly rich and complex data produced by a remarkably simple questionnaire.

In 1946, Forsyth and Katz made a critical step toward mathematization by proposing to replace the networks drawn in a process of trial and error with a square matrix, often referred to as 'adjacency matrix', in order to 'present sociometric data more objectively' (p. 341). While the goal was to display a graph[3] in a way that was less confusing than the hand-drawn sociograms, the authors also produced a quasi-algorithmic technique to manipulate the matrix simply by reordering rows and columns in a way that subgroups would become visible. The shift in mode of representation also opened the door for the application of relatively simple but powerful methods from matrix algebra (Festinger, 1949).

---

3   While the terms 'network' and 'graph' are frequently used synonymously, it should be noted that mathematicians often make a distinction based on levels of abstraction and formalization: 'There are hierarchies of mathematical models. A network is a model for empirical flows. A graph or digraph is a model for a network – it serves as a first approximation to a network with numerical or other values on its edges (or arcs) and maybe on its vertices. For a graph or digraph captures the structure of a network while suppressing the additional numerical information' (Harary, 1983, p. 355).

	node 1	node 2	node 3	...
node 1	0	1	0	
node 2	1	0	1	
node 3	0	1	0	
...				

A generic adjacency matrix describing an (undirected) graph. This square matrix uses binary values, but numerical values are often used as well if the data includes some measure of frequency or intensity for the relations between nodes.

Just like statistics provides a number of (standardized) techniques, for example, to establish a correlation coefficient between two variables, the matrix constitutes an intermediate form that points directly toward different operations that rely on linear algebra to produce 'views' on sociometric data, structural measures that are essentially 'order from order' (Chun, 2011, p. 101ff.), transformations of numbers into other numbers. We should not make the mistake, however, to dismiss such calculations as tautological, as essentially expressing the same thing as the original input; each calculation reveals some aspect of the data. In this sense, they are further examples for mechanical reasoning, transformations that become 'interpretations', ways of reading and making sense of the world in terms that are simultaneously reductionist (phenomena are reduced to a point-and-line model) and endlessly generative (the number of possible transformations is potentially infinite). Although Gerard Salton's work dealt with a different problem space and used the somewhat different term-document matrices, it was able to draw on the same space of mathematical technique, highlighting one of many (possible) intersections between trajectories.

Furthermore, the matrix approach made it possible to connect the work on sociometric data to a second line of development in the mathematization of social structure. During the 1940s, Bavelas (1948) had developed an innovative sketch for the mathematical expression of group structures, building on Kurt Lewin's *Principles of Topological Psychology* (1936). Using mostly geometric methods, he introduced such concepts as 'geodesic distance' and 'centrality' into the social network vocabulary. Unlike notions of statistical similarity (or distance), these measures were built on the idea of 'stepping' from one 'cell' (node) to the next. The distance between two nodes is thus the number of steps it takes to get from one to the other. As Festinger argued, the matrix approach proved useful here, because it could be directly applied to 'such concepts as diameter of [topological structures] and distance from one part of the structure to another' (Festinger, 1949, p. 157). The shift from the point-and-line diagram to the matrix representation thus reinforced the idea that social structure could become fully calculable and encouraged the import of techniques from algebra and geometry.

According to Barnes and Harary, the 'first indisputable application of graph theory to network analysis did not come until 1953' (Barnes and Harary, 1983, p. 237) when Harary and Norman's short volume *Graph Theory as a Mathematical Model in Social Science* (1953) was published. It marks a shift in disciplinary background similar to what we have seen in information retrieval: so far, most of the attempts at constructing mathematical methods for expressing and analyzing sociometric data had come from sociologists and psychologists with an interest in mathematics – with the notable exception of the statistician Leo Katz. But this was the work of two mathematicians with an interest in the social sciences. Frank Harary in particular established himself as the key figure in the 'mathematization' of sociometry, even before the publication of his seminal *Graph Theory* (1969), which not only standardized concepts, vocabulary, and methods, but also presented them in a pedagogical, applicable way that was crucial for the spread of graph theory and associated techniques.

While the more rigorous mathematical approach did not mean that ties with the social sciences were severed – Harary regularly collaborated with social scientists throughout his long career – there were nonetheless three important consequences. First, pictorial representations of networks and visual forms of analysis faded into the background. Network diagrams were still used, but rather as teaching aids in textbooks than as research tools in empirical work. Only the spread of graphical user interfaces in the 1990s and the development of layout algorithms, based for example, on force simulations, lead to a true renaissance of the now so familiar point-and-line diagrams. Second, network metrics and methods for mathematical analysis proliferated and became both conceptually and computationally more demanding, sometimes to a point where their empirical applicability became technically forbidding and methodologically questionable, even to scholars sympathetic to the general approach (cf. Granovetter, 1973, p. 1361). Third, although exchange between the mathematical methods of graph theory and empirical work in the social sciences has remained strong over the last decades, the movement toward abstraction and 'purification' implied by mathematization has led to a certain demarcation between the two. On the one side, graph theory has turned more and more into an 'immutable mobile' (Latour, 1986), an inscription that can travel from one setting to another without losing its shape. Stripped of the marks of their origin, these techniques – packaged in handbooks or software programs – are ready to be applied wherever a network can be found or formalized. On the other side, there has been a certain tendency, especially in less quantitative circles of sociology and social theory, to use the network model as an ontological concept rather than an analytical one, and to endow it with certain properties, for example, decentralization, uncontrollability, opposition to hierarchies, and so on.[4] This is largely at odds with the epistemological commitment that underpins the application of graph theory to social phenomena, which is not a commitment to the network as a positive empirical entity but primarily to concepts and methods for studying empirical phenomena that can be modeled as networks. Consider the following quote:

> As we have seen, the basic terms of digraph theory are point and line. Thus, if an appropriate coordination is made so that each entity of an empirical system is identified with a point and each relationship is identified with a line, then for all true statements about structural properties of the obtained digraph there are corresponding true statements about structural properties of the empirical system. (Harary, Norman, and Cartwright, 1965, p. 22)

What takes shape over these lines is a separation between the empirical and the analytical that is characteristic to quantitative empirical research and shifts the full epistemological weight onto the shoulders of 'formalization', that is, onto the 'appropriate coordination' between the two levels. I do not want to contest this separation in philosophical terms here, but rather put forward the much simpler critique that in order to produce a formalization of social phenomena that can be mapped unto the axioms of graph theory, a commitment has to be made, not to the network as an ontological category, but rather to a 'theory of the social' that supports and substantiates the formalization process, much like lay theories of language justified the representation of documents as term vectors in previous chapters. In Moreno's (1934) case, we find a theory of psychological 'attractions and repulsions' between 'social atoms' that bears the epistemological weight of formalization in the sense that it justifies the mapping of a relationship between two people onto two points and a line by conceiving 'the social' as a primarily dyadic affair.

4   This tendency has been particularly strong in media studies and adjacent fields where communication and computer networks proliferate. While these particular networks may indeed have very specific properties, graph theory does not imply a theory of the nature of empirical networks. This would seem obvious to a mathematician, but when reviewing three titles in media studies, Berry has to explicitly remind his readers that the 'network is not ontological it is analytical' (Berry, 2008, p. 365).

Computerization conveniently transforms this process from a matter of theoretical elaboration into one of design. The grammatization of operational entities, which spans data models, program logic, and interface elements, indeed 'produces' atomized entities and their relations: social media services, to use a recognizable example, do not *describe* empirical systems, but *fabricate* them by building communicative infrastructures where user profiles interact with each other in a variety of ways. Just like early information retrieval pioneers were comfortable processing language without more than a rudimentary theory of language, the treatment of accounts as nodes and friendship connections as links requires little in terms of epistemological commitment. The 'appropriate coordination' mentioned above, which keeps social scientists awake at night, comes easy when digital objects are no longer formalizations of something else, but 'natively' (Rogers, 2013, p. 1) digital objects that are *already* fabricated axiomatic entities, conveniently transposable into basic intermediate forms. I will come back to this question further down, after having looked at the historic development of a specific type of measure that develops against the backdrop I have just outlined: the recursive status index.

Recursive Status in Sociometry

While social theorists (Castells, 1996; Benkler, 2006) have regularly opposed network forms of social organization to hierarchies over the last decades, the empirical-analytical approach followed by small-group research makes no such opposition; quite to the contrary, graph theory is seen as a means to detect and to measure social hierarchies of different kinds. As already mentioned, despite the definition of sociometry as mathematical study, Moreno's mathematical toolkit was rudimentary. But the sociometric test yielded such rich and unconventional data that even basic counting could lead to curious discoveries, for example, concerning the distribution of interpersonal attraction. When asking people whom they liked best, had the most contact with, or admired the most, the resulting distribution would be invariably skewed. Transposing such a 'choice distribution' from the New York State Training School for Girls,[5] which Moreno used as his empirical playground, to New York City, he made an interesting observation:

> For New York, with a population of 7,000,000, the above percentages [taken from the Training School for Girls] would be after the 1st choice, 3,200,000

---

5   Gießmann (2009, p. 274) describes this reeducation camp for young girls, where Moreno worked, as a '*Dogville* in the US of the 1930s'.

individuals unchosen; after the 2nd choice, 2,100,000 unchosen; after the 3rd choice, 1,400,000 unchosen; after the 4th choice, 1,200,000 unchosen; and after the 5th choice, 1,050,000 unchosen. These calculations suggest that mankind is divided not only into races and nations, religions and states, but into socionomic divisions. There is produced a socionomic hierarchy due to the differences in attraction of particular individuals and groups for other particular individuals and groups. (Moreno, 1934, p. 250f.)

The idea that social structure is hierarchic, even in the absence of explicit, institutional modes of hierarchical organization, and that a network approach can identify these stratifications is recognizable in this passage, 80 years before a 'new' science of networks (Watts, 2004) began to find power-law distributions for connectivity in most of the places it looked. But Moreno's 'socionomic hierarchy' is only the beginning of a long-lasting relationship between applied network mathematics and rankings of various kind. The search for a social pecking order can indeed be seen as the central goal of sociometry and from the 1950s onward, new techniques based on structural measures were introduced at a regular pace.

A formal analysis of differences in 'status', 'authority', and 'influence', the three terms used most frequently – and often interchangeably – in this context, developed in line with the matrix approach outlined above. One of the techniques Festinger (1949) put forward consisted of simply squaring a matrix (multiplying it by itself), which results in a new matrix where each entry shows the number of two-step connections between two nodes. Cubing the matrix would get the numbers for three step paths, and so on. If applied to data from a sociometric test asking participants to indicate the persons whose opinion they valued most, this technique would show 'who influences the greatest number of people in less than a specified number of steps' (Festinger, 1949, p. 156). The question of social power becomes a matter of calculation.

Here, a specific paper, cited in both PageRank patents, stands out: in 1953, Leo Katz published 'A New Status Index Derived from Sociometric Analysis' in the journal *Psychometrika* and introduced the notion of a 'recursive' or 'cumulative' status index. Building on his earlier work on matrix representations of data collected by Moreno (Forsyth and Katz, 1946), Katz proposed a 'new method of computation' (Katz, 1953, p. 39) for calculating social status. Status measures were already common in studies using the sociometric test, but they were essentially based on simple counting, as seen in Moreno's discussion of socionomic hierarchies. Katz explicitly rejected this method and argued that 'most serious investigators [...] have been dissatisfied with the ordinary indices of "status," of the popularity contest type' because this 'balloting' of 'votes' would ultimately not allow to 'pick out the *real* leaders' (p. 39). His goal was not to measure popularity but social power, even if the latter term was not explicitly used. Therefore, Katz proposed a new index that takes into account '*who* chooses as well as how many choose' (p. 39), which means that votes from 'small fry' (p. 42) would simply count less. This shift rests on the idea that status is cumulative in the sense that the topology of a social network reflects a latent socionomic hierarchy, to stick with Moreno's term, in which the status of an individual largely depends on the status of her network neighborhood. Who you are is who you know.

Katz proposes a technically simple but conceptually challenging technique that transforms the initial sociometric choice matrix by first computing all paths between all nodes, then attributing a lower weight to longer paths through 'damping', and finally calculating a metric for every node based on the combined weight of their connections to all other nodes (Katz, 1953; Hanneman and Riddle, 2005). An individual that can reach far into the network in only a few steps will thus receive a higher status number than an individual that has a lot of immediate connections that do not lead deeper into the network. Similar measures to what is today known as 'Katz centrality' abound in the following decades and they are not only used for status measuring but also for other things, for example, to identify cliques (Hubbell, 1965). The contribution by the mathematical sociologist Phillip Bonacich (1972) is worth noting, because it consists of a metric based on the eigenvectors of a matrix, which means that not all paths between nodes are taken into account like in Katz's case, but only the shortest paths.[6] This makes the metric less dependent on local properties of networks and consequently more difficult to 'cheat' by adding nodes and connections locally. This resistance to what could be called 'link spam' is probably the reason why PageRank is a variant of eigenvector centrality rather than Katz centrality, although references to Bonacich's work are conspicuously absent from the patents.

Citation Analysis

A second arena where concrete techniques for the mathematical exploration and measurement of networks were pioneered – and directly applied to decision-making – is citation analysis, a field that shares a focus on scientific

---

6   For a deeper discussion of the various calculations and their differences, see Hanneman and Riddle (2005), Chapter 10.

literature with information retrieval. In 1963, the Institute for Scientific Information, founded by Eugene Garfield, printed the first edition of the Science Citation Index (SCI), an index of citations from 613 journal volumes published in 1961, manually extracted and sorted by computer (Garfield, 1963). With the first edition storing already 1.4 million citations on magnetic tape, this index was perhaps the first 'big data' network file available in the social sciences and several researchers used it over the following years to test different computational methods. One of these methods illustrates the considerable generativity of the graph representation: Henry Small's co-citation technique creates a new network on top of the citation data by looking not at direct references, but at 'the frequency with which two documents are cited together' (Small, 1973, p. 265), that is, cited in the same article. The technique thus creates a graph with variable link strength, since two papers may be cited together an arbitrary number of times, introducing a level of nuance that the underlying data lacks. Although Small knew Gerard Salton's work and, indeed, proposed co-citation as a measure of 'subject similarity', the relationship between information retrieval and citation analysis remained hesitant. Salton himself was aware of Garfield's index (cf. Salton, 1963), but his own experiments with citation data did not draw on the SCI, which was conceived as a commercial product from the beginning.

Garfield's initial strategy (1955) was to promote the SCI first and foremost as an 'association-of-ideas index', a tool for finding scientific literature that addressed the same problem space as information retrieval and again presented itself explicitly as an alternative to traditional subject headings and classifications. But it quickly became obvious that a series of evaluative metrics could be derived from the SCI without much effort. Thus, in 1972, Garfield presented a fleshed-out version of a concept he had initially introduced as a tool for the historiographical study of science, the (in)famous 'impact factor', claiming that '[p]erhaps the most important application of citation analysis is in studies of science policy and research evaluation' (Garfield, 1972, p. 478). When taking into account that the first attempt at citation ranking by Gross and Gross (1927) was designed to help university libraries decide which chemical journals they should subscribe to, it becomes clear that any evaluative metric would instantly face considerable normative and institutional entanglement, much more so than the mostly descriptive sociometry.

Highly applicable to questions concerning resource allocation, citation analysis – and all of scientometrics for that matter – oscillates between disinterested forms of metrological realism and the accounting realism of science management. The impact factor and its many variants provide measures of scientific recognition or success that resonate perfectly with contemporary 'audit cultures' that 'present themselves as rational, objective and neutral, based on sound principles of efficient management' (Shore and Wright, 2000, p. 61). Even if the 'engine of order' concept focuses primarily on integrated forms of performativity that revolve around computerization, digital infrastructures, and the tight coupling of data, analysis, decision, and application, citation analysis is one of many settings where we can observe how other kinds of 'operational assemblages', such as bureaucracies, produce their own forms of ordering based on calculation. As Burrows remarks, the performative character of 'quantitative control' has reached the point where 'academic metric assemblages are at the cusp of being transformed from a set of measures able to mimic market processes to ones that are able to *enact* market processes' (Burrows, 2012, p. 368). Another example is a particularly unexpected and mildly insidious application of social network analysis for a very literal form of ordering or arrangement: researchers used students' Facebook friendship networks, retrieved with the Netvizz application (Rieder, 2013), to break up the seating order during university exams to minimize cheating – with some success, apparently (Topîrceanu, 2017). Engines of order can be built out of various materialities.

The impact factor, calculated for scientific journals, is an extremely basic measure: it takes the number of citations the last two volumes of a journal received the following year and divides it by the number of articles published in these two volumes. This division highlights an important question – and certainly a central reason why literature from the citation analysis field is cited in the PageRank patents – that is not addressed in sociometry, namely the problem of size. If a journal publishes a large number of articles it is well positioned to receive more citations than a journal that publishes fewer; purely counting citations without taking publication volume into account would therefore be misleading and this is why the impact factor divides by the number of articles published (Garfield, 1972).

A 1976 paper by Pinski and Narin pushed things significantly further by pointing out two problems with Garfield's measure. First, citations have equal value in the impact factor scheme, although 'it seems more reasonable to give higher weight to a citation from a prestigious journal than to a citation from a peripheral one' (p. 298). Pinski and Narin therefore proposed a recursive index for importance, based on the same eigenvector calculations we found in Bonacich's work, although the authors were apparently not aware of sociometric techniques. Second, Pinski and Narin argued that the impact factor attributed disproportional importance to review journals that are referenced a lot for convenience rather than scientific contribution, and 'can therefore not be used to establish a "pecking order" for journal prestige' (p. 298). Again, they propose a solution by including an 'input-output' measure into their calculations (p. 300) where the 'influence weight' (W) of incoming citations (C) is divided by the number of outgoing citations (S):

$$W_i = \sum_{k=1}^{n} \frac{W_k C_{ki}}{S_i}$$

This formula basically states that the 'influence weight' (*W*) of a document should be the sum of the weight of the citations it receives, divided by the number of outgoing citations. If a document cites a lot of other sources (*S* = large), the 'value' it passes on to each of those sources will be lowered.

This means that the more papers an article cites, the lower the value 'transferred' to each of them. Review journals, which are not only cited a lot but also heavy citers themselves, are therefore no longer favored as brokers of influence. The exact same principle is at work in PageRank: the more outgoing links a site has, the lower the value of each link. This small twist shows how malleable these metrics are and how they react and adapt to new problems along the way. If we were to introduce a damping factor into this model, such as Katz's connection weight reduction scheme, in order to attenuate the 'free flow of citations in the referencing marketplace' (p. 298), we would essentially end up with PageRank, here in its canonical formulation:

$$r(A) = \frac{\alpha}{N} + (1 - \alpha) \left(\frac{r(B_1)}{|B_1|} + ... + \frac{r(B_n)}{|B_n|} \right)$$

PageRank basically applies a damping factor α (more on that further down) to Pinski and Narin's formula: *r(A)* is the weight to be calculated (equivalent of *Wi* in Pinski & Narin), *r(Bn)* stands for the weight of incoming links (*WkCki* above) and |*Bn*| for the number of outgoing links they have (*Si* above).

While Pinski and Narin do not quote the work of economist Wassily Leontief, unlike Hubbell (1965), who acknowledges this source of inspiration in his sociometric clique identification scheme, there is reason to believe that their version of an input-output model was equally inspired by economic thinking, in particular if we take into account that Pinski and Narin's metric was intended for a 'funding agency with its need to allocate scarce resources' (Pinski and Narin, 1976, p. 312).

This is one of many instances where we can observe clear affinities between algorithmic information ordering and market models. In their analysis of the effects of both the computer and the associated information concept on the discipline of economics, Mirowski and Nik-Khah (2017) indeed argue that 'what it meant to "know the truth" changed dramatically and irreversibly after World War II' (p. 1). They describe an epistemological nexus where concepts like 'equilibrium' or 'emergence' receive a decidedly computational interpretation: neoclassical economics, in particular, frame the market as 'the greatest information processor known to humankind' in the sense that it 'effectively winnows and validates the truth from a glut of information' (p. 7). While this book cannot provide a comprehensive analysis of the complex relationship between modern economics and algorithmic information ordering, the integration of economic thinking into the conceptual horizon can also be observed in sociometry and this merits closer attention.

From Sociometry to Social Exchange Theory

While the sociometric test was generally lauded for producing valuable data, Moreno's socio-psychological theory of attraction and repulsion between social atoms (Moreno, 1934, p. 6) was based on contested psychoanalytical assumptions and his goal to develop a 'technique of freedom' that reorganizes society by training individuals to transcend their social prejudices in order to liberate the forces of 'spontaneous attraction' did not go well with the sober and pragmatic mindset of most empirical sociologists. The sociometric papers working with Moreno's data therefore mostly subscribed to a vague version of the same atomistic and dyadic view of society, which enabled and justified the point-and-line formalization needed to apply graph theoretical methods, but they shunned the deeper aspects of the theoretical horizon behind it. Concepts like influence, status, importance, prestige, and so on filled the void, but they were defined in experimental terms reminiscent of Paul Lazarsfeld's empirical work[7] rather than as parts of robust theoretical frameworks. Influence, for example, if defined at all, was generally conceived as the capacity of an individual to change somebody else's 'opinion', as measured, for example, through voting in political elections. Even Kurt

---

7   Gitlin's (1978) critique of the 'dominant paradigm' in communications research can therefore be productively applied to sociometric concepts as well.

Lewin explicitly acknowledged that the goal of mathematization overruled other considerations:

> We have tried to avoid developing elaborate 'models'; instead we have tried to represent the dynamic relations between the psychological facts by mathematical constructs at a sufficient level of generality. (Lewin, 1964, p. 21)

And Kurt Lewin was certainly the sociometric scholar with the most substantial theoretical ambitions. Mullins (1973) squarely attributes the demise of small-group theory to the intellectual and theoretical vacuum left by Lewin's death in 1947. Granovetter's famous 'The Strength of Weak Ties' likewise ponders how '[s]ociometry, the precursor of network analysis, has always been curiously peripheral – invisible, really – in sociological theory' (Granovetter, 1973, p. 1360) and blames this not only on the difficulty to adapt methods to larger group sizes, but also on a lack of theoretical detail combined with 'a level of technical complexity appropriate to such forbidding sources as the *Bulletin of Mathematical Biophysics*' (Granovetter, 1973, p. 1361).

However, a glance at Granovetter's own work indicates where the field turned to find a new and more concise conceptual horizon: to social exchange theory, an approach that 'might be described, for simplicity, as the economic analysis of non economic social situations' (Emerson, 1976, p. 336). Here, power is no longer defined in vague psychological terms but in a serious, 'hard-knuckled' way as access to resources for economic advancement, to information on jobs, prices, opportunities, and so on. Since social exchange theory still relies on an atomistic and dyadic conception of social relations, it can accommodate graph theoretic models just as easily as attraction and repulsion did before. Having been turned into immutable mobiles by Harary and others, the mathematical concepts, methods, and metrics traveled effortlessly into the new conceptual space.[8] What in Moreno's view had to be produced through 'spontaneity training', namely the free association of individuals, now conveniently becomes a basic property of individuals conceived as free agents engaged in the rational choice of utility maximization.[9] While Mayer (2009) rightfully points to

---

8   As Emerson argues, social exchange theory is not a so much a theory, but 'a frame of reference within which many theories – some micro and some more macro – can speak to one another, whether in argument or in mutual support' (Emerson, 1976, p. 336).

9   'One answer, which we call "social atomism," suggests that social order is brought about through the free negotiations of autonomous individuals seeking to advance private interests. This view of social order is expressed in the 'social contract' theory associated with Hobbes,

the sociometric heritage of contemporary search engine metrics and its closeness with cybernetics and operations research, I would argue that this economic trajectory constitutes an equally important lineage. It supplied a rich new space for conceptual inspiration, similar to the already mentioned input-output model, and it provided a new home for the mathematical metrics and methods pioneered in sociometry.

It is a core paradox of mathematical network analysis that it affords powerful tools for examining concrete power relations empirically, which holds considerable critical potential, while also allowing to apply the measured hierarchies as operative mechanisms to allocate resources such as visibility or research funding. What the different strands I have discussed here furnish – and this is fundamental for any form of normative and operational application of evaluative metrics, whether in citation ranking or in web search – is a narrative that sustains what could be called 'the innocence of the link': whether it is spontaneous attraction, rational choice, or simply an inspirational account of scientific citation as solely based on intellectual merit, the application of the metrics to actual ranking, with concrete and tangible consequences, can only be justified if the link is kept reasonably 'pure'. Like the theory of 'revealed preference' in the last chapter, these narratives seek to 'protect' the integrity of behavioral data as indicators for contested concepts such as relevance, authority, or impact. In this context, the main enemies are therefore the 'deceitful linkers', whether they come as scientific citation cartels or their contemporary cousins, link farms. It is not surprising that a central argument against citation analysis as a means for research evaluation builds on a critique of the purity of actual citation practices.

Despite these resemblances, we must recognize that there is not a singular blueprint underpinning formalization. Theoretical and methodological frameworks, grammatization through technical forms, or simply exploration and experimentation can inform the identification and demarcation of entities and relationships that become materials for algorithmic treatment. Ideas from various fields, from mathematics and engineering to the social sciences, economics, and business management, can inspire the operational makeup of these algorithmic procedures. And there is little reason to believe that commonsense reasoning, tacit knowledge, and learning from practice and experience cannot play a

Locke, Rousseau, Spencer, and others. Contemporary variations of social atomism include types of social psychological theory, especially economic-type exchange theory' (Lewis and Weigert, 1985, p. 455).

central role in stirring the conceptual and technical imaginaries that inform technical creation.

So far, I have tried to sketch the historical background for certain core ideas present in PageRank in order to provide the material or 're-sources' (Chun, 2011, p. 20) for contextualizing this evaluative metric conceptually, in the sense that a critical reading of formulas or source code not only requires a capacity to understand technical languages but also interpretive ammunition to 'refill' computational artifacts that have most often been cleansed from easily accessible markers of context and origin. Historical investigation is indeed one way to reduce the opacity of software. If epistemological and methodological concepts such as the network model suggest a 'reading of reality' (Berry, 2008, p. 367), a historical approach can provide the material for an analysis of technicity that connects operation to a wider space of technical and nontechnical ideas. Such an analysis could seek to describe more general characteristics of the network approach, for example, the tendency to highlight 'the synchronic dispersal over the diachronic unfolding' (Berry, 2008, p. 367); it could situate it in relation to certain theories of the social and to specific mathematical methods, as I have tried to do in this section; but it could also attempt to home in further on technicity, which is the objective of the next section.

Two Moments of Commitment

To focus on the technical dimension of PageRank, I will develop two axes of mechanological interpretation, a comparative approach and a 'close reading' of a particular parameter, both organized around the question of how an understanding of metrics as 'descriptions' can help us apprehend how they become operative 'prescriptions' as engines of order. While citation metrics like the impact factor have quickly crossed the threshold between 'is' and 'ought', their use in 'science policy and research evaluation' (Garfield, 1972, p. 478) is hardly automated. Much like other statistical indicators before them, they have come to play an essential role in bureaucracies where ideals of so-called evidence-based governance privilege mathematical means of decision-making 'so constraining that the desires and biases of individuals are screened out', seeking to guarantee 'the rule of law, not of men' (Porter, 1995, p. 74). But even as integral parts of bureaucratic processes, these metrics retain both a certain visibility, which makes them amendable to critique, and margins of discretion in terms of how they are used. The rendering of graph theoretical methods in software is certainly significant on the descriptive side of things – just consider how SPSS[10] plays as role in orienting research practices in the social sciences (Uprichard, Burrows, and Byrne, 2008) – but prescriptive power is particularly enhanced when metrics are sunk into the system and become both invisible and inevitable, in the sense that margins of discretion are defined by the system itself. This is how algorithmic techniques inform engines of order in a very direct sense, 'conducting conduct' (Foucault, 2008, p. 186) by means of modulating what can be seen and what can be done in an online environment. When using Google Search, neither the ranking principles, nor their parameters are amendable to user intervention. We may change the query and apply certain filters, but the way the result list is put into sequence remains out of our hand.

This begs the question of how the concepts and metrics outlined above found their way into computing and became part of how the web is ordered. In 1992, Botafogo, Rivlin, and Shneiderman first explored the transposition – or 'freezing' – of sociometric methods into a navigational software environment as a means to solve the 'lost in hyperspace' problem, that is, the disorientation users often experience when navigating in a hypertext. Building on a paper by Harary (1959), the authors formalized hypertexts as directed graphs and began calculating metrics for the purpose of 'recovering lost hierarchies and finding new ones' (Botafogo, Rivlin, and Shneiderman, 1992, p. 143). The goal was not to identify the most important nodes for document retrieval but rather to assist hypertext authors in designing the structure of their text networks more explicitly, based on the idea 'that structure does reflect semantic information' (p. 148). Hierarchies were seen as helpful navigational devices and status metrics would help building them into the hypertext's topology. Interestingly, Botafogo, Rivlin, and Shneiderman explicitly argued that software would make it easy to implement different network metrics and thereby provide more than one view on the hypertext, granting 'the ability to view knowledge from different perspectives' (p. 148). Once again, we encounter the idea that algorithmic information ordering can provide the means for 'fini-unlimited' permutation, where the latent structures present in the network are modulated and arranged at will.

Taking the work in sociometry, citation analysis, and hypertext navigation together, one could argue that all the 'ingredients' for PageRank were available from the middle of the 1990s and all one had to do was to combine them.

10   SPSS (formerly Statistical Package for the Social Sciences) is one of the most commonly used tools for statistical analysis in the social sciences.

It is not the purpose of this chapter to judge the originality of Page and Brin's work but to show how network metrics were developed in different contexts and with different purposes in mind, and that they were indeed made operational in different ways and with different forms of performativity. This is where it is useful to connect back to Foucault's notion of the archive, understood not as a coherent 'paradigm' in Kuhn's (1962) sense, but as a wider 'conceptual field' (Foucault, 2002, p. 142) that allows for significant diversity and variation as well as regularity and 'transversal standardization' in the sense that similar metrics are applied in different domains.

The various metrics discussed over these last pages indeed define more general techniques for differentiation and distinction, but concrete calculative procedures and orchestrations can lead to very specific outputs. This means that an overarching critique of the reductionist and atomistic perspective espoused by the network model runs the risk of losing sight of the considerable margins for choice and expression available inside the conceptual space examined here. We therefore need to be attentive not only to moments of totalization, homogenization, and imposition but also to vectors of cumulative construction, heterogeneity, and fermentation. If algorithmic measurement increasingly means that 'authority no longer rests in the [social] relationships and instead migrates toward the measuring instrument' (Mayer, 2009, p. 68), the question of how we can better understand the way authority is concretely configured once it has migrated becomes virulent. Engaging PageRank as a model as well as an algorithmic technique can bring us closer to an answer. But this requires that we do more than capture its spirit; we have to examine its technical schema.

Flatlands and Two Ways to Make Hills

It is rather remarkable that, despite being initially conceived as a technique for finding scientific literature, citation analysis was not combined more thoroughly with existing techniques from information retrieval before the 1990s. The SCI's proprietary nature may have been a factor here, but it is safe to argue that the web, this gigantic and unruly mass of hyperlinked documents, played a significant role as catalyst in bringing together fields and methods that were largely separate until that point. Much like computerization and its different dimensions – including data availability, computing capability, and commercial opportunity – have informed the resurgence of information retrieval and its intermingling with artificial intelligence, the sheer size and complexity of the fledgling online spheres suggested that only algorithmic techniques would be capable of 'bringing order to the web' (Page et al., 1999).

The first fifteen years of web history essentially play through the earlier 'information wars' in fast forward: manually assembled catalogs like the commercial Yahoo! Directory (closed in 2014) or the volunteer project DMOZ (closed in 2017) used elaborate hierarchical classification systems – or 'hierarchical ontologies' in contemporary vocabulary – to provide searchers with well-ordered maps covering the masses of documents. The criticism leveled against these efforts is virtually the same as almost 50 years earlier:

> Human maintained lists cover popular topics effectively but are subjective, expensive to build and maintain, slow to improve, and cannot cover all esoteric topics. (Brin and Page, 1998, p. 117)

Automated search engines are presented as the answer, even if they have to deal with (partially) new problems, such as spamming and other forms of manipulation. Google Search has become almost synonymous with this automated approach. At first glance, it can be seen as a canonical information retrieval system that takes a query as input, searches through a (very large) document collection, and spits out a list of results. One could even make a legitimate comparison with coordinate indexing and argue that adding words to a query performs a Boolean AND and excluding words with the '-' operator a Boolean NOT. There is little reason to believe that Google's retrieval engine was initially all that different from the systems that Luhn and others had already experimented with in the late 1950s: word frequency counts, processing of document structure to identify 'privileged' text in titles or subheadings, statistical term-weighting schemes, and other techniques were well-known strategies for probabilistic, content-based indexing and already commonly used in web search. Put simply, the shift in perspective associated with Google Search did not concern retrieval techniques as such but rather the way the collection itself was conceptualized.

Indeed, PageRank is sometimes presented as an example for the field of unsupervised machine learning (Hastie, Tibshirani, and Friedman, 2009, p. 576), a set of techniques briefly discussed in Chapter 5 that are often used to 'map out' a dataset, either through forms of classification or through attribution of some numerical value to individual items. In this case, PageRank is the mechanism by which the web is no longer treated exclusively as a document repository, but additionally as a social system that is riddled with the very 'socionomic hierarchies' Moreno described. By applying a recursive status index inspired by sociometry and citation analysis to the index of web pages, every document in the corpus can be located in the stratified network/society and ranked according to its 'status' before searching even begins. Attributing an 'importance score' (Page et al., 1999, p. 3) to every document 'independent of the page content' (Bianchini, Gori, and Scarselli, 2005, p. 94) fundamentally means giving up the idea of a 'flat corpus' (Chakrabarti, 2003) of documents where relevance is only determined in relation to a query. While information retrieval generally conceives relevance with regard to a specific 'informational need', the socio- and scientometric attributions of status, influence, or impact are much closer to forms of aggregate description like mapping or clustering. As an unsupervised machine learning technique that tries to find an optimal description for specific aspects of a dataset, PageRank establishes a global 'pecking order' for the web. More precisely, because linking is framed as a form of citation and thus as rational attribution of importance by document authors, the hyperlink network can become a singular, universal network of 'authority' that the search system can combine with traditional ranking mechanisms to calculate a final score during the search process. This quote from the initial research paper on PageRank highlights this two-prone approach:

> The importance of a Web page is an inherently subjective matter, which depends on the readers interests, knowledge and attitudes. But there is still much that can be said objectively about the relative importance of Web pages. (Page et al., 1999, p. 1)

But how does this universalist component resonate with the larger argument for variation and perspectivism I have constructed over the last chapters? Comparing Google's algorithm to a close sibling points to moments of differentiation.

Just like PageRank, Jon Kleinberg's HITS (Hyperlink-Induced Topic Search) is an eigenvector-based evaluative metric that was introduced at nearly the same time as its more famous cousin (Kleinberg, 1999). Its virtually identical goal was to formulate 'a notion of authority' by processing the 'considerable amount of latent human judgment' encoded in hyperlinks, in order to solve the 'abundance problem' (p. 606) faced by web users. But there are two major differences.

First, HITS actually provides *two* eigenvector metrics, one for 'hubness' and another for 'authority'. Building on the idea 'that good hubs point to good authorities and good authorities are pointed to by good hubs' (Langville and Meyer, 2005, p. 136), Kleinberg makes a conceptual differentiation, entirely based on structural properties of the graph, resulting in a typology of nodes that, if implemented through an interface, could allow users to specify the type they are looking for. While metrics can indeed totalize and commensurate (Espeland and Stevens, 1998), there are many technical means to introduce differentiation and variation. In the domain of the fini-unlimited, one can not only calculate singular scores in countess ways but there is also no necessity to limit calculation to a singular score in the first place.

Second, HITS inverts the temporal sequence of authority ranking and document retrieval. Rather than calculate a universal or a priori landscape of authority like PageRank, documents matching a query are retrieved first and authority is calculated only second, taking only the link structure between found documents into account and not the full corpus. This means that in the HITS perspective, authority is dependent on a subject domain delineated through a query and a page that receives a high authority score for one search term may well get a much lower score for another. While this obviously does not abolish the notion of authority by any means, the concept is reconfigured, contextualized, and contained in the sense that HITS is less subject to what Barry and Browne (2006) euphemistically call 'topic drift' (p. 84), that is, the dominance of high-authority sites over a wide range of topics.

Algorithmic techniques do not exist in a disembodied state but become part of running systems where operations form (potentially recursive) sequences; simply rearranging these sequences may yield significant differences in terms of output. But being part of a running system also means that ideas compete on more than the merit of their results. Even if we may want to argue that the HITS perspective holds significant advantages over PageRank, the argument clashes with the fact that the computational requirements for HITS are much higher than for PageRank. While the latter can recalculate its universal landscape of authority at a set interval – before it fell silent on the topic, Google indicated a number of about once a month – the former would have to make an authority computation for every single search request. Certainly, the scores for the most popular queries could be calculated in advance, but a large disadvantage persists when it comes to both speed and cost. And the found documents for a given query may not even form a hyperlink network in the first place, reducing the system to traditional information retrieval metrics.

But even when looking inside the PageRank formula, we find space for variation and choice. In the next section, I will show how a single parameter encodes a significant theoretical and, consequently, operational commitment.

Objet petit α[11]

Just like Katz's (1953) 'status index', PageRank not only 'recursively propagate[s] weights through the link structure of the Web' (Brin and Page, 1998, p. 108), but includes 'a damping factor that limits the extent to which a document's rank can be inherited by children documents' (Page, 2004, p. 7). The question is how far through the network authority should propagate. The rationale put forward by Page et al. (1999) to explain rank 'decay' (p. 4) in PageRank is twofold: first, the actual problem in the context of a web search engine is that without damping, a 'rank sink' in the form of a closed loop between two or more pages could excessively accumulate rank at each pass of the iterative method used to compute the metric, the usual approach to calculation in absence of an analytical solution. Damping eliminates those undesired artifacts. Second, an 'intuitive basis' (p. 5) in the form of the model of a random surfer is introduced, where the damping factor α 'models the fact that users typically jump to a different place in the web after following a few links' (Page, 2004, p. 7). While PageRank is presented as 'an attempt to see how good an approximation to "importance" can be obtained just from the link structure' (Page et al., 1999, p. 4), neither the 'rank sink' nor the 'random walk' justification really account for damping in respect to the question of importance. The first justification concerns a technical problem arising from the particular computational solution used and the second fails to elaborate how a model of random user behavior actually relates to the calculation of an importance score. While PageRank can indeed be read as a scoring of the 'reachability' of a node in a graph, in the sense that more central sites would be stumbled upon more frequently if somebody was randomly following links, the transfer from dampened reachability to importance remains unexplained. It is not surprising that Google nowadays prefers the term 'useful' to 'important'.[12]

Much like the admittedly difficult question of how language and meaning relate, which received surprisingly little attention in early information retrieval, the move from socio- and scientometrics to the web correlates with a dramatic loss of interest in considerations that could be described as 'domain theoretic'. These considerations, which inform and justify the

---

11   In Lacan's psychoanalysis, the 'objet petit a' stands for an object of desire that remains forever unattainable, elusive. Žižek (1992) argues that it 'is not a positive entity existing in space, it is ultimately nothing but a certain *curvature of the space itself* which causes us to make a bend precisely when we want to get directly at the object' (p. 48).

12   https://www.google.com/search/howsearchworks/algorithms/, accessed 22 February 2017.

'appropriate coordination' between an empirical system and its formalization in the context of scientific description, are little more than inconveniences on the way toward computation. Terms like 'intuitive basis' signal the exchange of robust theoretical involvement for little more than commonsense reasoning, and this is really quite common in computing disciplines. We can, however, develop a line of mechanological interpretation that considers the explanations given by Katz and Bonacich for the inclusion of a damping factor into their own metrics.

Katz introduces the α factor as a means to adapt the calculation of his status index to 'both the group and the context' (Katz, 1953, p. 41) and provides an expressive example from the domain of information diffusion:

> For example, the information that the new high-school principal is unmarried and handsome might occasion a violent reaction in a ladies' garden club and hardly a ripple of interest in a luncheon group of the local chamber of commerce. On the other hand, the luncheon group might be anything but apathetic in its response to information concerning a fractional change in credit buying restrictions announced by the federal government. (Katz, 1953, p. 41)

One way Katz (1953) interprets α is as an estimate of the 'probability of effectiveness of a single link' (p. 41) for relaying information and he argues that this is highly dependent on context and, in particular, on the fit between the social setting and the message in question. In this sense, α encodes the probability that a piece of information is passed on from one person to the next and a researcher should choose an appropriate level based on her appreciation of the situation. A high level of damping means that information will not spread very far, even if high status individuals are involved. The 'conductivity' is considered to be low and status does not reach very far into the network. In contrast, if one looks at a military command structure, for example, conductivity can be considered to be very high since orders are generally followed from top to bottom. In this case, status would be strongly cumulative since a powerful individual like a general has full control over what happens further down the network hierarchy. If α is small, control over others is considered low and status ranking actually approaches the 'balloting' Katz criticized as dissatisfying, because status no longer propagates and the simple number of votes a person receives becomes the determining factor. Because already small differences in the factor can lead to significant variation in outcomes, the commitment to a particular estimation of the conductivity of a network – we must not forget that α is a manually set constant – has substantial consequences on the calculated hierarchies. Indeed, Bianchini, Gori, and Scarselli discuss α in PageRank in similar terms as the factor deciding how far the structure of a network should influence the status of a node:

> PageRank deeply depends on parameter [α]. When [α] is small, only the nearest relatives give an actual contribution to [PageRank], whereas, as [α] → 1, far ancestors are also significant for the evaluation of [PageRank]. (Bianchini, Gori, and Scarselli, 2005, p. 125)

The conceptual entanglements this modulation implies clears up further when examining the arguments behind Bonacich's (1987) decision to add a damping factor to his own 'power centrality' metric. In order to account for the results of an empirical study by Cook et al. (1983), which had shown a disjunction between network centrality and power in a bargaining network, Bonacich proposes a parameter β, which regulates the depth of influence in a very similar fashion to α by defining 'a radius within which power or centrality is being assessed' (Bonacich, 1987, p. 1174). What makes Bonacich's piece so interesting is his reflection on how β becomes a way to implement varying conceptions of what constitutes power in different social networks. The full quote is instructive:

> To some, the measure may seem hopelessly ambiguous; [power centrality] can give radically different rankings on centrality, depending on the value of β. However, the measure accentuates an inherent ambiguity in the concept of centrality. There are different types of centrality, depending on the degrees to which local and global structures should be weighted in a particular study and whether that weight should be positive or negative. When communication is typically over long distances, position in the global structure should count more than when all communication is local. In an organized hierarchy in which power is transitive, the power of those one has power over should be weighted more highly in determining overall power than when all relations are dyadic. (Bonacich, 1987, p. 1181)

We notice again that a single parameter is seen as encoding a fundamental appreciation of how influence or power operate in a given situation. Bonacich's β actually goes beyond α, because it is designed to work with negative values as well, so that connections to high status nodes are actually *detrimental* to rank. This allows the model to account for bargaining networks, where exchange theory considers it beneficial to be connected to a large number of low status nodes that can be more easily exploited because they lack information, for example, about prices. In this situation, 'power comes from being connected to those who are powerless' (p. 1171). Because β and α are set manually, they express a true commitment to a theory about the real-world properties of the network in question, even if that commitment is made with little consideration for its implications.

When applying this discussion to PageRank, two very different notions of status, authority, and importance emerge: with $\alpha \to 0$, the web is indeed conceived as a 'one person, one vote' type democracy[13] and collecting incoming links, no matter from where, would be the principal means of gaining rank; in a $\alpha \to 1$ setting, the web becomes a very different place – opaque, complex, and potentially Machiavellian, where success comes from either patronage by the already powerful or the patient and costly construction of large and spread-out strategic networks. While we have to keep in mind that this is a scale and not a binary decision, the first vision puts an emphasis on the local properties of the graph and makes it therefore possible for local changes, if significant in number, to affect the overall ranking of the system; the second builds on the global structure of the graph and local changes therefore have negligible effects on overall rankings. If we keep with the image of a social system, the respective models of transformation are 'populist/revolutionary' and 'conservative/reformatory'. While purely descriptive metrics make an epistemological commitment to a theory of power to represent social status, the prescriptive mode of PageRank as an engine of order in a technical system makes an *operational* commitment to reproduce and reinforce, in very practical terms, the hierarchy of social status it detects. The value Google usually communicated for α was 0.85 (Brin and Page, 1998, p. 110) and at this level, the often-heard interpretation of PageRank as essentially an expression of popularity (Diaz, 2008; Rieder, 2009) misses the target. While sheer numbers certainly do play a role, the idea that PageRank interprets the web as 'a gigantic popularity contest' (Roush, 2004, n.p.) does not capture how it 'brings order to the web'. At a level of 0.85, power is highly cumulative and an inlink from a high-status node will be much more valuable than from a site with lower status.

If we consider Google Search as a central site of power negotiation and arbitrage for the web, an analysis focusing on PageRank, which in practice

13   Whether voting is necessarily a core principle of democratic government is debatable, however. As Bernard Manin (1997) has shown, up to the French revolution, elections were generally associated with aristocracy and selection by lottery was seen as the truly democratic mode of assigning office.

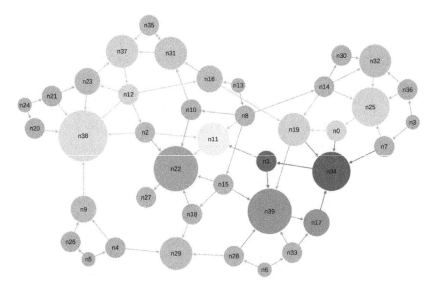

A network generated randomly with Gephi. Node sizes represent the number of inlinks and color represents PageRank ($\alpha = 0.85$), going from light to dark grey. We instantly notice that n1 has a high PR although it only receives a single inlink. This link comes from the highest status node (n34), however, and since that node links nowhere else, n1 receives a lot (85 percent) of its status.

Label	PR (α=0.85)	PR (α=0.7)	PR (α=0.55)	PR (α=0.4)	In-Degree	Out-Degree	Degree
n34	0.0944	0.0743	0.0584	0.0460	4	1	5
n1	0.0867	0.0617	0.0450	0.0345	1	2	3
n17	0.0668	0.0521	0.0423	0.0355	2	1	3
n39	0.0663	0.0541	0.0453	0.0388	5	1	6
n22	0.0619	0.0506	0.0441	0.0393	5	1	6
n27	0.0591	0.0451	0.0371	0.0318	1	0	1
n38	0.0522	0.0561	0.0542	0.0486	6	0	6
n11	0.0492	0.0372	0.0306	0.0274	3	1	4

A table of eight nodes from the same network as above, selected and ordered based on the highest values for PageRank ($\alpha = 0.85$). Four PageRank rankings were calculated. Note how n1 with just a single inlinks slips with lower values for α and n38 rises to the top of the ranking.

is certainly insufficient, would have to conclude that its authority-ranking mechanism applies, in a universal fashion, a largely conservative[14] vision of society to the document graph, one that picks out 'the *real* leaders' (Katz,

---

14   The term is used here in a rather literal sense as favoring the maintenance of the status quo. The difficulty to apply traditional concepts from political theory becomes evident when we take into account that the 'revolutionary masses' PageRank is set to defend against are mostly spammers and search engine optimizers.

1953, p. 39) and distributes visibility to them. Rather than showing us the *popular* it shows us the *authoritative*, or, to connect back to citation analysis, the *canonical* (Introna, 2007, p. 18). If we consider the link indeed as 'innocent', as a valid indicator of disinterested human judgment, PageRank shows us a *meritocracy*; if we take the link to be fully caught up in economic forces, however, we receive the map of a *plutocracy*. In either case, the search engine as an engine of order will accentuate the difference between high and low rank over time since pages with higher status will be more visible and thus have a greater chance of receiving further links.

Similar to the Bayesian classifier, computer scientists have studied the effects of α in great detail (Langville and Meyer, 2004, 2005; Bianchini, Gori, and Scarselli, 2005). But the above figure and table show the effects of changes in the value for α on a simple and actually rather 'egalitarian' network in a hopefully more accessible form than the papers written by specialists. While we cannot make any far-reaching generalizations based on a limited experiment, it is in line with the general finding that small variations in α can lead to significant changes in ranking. It also confirms that at high values for α the quality of inlinks is much more relevant than their number; a single link from a page with a high rank can be extremely valuable, especially if that page does not link anywhere else. When lowering α and thus adding more damping, the hierarchy shifts in favor of nodes with many inlinks. Although this is only a sketch, approaches involving tinkering or 'screwing around' (Ramsay, 2010) with algorithms should be considered as ways of studying them as 'beings that function' (Simondon, 2017, p. 151) in their natural habitat: eating numbers and spewing out different numbers at the rear end.

But again, computational requirements add an interesting caveat. While the level set for α has important conceptual and potentially political consequences, it also implies a cost factor, since a higher value means that the calculation will require a larger number of iterations to converge.[15] Langville and Meyer capture the dilemma:

> Consequently, Google engineers are forced to perform a delicate balancing act. The smaller α is, the faster the convergence, but the smaller α is, the less the true hyperlink structure of the web is used to determine webpage importance. And slightly different values for α can produce very different PageRanks. (Langville and Meyer, 2004, p. 346)

---

15   In the iterative power method for calculating PageRank, only an approximation to the eigenvector solution is calculated. The loop stops when the changes from one iteration to the next fall below a set level.

This means that a local theory of power is computationally and, because computation costs money, economically cheaper than a theory where status is based on global structural properties. In this case, the menace from spam apparently appeared as sufficiently substantial to convince Google that a larger radius of influence – and consequently a reduced capacity for local changes to affect global structure – was well worth the additional cost.

Variation and Combination

This chapter set out to examine what is 'in' the PageRank algorithm and it proceeded in two ways: It first situated this evaluative metric in a larger archive of statements, that is, of ideas, concepts, theories, methods, and techniques that developed in and around sociometry, citation analysis, social exchange theory, and hypertext navigation. This conceptual space constitutes, at least to a certain extent, the place of emergence from where PageRank became 'sayable' (cf. Foucault, 2002, p. 146). The fact that many of the papers discussed here are cited in the relevant patents adds concreteness and plausibility to this idea. The chapter deviated from the preceding ones by taking a contemporary technique as its narrative telos. Although an implicit focus on the present has guided my selections in earlier examples as well, there is a more specific reason for this choice: while information retrieval revolves around the conceptual and operational possibilities of computing machinery from the beginning and takes earlier work in information ordering mainly as negative inspiration, PageRank epitomizes a moment when a long and illustrious trajectory of calculative techniques finds a place and raison d'être in an information infrastructure supported by networked computing. Certainly, both sociometry and citation analysis were using computing machinery from the 1960s on and the latter, in particular, has been operating as an engine of order entangled in research evaluation and resource allocation almost from the beginning. But the shift from these 'ancestral' domains into document retrieval and ranking is much more abrupt that the rather steady accumulation of techniques discussed in previous chapters. These differences between trajectories indicate that algorithmic techniques are characterized by variation not only in terms of technicity and conceptual content, but also in terms of invention and evolution. If '[w]hat resides in the machines is human reality, human gesture fixed and crystallized in working structures' (Simondon, 2017, p. 18), there is no single way this 'fixing and crystallizing' happens, no canonical sequence of steps, and no singular discipline or materiality that holds everything together. PageRank illustrates how a heterogeneous archive of statements and practices finds expression in the particular form of an *algorithmic* technique, becoming ready-to-hand not only for software developers that want to use it in their own programs, but also for users engaged in the mapping practices mentioned at the beginning of this chapter: using a graph analysis toolkit like Gephi, PageRank becomes applicable to any network at the click of a button. Unsurprisingly, it asks its users to set a value for α, somewhere between 0 and 1.

Second, by comparing the algorithm to a close cousin and by examining a particular parameter in the model, the chapter tried to show that the concrete schema – the algorithmic technique, not the search engine – does not simply follow from the historical a priori. There are thousands of graph theoretical algorithms documented and hundreds of variants of the recursive status metrics I have focused on. Are they all based on a reductionist and atomistic vision of social relations? Quite possibly. Do they all encode the same logic, produce the same rankings, and commit to the same politics? Certainly not. There is variation and it is significant: even a single parameter can have extraordinary consequences for the actual ordering performed.

While my discussion of PageRank was more technical than earlier examples, the goal was to show how deeply entangled with social and cultural questions technicity can become, in particular when let loose into concrete application settings. Although Larry Page's proposition is basically just a way to transform one set of numbers into another set, what is actually expressed are not only mathematical functions but quite fundamental ideas about authority, importance, relevance, and so forth. Technicity, indeed, draws on different forms of imagination, even if the expression as a technical idea requires a capacity to function. The language used may be that of mathematics and code, but the expressed technical schema captures the outside world and, by becoming operational as part of a search engine, shows us that world in particular ways. Information retrieval's reluctance to formulate more elaborate theories of language, meaning, or knowledge does not prevent actual systems to enact operational interpretations of these things, simply by doing what they do. The orderings most of us are confronted with several times a day when querying Google Search are as much deliberate outcomes as the tree of knowledge Diderot and D'Alembert organized the *Encyclopédie* around. But the ways in which these outcomes come about could not be more different.

Like the techniques discussed in earlier chapters, network algorithms start from a common way of representing data as a graph, an intermediate form that implies a particular formalization of the empirical realities they target. While the feature vector 'sees' the world as sets of objects having certain properties, the graph frames objects in terms of their connections. We find a similar capacity for generalization and generativity: if a phenomenon can be fitted into an adjacency matrix, a large number of readily available techniques can be applied at will. While this chapter was mainly concerned with the various ways hierarchies of authority, influence, status, and so forth can be measured, this is only one of many things network algorithms can be used for. One could write a similar story for the detection of so-called 'cliques', for example, densely connected groups of friends in social networks, scientific disciplines or paradigms in citation networks, or sets of products that are bought together frequently. Or a story covering the various measures of 'betweenness' (Freeman, 1977) that seek to detect nodes that are 'bridging'[16] subgroups and can therefore not only access a potentially wider set of resources but also control the information flow between different parts of the network. The excitement around a science of networks that attempts to consider common aspects of networks across domains is indeed nourished by the fact that so many different phenomena can be productively modeled as graphs. We thus find the same ordering techniques applied to phenomena ranging from molecular interactions to collaborations between movie actors. But in all of these cases, mathematical transformations are coordinated with domain-specific interpretations in some way and the same metric will not necessarily express the same idea when applied to two different types of network, opening a space for interpretation and critique.

It should come as no surprise that the graph and the feature vector are not competing or mutually exclusive paradigmatic forms, but 'merely' pivotal instances in malleable spaces of technical expression. Ultimately, there is parallelism and abundant potential for connection in the field of algorithmic techniques and moving from one form or technique to another often requires little more than a change in perspective. The hyperlink network does not have to be treated strictly as a graph. We could, for example, consider a web document as a feature vector comprised not of words, but of the entities it links to. Akin to Henry Small's co-link analysis, we could then use Salton's similarity calculations to find pages that are 'related' because they link to similar places but are not directly connected. But the statistical technique does not really tell us what 'related' would actually mean here. Would we

---

16   Putnam (2000) distinguishes between two types of social capital: bonding capital is high for individuals that are central in a tightly knit group; bridging capital is high for those that connect disparate groups or circles. Many different algorithms have tried to formalize and calculate these ideas.

be able to find a theoretical framework to support and justify our idea or would we simply create and evaluate an experimental setup to demonstrate the capacity and utility of our system? Combining trajectories in the other direction, we could follow Luhn's idea and formalize co-occurrences of words in a text as a graph, submitting the resulting network to any number of centrality metrics, in the hope of finding the most 'important' words in the document. This technique, co-word analysis, is indeed quite common and we may rightfully ask what kind of 'capture' of language and meaning it implies. The functional forms of signification such operations may deploy in specific settings is not culturally neutral but also not easily aligned with cultural categories and dependent on the data under scrutiny.

While these are somewhat arbitrary examples, technical plasticity can be engaged more proactively and with a critical mindset. Connecting back to the discussion of software-making in Chapter 3, we can recognize that the plasticity software affords is not distributed equally, turning it into a site of political struggle. An example from my own work can illustrate what I mean. Almost fifteen years ago, I called for developer access to Google's search index, based on the idea that the enormous trust users place in the company should give rise to a 'symmetry of confidence' (Rieder, 2005) in the form of increased openness to (programmed) interaction with its products and infrastructures. To give concrete meaning to this proposal, I built a small web mashup on the basis of Yahoo!'s now defunct BOSS (Build your own Search Service) Web API. TermCloud Search would get 500 search results, each pretagged with a set of keywords, and then generate a word cloud based on these keywords. The cloud was meant to break with the linear hierarchy of the result list, to map the result space by providing an overview, and to furnish a visual representation that could be used to navigate the results by clicking on words. It was a basically a coordinate indexing system sitting on top of ranked search results. Multiple terms could be selected to create an AND query and the tool used simple keyword co-occurrence to show which terms appeared most commonly together.

This rather basic example is meant to show how engaging technicity does not require a deep dive into mathematical principles but may well begin with attentiveness to broad techniques, end-user functionalities, and interface arrangements. TermCloud Search can be understood as an attempt at critical contribution, in the form of an object, to the debate around the specific rationales information retrieval systems *should* implement. While Google Search generally emphasizes the capacity to deliver the right 'answer' to a 'question' in the least amount of time, my mashup considered the query not so much as a question, but as a way to evoke a potentially

termCloud Search

| bp | search |

assets (11) barack obama (13) bp america (15) **bp oil** (101) **bp plc** (98) bp shares (22) bp solar (9) british petroleum (23) business (17) ceo (18) claims (20) company (66) deepwater (40) disaster (17) dividend (9) energy (23) energy company (9) exploration and production (9) explosion (10) facebook (12) government (10) gulf (18) gulf coast (19) gulf of mexico (20) gulf oil (29) horizon (17) horizon oil (12) investors (11) leak (9) london (14) marketing (9) mexico oil (16) nasdaq (11) nyse (21) obama (19) oil (109) oil and gas (10) oil companies (9) oil company (20) oil disaster (14) oil giant bp (16) oil leak (11) oil rig (9) oil spill (125) oil well (12) president (17) price (9) products (9) quotes (19) reuters (19) rig (14) spill (37) stock (23) stock price (12) stock quote (21) stocks (30) the gulf (60) the gulf of mexico (69) tony hayward (23) ttm (9) twitter (17) united states (11) video (15) workers (9)

| terms + | terms - | show relations |

BP - Wikipedia, the free encyclopedia
http://en.wikipedia.org/wiki/BP
For other uses, see BP (disambiguation). For information on the oil ... BP has been involved in a number of environmental, safety and political controversies ...
bp | company | oil spill | bp connect | london | oil | deepwater | pipeline | british petroleum company | amoco | russia | 2go | bp express | bp shop | 1 may | iran | guardian | aioc | history | british petroleum
| inbound | related |

Gulf of Mexico Oil Spill Response - BP
http://www.bp.com/extendedsectiongenericarticle.do?categoryId=40&contentId=7061813
Updates from BP on work being done to address the Gulf of Mexico oil spill. With news, videos, claim submission information, and technical updates.
the gulf of mexico | gulf of mexico | oil spill | the gulf | bp america | gulf coast | subsea | deepwater | horizon | completion | relief well | leak | live feeds | livelihoods | search | internal investigation | milestone | harm | well kill | incident
| inbound | related |

Stock:BP (BP)
http://www.wikinvest.com/stock/BP_(BP)

The interface of termCloud Search, showing results for the query [bp]. Clicking on the term 'oil spill' would show the results tagged with that term and highlight the terms that co-occurred most often with it.

multifaceted or contested topic, and the result not as an answer, but as a crude overview and navigational interface into the different dimensions that topic may have. While this certainly overstates the conceptual reach of such a small experiment, one could say that the design objective was to induce a sensitivity for the plurality and composite character of an issue as well as to practically facilitate its exploration.

While the playful combination of techniques becomes clearly visible in this example, (almost) all software is a hybrid when looking behind the interface, even if design goals can certainly be less benign. Could we imagine a machine learning setup that sets α in PageRank dynamically, based on feedback, in order to delegate the inconvenient moment of human judgment and theoretical commitment to an empirical machine? If our goal is to deliver the 'best' results, we could very well calculate PageRank at different levels of α and submit each level to a randomly selected subset of our user base. In line with the notion of revealed preference, we may take it as a positive signal when a user actually clicks on the first link. If users select lower ranked links, we take this as negative feedback. The level of α with the highest percentage of positive signals wins and the problem is solved. Imagine similar games not for a single instance of algorithmic ordering, but for many: some concerning the formalization of document content, some concerning link structure, some concerning implicit or explicit feedback; others slicing users by location, by device form factor, or by movement speed in physical space; yet others personalizing based on use history or similarity with other users. If we imagine this huge network of possible factors and techniques – and probably a more complex appreciation of what success means – and we end up with a more accurate, albeit still superficial, appreciation of how systems like Google Search actually work and evolve over time. Google almost certainly scores on the basis of some intricate and adaptive combination of relevance (information retrieval), authority (network analysis), and feedback (machine learning) techniques, combining the different technical trajectories discussed in this book into a complex technical ensemble. Because each of the technical elements in play is complex and their (possible) interactions even more so, thousands of people with PhDs work at Google, not merely a few. As Peter Norvig, now Director of Research at Google, has recently argued, 'the competitive advantage really comes from the hard work of what you do with the algorithm and all the processes around making a product, not from the core algorithm itself' (r/Science and AAAS-AMA, 2018, n.p.). Technology is created from technical elements, but their arrangement and connection with the world increasingly relies on empirical processes that tie design, use, and evaluation tightly together into an object that is never entirely finished and therefore never fully 'detaches' from its producer the way Simondon describes (Simondon, 2014, p. 27). The study of algorithmic techniques gives us a handle on the vocabulary of functional expression, but the way technology is actually 'spoken' is increasingly hard to decipher.

Bibliography

Barabási, A.-L. (2002). *Linked: The New Science of Networks*. Cambridge: Perseus Publishing.

Barnes, J. A., and Harary, F. (1983). Graph Theory in Network Analysis. *Social Networks* 5(2), 235-244.

Bastian, M., Heymann, S., Jacomy, M. (2009). Gephi: An Open Source Software for Exploring and Manipulating Networks. In *International AAAI Conference on Weblogs and Social Media*. Retrieved from https://www.aaai.org/ocs/index.php/ICWSM/09/paper/view/154.

Bavelas, A. (1948). A Mathematical Model for Groups Structures. *Human Organization 7*(3), 16-30.

Benkler, Y, (2006). *The Wealth of Networks: How Social Production Transforms Markets and Freedom*, New Haven: Yale University Press.

Berry, D. M. (2008). The Poverty of Networks. *Theory, Culture and Society 25*(7-8), 364-372.

Berry, M. W., and Browne, M. (2006). *Understanding Search Engines: Mathematical Modeling and Text Retrieval* (2nd ed.). Philadelphia: Society for Industrial and Applied Mathematics.

Bianchini, M., Gori, M., and Scarselli, F. (2005). Inside PageRank. *ACM Transactions on Internet Technology 5*(1), 92-128.

Bonacich, P. (1972). Factoring and Weighting Approaches to Status Scores and Clique Identification. *Journal of Mathematical Sociology 2*(1), 113-120.

Bonacich, P. (1987). Power and Centrality: A Family of Measures. *American Journal of Sociology 92*(5), 1170-1182.

Botafogo, R. A., Rivlin, E., and Shneiderman, B. (1992). Structural Analysis of Hypertexts: Identifying Hierarchies and Useful Metrics. *ACM Transactions on Information Systems 10*(2), 142-180.

Brin, S., and Page, L. (1998). The Anatomy of a Large-Scale Hypertextual Web Search Engine. *Computer Networks and ISDN Systems 30*, 107-117.

Burrows, R. (2012). Living with the H-Index? Metric Assemblages in the Contemporary Academy. *Sociological Review 60*(2), 355-372.

Castells, M. (1996). *The Information Age: Economy, Society and Culture, Volume 1: The Rise of the Network Society*. Cambridge, Oxford: Blackwell.

Chakrabarti, S. (2003). *Mining the Web: Discovering Knowledge from Hypertext Data*. San Francisco: Morgan-Kauffman.

Chun, W. H. K. (2011). *Programmed Visions*. Cambridge, MA: MIT Press.

Cook, K. S., Emerson, R. M., Gilmore, M. R., and Yamagishi, T. (1983). The Distribution of Power in Exchange Networks: Theory and Experimental Results. *American Journal of Sociology 89*(2), 275-305.

Diaz, A. (2008). Through the Google Goggles: Sociopolitical Bias in Search Engine Design. In A. Spink and M. Zimmer (eds.), *Web Search: Multidisciplinary Perspectives* (pp. 11-34). Berlin: Springer.

Emerson, R. M. (1976). Social Exchange Theory. *Annual Review of Sociology 2*, 335-362.

Erdős, P. (1977). A Note of Welcome. *Journal of Graph Theory 1*(3), 3.

Espeland, W. N., and Stevens, M. L. (1998). Commensuration as a Social Process. *Annual Review of Sociology 24*, 313-343.

Festinger, L. (1949). The Analysis of Sociograms using Matrix Algebra. *Human Relations 2*(2), 153-158.

Forsyth, E., and Katz, L. (1946). A Matrix Approach to the Analysis of Sociometric Data: Preliminary Report. *Sociometry 9*(4), 340-347.

Foucault, M. (2002). *Archaeology of Knowledge* (A. M. Sheridan Smith, trans.). London: Routledge.

Freeman, L. C. (1977). A Set of Measures of Centrality Based on Betweenness. *Sociometry 40*(1), 35-41.

Garfield, E. (1955). Citation Indexes for Science: A New Dimension in Documentation through Association of Ideas. *Science 122*(3159), 108-111.

Garfield, E. (1963). Science Citation Index. In E. Garfield (ed.), *Science Citation Index 1961* (pp. v-xvi). Philadelphia: Institute for Scientific Information.

Garfield, E. (1972). Citation Analysis as a Tool in Journal Evaluation. *Science 178*(4060), 471-479.

Gießmann, S. (2009). Ganz klein, ganz groß. Jacob Levy Moreno und die Geschicke des Netzwerkdiagramms. In I. Köster and K. Schuster (eds.), *Medien in Zeit und Raum. Maßverhältnisse des Medialen* (pp. 267-292). Bielefeld: transcript Verlag.

Gitlin, T. (1978). Media Sociology: The Dominant Paradigm. *Theory and Society 6*(2), 205-253.

Granovetter, M. S. (1973). The Strength of Weak Ties. *American Journal of Sociology 78*(6), 1360-1380.

Gross, P. L. K., and Gross, E. M. (1927). College Libraries and Chemical Education. *Science 66*(1713), 385-389.

Hacking, I. (1990). *The Taming of Chance*. Cambridge: Cambridge University Press.

Hanneman, R. A., and Riddle, M. (2005). *Introduction to Social Network Methods*. Riverside: University of California, Riverside. Retrieved from http://faculty.ucr.edu/~hanneman/.

Harary, F. (1959). Status and Contrastatus. *Sociometry 22*(1), 23-43.

Harary, F. (1969). *Graph Theory*. Reading: Addison-Wesley.

Harary, F. (1983). Conditional Connectivity. *Networks 13*(3), 347-357.

Harary, F., and Norman, R. Z. (1953). *Graph Theory as a Mathematical Model in Social Science*. Ann Arbor: Institute for Social Research, University of Michigan.

Harary, F., Norman, R. Z., and Cartwright, D. (1965). *Structural Models: An Introduction to the Theory of Directed Graphs*. New York: John Wiley & Sons.

Hastie, T., Tibshirani, R., and Friedman, J. H. (2009). *The Elements of Statistical Learning: Data Mining, Inference, and Prediction* (2nd ed.). New York: Springer.

Hubbell, C. H. (1965). An Input-Output Approach to Clique Identification. *Sociometry 28*(4), 377-399.

Introna, L. D. (2007). Maintaining the Reversibility of Foldings: Making the Ethics (Politics) of Information Technology Visible. *Ethics and Information Technology 9*(1), 11-25.

Katz, L. (1953). A New Status Index Derived from Sociometric Analysis. *Psychometrika 18*(1), 39-43.

Kleinberg, J. M. (1999). Authoritative Sources in a Hyperlinked Environment. *Journal of the ACM 46*(5), 604-632.

Kőnig, D. (1936). *Theorie der endlichen und unendlichen Graphen*. New York: Chelsea.

Kuhn, T. (1962). *The Structure of Scientific Revolutions*. Chicago: University of Chicago Press.

Langville, A. N., and Meyer, C. D. (2004). Deeper Inside PageRank. *Internet Mathematics 1*(3), 335-380.

Langville, A. N., and Meyer, C. D. (2005). A Survey of Eigenvector Methods for Web Information Retrieval. *SIAM Review 47*(1), 135-161.

Latour, B. (1986). Visualization and Cognition: Thinking with Eyes and Hands. *Knowledge and Society: Studies in the Sociology of Culture Past and Present 6*, 1-40.

Lewin, K. (1936). *Principles of Topological Psychology*. New York: McGraw-Hill.

Lewin, K. (1964). *Field Theory in Social Science: Selected Theoretical Papers*. New York: Harper & Row.

Lewis, D., and Weigert, A. J. (1985). Social Atomism, Holism, and Trust. *Sociological Quarterly 26*(4), 455-471.

Manin, B. (1997). *The Principles of Representative Government*. Cambridge: Cambridge University Press.

Mayer, K. (2009). On the Sociometry of Search Engines: A Historical Review of Methods. In K. Becker and F. Stalder (eds.), *Deep Search: The Politics of Search beyond Google* (pp. 54-72). Piscataway: Transaction Publishers.

Mirowski, P., and Nik-Khah, E. (2017). *The Knowledge We Have Lost in Information*. Oxford: Oxford University Press.

Moreno, J. L. (1934). *Who Shall Survive? A New Approach to the Problem of Human Interrelation*. Washington, DC: Nervous and Mental Disease Publishing.

Mullins, N. C. (1973). *Theories and Theory Groups in Contemporary American Sociology*. New York: Harper & Row.

Page, L. (2001). Method for Node Ranking in a Hyperlinked Database. US Patent 6,285,999, filed 9 January 1998 and issued 4 September 2001.

Page, L. (2004). Method for Scoring Documents in a Linked Database. US Patent 6,799,176, filed 6 July 2001 and issued 28 September 2004.

Page, L., Brin, S., Motwani, R., and Winograd, T. (1999). The PageRank Citation Ranking: Bringing Order to the Web [technical report]. Stanford InfoLab. Retrieved from http://ilpubs.stanford.edu:8090/422/.

Pinski, G., and Narin, F. (1976). Citation Influence for Journal Aggregates of Scientific Publications. *Information Processing and Management 12*(5), 297-312.

Porter, T. (1995). *Trust in Numbers: The Pursuit of Objectivity in Science and Public Life*. Princeton: Princeton University Press.

Putnam, R. D. (2000). *Bowling Alone*. New York: Simon and Schuster.

r/Science, and AAAS-AMA. (2018). AAAS AMA: Hi, we're researchers from Google, Microsoft, and Facebook who study Artificial Intelligence. Ask us anything! *The Winnower*. https://doi.org/10.15200/winn.151896.65484.

Ramsay, S. (2010). The Hermeneutics of Screwing Around; or What You Do with a Million Books. In K. Kee (ed.), *Pastplay: Teaching and Learning History with Technology* (pp. 111-120). Ann Arbor: University of Michigan Press.

Rieder, B. (2005). Networked Control: Search Engines and the Symmetry of Confidence. *International Review of Information Ethics 3*, 26-32.

Rieder, B. (2009). Democratizing Search? From Critique to Society-Oriented Design. In K. Becker and F. Stalder (eds.), *Deep Search: The Politics of Search beyond Google* (pp. 133-151). Piscataway: Transaction Publishers.

Rieder, B. (2013) Studying Facebook via Data Extraction: The Netvizz Application. In H. Davis, H. Halpin, and A. Pentland (eds.), *WebSci '13 Proceedings of the 5th Annual ACM Web Science Conference* (pp. 346-355). New York: ACM.

Rogers, R. (2013). *Digital Methods*. Cambridge, MA: MIT Press.

Roush, W. (2004). Search beyond Google. *MIT Technology Review*, 1 March. Retrieved from https://www.technologyreview.com.

Salton, G. (1963). Associative Document Retrieval Techniques Using Bibliographic Information. *Journal of the ACM 10*(4), 440-457.

Shore, C., and Wright, S. (2000). Coercive Accountability: The Rise of Audit Culture in Higher Education. In M. Strathern (ed.), *Audit Cultures: Anthropological Studies in Accountability, Ethics and the Academy* (pp. 57-89). London: Routledge.

Simondon, G. (2014). *Sur la technique (1953-1983)*. Paris: Presses Universitaires de France.

Simondon, G. (2017). *On the Mode of Existence of Technical Objects* (C. Malaspina and J. Rogove, trans.). Minneapolis: Univocal Publishing.

Small, H. (1973). Co-citation in the Scientific Literature: A New Measure of the Relationship between Two Documents. *Journal of the American Society for Information Science 24*(4), 265-269.

Stigler, S. M. (1999). *Statistics on the Table: The History of Statistical Concepts and Methods*. Cambridge, MA: Harvard University Press.

Topîrceanu, A. (2017). Breaking Up Friendships in Exams: A Case Study for Minimizing Student Cheating in Higher Education Using Social Network Analysis. *Computers & Education 115*,171-187.

Uprichard, E., Burrows, R., and Byrne, D. (2008). SPSS as an 'Inscription Device': From Causality to Description? *Sociological Review 56*(4), 606-622.

Watts, D. J. (2004). The 'New' Science of Networks. *Annual Review of Sociology 30*, 243-270.

Zimmer, M. (2010). Web Search Studies: Multidisciplinary Perspectives on Web Search Engines. In J. Hunsinger, L. Klastrup, and M. Allen (eds.), *International Handbook of Internet Research* (pp. 507-521). Dordrecht: Springer.

Žižek, S. (1992). *Enjoy Your Symptom! Jacques Lacan in Hollywood and Out*. New York: Routledge.

Conclusion: Toward Technical Culture

Abstract
The conclusion synthesizes algorithmic information ordering into a typology of ordering gestures, paying particular attention to the modes of disassembly and reassembly that inform the underlying techniques. The attempt to distill an operational epistemology from the cacophony of techniques begs the question whether we are witnessing the emergence of a new *épistémè* (Foucault, 2005), a far-reaching set of regularities that characterize order is understood and operationalized. Furthermore, the chapter addresses the more immediately pressing need to understand how the capacity to algorithmically arrange individuals, populations, and everything in-between in dynamic and goal-oriented ways relates to contemporary forms of capitalism. To face this challenge, the chapter comes back to Simondon's mechanology and its broader cousin, technical culture, as a means to promote a 'widening' of technical imagination and appropriation.

Keywords: *épistémè*, operational epistemology, technical imagination, technical wisdom

Over the preceding chapters, I have attempted to develop a perspective on algorithmic information ordering that takes technicity as its main focus and considers ordering techniques as means for producing specific forms of function or behavior dealing with the 'arrangement and disposition' of data items that stand, more often than not, for something meaningful to human practice. While the chosen historical trajectories often dealt with books, articles, or other documents, I have argued that these techniques can be applied to any item that can be fitted into a common intermediate form like a feature vector or a graph. Other than that, little adaptation is required to transfer ordering gestures to new domains: calculating the similarity between user profiles on a dating site is hardly different from comparing text documents and deciding whether an applicant should

Rieder, B., *Engines of Order: A Mechanology of Algorithmic Techniques*. Amsterdam: Amsterdam University Press, 2020
DOI 10.5117/9789462986190_CONCL

receive credit can be handled the same way as spam filtering. Terms like 'computerization', 'datafication', or – at a lower level – 'formalization' all refer to processes that end up funneling different aspects of the world into the domain of algorithmic information ordering.

Technical objects, including online infrastructures, are built 'from elements that are already technical' (Simondon, 2017, p. 74) and algorithmic techniques constitute vocabularies of possible function that enable operation and serve as horizons for technical imagination. The notion of algorithmic technique indeed seeks to distinguish fundamental technical schemas from the arrangements and design choices they are embedded in. Even if technical objects are 'invented, thought and willed, taken up [*assumé*] by a human subject' (Simondon, 2017, p. 252), they depend on the *objective* technicities available at a particular stage of technical evolution. Their *objectal* integration into economic, social, and psychosocial relations occurs on the basis of their operational capabilities. An online music service can only make 'good' automated recommendations if there are techniques capable of producing outputs that match some standard of quality, for example, user satisfaction. The current debates around algorithms and artificial intelligence are stimulated by an expansion of actually attainable behavior. The widening of 'what computers can do' relies on the formulation of new algorithmic techniques, but practical applications also depend on factors like the proliferation of computerized task environments capturing human practice, continuously growing computational power, business models that take advantage of new opportunities, and forms of social interest or demand. One could easily imagine versions of this book that focus on these dimensions. My objective, however, was to address a small subset of the technical substance that lurks behind terms like 'algorithm' and to analyze it in ways that are attentive to specificity, variation, and relational embedding.

Seen from the perspective of techniques, software-making is neither an enactment of an autonomous technical telos nor a simple transposition of nontechnical ideas into technical form. It is the creation of a coherent system from disparate elements, a system that has internal consistency yet remains open to the world to a variable degree. If technical creation is indeed a form of communication as Simondon suggests, the 'message' a technical object carries is the operational substance it introduces into the networks that surround it, adding to and transforming them in the process. Mechanology is the hermeneutics of that message.

In this concluding chapter, I will attempt to give a clearer picture where a mechanology of algorithmic techniques may lead, first by distilling the epistemological dimension of algorithmic information ordering into a slightly more general classification of ordering gestures, second, by coming back to the question of how engines of order are tied to the social and economic logics of the present, and third by arguing that Simondon's notion of a 'technical culture' is a necessary correlate for societies that have made technology the very center of their mode of existence.

From Order to Ordering

One of the arguments I developed in the second part of this book held that traditional systems for bibliographic control like library classifications and subject headings were designed to further Enlightenment values such as universal education, while the special libraries and documentation centers multiplying after WWII reframed information as a resource for decision-making in business and government. These 'cultural' differences clearly played an important role in the story, but my main goal was to isolate elements of what could be called an 'operational epistemology' that emerges from the actual 'techniques involved in operationalizing distinctions in the real' (Siegert, 2013, p. 14) in these two settings. This project revolved around the notion of 'order', even if I worked with a broad definition that largely stuck to the OED's proposition as 'the arrangement or disposition of people or things in relation to each other according to a particular sequence, pattern, or method'.

As a means to discuss changing understandings of order, I set out from Deleuze's (1988) reading of Foucault's *The Order of Things* (2005), wondering whether we are witnessing the emergence of a new *épistémè*. In the classic *épistémè*, order was thought as pregiven, transcendental, and infinite, a 'perfect' or 'God' form (Deleuze, 1988, p. 125f.) where the variation of concretely existing things unfolds on a plane defined by eternal, unchanging principles. The scholar takes inventory of the regularities that characterize a world 'offered to representation without interruption' (Foucault, 2005, p. 224). This yields series of two-dimensional tables capturing and representing the order of things by positioning them with regard to their similarities and differences. The modern *épistémè*, however, trades idealism for empiricism. Order becomes the concrete result of contingent historical forces, namely the intrinsic processes of life, work, and language. Darwin's tree of life begins with a single organism and the myriad species that develop from it are the product of the mechanisms of mutation and selection playing out in geographies and ecologies where certain traits prime over others. Life is no longer an infinite variation of perfect forms but the outcome of the complicated yet finite evolution of contingent processes. We see a similar shift in economics: whereas the value of an item was previously based on the assessment of similarities and differences with other items, Smith and Ricardo now identify the hours of work necessary to produce something as the 'true' foundation of its value.

Deleuze's candidate for a new *épistémè* no longer revolves around transcendental grids or historical becoming, but around configurations where 'a finite number of components yields a practically unlimited diversity of combinations' (Deleuze, 1988, p. 131). Such a 'fini-unlimited' understanding of order would move from singular descriptions to 'kaleidoscopically transmuted tables whose expansion and open margins afford many formulations of similarity and difference' (Mackenzie, 2017a, p. 58), harbingers, as Dreyfus (2009) laments, of 'a postmodern, protean being ready to be opened up to ever new horizons' (p. 12). These formulations certainly resonate with the arguments presented in Chapter 4, where I measured the static and universalist ordering schemes of the nineteenth century against the combinatorial and perspectivist character of coordinate indexing that no longer attributes a fixed conceptual location to documents but retrieves and ranks them in response to a query that defines a conceptual location through the combination of search terms.

While distilling algorithmic ordering techniques into a single, idealized epistemological core can be useful, one risks losing sight of the operational dimension and its many specificities. I will therefore hold the fini-unlimited *épistémè* at bay for the moment and synthesize the previous chapters around two broad gestures I have mentioned numerous times: disassembly and reassembly. In both cases, the techniques involved cover considerable spaces of variation, even if shared intermediate forms play a pivotal role.

Disassembly

Moving the references in library catalogs from books onto cards arranged in filing cabinets already implied a gesture of detachment and atomization that prepared and enabled more fluid forms of reassembly. But disassembly was first a merely practical means for keeping a complete and up-to-date catalog, a boon to library management and knowledge access as collections grew. Since cards could be easily standardized and exchanged between libraries, the move actually furthered universalization rather than perspectivism. The uses of filing cabinets and other 'paper machines' (Krajewski, 2011) in business and government bureaucracies were more ambitious in terms of ordering and flowed directly into applications of digital database systems (cf. Gardey, 2008), but in libraries, the card catalog's potential for multiplying perspectives was hardly realized beyond the coexistence of subject headings, hierarchical classification, and alphabetical order. Disassembly and atomization were to serve political and epistemological universalism, not to challenge it. Indeed, while Paul Otlet envisioned a 'telematic cultural technique' (Hartmann, 2015, n.p.) where knowledge and information are chopped into fragments that users can combine and consult from a distance, his vision remained attached to stable and universal classification. Disassembly did not (yet) herald an understanding of order as a flexible process of ordering but served as a vehicle for access, transmission, and personal appropriation.

The information retrieval techniques taking aim at library practices were much more sensitive to the expressive power disassembly and reassembly afford. The advocates of coordinate indexing criticized hierarchical classification and precoordinated subject indexes for their practical complexity and for not taking full advantage of language's compositional qualities: words were combined too 'early' into compound concepts, they argued. Moving to single, disjointed keywords that are only 'coordinated' at query time would yield a whole range of benefits. Uniterms or descriptors, possibly taken from the documents themselves, would be faster, cheaper, and less subjective, that is, less exposed to human judgment and discretion. The idea that postcoordination reduces the biased influence of individuals on knowledge organization and retrieval is central, and this 'dispossession' is realized by eliminating syntactic possibilities from the indexing language. In coordinate indexing, the individual keyword is neither part of a classificatory hierarchy, nor capable of entering into precoordinated relationships with other terms. Even the order of keywords must be irrelevant. While the resulting intermediate form may resemble a list, the keywords attributed to a document are actually a *set* of unordered, detached items that can be intersected and queried through Boolean operators. Unlike a list, table, or tree, a coordinate index holds a latent form of order that only yields a specific arrangement when a query is made. However, as a versatile technique, it remains agnostic to the question of how keywords are selected, and we could easily imagine coordinate indexes that follow any of Hjørland's (2010, p. 74) four theories of knowledge, accommodating rationalist, empiricist, hermeneutical, or critical attitudes when creating a queryable keyword space.

In the context of the relational model for database management, the narrative concerning subjectivity persists on some level (Date, 2004, p. 401), but in organizational settings where records are continuously updated and data models can be expanded or changed, data integrity becomes the main objective. At least initially, normalization through decomposition and elimination of redundancy primarily serves this goal. But the outcome is similar. The fundamental restriction to the *relation* as intermediate form again installs a latent informational grid where each item is located in an unordered array of variables. Relations look like tables, but like sets, they are more abstract constructs. Syntactic purification once again assures the creation of homogenized data objects defined by independent attributes, even if these attributes can now be chosen from a larger variety of types. The goal is independence: from the hardware, the underlying storage systems, the larger organization of the database, and even the particularities of specific 'patterns of activity' (Codd, 1970, p. 379). The normative insistence on deduplication and decomposition through consecutive stages of normalization envisions the data-modeling process as an 'elimination procedure' (p. 381) that produces a space defined by atomized information coordinates, making the stored information ready for ad hoc ordering. The considerable 'linguistic power' (p. 381) of simple query languages based on first-order predicate calculus depends on the relation as intermediate form and on the adherence to these normalization principles. Database literature thus generally promotes a rationalist and analytico-synthetic perspective that is 'concerned with what the data *is*' (Date, 2004, p. 330) and commits to dissecting data into their smallest components. At the same time, however, relational database management systems like MySQL are not tied to these prescriptions and can be used as information stores without strict adherence to normalization. Concrete systems are again sufficiently general and flexible to accommodate data models that reflect various epistemological sensitivities. The technique is more inclusive than the conceptual horizon that drove its invention.

In areas dealing with full text or other types of 'unstructured' data, that is, data that are already digital but have not been fitted into a specific intermediate form or data model, the first question is how to disassemble them algorithmically. The early experiments performed by Luhn and Maron were, in fact, attempts to automate the construction of coordinate indexes to further reduce human influence. Both were aware that counting words in documents is a rather imperfect way to capture meaning, but the limitations of computing hardware and the encouraging results from working systems justified the approach. Coordinate indexing had already demonstrated how the description of items as sets of independent terms can yield considerable combinatorial power, but the experiments with full text showed that signals or measurements taken from the 'world' itself could be treated as variables or 'features' in similar fashion. Disassembly thus becomes an algorithmic process that selects or creates the attributes describing a group of items and funnels them into an intermediate form. Luhn and Maron arrive at almost the same point as Salton's more heavily formalized vector space model: documents are represented as unordered lists (sets) of terms and how often they occur. While names like 'frequency distribution' or 'feature vector' point to different mathematical fields and associated manipulation techniques, they basically refer to the same thing. From here, the selection or extraction of the attributes describing each item can expand in various directions: more elaborate features based on word-pairs, sentence structure, or document formatting can supplement word frequencies; various forms of propositional knowledge, from dictionaries to domain ontologies, can enhance feature quality; and weighting systems like tf-idf can assess their statistical specificity by calculating feature distribution over the full collection. These and many other possibilities show how formalization is rarely a mere effect of digitization but involves complex processes of delineation, selection, and (de)composition. Different techniques and rationales can inform the construction of feature vectors and the rather basic theories of language and meaning encountered over the last chapters do not preclude deeper engagement with the objects under scrutiny. Finally, if the relational model suggests a rationalist approach to disassembly, the statistical techniques dominating information retrieval favor an empiricist attitude, where informational grids are not modeled in advance but extracted from the world through iterative experimentation and optimization under the auspices of practical objectives.

In the context of network algorithms, lastly, the pathways toward disassembly and formalization are remarkable in at least two respects. First, while sociometric work is clearly focused on measuring and method, it draws more explicitly on domain theorization: Moreno's psychoanalytical ideas, social exchange theory, and the various brands of social network theory describe society as a collection of individuals and reduce social structure to the patterns of interaction between these social atoms. This may not be a particularly extravagant model, but it shows how formalization can be guided by more explicit forms of domain theorization. Rodgers's (2011) 'age of fracture', which is closely related to theories building on 'microfoundations' in economics, political science, and sociology, can thus be seen as providing the intellectual fuel that drives this particular vector of atomization. Second, the network model introduces an intermediate form tied to graph theoretic concepts and computations, adding to already available set-theoretic, statistical, and algebraic techniques. Constructs like (geodesic) distance and centrality draw directly on the underlying shift in representation, even if graphs can also be treated as sets, vectors, or distributions. The network perspective adds relationships between items as 'material' but sticks to the familiar logic of syntactic reduction: links rarely carry more information than direction and connection strength. The broad calculative potential again depends on this reduction.

In summary, there are different ways to capture application domains into information granules and intermediate formalizations. More deliberate approaches to modeling contrast with more empirical methods that instantiate heavily mediated forms of 'listening to the world'. All of them serve to get the world into the computer in ways that facilitate subsequent reassembly gestures. Disassembly draws on these different processes to produce forms of raw data, understood not as found or untreated, a notion that has been rightfully criticized (cf. Gitelman, 2013), but raw like the cleaned, peeled, and chopped vegetables in supermarkets that have been prepared as ingredients ready to be submitted to one of many available recipes. For Foucault (2005), classification inescapably entails the creation of 'a common ground' and we can think about formalization as a means to produce such a 'mute ground upon which it is possible for entities to be juxtaposed' (p. xviii). This already involves forms of interpretation, even if they can seem purely mechanical, haphazard, or dispersed. While disassembly may occur as a contained gesture, deliberately applied by some actor at some point in time, maybe in the context of experimentation, research, or decision-making, its contemporary cultural significance draws on the observation that human life increasingly revolves around infrastructures built from the ground on up atomized units and decomposed data granules. One could argue that formalization in computerized environments already begins at the earliest stages of systems design, when primary functionalities and data models are mapped out. The basic setup of Facebook as a series of user profiles that connect through friendship relations and communicate through messages already defines and prepares the raw material available for algorithmic information ordering to latch onto.

Reassembly

Intermediate forms such as feature vectors or graphs thus point in two directions. On the one side, they connect with the 'world' and the different ways application domains can be funneled into computation. On the other side, they highlight the considerable calculative potential that is unlocked when data are made ready for algorithmic ordering. The techniques for reassembly again differ in both what they do and how they do it. On a very general level, they are held together by a broad allegiance to the fini-unlimited: when applied to large collections of multidimensional data, all of the techniques discussed in this book allow for almost endless recombination. Order is no longer a stable structure but dissolves into instances of ordering that generate perspectives on the data items under scrutiny and, by extension, on the world they capture. Even if we consider that machines consist of 'human gesture fixed and crystallized in working structures' (Simondon, 2017, p. 18), the ways these perspectives are produced have become increasingly nonanthropomorphic, simply because the sheer number of small steps even simple techniques entail can no longer be handled by human beings.

Instead of rehashing my chapter outline, I propose to synthesize the almost limitless number of techniques and interface arrangements around three fundamental ordering gestures. The borders between these gestures are not clear-cut, but a broader systematization can inform a perspective that sits between the sprawling park of algorithmic techniques and their far-reaching idealization as a fini-unlimited *épistémè*. This middle ground may, in turn, facilitate the conceptual coordination between techniques and their application domains.

The first gesture is the *aggregate description* of populations of items. Traditionally the core domain of statistics, I have dedicated little space to notions such as averages or correlations between variables in a dataset, since my main interest was information ordering understood as arrangement of items. Certain overall descriptions of datasets did seep in, however. Tf-idf and similar weighting procedures use statistical horizons to decide whether a given attribute is more or less specific and therefore a good signal or 'clue'. And unsupervised machine learning techniques such as PageRank or the *k*-means algorithm briefly mentioned in Chapter 5 seek to provide some overall assessment of a dataset, even if their main target is the individual item. One could add techniques that I have not discussed at all, for example, generative statistical models like Latent Dirichlet Allocation (Blei, Ng, and Jordan, 2003), used in text mining to detect 'topics' in document collections. But I mainly mention aggregate description to remind us that the information retrieval island is part of a much larger archipelago of concepts and techniques that it connects with in myriad ways. One could easily use a coordinate index for descriptive purposes, for example, by counting the most common terms in a given collection to get an overview of the subjects covered. One could also map the topic space with a network representation on the basis that two keywords should be linked if they are attributed to the same item. Luhn's 'lattice of word-pair linkages', discussed in Chapter 5, applied a similar principle to 'map' the content of a document. Much of the power of the relational model in organizational settings comes from the capacity to summarize, to establish relationships between attributes or variables, and to trace change over time. Even if these practices are not necessarily ordering in the sense of ranking or classifying items, they imply an appreciation of patterns in a population and can thus form the basis for decision-making. Once information has been formalized into intermediate forms, it can certainly be retrieved in various ways, but it also becomes part of a broader 'avalanche of numbers' (Hacking, 1990, p. 2) and thus susceptible to the analytical gestures and ways of knowing that have been developed in statistics since the eighteenth century. And the specific forms of algorithmic intervention that permeate digital infrastructures and interfaces necessarily imply moments of representation where some kind of description is established (cf. Hacking, 1983).

The second gesture I want to address, *grouping*, moves more clearly toward direct action on the items under scrutiny. Grouping can be under-stood as a form of distinction- or border-making that may rely on various techniques. Logic-based systems like coordinate indexing and the relational model allow for the deliberate specification of criteria to make selections of items. In fact, any intermediate form that frames items as objects and properties can be subjected to such 'hard' forms of border-making. We can distinguish different logical or set-theoretic formulations, but what is important here is that information ordering often implies moments where criteria for inclusion and exclusion are set without any kind of iterative processing or complex transformation. If a document does not have any of the keywords given in a query, it is not retrieved. If an entry in a database table does correspond to a variably complex condition, it is not part of the result set. If two nodes in a friendship network are not connected, they are not able to interact or access each other's profiles. The pruning of information through clearly defined criteria is certainly not a new practice; but detailed, multidimensional data and powerful query languages allow for the expression of exceedingly complex rules for drawing such lines. That said, dynamic and interactive settings make it easy to change queries on the fly and, as Luhn and Salton have shown, borders can be shifted automatically, for example, by extending a query along similarity pathways if the number of results is too small. Further into that direction, we encounter techniques like machine learning as a means to make probabilistic distinctions in situations where criteria cannot be easily specified. In the case of supervised machine learning, exemplified by the Bayes classifier, an already labeled training set or continuous feedback data can serve as the guiding input a system uses to derive the 'rules' that define borders by linking each feature or attribute probabilistically to each class or target variable. Unsupervised machine learning techniques, on the other hand, generate classes through iterative calculations looking for optimal distributions of differences and similarities. While the deliberate forms of selection we find in logic-based systems rests on some theory or understanding of the underlying criteria or process, these forms of inductive classification focus on desired outcomes and delegate the generation of the selection mechanism to the algorithmic process. In the end, grouping is a gesture that can be seen in descriptive terms but often prepares differential treatment: certain documents are retrieved, certain emails are discarded as spam, certain users are held at the border, certain applicants are invited for an interview, certain ads are shown to certain user groups, and so forth. Depending on how information ordering is embedded in bureaucratic or technical systems, grouping can inform decision-making processes or automate them entirely.

The third gesture is *attribution* and involves the assignment of a rank or numerical value to items or relationships. This could, for example, be a calculation of relevance numbers for documents in a collection in relation to a specific query. It could concern the degree of similarity between two documents. It could also refer to the attribution of an authority measure like PageRank to each node in a social, citation, or hyperlink network. It could simply mean putting a list in alphabetical order or along some numerical variable. A typical output would be a ranked list that establishes a specific sequence. But it could also mean positioning on a numerical scale. The frontier between attribution and different forms of grouping is clearly porose, in particular from a technical perspective, not only because classes could be based on numerical intervals, but also because probabilistic classification can be seen as a multidimensional attribution process where each item receives a relevance number for each class and ends up receiving the label of the class with the highest value. Numerical cutoffs constitute clear instances where deliberate design choices shape algorithmic behavior and the decision to ignore the lowest frequency words in a document collection, to divide search results into pages of ten, to flag content as copyright infringement or terrorist propaganda above a certain detection threshold, or to deny credit or parole to people receiving a certain probability assessment shows how attribution can be used to set hard group boundaries. Document search is traditionally a combination of grouping and ranking. However, distinguishing the two gestures serves as a reminder that the particular operational embedding of techniques is far from irrelevant, that the same outputs for an algorithmic process can be arranged into decisions in various ways.

These three gestures and the many ways they are implemented and combined in actual technical systems can work on individuals, populations, and anything in between, making scale a factor that can be manipulated freely. And one could add other gestures to the list. Although I have not specifically talked about forecasting in this book, it is clearly relevant. Techniques concerned with prediction over time indeed point toward their own intermediate forms, such as time-series data. But description, grouping, and attribution are already gestures concerned with 'the future' if orchestrated in specific ways. Techniques necessarily work on the basis of available data, and in a statistical context the term 'prediction' merely signals that some inference is being made. This ambiguity shows how techniques, understood as computational transformations, do not necessarily map neatly onto ordering gestures, highlighting the difficulty of aligning technical operation with common cultural categories.

The fuzziness of my taxonomy of gestures is also an effect of the great variability, malleability, and diversity in application domains information ordering has come to know. If we uphold the parallel between technicity and language as two means of expression, the identification of basic 'speech acts' of information ordering can hardly capture the complex realities of local arrangements. What broadly runs through the different techniques, however, are forms of apprehension or formalization that frame the world as a series of atomized items defined by loose properties or relationships. Instead of placing them into an a priori system of order, they are kept in an intermediate state: already captured and transformed, but sufficiently mobile to support dynamic and multifaceted forms of reassembly, operations on differences and similarities that become descriptions, groupings, and attributions that can then be pushed back into the domains they cover.

Operational Epistemology

While the purpose of this book was not to funnel the jagged terrain of algorithmic techniques into broad idealizations, both Simondon's framing of technology as mode of existence and the cultural techniques tradition suggest that technological change can have profound effects on the makeup of human reality. If we paraphrase Siegert (2013, p. 57) and argue that order *as such* does not exist independently of ordering techniques, we must expect the developments I have examined over the last chapters to have far-reaching consequences. The following passage from *The Order of Things* hints at the

deeper repercussions information orderings' operational epistemology
may carry:

> Order is, at one and the same time, that which is given in things as their
> inner law, the hidden network that determines the way they confront
> one another, and also that which has no existence except in the grid
> created by a view, an attention, a language; and it is only in the blank
> spaces of this grid that order manifests itself in depth as though already
> there, waiting in silence for the moment of its expression. (Foucault, 2005,
> p. xxi, translation amended)

Leaving the obvious Kantian undertones (cf. Djaballah, 2008) aside, Foucault's point, here, is to argue that any *épistémè* or discursive formation
carries a view, attention, and language containing certain preconceptions
concerning the 'inner law' of things. If we substitute the more idealistic
notion of 'view' with that of 'technique', we can indeed ask how algorithmic
information ordering makes the world 'manifest itself' in broader terms. The
question has been asked many times in other areas, for example, around
statistics. The common saying that 'correlation does not imply causation'
expresses skepticism about the statistical method, but also confidence in
a world operating according to causal principles. Causes exist, the saying
claims implicitly, even if statistics may not suffice to uncover them. But,
as Hacking (1990) argues, for statisticians as illustrious as Karl Pearson
himself, correlation may well have 'destroyed causes' (p. 188) and not just
our means to observe them. Conceptions of reality are at stake in debates
concerning method and technique. Box's famous assertion that 'all models
are wrong but some are useful'[1] can be read as a pragmatic response, where
the 'whole truth' is no longer to be had, but good approximations can still
yield advantageous results in practical applications.

Similar debates occur in and around computing. In his rebuttal of Chomsky, Norvig not only puts forward the 'engineering success' of statistical
machine translation but argues that '[m]any phenomena in science are
stochastic' (Norvig, 2015, n.p.), that is, random. This is clearly an assessment
of the nature of reality itself, and one that evokes the much longer 'erosion
of determinism' that Hacking (1990) links to the emergence of statistics in
the nineteenth century. Extreme forms of computationalism, like Stephen

---

1   Followed by this longer explanation: 'Now it would be very remarkable if any system existing
in the real world could be exactly represented by any simple model. However, cunningly chosen
parsimonious models often do provide remarkably useful approximations' (Box, 1979, p. 205).

Wolfram's (2002) principle of 'computational equivalence', which holds that 'any process whatsoever can be viewed as a computation' (p. 716), are examples of the blurring between technique and ontology. And I have already mentioned the work of Mirowski and Nik-Khah (2017), who argue that the neoclassical idea that 'truth is the output of the greatest information processor known to humankind – namely, The Market' (p. 7) could not have been envisaged without the computer and the associated understanding of information as computable resource.

Contemporary life in economically developed societies is indeed organized around digital devices and environments that grammatize, formalize, and capture activities, yielding masses of granular data in the process. This has the practical effect that the world is increasingly revealed through computational methods combing through these data troves. If, as Burrows (2009) argues, social 'associations and interactions are now not only *mediated* by software and code, they are becoming *constituted* by it' (p. 488), one result is an overflow of data as an obvious resource to draw on, feeding a powerful drive toward machinic modes of analysis and action. Computerization has become a self-reinforcing process where data generated by some kind of machine require other machines to make sense of them. Much like the increase in documentary production – first in libraries, information centers, and bureaucracies and then on the web – has fueled the 'information overload' narrative, paving the way for algorithmic information ordering, the explosive production of data in almost every domain makes broad swaths of the world appear as intrinsically 'multifaceted' (Weinberger, 2008, p. 82) and 'too big to know' (Weinberger, 2012), continuously expanding the utility and allure of techniques that are designed to combine 'many small and individually ambiguous clues' (Spärck Jones, 1999, p. 277f.) into *useful* descriptions and decisions.

This feeds directly into Floridi's assessment that our ever-expanding 'infosphere' has the epistemological effect that 'the world itself [...] will be increasingly understood informationally' (Floridi, 2014, p. 50). Techniques and experiences associated with computing trickle into the 'view, attention, and language' of our time. We find an interesting parallel in Foucault's later work on the art of governing, where the emergence of the problem of the population (Foucault, 2009, p. 29ff.) mirrors the shift from the classic to the modern *épistémè*. Through the study of epidemics and spirals in economic production, in particular the regular nutrition shortages during the seventeenth and eighteenth century, mercantilist theorizations of the state modeled on the household appeared as no longer viable. The notion of 'population' consequently emerged as a conceptual entity with a specificity of its own, that is, with its own irreducible laws, regularities, and forces.

Foucault attributes this 'discovery' of the population to physiocrats like Quesnay and Turgot but also singles out the nascent discipline of statistics as crucial to the conceptualization of the newly identified entity: the modes of aggregate description and analysis that statistics provides make the populations' particular character visible and amendable to scientific investigation.

While the term 'population' remains with us in statistical language to designate any set of items or cases, what increasingly separates us from the modern *épistémè* is a declining belief that there are irreducible 'social forces' driving history in the making. We find clear indications of such a shift in the social sciences. In Latour's (2005) full-fledged attack on the very idea of 'social force' – appropriately named *Reassembling the Social* – he writes that the '"social" is not some glue that could fix everything including what the other glues cannot fix; it is what is glued together by many other types of connectors' (p. 5). The social, in this reading, is seen 'not as a special domain, a specific realm, or a particular sort of thing, but only as a very peculiar movement of re-association and reassembling' (p. 5). Society is no longer a specific sphere characterized by specific forces, but rather the outcome of networks connecting 'heterogeneous elements', 'actors', or 'atoms' (p. 217). It is not surprising that such a perspective would be interested in the fini-unlimited possibilities of information ordering, where computation can do much more than describe coherent wholes. The goal is no longer to 'go from the particular to the general, but from particular to *more* particulars' (Latour et al., 2012, p. 599) by 'aggregating and disaggregating according to different variables' (p. 607). Methodology and ontology once again entwine:

> 'Specific' and 'general', 'individual' and 'collective', 'actor' and 'system' are not essential realities but provisional terms that depend rather on the ease with which it is possible to navigate through profiles. (Latour et al., 2012, p. 593)

Is there a parallel between the discovery of the population through the lens of statistical aggregation and its conceptual dissolution through 'the practical experience of navigating through data sets' (Latour et al., 2012, p. 602)? The analytical expressivity and plasticity that computational tools for data analysis confer is certainly highly suggestive. Is this the end of one way of 'thinking', of one view, attention, and language, and the beginning of another? The cultural techniques perspective cautions against hasty periodization but leaves little doubt that transformations in dominant techniques will have critical consequences, in particular if we consider Lash's (2006) argument that the information paradigm heralds a 'collapse of ontology and epistemology' where 'modes of knowing are increasingly also modes of being' (p. 581). New *épistémè* or not, the world changes in front of our eyes and everywhere we look, we find computers.

Engines of Order

These more speculative epistemological considerations are important in their own right, but I have situated my inquiry in the particular technicities of software and software-making, which endow algorithmic information ordering with a particular kind of performativity. Software allows for the formulation of techniques that could not exist without the iterative capacities of computing machinery. And software defines the digital environments where information ordering serves as a means of production for the generation of economic value, as a mechanism for 'programmed coordination' (Bratton, 2015, p. 41), and – in extremis – as a technology of power, that is, a way to 'conduct conducts' (Foucault, 2008, p. 186). While Simondon suggests that we think of technical evolution as a combination of invention and concretization that is largely independent from economic or social considerations (cf. Bontems, 2009), he writes at a time where the 'coating' of consumer capitalism is still thin and the endless proliferation of small variations drawing on the same technicities is not yet the dominant form of technical creation. He also writes long before pervasive online infrastructures allow for much tighter integration between design, deployment, and empirical evaluation, transforming the process of technical creation – at least in certain areas – into an ongoing practice that never releases anything like a 'final' product. I certainly kept with the idea that the objective dimension of technicity, which concerns the accumulation of new technical schemas, is not a mere manifestation of external forces, but I also argued that technical creation carries deeply into the objectal, for example, when business logics are modeled with standard components. Due to its artisanal character, software remains open to context, which means that the specific ways operation is arranged can reflect social and cultural embeddings to a high degree. The orchestration of techniques into a technical object or 'product' is crucial.

Orchestration

Frozen into ready-to-hand code modules or programmed from scratch, algorithmic ordering techniques can be arranged and combined in countless ways. Many software packages will implement more than one ordering gesture: any relational database management system, for example, already incorporates features for description, grouping, and attribution. A single library like the Natural Language Toolkit for Python will provide access to tens or hundreds of techniques that can be integrated into larger programs. Google Search combines an information retrieval mechanism scoring some query-related form of relevance with a network algorithm trying to express a notion of authority and a learning system that relies on user feedback for optimization. And Google Search incorporates many other instances of technicity, from web crawlers to data center architectures and device-specific user interfaces. The actual process of ordering concrete items in concrete task settings is never just the 'application' of a singular algorithmic technique to some disembodied dataset. It is the connection between a particular domain of practice, particular forms of capture, particular data representations, particular implementations of particular techniques, and particular dispositions of outputs that may directly reach back into the realities data were initially gleaned from. Technical individuals or ensembles necessarily imply specific *orchestrations* of disparate elements.

Consider the following example: A researcher working with social media data may want to analyze some form of online interaction, for example, 'mentioning' on Twitter. Her dataset is based on a keyword search submit-ted to a particular web API that shapes data in certain ways and imposes certain access limits. The data was collected with the help of a software package such as DMI-TCAT (Borra and Rieder, 2014), which adds its own idiosyncrasies to the chain when the collected data is parsed to represent users and their interactions as a network file. The researcher opens the file in a graph analysis program like Gephi (Bastian, Heymann, and Jacomy, 2009) to examine and visualize its contents. Since she is interested in social hierarchies and thematic authority, she applies Gephi's implementation of PageRank (leaving α at the default level of 0.85), which adds a variable to each node. She uses the new variable to color nodes in a network visualization, a form of output that relies not only on the full battery of technicity behind contemporary GUI-based software and on the specific forms and functions Gephi provides, but also on algorithmic techniques for transforming the multidimensional graph into a two-dimensional point-and-line diagram that reveals some aspect of its structure. This orchestration of PageRank as part of a research method is obviously very different from the algorithm's integration into the vast technical ensemble we encounter when searching on google.com, but even this rather contained practice is fully caught up in large networks of operation that afford and require many choices to be made.

This is one of several reasons why computing cannot be sufficiently described as 'applied logic' and subfields like machine learning are not simply 'applied statistics'. Algorithmic techniques, seen as *elements*, define the objective possibilities for software behavior but do not determine the objectal variations emerging trough orchestration into *individuals* and *ensembles* in concrete settings. The term 'applied' hides the myriad connections and decisions that inevitably emerge, and it sterilizes the 'qualculative' (Cochoy, 2008) injunction of judgment into calculation. The notion of algorithmic technique and its characterization as a technical element is indeed designed to battle the tendency to singularize 'algorithms' into a monolithic cultural form, trivializing the variability, complexity, and depth of modern technology. As Bogost (2015) plainly, states, '[c]oncepts like "algorithm" have become sloppy shorthands, slang terms for the act of mistaking multipart complex systems for simple, singular ones' (n.p.), further cementing us in a culture that has little patience for the technical principles informing the infrastructures and environments that constitute our real.

If there are indeed so many possibilities for orchestration and design and so many choices to be made, how can we better understand the choices that *are* being made? As I have argued, a system's makeup is tied to its purpose and since information ordering has become part of many different application domains, a large variety of purposes inform concrete arrangements. Starting from the traditional information retrieval setup, where a searcher tries to extract references or documents from a collection, we can see more clearly where things have been heading. Bearing in mind Shera's idea, echoed five decades later by commentators like Weinberger,[2] that future classifications of knowledge would imply 'widely varying schematisms, each constructed for a specific purpose [...] in accordance with a particular point of view or philosophic orientation' (Shera, 1952, p. 17), one could indeed argue that local schematisms have become the norm as information ordering has moved beyond public libraries. Coordinate indexing made it easy to formulate site-specific vocabularies, possibly taken from the data themselves. This basic setup has since widened from the familiar bibliographic mission to 'connect the right information with the right users at the right time' to forms of data processing that 'help users analyze and digest information and facilitate decision making' (Aggarwal and Zhai, 2012, p. 2). A wide variety of datasets now regularly meets an equally broad diversity of algorithmic techniques.

---

2   Referring to mapmakers' decisions what to include and exclude, Weinberger argues: 'The line between the implicit and the explicit isn't drawn by the intellect. It's drawn by purpose and thus by what *matters* to us' (Weinberger, 2008, p. 158).

While 'data' used to mean 'text documents' and ordering was mainly retrieval, we now see a much wider range of datafied domains and a much larger set of techniques that inform different gestures at the level of the interface. Orchestrations into concrete application arrangements vary heavily. Although Bowker's (2005) call to build databases and information systems with 'a view to designing for maximum flexibility and allowing as much as possible for an emergent polyphony and polychrony' (p. 184) has been largely realized if we consider the masses of atomized data collected in relational databases and elsewhere, access to the facilities for reassembly, which define the actual flexibility available to end-user, is a different matter entirely.

Expert users now have impressive tools for retrieval and analysis at their fingertips, boosting their capacity to multiply analytical perspectives at will, but the instances of information ordering integrated into online environments and platforms point in a different direction. Starting from the introduction of statistical ranking, based on frequency or specificity of terms, there has been a tendency to reduce expressivity at the query level, or at least to add modes of processing that are not user amendable. Google's dominant web search engine, for example, continues to provide considerable end-user expressivity through free-form queries, some basic syntactic possibilities, and a (small) set of accessible parameters, but it also relies on a large number of intractable techniques that affect the result set and sequence. Authority-based document scoring, learning through feedback, personalization, and localization imply moments of ordering that are neither clearly identifiable, nor easily influenced from the outside. If we look at recommender systems or other instances of automatic modulation, there is even less explicit user input and influence. The canonical application example for machine learning, spam filtering, initially relied on explicit, proactive labeling by users and sometimes mail clients even provided access to the derived model. But much of this work has been moved into the server architectures of email providers, who employ a whole battery of techniques in the background. The orchestration of algorithmic techniques in contemporary infrastructures is increasingly arranged around forms of implicit feedback that basically take user behavior as revealed preference, that is, as a stand-in for an interest or desire previously expressed through a query or other explicit gesture. Who is the real user of information ordering in these contexts?

Digital Capitalism

The capacity to orchestrate technical elements around different application logics, to funnel digital items interchangeably into intermediate forms, and to connect interfaces to algorithmic ordering in various ways means that software has become an important means of production for generating economic value in the massive, marked-based interaction infrastructures discussed at the beginning of this book. While people continue to search for contents or pieces of information, relying on algorithmic techniques to retrieve or analyze, human beings and their practices have themselves become 'documents like any other' (Ertzscheid, 2009), disassembled into databases and reassembled at will. The capacity to examine and order a datafied 'social' in myriad ways fascinates not only academic researchers but also commercial and governmental users that have the resources to exploit these data much more thoroughly to further their operational goals. In 1949, Heidegger (1977) analyzed technology as a mode of 'revealing' (*Entbergen*) and claimed that the essence of modern technology consisted in revealing nature exclusively as a *resource*, as a stock of energy and raw material. He claimed that '[u]nlocking, transforming, storing, distributing, and switching about are ways of revealing' (p. 16). While I have tried to argue that there is no intrinsic or necessary connection between computing and the logic of *Gestell*, it is hard to ignore how computerization and datafication have turned human life into a resource that can be arranged and exploited in various ways, from aggregations of the 'free labour' (Terranova, 2004) of Internet users into knowledge products to the general framing of practice and experience 'as free raw material for translation into behavioral data' that generates 'a proprietary *behavioral surplus*' (Zuboff, 2019, p. 8). One cannot talk about software-making without naming the economic order it is embedded in. An analysis of software as technology of power requires constant attention to both objective and objectal dimensions and Zuboff's (2019) recent take on 'surveillance capitalism' indeed traces a particularly scathing trajectory into the 'fusion of digital capabilities and capitalist ambitions' (p. 27).

In this context, the capacity for constant empirical adaptation to feedback signals certainly stands out: the automation of *interested* readings of reality opens various directions for *interested* forms of optimization that range from personalization to iterative product development via A/B/*N* testing. Integrated digital infrastructures facilitate the 'transition to market-based relationships' (Agre, 1994, p. 120) where algorithmic information ordering serves as coordination mechanism, but they also affect production processes overall, tying the quest for economic value ever more closely to algorithmic articulations of data streams. Some of these articulations may indeed take the form of automated optimization through machine learning, but the logistical functions we encountered around the card catalog and the role of the relational model as a broad instrument for all kinds of 'business intelligence' practices should remind us that the different gestures for description and ordering can be applied to value chains in a variety of ways. Algorithmic techniques affect existing products and services, inform the creation of entirely new product categories, such as self-driving cars or voice assistants, and play various roles in the managerial quest for competitive advantage.

In line with Simondon's insistence that technical evolution is mainly driven by intrinsic factors, I have been hesitant to use concepts like ideology to explain how algorithmic techniques are invented, even if my account included 'culturalist' factors such as the pessimism about human reason (Heyck, 2012, p. 100) and the alleged pragmatism of individuals and institutions subscribing to accounting realism (Desrosières, 2001). Whether one emphasizes technicity or ideology, it is clear that computing has been deeply caught up in the emergence of what Thrift (2005) calls 'knowing capitalism', which revolves around forms of analysis, modulation, and commodification of everyday life that are intrinsically tied to software as 'analytical procedures', 'templates for decision-making', and a 'key technology of government for both the state and commerce' (p. 172). While some readers may have hoped for more attention given to the cultural and ideological connotations of information ordering, Thrift's emphasis on the constitutional capacities of software leaves room for a radical argument: What if the arrow of causality, to put it simply, points from technicity to ideology and not the other way around? If techniques are indeed 'always older than the concepts that are generated from them' (Macho, 2003, p. 179), we may have to reconsider how we investigate and describe the formation of culture. Is Wiener's idea of feedback a 'concept' with serious substance before it gets implemented in physical machinery? Is the transgression of ontological domains Thrift (2005, p. 13) ascribes to cybernetics an actual 'idea' before concrete techniques for the description and, crucially, the mechanical production of teleological behavior are developed? Is the advent of Rodgers's (2011) 'age of fracture' first and foremost a transformation in modes of thinking or is it, on the contrary, an effect of techniques based on analytical disassembly and synthetic reassembly? Does digital capitalism create a 'favorable environment' or a 'demand' for information ordering or should we see phenomena like information overload and the extension of market forms as consequences of computerization that create new economic opportunities?

Even if we do not install the computer as the root cause for epistemological perspectivism and knowing capitalism, we can clearly see how algorithmic techniques give concrete operational meaning to notions like modulation, optimization, and emergent coordination. Whether we consider 'ideas' or 'techniques' to come first, or subscribe, as I would suggest, to a relational perspective that emphasizes contingent composition over idealization, there are clearly affinities, resemblance, and synergies between the 'spirit' of contemporary capitalism (Boltanski and Chiapello, 2005) and the technical schemas discussed over the last chapters.

Orchestration binds objective technical potential into objectal relations and thus into social, economic, or political arrangements, transforming them in the process. The relational model, for example, is indeed a highly flexible means to organize information in such a way that it can be queried and ordered at will, but its broad potential for epistemic pluralism is constrained in actual databases, first by the chosen data model and then by the larger processes and practices it connects with. The human subject registered in such a database would hardly care whether their bureaucratic existence is governed by a navigational or a relational database, but for the designer and manager, the compositional qualities of a well-normalized database provide the means to interrogate, aggregate, discover, and optimize. The structural openness of software is certainly an opportunity for critical experimentation, but also a means to align digital tools and infrastructures with operational objectives and managerial practices. My emphasis on expression, plasticity, and variation in technical creation may seem to contradict a perspective sensitive to larger societal power relations and modes of economic organization. I have indeed argued that software, due to its modular character and effortless reproducibility, remains linked to artisanal forms of production, resulting in artifacts that have a high degree of 'internal contingency' and leave 'the path open for new possibilities' (Simondon, 2017, p. 29). But expression in the medium of function concerns, first and foremost, those who make software. Commentators often associate the creative aspects of software-making with phenomena like free and open-source software, artistic experimentation, civic technology, or even startup culture. Experimental design and code sprints show how quickly impressive and innovative pieces of software can be stitched together out of rich layers of abstracted and modularized function. While these examples are relevant, it should be clear that plasticity is no less available to (large) companies or governmental entities, even if more restrictive management structures may well reduce some of its spontaneity.

Building on Moor's (1978) relational demarcation between hardware and software, where the latter is 'those programs [...] which contain instructions the person can change' (p. 215) and '[w]hat is considered hardware by one person can be regarded as software by another' (p. 216), I have argued that the capacity to build is largely a question of resources. Software allows a single developer to do astonishing things, but a company with many competent employees, sizable server farms, robust technical foundations, and lots of user data can do much more. The means of production necessary to build an online platform capable of hosting thousands of interactions per second are daunting. This is the main reason I approached algorithmic techniques in close connection with the concept of 'engine'. The latter only emerges in its full sense when a program grows into an infrastructure for human practice, when an element integrates into a technical individual or ensemble and, through it, becomes 'an active force transforming its environment, not a camera passively recording it' (MacKenzie, 2006, p. 12). In this moment, the plasticity of software is fully caught up in the exercise of power, which 'is an ensemble of actions on possible actions: it operates on the field of possibility where the behavior of acting subjects is inscribed: it incites, it induces, it diverts, it makes easier or more difficult, it broadens or limits, it renders more or less probable; in the most extreme, it constrains or prevents absolutely' (Foucault, 1982, p. 789, translation amended). PageRank can be used by researchers to analyze power relations in interaction networks, but as part of Google Search, it affects the navigational practices of billions of users and distributes visibility and economic opportunity on a global scale. While Morozov (2019) rightfully points out that the 'behavior modification' at the heart of Zuboff's surveillance capitalism is only one of many different ways capitalism can draw on computing to generate surplus, algorithmic techniques most clearly become technologies of power when they begin to modulate navigational distances, access to information and resources, or groupings that affect the possibilities and probabilities of concrete practice. Software-makers design 'rules of conduct able to be applied to determinate situations' (Thrift, 2005, p. 172) by putting in place forms and functions, including the margins of indetermination that allow for articulation and adaptation during use. Information ordering and other algorithmic techniques have significantly extended what these rules of conduct can look like, moving from static grammars of action to adaptive structures that enable 'soft' forms of control (cf. Cheney-Lippold, 2011). Online platforms, in particular, act as engines of order when algorithmic techniques engage in the programmed coordination of large numbers of participants, enabling, capturing, and steering interactions in ways that promote specific operational goals, in particular those of the platform itself. This is what Bratton (2015) means when he argues that 'it is far less important how the machine represents a politics than how "politics" physically *is* that machinic system' (p. 44).

How well actors are able to integrate computing into their search for profit and power has already become a central factor for success. At the end of 2018, the five largest companies in the world, measured by market capitalization, are Apple, Alphabet, Microsoft, Amazon, and Tencent, with Facebook and Alibaba not far behind. While my foray into software-making and algorithmic techniques has focused on technicity, it is a mark of contemporary computing that its sprawling reservoirs of technique and knowledge have been funneled very successfully into business endeavors, to a point where Andreessen's (2011) assessment that 'software is eating the world' receives a somewhat darker meaning. Looking at these large IT companies, we notice that most of them have been engaging in 'concentric diversification', a business strategy 'where the firm seeks to move into activities which mesh to some degree with the present product line, technological expertise, customer base, or distribution channels' (Thompson and Strickland, 1978, p. 69). Software plays a role here. Stucke and Grunes (2016) have convincingly argued that both monopolization and expansion into new sectors are supported by the cross-market utility of collected data, and I would suggest that the generalizability and transferability of algorithmic techniques has similar effects. Computerization and datafication bring ever more practices into the scope of computation, allowing for the application of similar techniques to very different task domains. Artificial intelligence and automation are currently the two terms that evoke this process most clearly, and the companies that master the computational means of production have good chances to extend their domination to new sectors at a brisk pace. Both the plasticity of software and the role of purpose or interest in information ordering appear quite differently when we move from Latour's research lab to the economic and governmental spheres that rely heavily on computing in their core activities.

What we have been witnessing over the last 70 years is the progressive emergence of a new 'technical system' (Gille, 1986), an expanding sphere of interoperability built around computing as core technology that generates self-stabilizing synergies and affects social and economic organization more generally, pushing for further waves of computerization and datafication in the process. Algorithmic information ordering emerges as a central means to know and to act in this system, providing advantages to those who master its design and application. These developments manifest themselves in various ways through many larger and smaller 'problems' or 'issues', but their broader repercussions demand that we interrogate the modes of thinking required to develop adequate responses.

Among Machines

Over the preceding chapters, I have tried to develop a perspective on technic-ity that is intentionally irreverent with regard to disciplinary conventions. Rather than narrate the history of algorithmic information ordering as a scientific field, I have presented the various techniques as technical ideas and artifacts that end up in the hands of programmers applying them with little regard to where they came from. Information scientists may have been appalled with my treatment of their discipline. Why did I not provide an overview of the canonical set-theoretic, algebraic, and probabilistic models for information retrieval first and then walk through each of them systematically? Why did I mention the concept of 'information need', the very foundation of the field, only in passing? In the introduction of this book, I have argued that I would engage with algorithmic techniques as a software developer interested in functional possibilities, not as an information scien-tist invested in paradigmatic coherence, nor a historian of science retracing the emergence of a discipline. The developer who encounters techniques through software libraries indeed does not have to care whether a quantified list of properties is understood as frequency distribution or feature vector as long as the proposed function solves their specific problem. As a media scholar interested in the 'levers on "reality"' (Goody, 1977, p. 109) techniques provide, I sought to align myself with a form of technical practice that has a pragmatic interest in operation first and foremost. This alignment clearly did not result in a textbook for programmers but inspired an appropriation of algorithmic techniques that followed its own intellectual agenda.

In Turkle and Papert's (1990) classic study on 'styles and voices within the computer culture' the authors observe an 'epistemological pluralism' when groups of students begin to program, a diversity of approaches that is progressively funneled into a (gendered) 'canonical style' based on for-malization, which is then imposed as the correct and superior way of doing things. One of the goals of this book was to find a form of engagement with technicity that not only emphasizes variation and pluralism but actively promotes a perspective that does not bind itself to the epistemological horizon of the computing disciplines while remaining close to the technical substances at hand. I have tried to demarcate a level of analysis that is sufficiently technical to capture the core of the discussed techniques and sufficiently anchored in a media theoretical perspective to connect these technicities to broader and more speculative questions concerning cultural ramifications and significance. This approach has largely been inspired by Simondon's mechanology and the cultural techniques tradition, which both eschew foundationalist idealizations and instead focus on operation and on the contingency and promiscuity of ontic coupling. The present state of technicity, in this perspective, is the result of sedimentation and layering, of continuous contingent construction and widening of functional possibilities rather than the effect of straightforward scientific progress or of singular incursions that determine what comes afterwards.

But the desire to break through the 'canonical style' of presenting and discussing technical matters is not simply a question of intellectual *coquetterie*. Running through this project is the question of how to move beyond the alienation that characterizes a technological society marked by an 'ignorance or resentment' of the machine, by 'non-knowledge of its nature and its essence' (Simondon, 2017, p. 15f.). One could indeed argue that the objective dimension of technology has been handed over to specialized disciplines and only its objectal integration figures as subject of larger social debates. The often-lamented 'autonomy' of technology can then be seen as a consequence of its reduction to some utility or 'social effect'. Simondon argued that solving the problem of alienation would require reconciliation between 'culture' and 'technology', including the recognition that technical objects are expressions that have meaning independent of their use. A 'technical culture' or 'technical wisdom' (Simondon, 2017, p. 159) would be sensitive to technicity in a way that is not limited to the *hic et nunc* of technical work but attuned to its historical and relational becoming. To create such an awareness is one of the tasks of mechanology. Debates about 'digital skills' and programming courses for humanities scholars certainly have their place, but my hope was to sketch a mechanological approach to software that mobilizes its own view, attention, and language. My relatively gentle entrance into the meandering roads of algorithmic information ordering discussed rather simple operations on words in documents and indexes, basic elements of Boolean logic, forms of counting and comparing, some calculations on networks, and the general setup of feedback going into a learning machine. Yes, one could go much deeper into these techniques and I have certainly glossed over many details and nuances. But these are nonetheless the broad elements that a system as complex as Google Search is made of.

I have taken care not to present a singular line through information retrieval, machine learning, and network algorithms, but to conceive techniques and their variations as elements, as building blocks of concrete systems. A document search engine may build on manually created indexes, implement collaborative tagging, or extract word frequencies from text contents, taking into account document structure, word co-occurrence, or formatting. It could use a term-weighting scheme like tf-idf to add dis-criminatory power. It could model a query language using Boolean or more intricate parameters, or it could sway into another direction and attempt to map the document space using something like PageRank or even a clustering technique that provides an overview to users rather than a ranking. The system could incorporate a feedback loop, use personalization, take into account location, device type, or time of day as means to differentiate. And each one of these things could be done in many different ways. To recognize these spaces of variation and choice is startling, because it means that technologies like computing or even algorithmic information ordering can-not be totalized into a singular logic, as convenient as that would be. There are myriad systems composed of disparate elements performing myriad tasks in myriad settings. But in early 2019, popular media and scholarly publications are full of anxieties and far-reaching proclamations about 'algorithms', including worries concerning their power, their effects, their opacity, their nonaccountability, their biases, their ideologies. Over the final pages of this book I want to come back to this problem space through the lens of the preceding chapters, not to formulate a short-term action plan, but to think more broadly about technical culture and the role of the humanities in societies where life is increasingly lived 'among machines' (Simondon, 2017, p. 12).

There have certainly been promising efforts to 'study the algorithm' (Lazer et al., 2014, p. 1205). Journalists have adapted their 'traditional watchdog-ging [to] algorithmic accountability reporting' (Diakopoulos, 2015) and use reverse engineering techniques to reconstruct decision procedures, for example, those involved in adaptive pricing on web shops. Sandvig and colleagues (2014) have proposed a classification of different empirical approaches, including code auditing, interface scraping, or crowdsourced collection of outputs. Due to various legal, economic, and technical fac-tors, these approaches have important limitations (Ananny and Crawford, 2017), one of them stemming from the recognition that actual outcomes are distributed accomplishments that include multilayered technicities, disparate use practices, and large, complex data streams (Rieder et al., 2018). But, as Manovich points out, another part of the conundrum concerns the adequate level and detail of technical description:

> As more and more of our cultural experiences, social interactions, and decision making are governed by large-scale software systems, the ability of nonexperts to discuss how these systems work becomes crucial. If we reduce each complex system to a one-page description of its algorithm,

will we capture enough of software behavior? Or will the nuances of
particular decisions made by software in every particular case be lost?
(Manovich, 2013a, n.p.)

What constitutes 'enough' will of course depend on the system under scrutiny, but any answer will require at least a somewhat robust understanding
of algorithmic techniques and systems design. The empirical approaches
currently being proposed to make sense of actual working systems crucially
depend on our capacity to create adequate conceptual representations
of the objects under scrutiny. We cannot study the makeup of a technical system if we lack the capacity to imagine how such a system *could* be
constructed. Which techniques could have been used and how could they
have been adapted and combined? What was the range of choices that had
to be made? My attempt to highlight plasticity and variation served this
very goal; comparing PageRank with HITS and looking at the α parameter
were just two ways of probing, but one could easily multiply such attempts
at counterfactual thinking, moving down into crawling and indexing or
up to the level of the interface. If there is any hope of ever gaining something resembling a sufficient understanding of things like Google Search,
Facebook's News Feed, or much more contained systems used in hiring,
credit assessment, or criminal justice, there needs to be a real vocabulary
of technical possibility, which means knowledge of elements and their
potential arrangements. Only a perspective that recognizes the moments of
plasticity and choice developers – and by extension the organizations they
report to – regularly face will be able to articulate the political dimension
of technology.

The consolidation of efforts to detect, for example, unacceptable forms of
discrimination and to create accountability for algorithmic decision-making
are indeed breaking necessary new ground, and there is much to learn
from such attempts to study concrete empirical objects. It is particularly
encouraging that approaches currently being developed and tested often
focus on entire systems and their specific embeddings. Attention is paid
to data inputs, to the technical dimension of processing and ordering,
and to the generation, presentation, and application of outputs, including,
for example, discussions of cutoff points that transform probabilistic assessments into binary classifications. Intellectual investment in making
algorithmic techniques more broadly intelligible can help deepen these
efforts not only in terms of general technical literacy, but more specifically
when it comes to the questions to ask and the possibilities to consider. A
sense of technicity, a 'knowing one's way in something' (*sichauskennen*) to

use Heidegger's (1989, p. 14) term, is necessary to overcome the persistent rift between 'technical' and 'social' approaches. Broader cultural understanding of algorithmic techniques in both objective and objectal terms would allow for a deeper appreciation of the fundamental operationality specific technical trajectories are introducing into the fabric of life.

As computing continues to penetrate into human practice, the border with other domains crumbles. Are real-time auction models, like the one Google uses to sell ad space, or pricing mechanisms, like Uber's surge pricing, applications of economic theory or a particular kind of 'computer solution' (Muniesa, 2011)? Such distinctions look increasingly undecidable as software becomes the preferred mode of expression for operational concepts and ideas. This means that there is dire need for interpretations that either bring these techniques back into more familiar territory or help us move closer to their vernaculars. Recent work by scholars like Burrell (2016) and Mackenzie (2015, 2017a) has indeed begun to flesh out ways to analyze and describe how specific techniques 'think', that is, how they construct complex forms of 'cognitive' behavior out of iterative executions of small steps or calculations. In addition to providing a framework for an understanding of software-making as the assembly of techniques into larger systems, this book sought to make its own contribution to these efforts.

On a broad level, describing the forms of cognition algorithmic techniques instantiate as (variably) 'nonanthropomorphic' means recognizing that a statistical bias is something very different than the prejudice or partiality the term implies when applied to humans, even when it has similar outcomes or effects. The former demands a different critique and different remedies, which requires that we develop forms of moral and political reasoning capable of operating within the modes of ordering algorithmic techniques deploy. And these modes may well remain strange to us. Just like Foucault's (1995, p. 36f.) reminder that half-proofs could lead to half-punishments in legal proceedings until the Renaissance rings profoundly alien today, new forms of normative reasoning may not necessarily appear intuitively consistent from the start. It is increasingly clear, for example, that concepts like 'fairness' do not easily map onto algorithmic techniques, not because computers have some inherent limitation, but because fairness is an unstable and contested outcome of highly contextualized attempts at balancing social trade-offs (cf. Kleinberg et al., 2016). Technological solutions can render moral commitments invisible by sinking them into digital tools and infrastructures, but they hardly disappear. How competing conceptions of justice prevail in contemporary societies may increasingly become a question of design and the humanities have the capacity and responsibility to investigate how algorithmic techniques affect how such matters are framed and resolved. This must include an interest for the many different practices involved in the making of technical artifacts: indeed, if decision-making is relegated to design and control practices, the whole lifecycle of a program or service becomes relevant for its analysis.

A study of algorithmic techniques is clearly not enough to capture the broader infrastructural qualities and the normative thrust technical individuals and ensembles exercise when they combine these elements into the specific forms and functions of working systems. A critical reading of PageRank is by no means sufficient for getting a grip on the technical makeup of Google Search and the way it orders the web. An analysis of Facebook's News Feed filtering mechanism cannot account for the service's pervasive role as infrastructure for sociability. Since algorithmic information ordering has come to play a pivotal role in these systems, however, it requires special attention and can constitute an entry point into broader forms of analysis that cover grammatization, value creation, and other aspects. The challenge is to connect the objective technical makeup of a system to its objectal embedding, using one 'side' to shed light on the other. In my analysis of PageRank, I have proposed a reinterpretation of the functional principles at work that operated in a similar discursive register as Google's 'voting' narrative, even if my conclusions were quite different. Such reinterpretations take operational mechanisms as crystallized human gesture and read them as such. While these readings can take more abstract directions, they benefit from localized or at least application-specific focus since cultural dimensions tend to become clearer when technicity is bound into working systems.

Nourished with technical imagination, we would be prepared to probe the character of algorithmic techniques more thoroughly, in particular around the tensions between technique and application domain. Investigations into biases can call attention to certain social effects of machine behavior, but the normative thrust of algorithmic techniques is not simply oscillating between 'neutrality' and 'bias'. Norms and values are often domain-specific and behavior that is deemed desirable in one area may be considered problematic in another. What constitutes a 'good' recommendation in the context of a music service may produce troubling effects when applied to politically salient content: the same capacity to drill deeper and deeper into specialized genres may yield hidden gems on Spotify but lay pathways to increasingly radicalized political positions on YouTube. Content filtering optimized for user engagement may produce benign results in one kind of context but stir violence in another. As Grimmelmann (2009) has argued, the search terms

'Jew' and 'gerbil' do not have the same cultural significance and handling them with the exact same retrieval and ranking mechanisms is bound to produce trouble.

Indeed, in the technical publications I have cited over the last chapters and the many more I have consulted during my research, the lack of 'domain theorization' stands out. Terms like 'aboutness' and 'intuitive basis', but also the recurring use of the qualifier 'reasonable' to justify ad hoc decisions, signal how commonsense and largely unexamined arguments flow into algorithmic techniques. There is extensive research going into the invention, development, understanding, implementation, and application of algorithmic techniques, but even concrete experiments often refrain from entering into a more substantial dialogue with the domain space they target. The process of formalization into intermediate forms is often almost disappointingly lacking in theoretical elaboration. This does not mean that all algorithmic techniques eschew more intricate attempts to conceptualize the world they operate on, but even PageRank, which explicitly draws on decades of research in sociometry and citation analysis, makes a clear epistemological break with these disciplinary spaces and prefers to emphasize the crude model of a random user clicking on links. Hans Peter Luhn, who almost single-handedly invented the field of text mining, was neither a linguist with a deep interest in the structure of language, nor a cybernetician pursuing a computational theory of meaning, but an engineer equipped with a mix of capability, curiosity, and the resources of IBM. He was someone with 'sensitivity to technicity' (Simondon, 2017, p. 74) who conveniently worked at the center of a 'technical system' (Gille, 1986) getting ready to begin its march toward domination. He looked at the library problem through the lens of that system and mobilized the existing reservoirs of knowledge and technique to the fullest, further adding to them in the process. My point is that all of this requires surprisingly little in terms of belief or ontological labor.

The humanities and social sciences have the capacity to play a more proactive role in these settings than merely pointing out the insufficiencies, limitations, and blind spots of computing. Broader conceptual or domain-specific contributions to technical imaginaries are within the realm of possibility and my irreverence to disciplinary conventions indeed tried to convey a sense of possibility that is not immediately neutered by the forbidding complexity of formal notation and jargon. Making actual contributions to invention and adaptation is certainly easier said than done but attempts to intensify technical speculation and active engagement could draw on existing spheres in the humanities and social sciences where scholars are involved in the making of technical objects. Fields like digital methods and the digital humanities should not be afraid to translate their own burgeoning technical expertise into 'critical technical practice' (Agre, 1997b) – propositions that go beyond the domain of research methodology and drive a 'widening' of technical imagination. The work of scholars like Johanna Drucker (2011, 2013), for example, is not only suited to complicate visual displays of quantitative information in humanistic projects but could be extended to the question of how interfaces can show and capture nuance, doubt, or the probabilistic assessments that often underlie binary outcomes. The recognition that technical work is generally 'qualculation', an entanglement of calculation and judgment, indeed creates a huge opening both for critique and contribution. What kind of domain knowledge could be integrated into algorithmic techniques? Which kind of nuances could one specify? Are there alternatives to atomization that are not painstaking forms of logical description? More generally, can we pick up on Agre's (1997a) critique, which holds that fields like artificial intelligence limit, exclude, and stifle themselves by requiring that every idea must be 'proven' in the form of a working system, to build the conditions for more open-ended technical conversation and speculation? The contingent and constructive accumulation of techniques will not come to an end any time soon and the concept of path dependence should remind us that existing trajectories were not inevitable at one point in time and new directions can be still forged, as difficult as that may be.

A life 'among machines' demands that we connect analytical capacities more tightly to forms of normative reasoning that do not eschew prescriptive arguments. Referring to Benjamin's recognition of technology's social potential, Bunz remarks:

> [O]ur questioning of technology (and our social relationship to it) has become worse over time. Today, we mostly ask technology for profitable business, but not for a better society. [...] It seems that ensuring a distance between man and technology is the ideology of our time. (Bunz, 2014, p. 61)

Interestingly, technical artifacts or services are often described and justified by their creators with reference to moral values or social benefits. Facebook's mission statement to 'give people the power to build community and bring the world closer together' (Zuckerberg, 2017) is a particular far-reaching example, but we regularly find broadly emancipatory narratives next to 'obvious' perks like user-friendliness, convenience, or security. User privacy is quickly becoming a value companies can hardly ignore, at least in their rhetoric. Google continues to liken links to votes[3] and used to underscore the 'uniquely democratic nature of the web'[4] to justify link counting, even if PageRank's core objective is to attribute differential value to each vote. Terms like 'disruption' or 'disintermediation' are often used to frame new tools or services as attacks on vested interests or expert governance, echoing the attempts to delegitimize librarians we encountered over the last chapters.

It is easy to dismiss such claims as cynical or naive, but they signal that there is an opportunity for narrating technical artifacts in cultural terms. Following Spärck Jones's (1990) argument that information retrieval and artificial intelligence experiments evaluate a technique's capacity to satisfy specific needs or purposes, thus delivering 'measures of acceptability not of truth' (p. 281), the notion of 'acceptability' stands out as a way to interrogate the real and potential performativity that arises in concrete situations. This opens a larger register for critique than potentially limited and limiting concepts such as truthfulness or bias, which capture only a part of what is at stake. Commercial actors playing a dominant role in defining the emerging infosphere certainly use various strategies to present their products as *acceptable* and current debates about the power of algorithms, platforms, and data practices already invoke counternarratives that include questions of technical design. What are the conditions of acceptability one can put toward something like Google Search? Can we formulate normative elements that are not simply the revealed preference of market behavior? How can they find expression in the form of algorithmic techniques? Should they? These efforts can profit from a conceptual frame that makes technicity addressable in these terms and points toward forms of contribution that include experimentation and creation. Critical investigations into potential biases in datasets (cf. O'Neil, 2016) and broader social effects (cf. Eubanks, 2018) could then be seen as starting points for concrete design-oriented reflections, from designing for 'auditability' (Sandvig et al., 2014) to explicitly domain- and value-sensitive methodologies for software-making.

An exclusively reactive stance is not enough when it comes to dealing not only with individual techniques, but with pervasive technical infrastructures that function as globe-spanning 'agencies of order' (Peters, 2015, p. 1). The idea that we can hope for little more than to detect and (maybe) correct the practical or moral 'mistakes' of all-powerful companies and institutions leaves us stuck in a situation where alternative arrangements seem always

3   https://support.google.com/webmasters/answer/40349?hl=en, accessed 22 February 2017.
4   https://web.archive.org/web/20001109080600/http://www.google.com/technology/index. html, accessed 22 February 2017.

further out of reach. It is certainly not surprising that mostly defensive norms like transparency, accountability, and privacy take the center stage when always larger parts of our digital environments are dominated by a handful of actors. The sheer economic power of these large companies is alarming, their technological prowess is intimidating, and their seemingly inescapable monopoly positions make it hard to envisage other scenarios. But critical work must not confine itself to a reactive position that thinks exclusively in terms of freedom *from*, not freedom *to*. Search engines that function just like Google, social networks looking just like Facebook or Twitter, a little less capable and convenient maybe but with respect for users' privacy – this is hardly inspiring. Is there a space for some form of technological utopianism that is neither Silicon Valley solutionism (Morozov, 2013) nor a retreat into a kind of liberal minimalism where technology is to be tamed rather than molded with ambition? Can we envision a mandate for computing that mirror's the public library's commitment to Enlightenment values? Can we ask technology for more than we are currently getting?

My emphasis on the plasticity of technicity, on functional abstraction as opportunity, and on epistemological pluralism indeed has a normative, prescriptive component: while domination of and through technicity can hardly be ignored, a widening of technical imagination is necessary to combat a further reduction of what we ask of technology. An appreciation of algorithmic techniques and how they are assembled into working systems can hopefully inspire and substantiate forms of contribution to technical creation that range from participation in design processes to the speculative generation of ideas. Despite its entanglement with globe-spanning corporate infrastructures, the domain of software remains a fertile playground for all kinds of critical and creative engagement seeking to reclaim plasticity. Simondon's philosophy indeed envisages technical culture and imagination as a balance between artisanal and industrial modes of creation, drawing on the powerful engine of concretization while making sure that technical objects remain open and sensitive to local circumstances. Human beings would act as coordinators and inventors that are 'among machines' rather than above or below them (Simondon, 2017, p. 18). This does not boil down to generalized technical training but starts from the recognition of the inescapable centrality of technology to human life and asks for a deeper involvement with current arrangements of technicity. Because Simondon would certainly caution us that the mere exchange of one set of values or finalities for another would again keep technology 'small', ignoring its specific substance and capacity for expression. But from artistic experimentation to civic technologies, from open-source software to algorithmic accountability efforts, there are many examples where people are asking more from technology while embracing its unique potential. These efforts deserve much more visibility and support. And they may well include moments of outright refusal. But even here, technical culture is an asset and not a liability: as prolific hacker Maxigas (2017) states, '[t]echnical expertise is essential for mounting a challenge to technological innovation' (p. 850).

If we agree with Latour (1991) that 'technology is society made durable', we cannot limit ourselves to quick fixes but need to question much more thoroughly how this process of 'making durable' can be governed in ways that are more inclusive, ambitious, and born out of debate. As scholars critiquing YouTube's recommendation system, for example, we cannot merely ask for some vague value change that implements 'plurality' and keeps users from spiraling into radicalization, shifting the burden of far-reaching design decisions to actors that have acquired quasi-governmental forms of power. Dare we ask the question of how YouTube *should* work, from interface to recommender system? Or at least how it *could* work differently? Can we imagine forms of 'cooperative responsibility' for organizational and design decisions concerning large online platforms? (cf. Helberger et al., 2018) What would this look like, which institutions, forms of deliberation, and modes of application would be suitable? Taking technicity seriously would require more technical acculturation, yes, but also the realization that we are designing and negotiating increasingly fundamental operating mechanisms of society.

When technical systems become social systems and vice versa, technical critique and social critique increasingly depend on each other. The discussion of algorithms in criminal justice, for example, is right to address the real and potential effects of concrete technical practices on particular populations, but it cannot stop short of interrogating the broader goals criminal justice systems pursue. We can isolate instances of decision-making and analyze their procedural component, but the question of justice is necessarily much larger. What makes biases in domains like criminal sentencing or parole so fraught with anger and anxiety is that we ultimately know that these decisions are part of larger systems of injustice, where individuals are taken out of circumstances marked by social and economic inequality and put into carceral structures that further destroy their chances to participate meaningfully in society. How would a critique of technicity look like that builds on Angela Davis's (2003) foundational denunciation of mass incarceration? Or, put differently, how could algorithmic techniques contribute to a criminal justice system that had rehabilitation as its central focus? Could machine learning be used to identify the most effective resources for reintegrating an offender into society rather than to operationalize the contestable notion of recidivism? These speculations may seem far-fetched, but my insistence on the notion of 'purpose' and 'interest' ultimately means that algorithmic information ordering cannot be detached from the larger power structures it is embedded in.

Make no mistake, the positive view of technicity and technical creation I have defended over the course of this book does not mean that I ignore the highly problematic role technology has come to play. At the present moment, engines of order are instrumental in tightening the '"iron cage" of consumerism' (Jackson, 2009) and in making 'surveillance capitalism' (Zuboff, 2019) a concrete reality. What I believe, however, is that this is not an inevitability. The redefinition of existing modes of knowing and acting can be an opportunity, if seized upon. If technical work is indeed qualculative, we need to develop an understanding of technicity that does not try to eliminate the part of judgment, but makes it visible, debatable, and amendable to change. Although calculation is still often seen as a guardrail against the capriciousness of human judgment, I hope that this book has clearly shown that the myriad moments of choice render algorithmic operation riddled and wrought with ideas and values that are far from uncontested. If technology is human gesture, how could it be otherwise? Instead of seeking to eliminate judgment from technicity, we must invest more in our normative capacities as they intersect with technicity. The most important contribution the humanities can make to our technological society is to articulate how human judgment, expressed as technical artifact or not, can bloom in ways that do not fall back into structures of domination. Technological societies that have self-optimizing infrastructures and techniques for dynamic and fine-grained distinction-making at their disposal will have to combine knowledge of machines with political and moral sensitivity. What is the 'glue' (Latour, 2005) that holds societies together when every little data point can become a variable in techniques whose very purpose is to differentiate? That challenge requires more than technical imagination; it requires political imagination capable of integrating technicity into visions of society that seek deliberation, cooperation, and justice.

Bibliography

Aggarwal, C. C., and Zhai, C. (eds.). (2012). *Mining Text Data*. New York: Springer.

Agre, P. E. (1994). Surveillance and Capture: Two Models of Privacy. *The Information Society 10*(2), 101-127.

Agre, P. E. (1997a). *Computation and Human Experience*. Cambridge: Cambridge University Press.

Agre, P. E. (1997b). Toward a Critical Technical Practice: Lessons Learned in Trying to Reform AI. In G. C. Bowker, S. L. Star, W. Turner, and L. Gasser (eds.), *Social Science, Technical Systems, and Cooperative Work: Beyond the Great Divide* (pp. 131-158). New York: Psychology Press.

Ananny, M., and Crawford, K. (2017). Seeing without Knowing: Limitations of the Transparency Ideal and Its Application to Algorithmic Accountability. *New Media & Society 33*(4), 973-989.

Andreessen, M. (2011). Why Software Is Eating the World. *Wall Street Journal*, 20 August. Retrieved from http://online.wsj.com.

Bastian, M., Heymann, S., Jacomy, M. (2009). Gephi: An Open Source Software for Exploring and Manipulating Networks. In *International AAAI Conference on Weblogs and Social Media*. Retrieved from https://www.aaai.org/ocs/index.php/ICWSM/09/paper/view/154.

Blei, D. M., Ng, A. Y., and Jordan, M. I. (2003). Latent Dirichlet Allocation. *Journal of Machine Learning Research 3*, 993-1022.

Bogost, I. (2015). The Cathedral of Computation. *The Atlantic*, 15 January. Retrieved from https://www.theatlantic.com.

Boltanski, L., and Chiapello, E. (2005). *The New Spirit of Capitalism* (G. Elliott, trans.). London: Verso.

Bontems, V. (2009). Gilbert Simondon's Genetic 'Mecanology' and the Understanding of Laws of Technical Evolution. *Techné: Research in Philosophy and Technology 13*(1), 1-12.

Borra, E., and Rieder. B. (2014). Programmed Method: Developing a Toolset for Capturing and Analyzing Tweets. *Aslib Journal of Information Management 66*(3), 262-278.

Bowker, G. C. (2005). *Memory Practices in the Sciences*. Cambridge, MA: MIT Press.

Box, G. E. P. (1979). Robustness in the Strategy of Scientific Model Building. In R. L. Launer and G. N. Wilkinson (eds.), *Robustness in Statistics* (pp. 201-236). New York: Academic Press.

Bratton, B. H. (2015). *The Stack: On Software and Sovereignty*. Cambridge, MA: MIT Press.

Bunz, M. (2014). *The Silent Revolution*. Basingstoke: Palgrave Macmillan.

Burrell, J. (2016). How the Machine 'Thinks': Understanding Opacity in Machine Learning Algorithms. *Big Data & Society 3*(1), 1-12.

Burrows, R. (2009). Afterword: Urban Informatics and Social Ontology. In M. Foth (eds.), *Handbook of Research on Urban Informatics: The Practice and Promise of the Real-Time City* (pp. 450-454). Hershey: Information Science Reference.

Cheney-Lippold, J. (2011). A New Algorithmic Identity: Soft Biopolitics and the Modulation of Control. *Theory, Culture & Society 28*(6), 164-181.

Cochoy, F. (2008). Calculation, Qualculation, Calqulation: Shopping Cart Arithmetic, Equipped Cognition and the Clustered Consumer. *Marketing Theory 8*(1), 15-44.

Codd, E. F. (1970). A Relational Model of Data for Large Shared Data Banks. *Communications of the ACM 13*(6), 377-387.

Date, C. J. (2004). *An Introduction to Database Systems* (8th ed.). London: Pearson Education.

Davis, A. Y. (2003). *Are Prisons Obsolete?* New York: Seven Stories Press.

Deleuze, G. (1988). *Foucault* (S. Hand, trans.). Minneapolis: University of Minnesota Press.

Desrosières, A. (2001). How Real Are Statistics? Four Possible Attitudes. *Social Research 68*(2), 339-355.

Diakopoulos, N. (2015). Algorithmic Accountability. *Digital Journalism 3*(3), 398-415.

Djaballah, M. (2008). *Kant, Foucault, and Forms of Experience*. London: Routledge.

Dreyfus, H. (2009). *On the Internet* (2nd ed.). London: Routledge.

Drucker, J. (2011). Humanities Approaches to Graphical Display. *Digital Humanities Quarterly 5*(1), n.p.

Drucker, J. (2013). Performative Materiality and Theoretical Approaches to Interface. *Digital Humanities Quarterly 7*(1), n.p.

Ertzscheid, O. (2009). L'Homme, un document comme les autres. *Hermès 53*(1), 33-40.

Eubanks, V. (2018). *Automating Inequality: How High-Tech Tools Profile, Police, and Punish the Poor*. New York: St. Martin's Press.

Floridi, L. (2014). *The Fourth Revolution: How the Infosphere Is Reshaping Human Reality*. Oxford: Oxford University Press.

Foucault, M. (1982). The Subject and Power. *Critical Inquiry 8*(4), 777-795.

Foucault, M. (1995). *Discipline and Punish: The Birth of the Prison* (A. Sheridan, trans.). New York: Vintage Books.

Foucault, M. (2005). *The Order of Things: An Archaeology of the Human Sciences*. London: Routledge.

Foucault, M. (2008). *The Birth of Biopolitics: Lectures at the Collège de France, 1978-79* (G. Burchell, trans.). Basingstoke: Palgrave Macmillan.

Foucault, M. (2009). *Security, Territory, Population: Lectures at the Collège de France, 1977-78* (G. Burchell, trans.). Basingstoke: Palgrave Macmillan.

Gardey, D. (2008). *Écrire, calculer, classer. Comment une evolution de papier a transformé les sociétés contemporaines (1800-1940)*. Paris: La Decouverte.

Gille, B. (ed.). (1986). *The History of Techniques, Volume 1: Techniques and Civilizations* (P. Southgate and T. Williamson, trans.). Montreux: Gordon and Breach.

Gitelman, L. (2013). *Raw Data Is an Oxymoron*. Cambridge, MA: MIT Press.

Goody, J. (1977). *The Domestication of the Savage Mind*. Cambridge: Cambridge University Press.

Grimmelmann, J. (2009). The Google Dilemma. *New York Law School Law Review 53*, 939-950.

Hacking, I. (1983). *Representing and Intervening.* Cambridge: Cambridge University Press.

Hacking, I. (1990). *The Taming of Chance.* Cambridge: Cambridge University Press.

Hartmann, F. (2015). Paul Otlets Hypermedium. Dokumentation als Gegenidee zur Bibliothek. *LIBREAS Library Ideas 28,* n.p.

Heidegger, M. (1977). *The Question Concerning Technology, and Other Essays* (W. Lovitt, trans.). New York: Garland.

Helberger, N., Pierson, J., and Poell, T. (2018). Governing Online Platforms: From Contested to Cooperative Responsibility. *The Information Society* 34(1), 1-14.

Heyck, H. (2012). Producing Reason. In M. Solovey and H. Cravens (eds.), *Cold War Social Science* (pp. 99-116). New York: Palgrave Macmillan.

Hjørland, B. (2010). The Importance of Theories of Knowledge: Indexing and Information Retrieval as an Example. *Journal of the American Society for Information Science and Technology* 62(1), 72-77.

Jackson, T. (2009). *Prosperity without Growth: Economics for a Finite Planet.* London: Earthscan.

Kleinberg, J., Mullainathan, S., and Raghavan, M. (2016). Inherent Trade-offs in the Fair Determination of Risk Scores. ArXiv:1609.05807 [Cs, Stat]. Retrieved from http://arxiv.org/abs/1609.05807.

Krajewski, M. (2011). *Paper Machines: About Cards & Catalogs, 1548-1929* (P. Krapp, trans.) Cambridge, MA: MIT Press.

Lash, S. (2006). Dialectic of Information? A Response to Taylor. *Information, Communication & Society* 9(5), 572-581.

Latour, B. (1991). Technology Is Society Made Durable. In J. Law (ed.), *A Sociology of Monsters: Essays on Power, Technology and Domination* (pp. 103-131). London: Routledge.

Latour, B. (2005). *Reassembling the Social: An Introduction to Actor-Network-Theory.* Oxford: Oxford University Press.

Latour, B., Jensen, P., Venturini, T., Grauwin, S., and Boullier, D. (2012). 'The Whole Is Always Smaller Than Its Parts': A Digital Test of Gabriel Tarde's Monads. *British Journal of Sociology* 63(4), 590-615.

Lazer, D., Kennedy, R., King, G., and Vespignani, A. (2014). The Parable of Google Flu: Traps in Big Data Analysis. *Science* 343(6176), 1203-1205.

Macho, T. (2003). Zeit und Zahl: Kalender- und Zeitrechnung als Kulturtechniken. In S. Krämer and H. Bredekamp (eds.), *Schrift, Zahl: Wider die Diskursivierung der Kultur* (pp. 179-192). München: Wilhelm Fink Verlag.

Mackenzie, A. (2015). The Production of Prediction: What Does Machine Learning Want? *European Journal of Cultural Studies* 18(4-5), 429-445.

Mackenzie, A. (2017a). *Machine Learners: Archaeology of a Data Practice.* Cambridge, MA: MIT Press.

MacKenzie, D. (2006). *An Engine, Not a Camera: How Financial Models Shape Markets*. Cambridge, MA: MIT Press.

Manovich, L. (2013a). The Algorithms of Our Lives. *Chronicle of Higher Education*, 16 December. Retrieved from https://www.chronicle.com.

Maxigas. (2017). Hackers against Technology: Critique and Recuperation in Technological Cycles. *Social Studies of Science 47*(6), 841-860.

Mirowski, P., and Nik-Khah, E. (2017). *The Knowledge We Have Lost in Information*. Oxford: Oxford University Press.

Moor, J. H. (1978). Three Myths of Computer Science. *British Journal for the Philosophy of Science 29*(3), 213-222.

Morozov, E. (2013). *To Save Everything, Click Here*. New York: Public Affairs.

Morozov, E. (2019). Capitalism's New Clothes. *The Baffler*, 4 February. Retrieved from https://thebaffler.com.

Muniesa, F. (2011). Is a Stock Exchange a Computer Solution? Explicitness, Algorithms and the Arizona Stock Exchange. *International Journal of Actor-Network Theory and Technological Innovation 3*(1), 1-15.

Norvig, P. (2015). *On Chomsky and the Two Cultures of Statistical Learning*. Retrieved from http://norvig.com/chomsky.html.

O'Neil, C. (2016). *Weapons of Math Destruction: How Big Data Increases Inequality and Threatens Democracy*. New York: Crown.

Peters, J. D. (2015). *The Marvelous Clouds: Toward a Philosophy of Elemental Media*. Chicago: University of Chicago Press.

Rieder, B., Matamoros-Fernández, A., and Coromina, Ò. (2018). From Ranking Algorithms to 'Ranking Cultures': Investigating the Modulation of Visibility in YouTube Search Results. *Convergence 24*(1), 50-68.

Rodgers, D. T. (2011). *Age of Fracture*. Cambridge, MA: Harvard University Press.

Sandvig, C., Hamilton, K., Karahalios, K., and Langbort, C. (2014) Auditing Algorithms: Research Methods for Detecting Discrimination on Internet Platforms. Paper presented to 'Data and Discrimination: Converting Critical Concerns into Productive Inquiry', a preconference at the 64th Annual Meeting of the International Communication Association. Seattle, WA, 22 May. Retrieved from https://pdfs.semanticscholar.org/b722/7cbd34766655dea10d0437ab10df3a127396.pdf.

Shera, J. H. (1952). Special Librarianship and Documentation. *Library Trends 1*(2), 189-199.

Siegert, B. (2013). Cultural Techniques; or The End of the Intellectual Postwar Era in German Media Theory. *Theory, Culture & Society 30*(6), 48-65.

Simondon, G. (2017). *On the Mode of Existence of Technical Objects* (C. Malaspina and J. Rogove, trans.). Minneapolis: Univocal Publishing.

Spärck Jones, K. (1990). What Sort of a Thing Is an AI Experiment? In D. Partridge and Y. Wilks (eds.), *The Foundations of Artificial Intelligence* (pp. 276-281). Cambridge: Cambridge University Press.

Spärck Jones, K. (1999). Information Retrieval and Artificial Intelligence. *Artificial Intelligence 114*, 257-281.

Stucke, M. E., and Grunes, A. P. (2016). *Big Data and Competition Policy*. Oxford: Oxford University Press.

Terranova, T. (2004). *Network Culture: Politics for the Information Age*. London: Pluto Press.

Thompson, A. A., and Strickland, A. J. (1978). *Strategy and Policy: Concepts and Cases*. Dallas: Business Publications.

Thrift, N. (2005). *Knowing Capitalism*. London: Sage.

Turkle, S. and Papert, S. (1990). Epistemological Pluralism: Styles and Voices within the Computer Culture. *Signs 16*(1), 128-157.

Weinberger, D. (2008). *Everything Is Miscellaneous*. New York: Henry Holt.

Weinberger, D. (2012). *Too Big to Know*. New York: Basic Books.

Wolfram, S. (2002). *A New Kind of Science*. Champaign: Wolfram Media.

Zuboff, S. (2019). *The Age of Surveillance Capitalism: The Fight for a Human Future at the New Frontier of Power*. New York: PublicAffairs.

Zuckerberg, M. (2017). Bringing the World Closer Together [Facebook message], 22 June. Retrieved from https://www.facebook.com/zuck/posts/10154944663901634.

About the Author

Bernhard Rieder is Associate Professor of New Media and Digital Culture at the University of Amsterdam and a collaborator with the Digital Methods Initiative. He writes about the history, theory, and politics of software and develops research tools for data extraction and analysis.

Index